MUSIC
in theory and practice

MUSIC in theory and practice

second edition

Bruce Benward   Volume I

University of Wisconsin, Madison

wcb
Wm. C. Brown Company Publishers
Dubuque, Iowa

wcb group

Wm. C. Brown
Chairman of the Board

Mark C. Falb
Corporate Vice President/Operations

Book Team

Louise Waller
Editor

**Natalie Gould/Joyce S. Oberhausen/
Anne Caylor Cody**
Production Editors

William J. Evans/Barbara Grantham
Designers

Paula S. De Fontaine
Design Layout Assistant

Mavis M. Oeth
Permissions Editor

**wcb Wm. C. Brown Company Publishers,
College Division**

Lawrence E. Cremer
President

Raymond C. Deveaux
Vice President/Product Development

David Wm. Smith
Assistant Vice President/National Sales Manager

David A. Corona
Director of Production Development and Design

Matthew T. Coghlan
National Marketing Manager

Janis M. Machala
Director of Marketing Research

William A. Moss
Production Editorial Manager

Marilyn A. Phelps
Manager of Design

Mary M. Heller
Visual Research Manager

Consulting Editor
Frederick W. Westphal
California State University, Sacramento

Project Consultant
Dominic Intili
Indiana University of Pennsylvania

Cover photo by Israel Kopmar

Copyright © 1977, 1981 by Wm. C. Brown Company Publishers

Library of Congress Catalog Card Number: 80–65684

ISBN 0–697–03423–2

All rights reserved. No part of this publication may be reproduced, stored in a retrieval system, or transmitted, in any form or by an means, elecronic, mechanical, photocopying, recording, or otherwise, without the prior written permission of the publisher.

Third Printing, 1982

Printed in the United States of America

Contents

Preface ix

Introduction 3 — Sound 3. The Four Properties of Sound 4: *Pitch* 4, *Intensity* 4, *Duration* 4, *Timbre* 5. Summary 6.

1 Notation 7 — History 7: *Neumatic Notation* 7, *Mensural Notation* 8, *Tablature Notation* 9, *Present Notation* 10. Notation of Pitch 10: *The Staff* 10, *Letter Names* 10, *Solfeggio Syllables* 11, *The Clefs* 12. Octave Identification 14. Intervals 14. Accidentals 15: *Enharmonic Equivalents* 15. Notation of Duration 16: *The Tie* 16, *The Dot* 16, *Meter Signatures* 17. Dynamic Markings 20. Some Directions for Notation in Manuscript 20.

2 Scales, Modes, Intervals, Tonality, Key 27 — Scale 27. Diatonic Scales 28: *Major Scale* 28, *Natural Minor Scale* 31, *Harmonic Minor Scale* 32, *Melodic Minor Scale* 33. Scale Tuning 34: *Pythagorean Tuning* 34, *Mean-Tone Tuning* 35, *Equal Temperament Tuning* 35. Scale Relationships 37: *Relative Relationship* 37, *Parallel Relationship* 39. Other Diatonic Scales 41: *Pentatonic Scale* 41. Nondiatonic Scales 42: *Chromatic Scale* 42, *Whole-Tone Scale* 43. The Modes 44: *Greek Modes* 44, *Church Modes* 44. Intervals 48: *Major, Minor, and Perfect Intervals* 48, *Augmented and Diminished Intervals* 49, *Enharmonic Intervals* 50, *Inversion of Intervals* 51. Tonality 54: *Key* 54, *Pitch Inventory* 54.

3 The Anatomy of Harmony 57 — Harmony 57. Chord 57: *Triad* 57, *Triad Roots* 58. Scale Degree Names 60: *Triad Stability* 64, *Triad Inversion* 64, *Triad Position* 64. Triad Analysis Symbols 65. Figured Bass 66: *Continuo* 66, *Figured Bass Symbols* 67. Cadence 72: *Authentic Cadence* 72, *Half Cadence* 73, *Plagal Cadence* 73, *Deceptive Cadence* 74. Nonharmonic Tones 74: *Nonharmonic Tone Types* 76. Harmonic Rhythm 88.

4 The Anatomy of Melody 93 — Melody 93: *Step Progression* 93. Hierarchy of Melodic Components 94: *Structural Tone* 94, *Secondary Tone* 97, *Embellishing Tone* 98.

5 Melodic Organization 103 — The Organization of Melodic Thought 103: *The Motive* 103, *Phrase Member* 104, *Phrase* 104, *Period* 104, *Three-Part Period* 107, *Double Period* 109, *Song Form* 110, *Modifications of the Phrase* 110, *Other Melodic Organization* 112.

6	**Instruments and Voices 119**	Voice Ranges 119. Instrumental Ranges 119: *Nontransposing Instruments* 119, *Transposing Instruments* 119. Tessitura 123.
7	**Voice Leading in Four-Part Chorale Writing— Model Analysis 127**	Chorale by Johannes Crüger 127. Analysis of the Chorale 129: *Pitch Inventory* 129, *Scale* 129, *Key* 129, *Melody* 129, *Harmony* 130, *Rhythm* 131, *Texture* 131. Voice Leading 131: *Doubling* 134, *Spacing* 134, *Modulation* 135. Summary 135: *Fixed Practices* 135, *Preferred Practices* 136.
8	**Harmonic Progression 141**	The Relationship of Chords 141: *Root Relationships* 141. Chord Progressions 142: *Progression Patterns* 142. $^6_4$ Chords 152. Chord Selection 153. Summary 160.
9	**Style Periods 165**	Style 165: *Renaissance Period* 166, *Baroque Period* 166, *Classical Period* 166, *Romantic Period* 167, *Post-Romantic and Impressionistic* 167, *Contemporary Period* 168.
10	**Approach to Style Analysis 171**	Analysis 171: *Analytical Procedure* 171. Style Analysis 171: *Pitch Inventory* 172, *Scale* 172, *Key or Mode* 172, *Tonality* 172, *Melody* 172, *Harmony* 172, *Rhythm* 172, *Texture* 172, *Form* 173, *Contrapuntal Applications* 173.
11	**The Major-Minor Dominant Seventh Chord 175**	The Seventh Chord in General 175: *History* 175, *Analysis Symbols* 176. The Major-Minor Dominant Seventh Chord 178. Inversion of Seventh Chords 178: *Positions* 179. Resolution of Seventh Chords 179: *Circle Progression* 179, *Noncircle Progression with Resolution* 182, *Nonresolution* 183. Part-Writing Procedures for V^7 185.
12	**The vii^{ø7} and vii$^{°7}$ Chords 193**	Dominant Tendencies 193: *Progressions from vii^{ø7} and vii$^{°7}$* 194. Historical Use 198: *Renaissance* 198, *Baroque* 198, *Classical* 199, *Romantic* 200, *Post-Romantic and Impressionistic* 201, *Miscellaneous* 202.
13	**Modulation 203**	Modulation 203: *Common Chord Modulation* 203, *Static Modulation* 206, *Chromatic Modulation* 207, *Enharmonic Modulation* 208. Harmonizing Melodies that Modulate 218.
14	**Nondominant Seventh Chords 225**	Nondominant Seventh Chords 225: *Analysis Symbols* 226, *Resolutions* 227, *VI^7 in Minor* 233. Summary 233: *Part-Writing of Nondominant Seventh Chords* 233, *Harmonizing Nondominant Seventh Chords* 238.
15	**Secondary Dominant Chords 243**	Secondary Dominant Chords 243: *Characteristics* 243, *Secondary Dominant Types* 245. History 248: *Baroque Period* 248, *Classical Period* 248, *Romantic Period* 249, *Post-Romantic and Impressionistic Period* 251. Treatment 251: *As V of (V/)* 251, *As V^7 of (V^7/)* 252, *As vii$^{°6}$ of (vii$^{°6}$/)* 253, *As vii^{ø7} of (vii^{ø7}/)* 253, *As vii$^{°7}$ of (vii$^{°7}$/)* 254. Summary 256: *Part-writing Procedures* 256. Selecting for Chord Progressions 261.

16   **Two-Part (Binary) Form**   **275**

Two-Part Form 275: *Similar Material* 275, *Different Material* 276, *Both Similar and Different Material* 276. Rounded Binary Form 281: *Four-Phrase Level* 282, *Five-Phrase Level* 282. History 284: *Middle Ages* 284, *Renaissance* 285, *Baroque* 285, *Classical Period* 285, *Romantic Period* 287, *Post-Romantic and Impressionistic Period* 287, *Contemporary Period* 288.

17   **Three-Part (Ternary) Form**   **295**

Three-Part Form 295: *Three-Phrase* 295, *Song Form* 296, *Song Form Expanded* 298, *Song Form with Trio* 298. History 302: *Medieval and Middle Ages* 302, *Renaissance and Baroque* 302, *Classical Period* 302, *Romantic Period to Present* 303.

18   **American Popular Song**   **309**

Popular Music Symbols 309. Form 314. Key 315. Rhythm and Meter 316. Melody 316. Harmony 316: *Harmonic Progressions* 318, *Typical Circle-of-5ths Chord Patterns* 320, *Summary* 323, *Four-Chord Formulas* 329, *Turnarounds* 331.

19   **Blues, Boogie, and Jazz**   **335**

Blues 335: *Harmony* 335, *Melody* 338. Boogie-Woogie 341: *Harmony* 341, *Melody* 341, *Rhythm* 342, *Texture* 342. Jazz 343: *Jazz Rhythm* 343, *Jazz Harmony and Altered Chords* 346, *Jazz Melody and Improvisation* 349. References 356.

Appendix 1   359
Appendix 2   361
Appendix 3   365
Glossary   367
Index   379

Preface

To the Student

Before you begin your study of music theory I would like to discuss the subject in general and explain what you may expect to gain from its study. The chances are that you have had little previous experience in music theory and you may very well wonder why you should occupy (or perhaps be required to occupy) your time with it.

If you are typical of most young musicians beginning a serious study of your art, you already play an instrument or sing well, but you are interested in acquiring further technical skills and interpretive insights. You probably have been a performer for some years and have had success in public concerts either as an individual or as part of a group (band, orchestra, or chorus). From these experiences you have developed a keen musical intuition and wish to strengthen it further. *Intuition* is knowledge that comes to a person without conscious remembering or reasoning. Your music intuition includes a vast storehouse of familiar sounds, established patterns of melody, harmony, and rhythm, and an instinctive consciousness that you draw upon thousands of times in the performance of a single composition. Bits of information you have accumulated since your first musical experience are stored in your memory and are shaped into thoughts or judgments that you apply daily. You make split-second decisions about the phrasing of a melody, the application of dynamics (louds and softs), and the tempo of the music you play. And yet, you are seldom able to say precisely where this knowledge came from. Your musical intuition has become a part of you through your experience and, indeed, is one of the most valuable gifts in your possession.

As your musical intuition has already told you, music is a complex and highly organized combination and arrangement of tones. Besides providing a rational knowledge of music, a study of music theory interacts with intuition—honing, sharpening, and enhancing it with further insights and perception not available from any other source. Much of what you learn from this book will at first be simply surface information that you apply in a cursory manner, but as the concepts and ideas mature in your mind they will become a part of your musical makeup and will eventually amplify and broaden your musical intuition.

This book is essentially a study of patterns in music. It seeks to look at music literature as highly organized, ordered tonal designs. Your task is to observe and take part in the search for these patterns. With few exceptions, the terms I employ are in common use, and many of the procedures I use in analysis and composition are standard practice. The conclusions I reach, however, may differ at times with your judgments or with those of your professor. As long as your analysis is backed by logical reasoning and is a true assessment of the sounds you hear, such differences of opinion are healthy and are positive indications that you are developing your own convictions—certainly one of the objectives of the course.

Included in the book are a large number of musical examples. Each one illustrates a point I make in the text, so it is critical that you study the musical illustrations and, if possible, play them on the piano. Descriptions and definitions are often explained better through music illustrations than by long, involved written explanations, so you may find my narrative material rather short and to the point. If you go no further than the words in the text, you will miss much of the information I have for you.

It is of little value to memorize definitions of terms unless you can also recognize illustrations of them in musical compositions. It does not suffice simply to know terms—you must go one step further and make these terms and ideas a familiar and practical part of your entire approach to music.

The assignments in the text are fairly numerous and are designed to allow you to apply the information you acquire to music literature. They are of three types, and each has its specific purpose:

1. Concentrated drill on a particular musical pattern or patterns is provided. Many patterns do not occur in sufficient quantity in a single composition to give you enough practice in identifying them, so these drills contain patterns extracted from their musical setting to let you work on a large variety in a shorter space of time.
2. The next step is a search for patterns and relationships in a music composition. This exploration often inspects all aspects of a work and seeks those components that create musical style. Skill in analysis is of critical importance to all musicians.
3. The ultimate test of your comprehension is composition. If you can manipulate musical devices successfully in a composition you will have achieved perhaps the single most important goal of the text. Creativity within the framework of a particular style or form is one of the best indications of superior musicianship.

In summary,

1. Your musical intuition is a very valuable asset. Use it often.
2. In addition to your intuition, a study of musical logic (music theory) makes you think consciously about the patterns in music. Without patterns, music could communicate very little.
3. The study of music theory will enhance and reinforce your musical intuition.
4. Although terms and procedures are objective, conclusions in the analysis of music are often subjective, and thus differing logical viewpoints should be expected and accepted.
5. The music illustrations are even more important than textual material. Study the illustrations at least as diligently as the written material.
6. Application of terms and concepts to actual musical situations is of the utmost importance. The memorizing of definitions is of itself of little significance.
7. In the world of music the highest premiums go to those with the most perceptive, imaginative, and creative minds. As most musicians will tell you, creativity combined with a thorough knowledge of music is the best guarantee for a successful career in music.

To the Instructor

In the words of the composer George Crumb, "Music might be defined as a system of proportions in the service of a spiritual impulse." In the same vein, music theory might be defined as the study of the artful designs, ingenious proportions, and inventive patterns in music that are transformed by the mind into aesthetic experience.

The purpose of this two-volume text is to present the basic ingredients of the art of music, so that structure, design, and language are made clear and accessible to the student examining the array of tonal configurations found in music literature. The text provides a basis for the integration of the following skills and knowledge, which are important in any undergraduate theory program:

ANALYSIS SKILLS	The ability to discern the design, proportion, and patterns of music.
HISTORICAL PERSPECTIVE	An understanding of the rich heritage of the past and the styles of music that evolved during the different periods of musical writing.
COMPOSITIONAL SKILLS	Insight into the ways in which music is put together and into the forms, elements, and resolutions required of the composer.
A "SEEING" EAR	The ability to hear music and determine the nature of the musical devices, the melody, the harmony, the rhythm, and the form. Although this book does not address itself specifically to the topic, the professor may utilize materials from it for this purpose. (Additional material may be found in my book, *Workbook in Ear Training.*)
A "HEARING" EYE	The ability to look at music and determine from sight alone how it will sound. (Additional material to develop this skill may be found in my book, *Sightsinging Complete.*)
PERFORMANCE	This book does not address itself specifically to performance; however, it provides ample opportunity for the developing musician to improve performance skills while gaining analytical, historical, and compositional perspectives.

Although this text is written from a traditional background, the following features distinguish it from more conventional books in music theory:

1. *The text begins at the beginning.* No previous knowledge of music theory is required; however, the ability to read music and play an instrument or sing is assumed.
2. *Four-part harmonization is included as a discipline.* This instruction represents a microcosm of devices and procedures found in the large body of music written during the period of tertian functional harmony.
3. *A thorough study of melody is included.* Particular stress is placed on basic melody, melody writing, melodic analysis, melodic devices, and melodic form.
4. *The text offers a historical perspective.* Frequent comparisons of style afford the opportunity to examine the framework and progress of music history.
5. *Music from the Renaissance to the contemporary period is examined in both volumes.* Compositional devices are studied in the light of stylistic trends.

6. *The text includes a study of music indigenous to American culture.* Volume 1 investigates the popular song, jazz, blues, and boogie.
7. *The twentieth century is well represented.* Volume 2 includes a variety of this century's music literature and provides diverse assignments in this area.
8. *Specific compositions are studied.* The text continually directs attention to the music examples and encourages class discussion of them.
9. *The in-class composition and performance of musical works is encouraged.* Many of the assignments found at the ends of chapters and in the accompanying workbooks are designed to promote student interest in developing composition skills.
10. *The two volumes provide a complete basis for the study of music theory.* Volume 1 is usually completed in the first year of instruction and volume 2 in the second or third year of study.
11. *The chapters may be studied in the order preferred by the instructor.* Chapters that may be covered in different order are listed in the *Instructor's Manuals* that accompany volumes 1 and 2.
12. *An outline format is maintained throughout the two volumes.* This format ensures conciseness, efficiency, and ease in locating specific topics.

Acknowledgments

Grateful acknowledgment is extended to William Hyman for his more than generous assistance in preparing two chapters, "The American Popular Song" and "Blues, Boogie, and Jazz"; to Robert McCurdy for his patience in transcribing music from recorded material; and finally, to Dale Gilbert, director of the School of Music at the University of Wisconsin, Madison, for the many intangibles of friendship without which this book would have been impossible.

Bruce Benward

MUSIC
in theory and practice

Introduction

Sound
Vibration
Compression
Rarefaction

Frequency
Pitch
Tone
Intensity

Duration
Meter
Rhythm
Timbre

Harmonic Series
Partials
Fundamental

In order to understand the nature of music, it is important to know something about its basic ingredient—sound. All compositions—past, present, and future—are simply manipulations of the four properties of sound: *pitch, intensity, duration,* and *timbre*. No matter how complicated the composition, the composer and (to an extent) the performer have only these four variables with which to work. The following definitions are important to an understanding of sound.

SOUND

Sound is the sensation perceived by the organs of hearing when vibrations (sound waves) are produced in the air.

Vibration

Vibration is the periodic motion of an elastic body (such as a string, a column of air, or vocal cords).

Compression and Rarefaction

These terms refer to the alternation of increased *(compression)* and decreased *(rarefaction)* pressure in the air caused by an activated (vibrating) surface or air column. One complete cycle of compression and rarefaction produces a vibration, or sound wave.

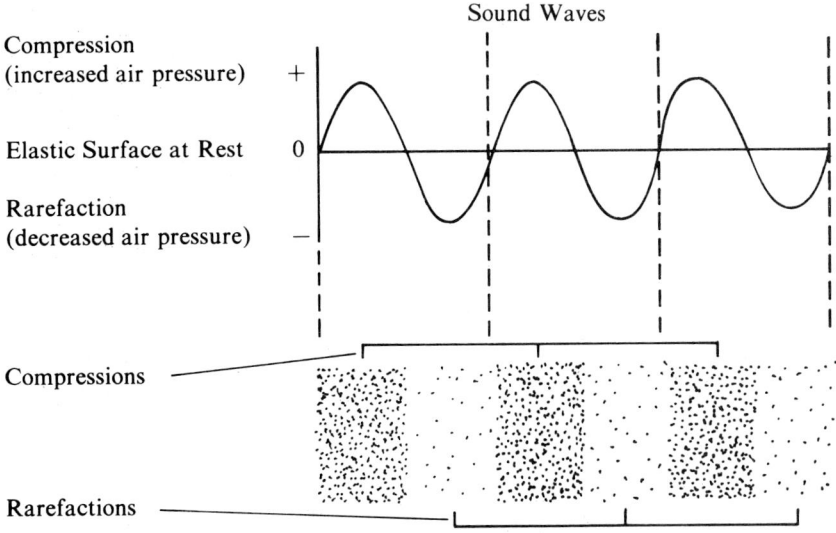

Frequency
: *Frequency* refers to the number of compression-rarefaction cycles that occur per unit of time, usually one second. Audible sounds for the human ear range from 20 to 20,000 cycles per second (cps).

THE FOUR PROPERTIES OF SOUND
: The four properties of sound as these relate to music are described in the following terms.

Pitch
: *Pitch* is the highness or lowness of a sound. Variations in frequency are what we hear as variations in pitch: the greater the number of sound waves produced per second by the vibration of an elastic body, the higher the sound we hear; the fewer sound waves per second, the lower the sound.

Tone
: A *tone* is a musical sound of definite pitch.

Intensity
: *Intensity* (amplitude) is heard as the loudness or softness of a pitch. In *acoustics* (the science of sound), intensity is the amount of energy affecting the vibrating body, and the physicist measures intensity on a scale from 0 to 130 in units called *decibels*. The composer uses symbols to indicate gradations of loudness or softness in a composition.

ITALIAN WORD	SYMBOL	TRANSLATION	AVERAGE DECIBELS
PIANISSIMO	*pp*	VERY SOFT	40
PIANO	*p*	SOFT	50
MEZZO PIANO	*mp*	MODERATELY SOFT	60
MEZZO FORTE	*mf*	MODERATELY LOUD	70
FORTE	*f*	LOUD	80
FORTISSIMO	*ff*	VERY LOUD	100

Duration
: *Duration* is the length of time a pitch, or tone, is sounded. For patterns of duration the following terms are used: *meter* and *rhythm*.

Meter
: *Meter* describes regularly recurring notes of equal duration, generally grouped into patterns of two, three, four, or more with the first note in each group accented. These patterns of strong (−) and weak (⌣) pulses are called *beats*. For example:

Duple meter: − ⌣ / − ⌣ / − ⌣ =

Triple meter: − ⌣ ⌣ / − ⌣ ⌣ / − ⌣ ⌣ =

The recurring patterns of a *duple* (two-beat) *meter* or a *triple* (three-beat) *meter* are the two basic meters. All other meters result from some combination of these two.

Rhythm

Composers superimpose note values (durations) of varying lengths on these metrical patterns in order to give expression to their musical ideas. This relationship between the specific durations, which express (externalize) musical ideas, and the meter(s), on which these ideas are superimposed, becomes one of the most important aspects of rhythm.

Timbre

Timbre is the tone quality or color of a sound. It is the property of sound that permits us, for instance, to distinguish between the sound of a clarinet and the sound of an oboe.

This individual quality of sound is determined by the shape of the vibrating body, its material (metal, wood, human tissue), and the method used to put it in motion (striking, bowing, blowing). It is also the result of the human ear's blending into one sound what is indeed a series of tones or pitches produced simultaneously by the vibrating body.

Harmonic Series

A *harmonic series* includes the various pitches produced simultaneously by a vibrating body. This physical phenomenon results because the body vibrates in sections as well as in a single unit. A string, for example, vibrates along its entire length as well as in halves, thirds, quarters, and so on until it comes to rest.

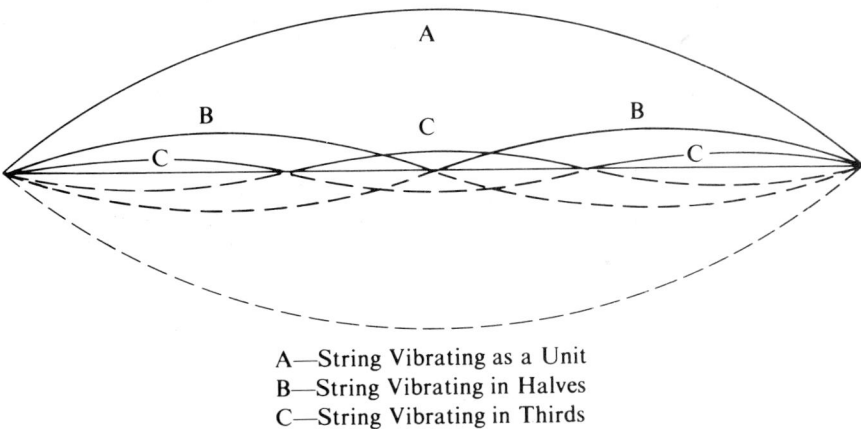

A—String Vibrating as a Unit
B—String Vibrating in Halves
C—String Vibrating in Thirds

The pitches produced simultaneously by the vibrating sections are called *partials*, or *harmonics*. The first partial, often called the *fundamental*, and the series of partials produced simultaneously by the vibrating body constitute a musical tone. Since the fundamental is the lowest frequency and is also perceived as the loudest, the ear identifies the fundamental as the specific pitch of the musical tone.

Although the harmonic series theoretically goes to infinity, there are practical limits; the human ear is insensitive to frequencies above 20,000 cps. The following illustration carries the harmonic series to the sixteenth partial:

Harmonic Series of C

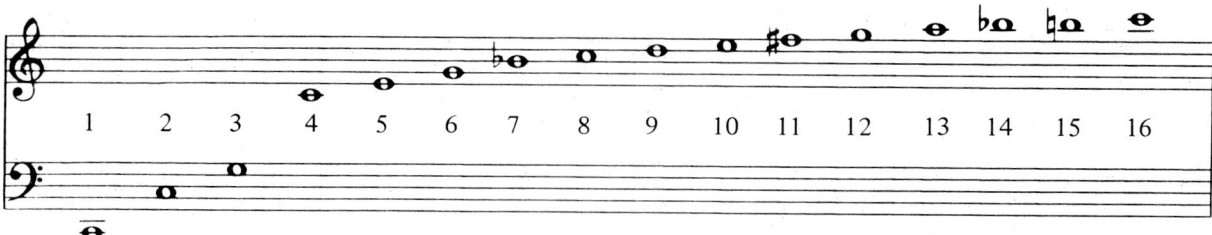

Fundamental

The individual partials that make up a musical tone are not distinguished separately, but are heard by the human ear as a blend that characterizes timbre.

An instrument like the clarinet tends to favor the odd-numbered partials (1, 3, 5, 7, 9, and so on) due to its nature and the makeup of its vibrating air column. This suppression of the even partials is what gives the clarinet its particular quality of tone.

SUMMARY It is important to remember that the characteristics of a musical tone—pitch, duration, intensity, tone quality—are present simultaneously and that no practical separation of these is really possible. The principal concern is to determine how these musical tones interact with each other to produce a musical grammar.

1 Notation

Neumatic Notation	*C Clef*	*Notation of Duration*	*Dot*
Mensural Notation	*Alto Clef*	*Whole Note and Rest*	*Meter Signatures*
Tablature Notation	*Tenor Clef*	*Half Note and Rest*	*Simple Meter*
White Notation	*Octave Identification*	*Quarter Note and Rest*	*Compound Meter*
Staff	*Intervals*	*Eighth Note and Rest*	*Asymmetrical Meters*
Letter Names	*Sharp*	*Sixteenth Note and Rest*	*Decimal Meter*
Solfeggio Syllables	*Flat*	*Thirty-Second Note and Rest*	*Fractional Meter*
Treble Clef	*Natural*		*Mixed Meter*
Bass Clef	*Double Sharp*	*Sixty-Fourth Note and Rest*	*Polymeter*
Grand Staff	*Double Flat*		*Dynamic Markings*
Ledger Lines	*Enharmonic Equivalents*	*Tie*	*Manuscript Notation*

When we transcribe speech, we are involved in writing symbols that will call to mind only the spoken words. The words we write do not show who should speak them or how fast or how loud they should be said. When we notate music, however, we write symbols that show three of the four properties of sound: pitch and duration are given accurately and relative intensity is indicated. Furthermore, pitch and duration are shown simultaneously. Music notation is therefore of necessity far more complicated than written words.

HISTORY

Neumatic Notation

From about A.D. 650 to A.D. 1200, music notation consisted of a set of symbols called *neumes* (pronounced "newms"). These symbols took their name from the Greek word meaning gesture. Written above the Latin texts associated with the liturgy of the Roman Catholic church, neumes could not convey pitch or duration, but rather served as a memory aid in recalling previously learned melodic lines.

EARLY TYPES OF NEUMES

/   .   ✓   ∧

VIRGA   PUNCTUM   PODATUS   CLIVIS

The following example of neumatic notation is from a twelfth-century gradual taken from a manuscript in the New York Public Library.*

---

*Curt Sachs, *Our Musical Heritage: A Short History of Music,* 2nd ed. © 1955, Plate II. Reproduced by permission of Prentice-Hall Inc., Englewood Cliffs, New Jersey.

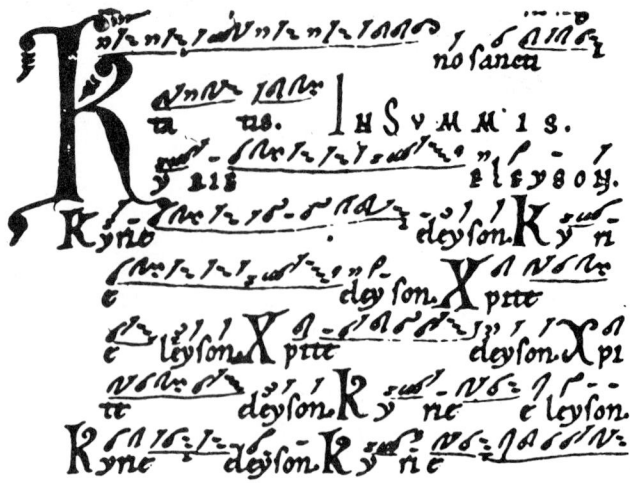

In the tenth century, a horizontal red line was drawn above the text to indicate F. The neumes were written on, above, and below this line, and their position in relation to it indicated their approximate pitch. Later a second line to indicate C was drawn in yellow above the red line.

In the eleventh century, a four-line staff appeared that included the F line, the C line, and two additional lines. Neumes were square- or diamond-shaped. Combined with the staff, neumes now had the capability for indicating specific pitches. The four-line staff is still used to notate Gregorian chant.

Four-line staff and later types of neumes*

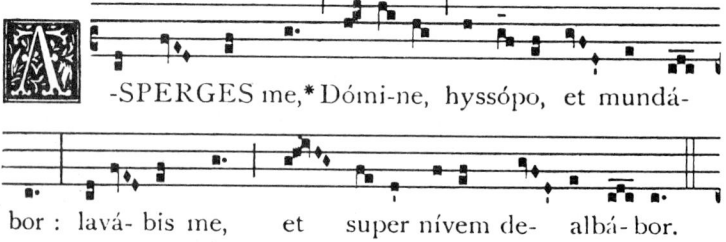

Transcribed into modern notation:

Mensural Notation

Mensural (measured) notation, a system that included durational values as well as pitch, developed during the thirteenth century as the single melody and free rhythm of Gregorian chant or plainsong gave way to measured music that included parts, descant, and later harmony and counterpoint.

*An antiphon in Gregorian chant from *The Liber Usualis, No. 801*, ed. the Benedictines of Solesmes. (Boston: McLaughlin & Reilly Co., 1938) p. 11.

LATE THIRTEENTH-CENTURY MENSURAL NOTATION

DUPLEX LONGA   LONGA   BREVIS   SEMIBREVIS

From approximately 1250 to 1450, notes were predominately black (heads filled in). From 1450 to about 1600 (the Renaissance period), composers used white notation (note heads not filled in).

RENAISSANCE NOTATION

NOTE NAME	SYMBOL	CORRESPONDS TO OUR
MAXIMA	⊐	NONE
LONGA	⊐	NONE
BREVIS	▭	𝅜
SEMIBREVIS	◇	o
MINIMA	◇ (stem)	♩ (half note)

Tablature Notation

Tablature notation was a type of instrumental notation found in the fifteenth, sixteenth, and seventeenth centuries. Pitch was illustrated by numbers or letters placed on a series of lines that was not a staff but represented the strings, keyboard, or holes of the individual instrument.

The following example illustrates a type of Italian tablature for the *chitarra* (guitar). The numbers represent frets where the fingers should be placed (O means open string), and the lines are the strings of the instrument. Beneath the tablature is the same music in modern notation.

Bergamasca   Intavolatura di Chitarra e Chitarriglia (1646)*

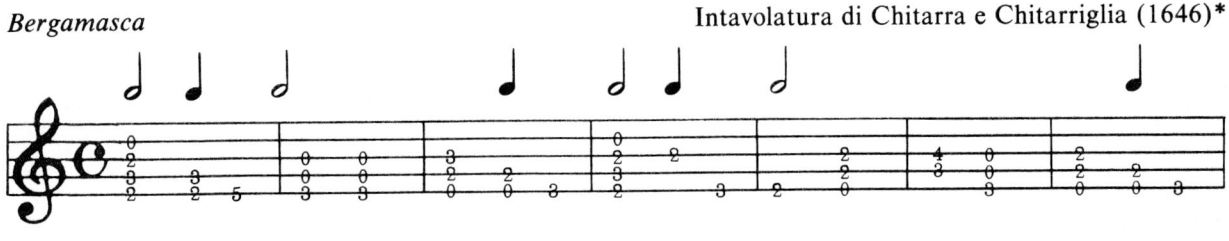

Tablature in modern notation:

*Johannes Wolf, *Notationskunde* (Leipzig: Breitkopf & Härtel, 1919).

Present Notation

Our present system of notation evolved from thirteenth-century practices. The treatise on mensural notation *De Musica Mensurabili (Ars Cantus Mensurabilis)*, by Franco of Cologne (active 1250–80), contains fundamental rules of modern notation. The five-line staff appeared in the thirteenth century. Present-day conventional notation is more directly related to fifteenth- and sixteenth-century mensural notation. The later use of bar lines and square- or diamond-shaped notes brought notation very close to the type found today. The chart below shows the evolution of some of the more common notational signs.

HISTORICAL DEVELOPMENT OF NOTATION

DEVELOPED APPROXIMATELY	TYPE	EXAMPLES OF NOTATION
A.D. 650	NEUMES	/ ·
A.D. 1250	BLACK MENSURAL	▌ ▪ ♦
A.D. 1450	WHITE MENSURAL	▯ ▭ ◇ ◇ ♦ ♪
A.D. 1600	MODERN	▭ o 𝅗𝅥 ♩ ♪

The sixteenth century introduced the short *ledger lines* that made it possible to extend the range of the staff. Our round notes developed when it was realized that they were easier to write and print. Although a fairly basic system has prevailed during the past three hundred years and we often think of the present system as static, notation is at this moment undergoing transformation.

NOTATION OF PITCH

The Staff

Five lines:
═════════

Letter Names

The various pitches are referred to by the first seven letters of the alphabet (A B C D E F G).

Solfeggio Syllables

Certain systems of *solfeggio* (vocal exercises sung to a vowel, syllables, or words) use the syllables do, re, mi, fa, sol, la, ti to indicate the pitch.

The present solfeggio system derives from Guido d'Arezzo, an eleventh-century monk, who sought to teach sight-singing through the use of a well-known hymn to St. John, *Ut queant laxis*. The hymn contains six phrases of text, and the beginning notes of the phrases of Guido's melody form the first six notes of the scale: C, D, E, F, G, A. The syllables beginning these phrases are ut, re, mi, fa, sol, la.

Scale degree:	C	D	E	F	G	A
Syllable:	ut	re	mi	fa	sol	la

Hymn to St. John *(Ut queant laxis)*

The significance of this system lay in the location of the half step which occurred between the syllables mi and fa. The *hexachord* (a scale of six notes) could begin on C, and on G or F as well. In the hexachord on F, a B-flat was added to insure the half-step interval between mi and fa. The first syllable was eventually changed from ut to do.

The Clefs

A *clef* is a symbol placed at the beginning of a line of music that establishes the letter names of the lines and spaces of the staff.

Treble Clef (G)

The *treble clef* or *G clef* is an ornate letter G. The curved line terminates at the second line of the staff, thus designating the letter name of a note on that line as G.

Staff with Treble or G Clef

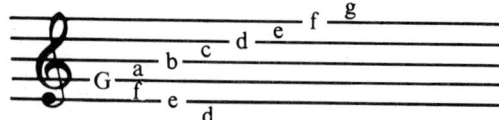

Bass Clef (F)

The *bass clef* resembles a large comma followed by a colon. It is called the *F clef* because it derives from the letter F (𝄢 becomes 𝄢). The dots of the colon are placed above and below the fourth line of the staff, designating that line as F.

Staff with Bass or F Clef

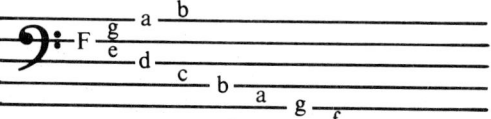

Grand Staff

Together, the treble and bass staves make up the *grand staff* associated with keyboard music. The illustration shows the point at which both clef signs converge. The two Cs are the same pitch. The pitch is called *middle C*.

Grand Staff

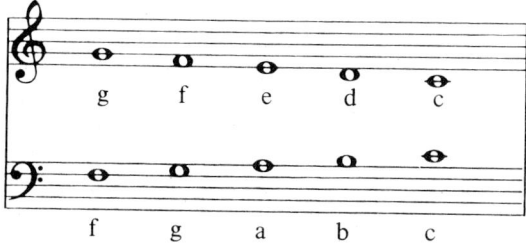

Ledger Lines

Pitches that go beyond the limits of the staff are written by adding *ledger lines* above or below the staff. Ledger lines, which parallel the staff, accommodate only one note.

12   Notation

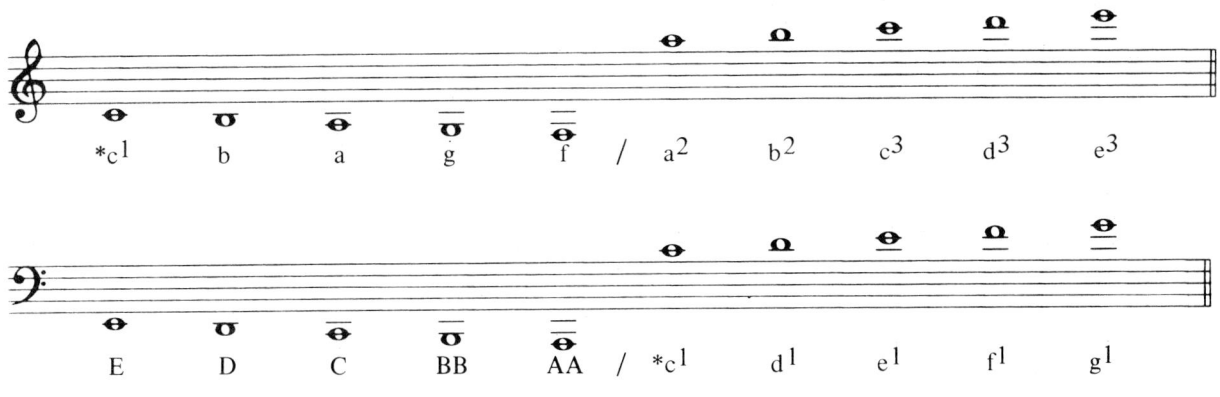

C Clef

A *C clef* may be placed on any line of the staff. It is a movable clef. The notch of this elaborate symbol points to the line that will designate the pitch of middle C.

Alto Clef

The *alto clef* is a C clef that notches or designates the third line of the staff as middle C. It is the standard clef used in music for viola.

Tenor Clef

The *tenor clef* is a C clef that notches or designates the fourth line of the staff as middle C. The tenor clef is occasionally found in music written for cello, bassoon, or trombone.

Soprano, Mezzo Soprano, and Baritone Clefs

The *soprano, mezzo soprano,* and *baritone clefs* are C clefs less often used than the alto and tenor clefs. In each case the line indicated by the notch of the clef is designated as middle C.

ASSIGNMENT 1 Write the letter name of each note in the blanks below the staff.

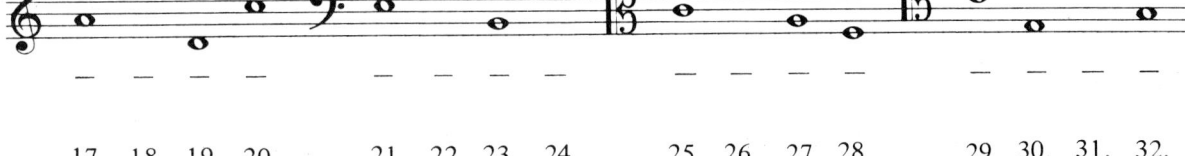

---

*Numbers are used to identify pitches with a specific octave (see page 14).

OCTAVE IDENTIFICATION

Since the pitch spectrum is so wide, it is often necessary to identify a specific note by the octave in which it appears. Thus, middle C is distinguished from any other C in the pitch spectrum by the written designation c^1.

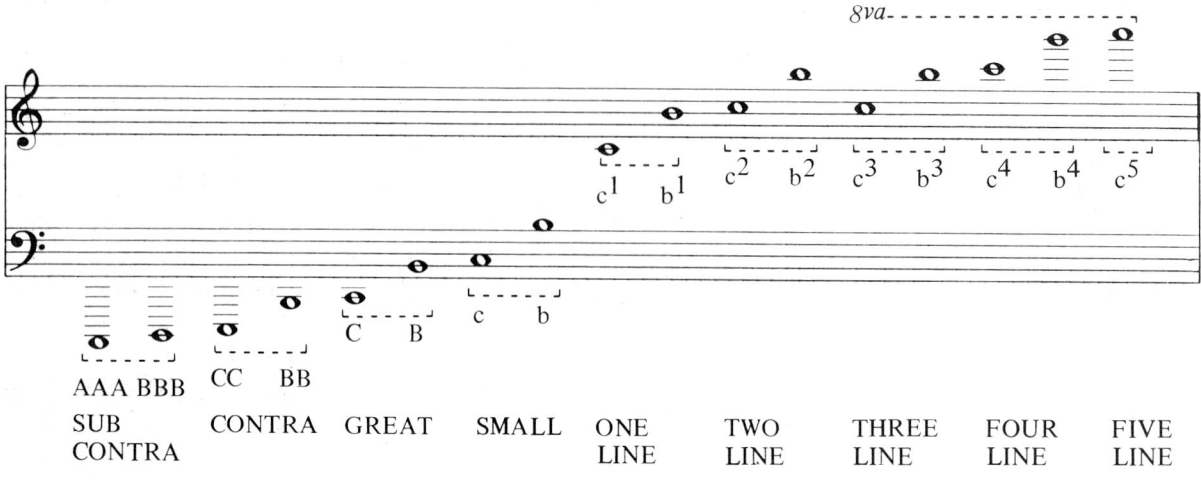

ASSIGNMENT 2 Write the letter name for each note and indicate the octave identification.

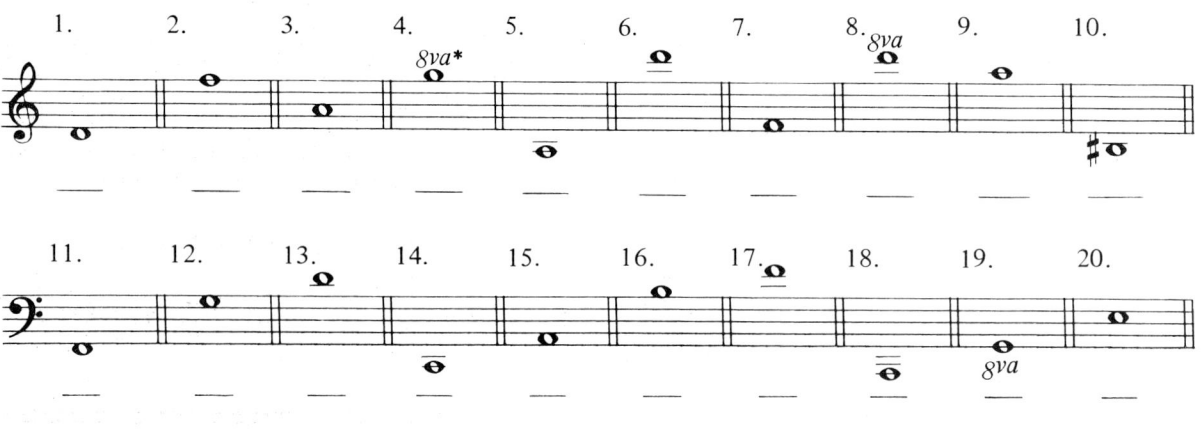

INTERVALS

An *interval* is the difference in pitch between two tones. In Western music the half step is the smallest interval used. It is the interval between any two adjacent tones in the pitch spectrum.

*"8va" above a note indicates that it sounds an octave higher than written. Below the note indicates that it sounds an octave lower than written.

ACCIDENTALS *Accidentals* are symbols that are placed to the left of the note heads to indicate the raising or lowering of a pitch.

Sharp (♯)—raise the pitch a half step.
Flat (♭)—lower the pitch a half step.
Natural (♮)—cancel any previous sharp or flat and return to the natural, or unaltered, pitch.
Double Sharp (𝄪)—raise the pitch two half steps.
Double Flat (♭♭)—lower the pitch two half steps.

G Sharp   G Flat   G Natural   G Double Sharp   G Double Flat

Enharmonic Equivalents *Enharmonic equivalents* are tones that have the same pitch but different letter names.

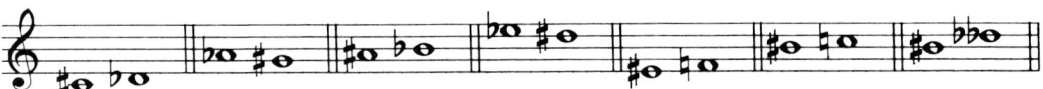

In passages of music involving half-step motion, flatted tones are most often followed by a tone with a different letter name a half step lower.

USUALLY FOUND: LESS OFTEN FOUND:

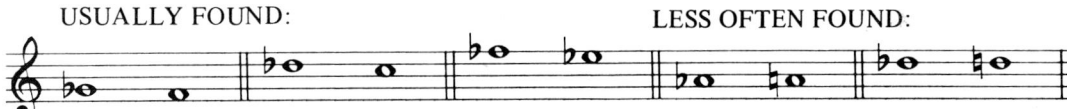

In passages of music involving half-step motion, sharped tones are most often followed by tones with a different letter name a half step higher.

USUALLY FOUND: LESS OFTEN FOUND:

ASSIGNMENT 3
1. Below are ten notes.
2. Among the ten notes are five pairs of enharmonic equivalents (tones that have the same pitch but different letter names).
3. Using the numbers below the staff, pair up the enharmonic equivalents:

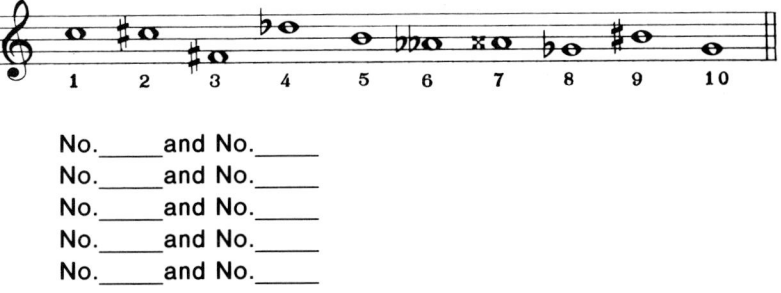

No.____ and No.____
No.____ and No.____
No.____ and No.____
No.____ and No.____
No.____ and No.____

NOTATION OF DURATION

Notation of duration is illustrated in the following chart:

NAME	NOTE	REST	EQUIVALENTS	
Breve (double whole note)	𝄺		Two Whole Notes	𝅝 𝅝
Whole Note	𝅝		Two Half Notes	𝅗𝅥 𝅗𝅥
Half Note	𝅗𝅥		Two Quarter Notes	♩ ♩
Quarter Note	♩		Two Eighth Notes	♫
Eighth Note	♪		Two Sixteenth Notes	
Sixteenth Note			Two Thirty-second Notes	
Thirty-second Note			Two Sixty-fourth Notes	
Sixty-fourth Note			Two One Hundred Twenty-eighth Notes	

The Tie

The *tie* is a curved line that connects two adjacent notes of the same pitch into a single sound with a duration equal to the sum of both note values.

The Dot

Placed to the right of a note head, the *dot* lengthens the value of the note by half again its value. A *second dot* lengthens the dotted note value by half the length of the first dot:

Dots may also be used with rests and affect them in the same way:

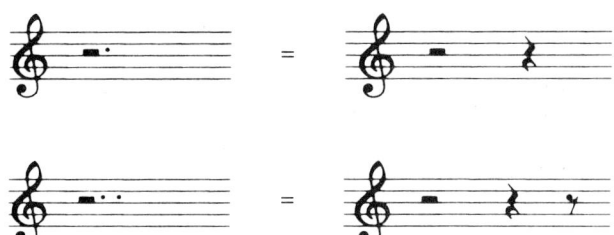

Meter Signatures

Meter may be defined as a regular, recurring pattern of strong and weak pulses of equal duration. This recurring pattern of durations is identified at the beginning of a composition by a *meter signature* (time signature) of two numbers.

The upper digit indicates the number of basic durations per measure. It may or may not indicate the number of pulses per measure (as will be seen later in compound meters).

The lower digit indicates the note value of the basic duration: 2 signifies a half note, 4 refers to a quarter note, 8 to an eighth note, and so forth.

Simple Meter

In *simple meter,* each beat is divided and subdivided by two. The upper numbers in simple meter signatures are usually 1, 2, 3, or 4. Some simple meters showing the duple division of the beat:

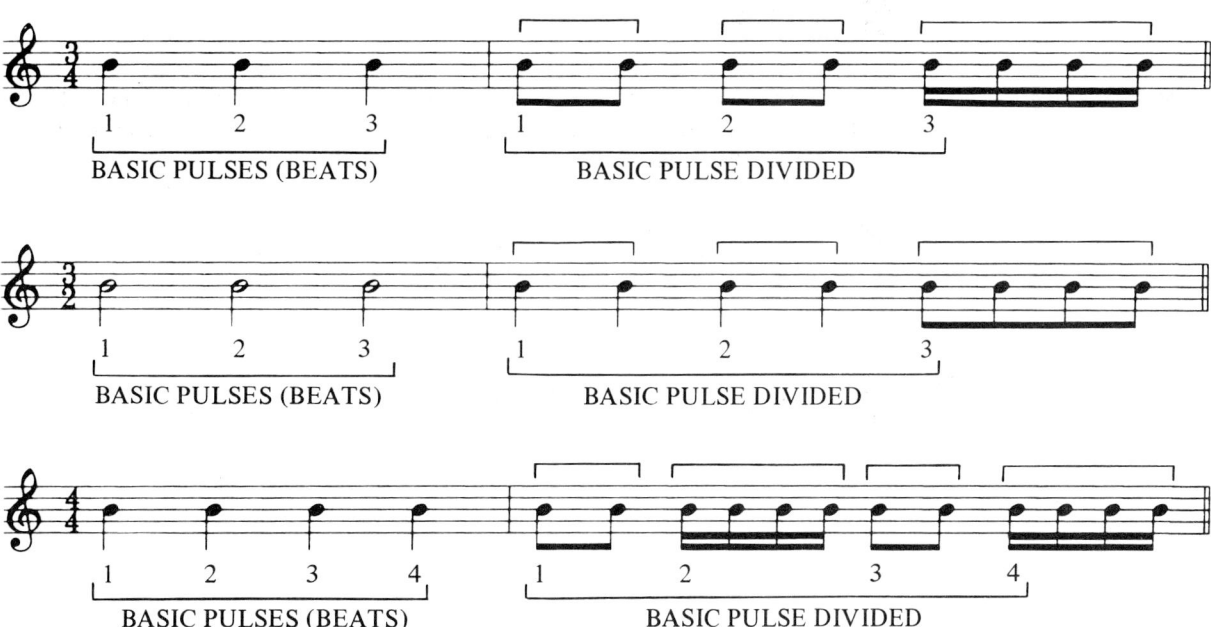

Compound Meter   In *compound meter,* each pulse combines beats into groups of three. The most common compound meter signatures are 6/8, 9/8, and 12/8.

Compound meter signatures often utilized:

6	6	6		9	9	9		12	12	12
4	8	16		4	8	16		4	8	16

Musicians consider only two basic pulses in 6/8 meter, three in 9/8 meter, and four in 12/8 meter.

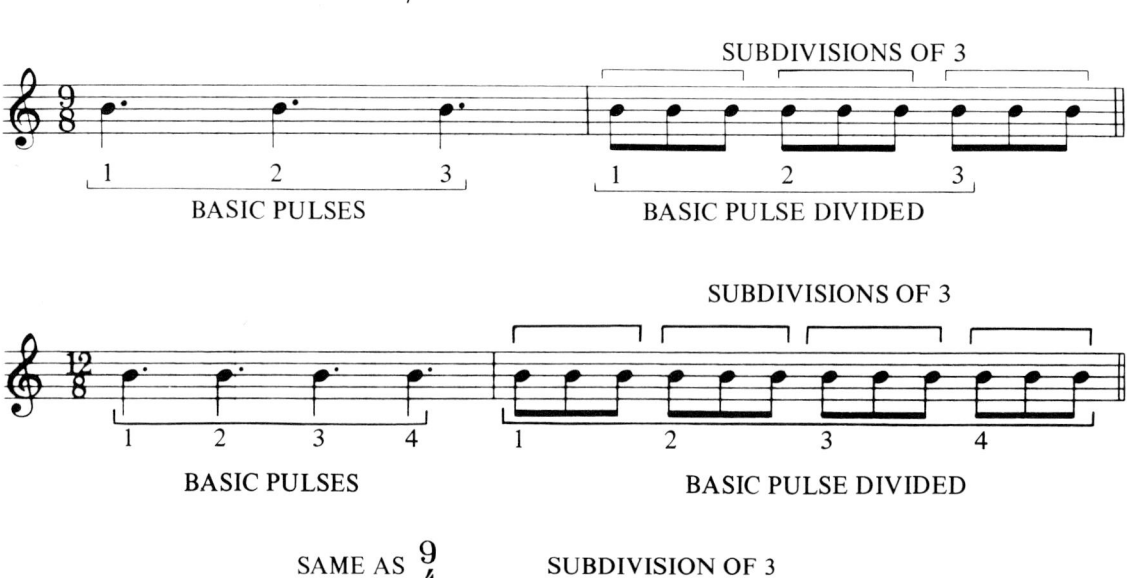

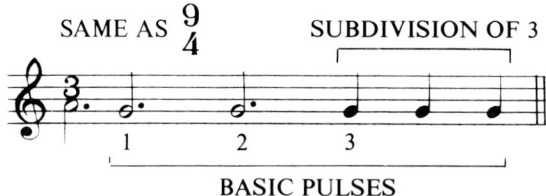

18 Notation

Note that the basic pulse will be some kind of dotted note value:

Asymmetrical Meters The term *asymmetrical* means not symmetrical and applies to those meter signatures that indicate the pulse cannot be divided into equal groups of 2, 3, or 4.

Asymmetrical Divisions *Asymmetrical divisions* are sometimes unconventional divisions of a measure (which might otherwise be fitted into a simple or compound meter) that are used consistently throughout a composition or an extended section.

Asymmetrical division of 9/8 $\quad \dfrac{4 + 2 + 3}{8}$

Asymmetrical division of 8/8 or 4/4 $\quad \dfrac{3 + 2 + 3}{8}$

New Trends Innovations in music of the twentieth century include the use of meters in which the lower number is replaced by a note value, decimal meters, fractional meters, mixed meters, and polymeters.

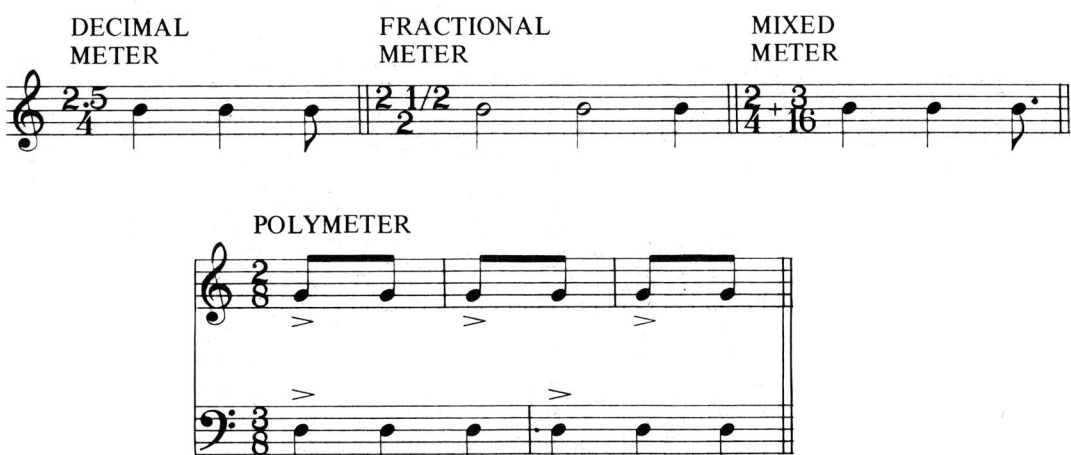

Notation 19

DYNAMIC MARKINGS

Dynamic marks indicate the general volume (amplitude) of sound. Although imprecise, such marks denote approximate levels of intensity. The following words, abbreviations, and signs are common:

SYMBOL	TERM	DEFINITION
pp	PIANISSIMO	VERY SOFT
p	PIANO	SOFT
mp	MEZZO-PIANO	MODERATELY SOFT
mf	MEZZO-FORTE	MODERATELY LOUD
f	FORTE	LOUD
ff	FORTISSIMO	VERY LOUD
<	CRESC. OR CRESCENDO	BECOME LOUDER
>	DECRESC., DECRESCENDO, OR DIM., DIMINUENDO	BECOME SOFTER
sfz sf	SFORZANDO, SFORZATO	SUDDEN ACCENT ON A SINGLE NOTE OR CHORD
sfp	SFORZANDO FOLLOWED BY PIANO	SUDDEN ACCENT FOLLOWED IMMEDIATELY BY SOFT
fp	FORTEPIANO	LOUD FOLLOWED IMMEDIATELY BY SOFT

SOME DIRECTIONS FOR NOTATION IN MANUSCRIPT

1. The stems of single notes within the staff should be about one octave in length.

One Octave

2. When a staff contains a single melody line only, stems go down on those notes above the middle line and up when the notes are below the middle line. When the note is on the middle line, the stem is usually taken down except when the stems of adjacent notes are in the opposite direction.

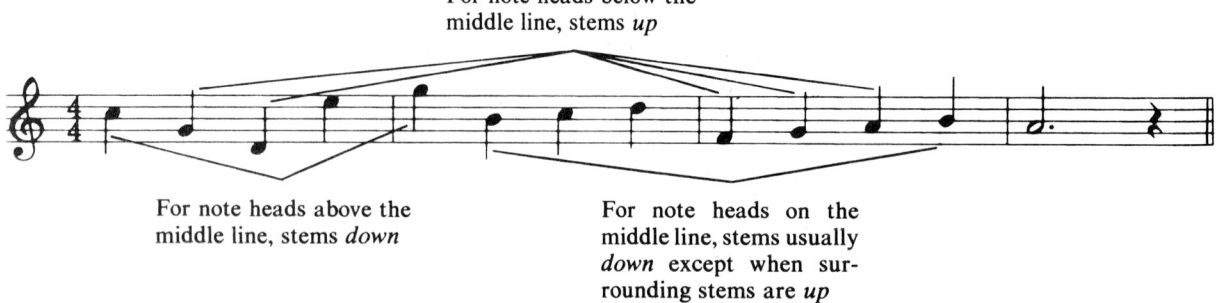

For note heads below the middle line, stems *up*

For note heads above the middle line, stems *down*

For note heads on the middle line, stems usually *down* except when surrounding stems are *up*

3. When stemmed notes are placed on ledger lines, the stems should extend to the middle line of the staff.

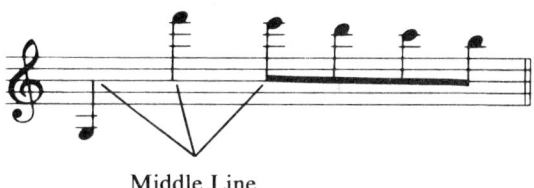

Middle Line

4. When connected by beams, stemmed notes should be modified so that the beams are slanted to cross no more than one line of the staff for each set of two notes.

Beam does not pass more than one staff line per two notes

5. When two melodies occupy the same staff, the stems for one melody are up and for the other down. This makes it possible to distinguish each separate melody.

6. Beam groups of eighth notes (also smaller values) according to unit beats.

7. Use flags for eighth or shorter value notes that are not grouped to permit beaming.

8. Avoid connecting (by beams) more than six notes unless all are a part of one beat.
9. Avoid mixing flagged and beamed notes except when notating vocal music. In vocal music using shorter note values (eighth notes or smaller), flagged notes should be used when the text-music relationship involves one note for each syllable.

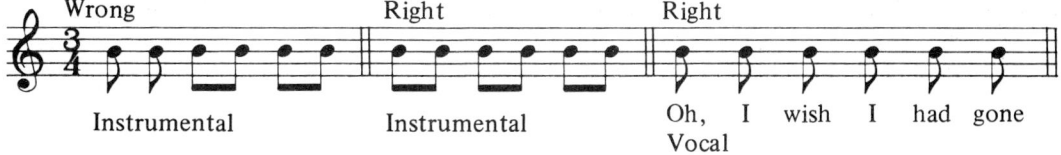

Instrumental   Instrumental   Oh,   I   wish   I   had   gone
                                                                   Vocal

10. Irregular divisions of a beat or measure are indicated by showing the number of notes in the resulting group by means of an arabic number.
    The note values of the irregular group are notated the same as the regular group providing the number of notes in the irregular group is less than twice that of the regular, e.g., a triplet retains the same note values as a regular duplet.

Regular group is 8th notes   Irregular group is also 8th notes.

When the number of notes in the irregular group is more than twice the number of the regular, then the next smaller note value is used, e.g., a quintuplet would employ the next smaller note value.

Regular group is 8th notes   Irregular group is 16th notes (Contains more than twice the notes of the regular group)

11. In compound meter, try to show the basic pulse structure of the measure and the subdivision (of three) as clearly as possible.

12. The whole rest (▬) can be used to indicate a full measure rest in any meter.
13. Avoid half rests in 3/4 meter; use two quarter rests.

14. When notes of a chord are on an adjacent line and space, the higher of the two is always to the right regardless of the direction of the stem.

Higher note to the right

15. When a dotted note is on a line the dot is usually placed slightly above the line. When two separate voices are placed on a single staff, the dots are below the line on the notes with stems down.

Dots *above* the line except in two voices

16. Dynamic markings should be added above, between, or below staves according to the nature of the music or score:

    Instrumental Music: The markings are usually placed beneath the staff to which they refer. Sometimes, because of inadequate space, it is necessary to place markings above the staff.

    Vocal Music: The markings are usually placed above the staff to which they refer. This is done to avoid confusion with the words of the text.

    Piano Scores: The markings are placed between the staves if the markings are to apply to both staves. If markings are needed for each staff individually, the markings should go just above or below the staff to which they refer.

    Generally avoid placing markings directly on the staff, although some like the crescendo ⟨ and diminuendo ⟩ will protrude into the staff on occasion.

ASSIGNMENT 4 Below are five melodies without meter signatures. Indicate the meter signature, or in some cases, the two meter signatures, that renders the notation correct.

No. 1 _____ and _____
No. 2 _____ and _____
No. 3 _____ and _____
No. 4 _____ and _____
No. 5 _____ and _____

ASSIGNMENT 5 Below are sixteen measures of music. In each the notation is either confusing or incorrect.
Rewrite each measure on the staff provided and clarify or correct the notation.

ASSIGNMENT 6

1. Select a meter signature from either subheading "Asymmetrical Meters" or "New Trends" on page 19.
2. Write a measure in a rhythm you think is "catchy." Include or exclude pitch as you wish.
3. Play the rhythm in class and repeat it at least five times.
4. Ask each of the other members of the class (individually) to repeat your rhythm.
5. Then, ask each class member to notate the rhythm on score paper.
6. You must decide whether each notation is correct (even if it is different from your way of notating it) or incorrect.

ASSIGNMENT 7

1. Write a rhythmic composition of sixteen measures that contains rhythmic patterns each lasting two measures and repeated once. Continue these patterns through the sixteen measures. You should end up with four different rhythmic patterns, each repeated once.
2. Add melodic pitches or make your composition exclusively rhythmic—as you wish.
3. Play your sixteen-measure composition in class. Repeat it several times.
4. Appoint individual class members to remember each of the four rhythms in your composition—one class member per rhythm.
5. Then, ask these four members to play your four rhythms, each playing the rhythm you asked the individual to remember and in the same order you had played them, of course.

2 Scales, Modes, Intervals, Tonality, Key

Scale Pitches
Diatonic Scales
Major Scale
Transposition
Circle of Fifths
Natural Minor Scale
Harmonic Minor Scale
Melodic Minor Scale

Scale Tuning
Pythagorean Tuning
Mean-Tone Tuning
Equal Temperament
Relative Relationship
Parallel Relationship
Pentatonic Scale

Nondiatonic Scales
Chromatic Scale
Whole Tone Scale
Greek Modes
Church Modes
Major, Minor, Perfect Intervals

Augmented and Diminished Intervals
Enharmonic Intervals
Inversion of Intervals
Tonality
Key
Pitch Inventory

SCALE

A *scale* is a series of ascending and descending pitches. Musicians use a scale as a convenient way of displaying the tones used in a melody or harmony. In the following example, the melody consists of twenty-four notes but only seven different letter names. These letters are arranged in ascending order to form a scale.

Although an infinite variety of pitch combinations are available, the following scales represent those in most common use during the past 200 years.

DIATONIC SCALES

Diatonic (literally "across the tones") defines a scale of mixed half and whole steps (and an occasional step-and-a-half) in which each individual tone plays a role. The first tone (the *tonic*) of a scale is a point of rest and is considered to be the most stable. Other tones lead toward or away from it creating varying degrees of tension or relaxation.

Since the *tonic* (the first note) is the focal point of the scale, the most stable note, and the point of greatest relaxation, diatonic melodies are frequently shaped by composers to end on the tonic note. At times the word "diatonic" is used to indicate a tone that is part of a particular scale pattern—as distinguished from a *nondiatonic* tone that does not belong to the scale pattern.

Major Scale

The *major scale* is a scale of seven different pitches with whole steps separating adjacent tones except for half steps between the third and fourth degrees and between the seventh and eighth (or first) degrees. The eighth pitch has the same letter name as the first and thus is treated as a duplication.

Since all adjacent keys (black and white) on the piano are a half step apart, the following illustration shows that by beginning on C and playing in order only the white keys to the next C, a *C major* scale results.

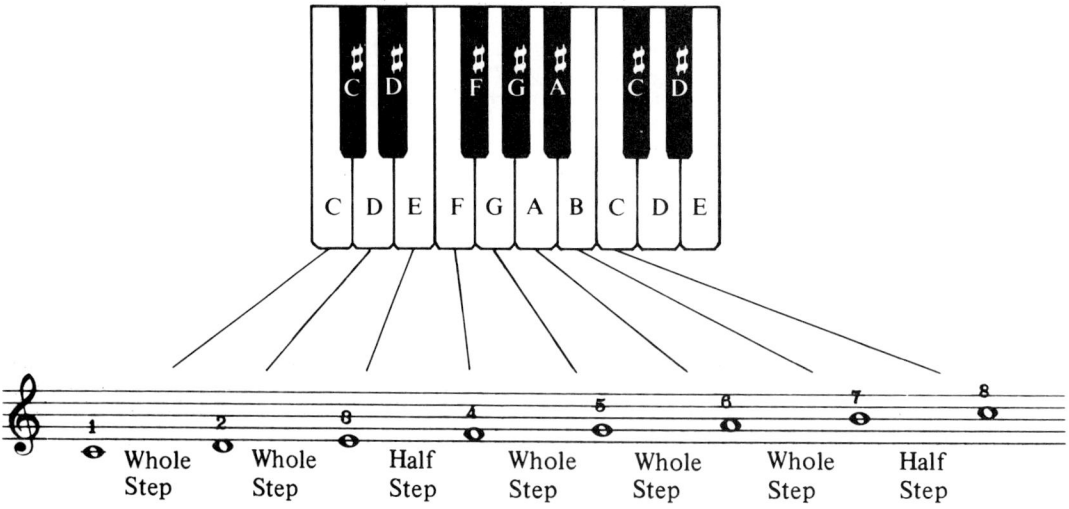

The following melody utilizes the notes of the C major scale:

Duke Street   Hymn Tune

28 Scales, Modes, Intervals, Tonality, Key

Transposition This same major-scale pattern of half and whole steps can be duplicated at any pitch. Such rewriting is called *transposition*. In the following example, the major scale is transposed so that its first tone is G and it is called the *G major scale*:

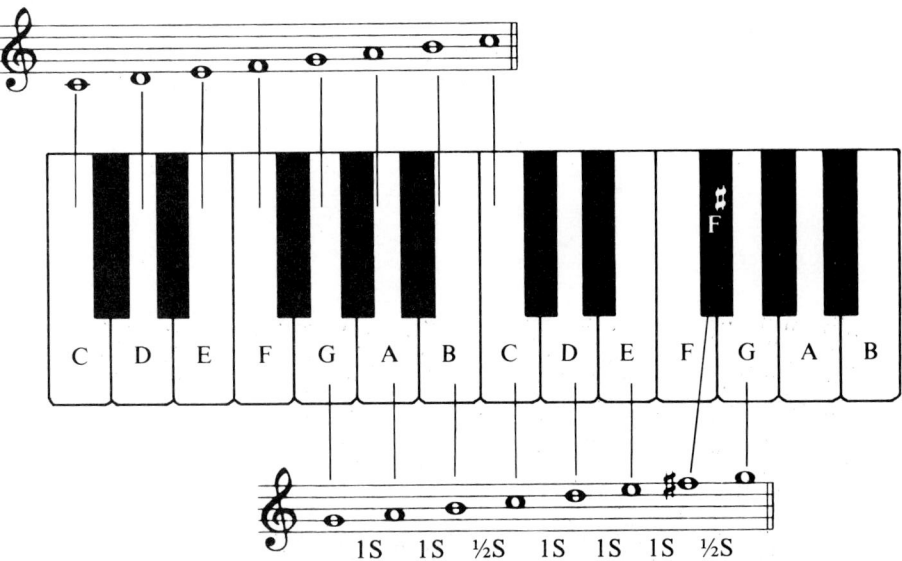

From the preceding illustration of the G major scale, it can be seen that a sharp is necessary if the major-scale pattern of half and whole steps is to be carried out in the transposition. The following chart provides a convenient way to memorize the sharps or the flats needed when the scale begins on various pitches. The arrangement of the necessary sharps or flats is called a *key signature* and appears at the beginning of each staff in a composition. Notice that each successive tonic, or beginning note, is a *perfect fifth,* or a *P5* (five scale degrees), above the previous tonic. A new sharp is added to the key signature for each succeeding P5, and in the flat signatures, a flat is dropped for each succeeding P5.

MAJOR KEY SIGNATURES

TONIC (BEGINNING NOTE)	NUMBER OF SHARPS OR FLATS	KEY SIGNATURE AND TONIC NOTE
C	NONE	
G	1 SHARP	
D	2 SHARPS	
A	3 SHARPS	
E	4 SHARPS	
B = C♭	5 SHARPS / 7 FLATS	
F♯ = G♭	6 SHARPS / 6 FLATS	
C♯ = D♭	7 SHARPS / 5 FLATS	
A♭	4 FLATS	
E♭	3 FLATS	
B♭	2 FLATS	
F	1 FLAT	

Another way to visualize the relationship of major scales one to another is to show the entire circle of transposition by P5s from C back to C.

Scales, Modes, Intervals, Tonality, Key

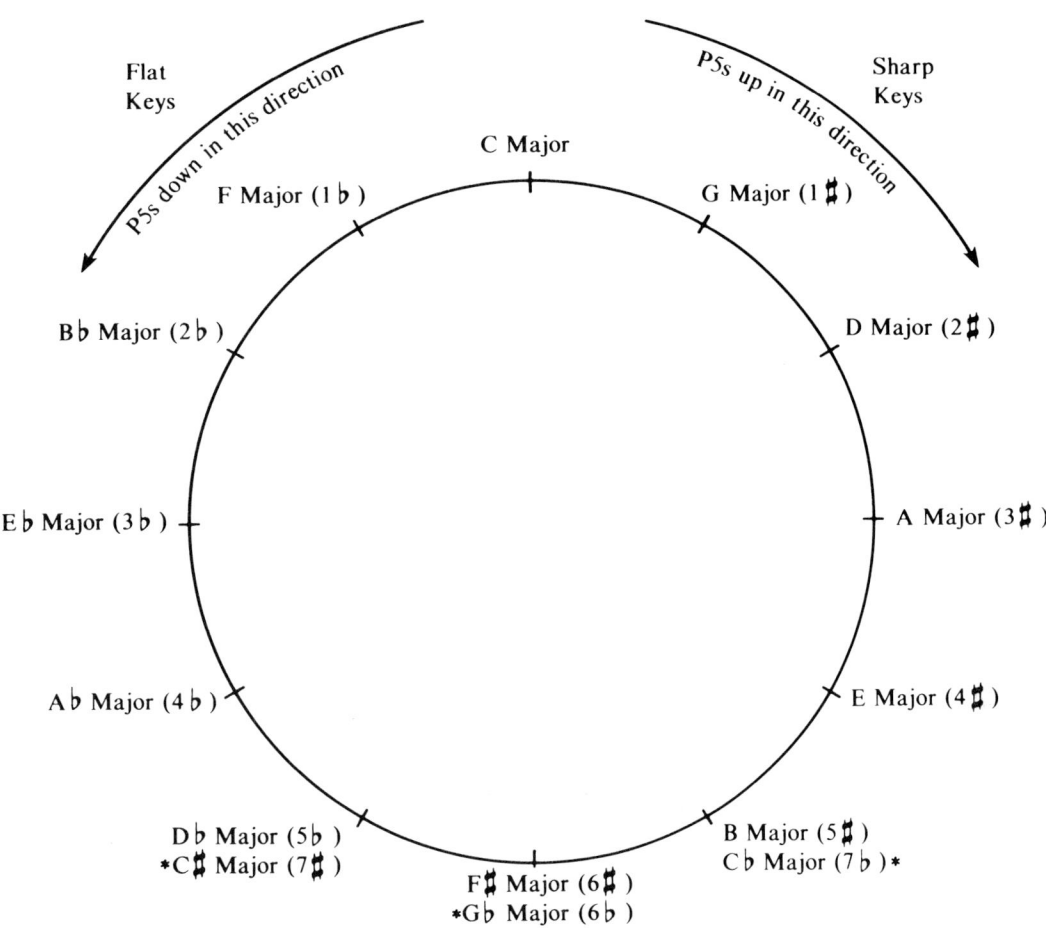

*Enharmonic Equivalents

Natural Minor Scale   The *natural minor scale* is a scale of seven different pitches with whole steps separating adjacent tones except for half steps between the second and third degrees and between the fifth and sixth degrees. Its pitches are those of the white keys of the piano from A to A:

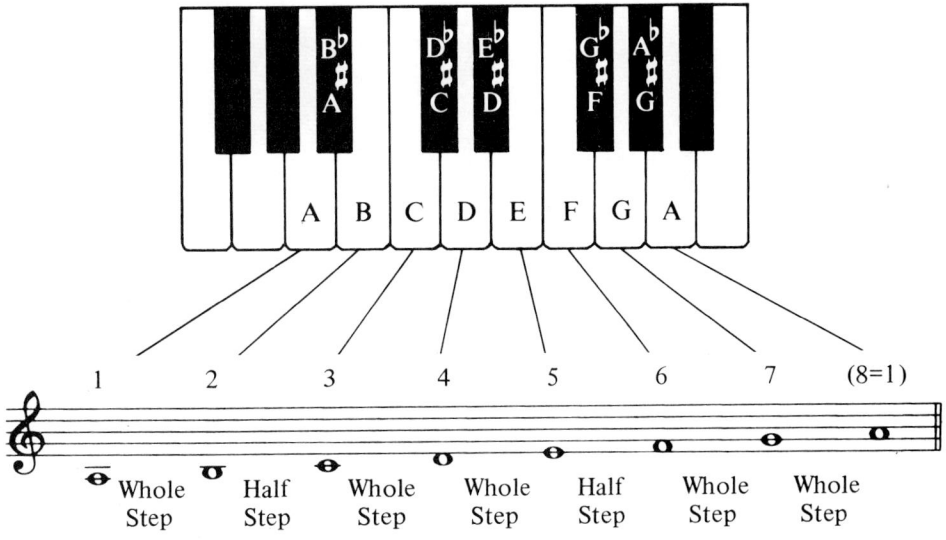

Scales, Modes, Intervals, Tonality, Key   31

The natural minor scale can be conveniently thought of as a major scale from the sixth to the sixth degree.

The following carol is an example of a melody utilizing the natural minor scale:

Harmonic Minor Scale   The *harmonic minor scale* is the natural minor scale with a raised seventh degree. The added impetus of a raised seventh degree gives more melodic thrust toward the tonic and provides for a major dominant triad. Raising the seventh degree causes a step-and-a-half to develop between the sixth and seventh degrees and a half-step between the seventh and eighth degrees. Accidentals used to raise the seventh degree do not appear in the key signature. The pattern of half steps (2–3, 5–6, 7–8) is shown in the following illustration:

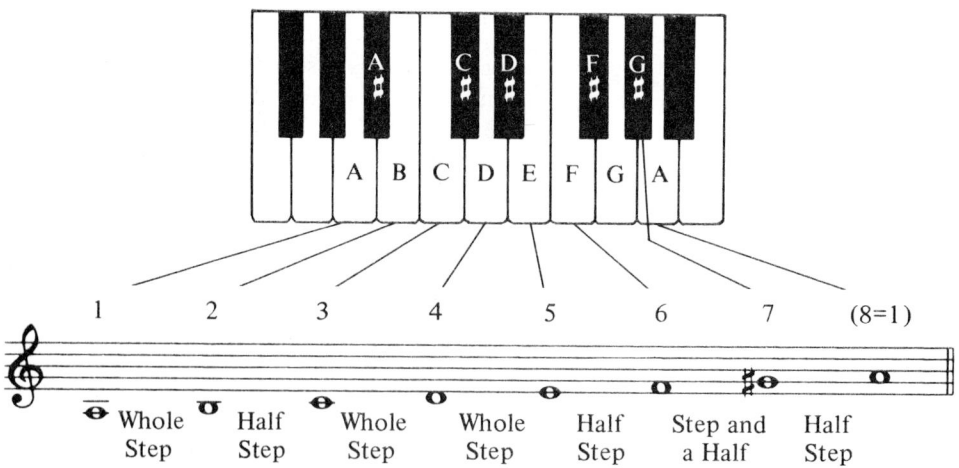

32   Scales, Modes, Intervals, Tonality, Key

This Mozart excerpt utilizes the harmonic minor scale. Notice the presence of G-sharps in measures 2, 4, 7, 8.

Mozart: *Piano Sonata in A Minor,* K. 310 (first movement)

Melodic Minor Scale

The *melodic minor scale* appears in both an ascending and a descending form. The ascending form includes raised sixth and seventh degrees, producing half steps between the second and third and seventh and eighth degrees. The descending form coincides exactly with the natural minor.

The melodic minor scale developed because composers liked the urgency of the raised seventh, but found the step-and-a-half interval between the sixth and seventh degrees of the harmonic minor scale too rough especially for smooth vocal writing. Thus, the melodic minor scale evolved. In descending melodic passages, no need exists for the raised seventh, so composers most often used the natural minor with the lowered seventh and sixth degrees.

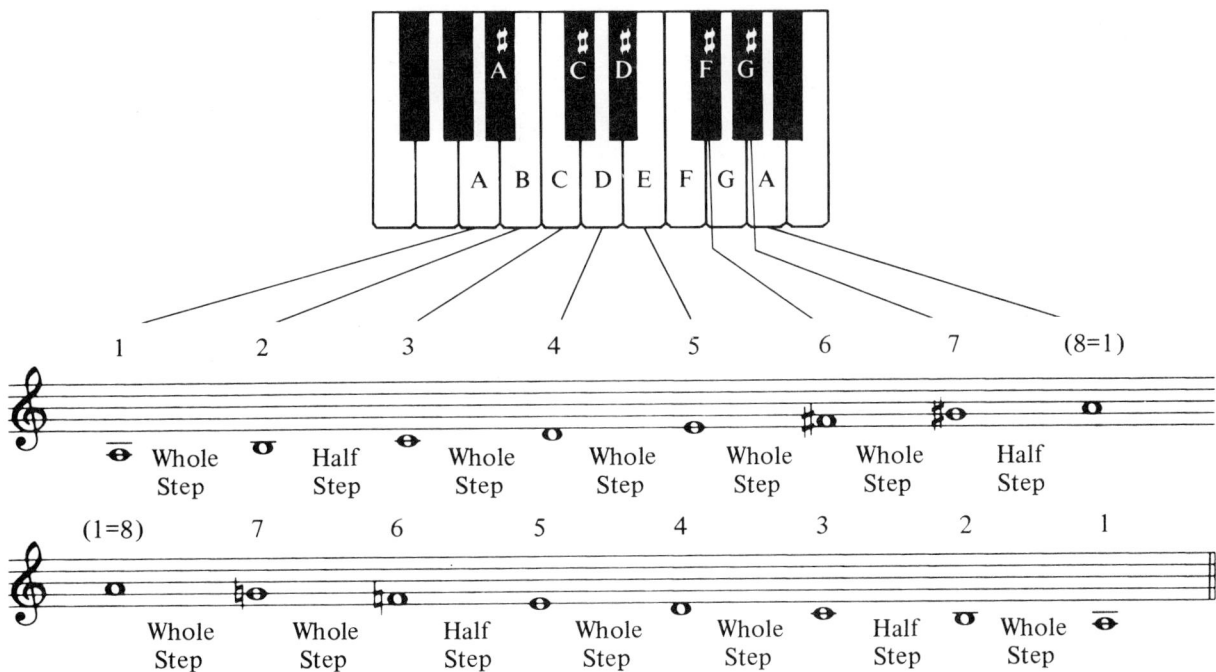

Scales, Modes, Intervals, Tonality, Key   33

The following excerpt includes the ascending and descending forms of the melodic minor scale:

Schwing' dich auf zu deinem Gott
(Soar Upward to Thy God)   Chorale

In practice, two or even all three forms of the minor scale may be used by composers in a single composition. Certainly an examination of music literature, especially vocal and choral, reveals that composers considered the natural, harmonic, and melodic minor as arrangements of the same scale with each form to be used according to need. This excerpt, by Bach, utilizes the various forms of the *A minor scale* in a single phrase of music:

Bach: *Herr Jesu Christ, du höchstes Gut*
(Lord Jesus Christ, Thou Highest Good)

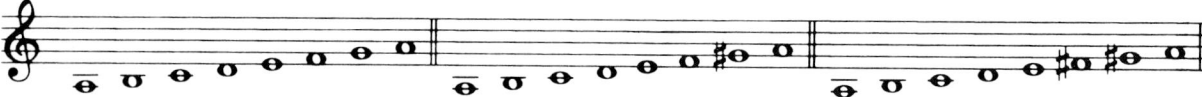

SCALE TUNING	Since the mid-nineteenth century, the *equal temperament system* of tuning has been accepted as the standard for nearly all music written in the Western world. Most musicians trained in the twentieth century find it difficult to conceive that other systems of tuning were ever in use. Nevertheless, the history of music reveals a variety of methods that preceded equal temperament. The two most important of these were Pythagorean tuning and mean-tone tuning.
Pythagorean Tuning	Attributed to the philosopher Pythagoras in the sixth century B.C., *Pythagorean tuning* prescribes the tuning of scale pitches that conform to the *pure fifth*. The harmonic series, illustrated on page 6, shows the pure fifth between the second and third partial (c to g). Thus, if the g were vibrating at 300 cycles per second, the c below it would be vibrating at 200 cycles per second—a ratio of 3:2. The following illustration demonstrates how a C scale could be derived by applying a series of 3:2 ratios:

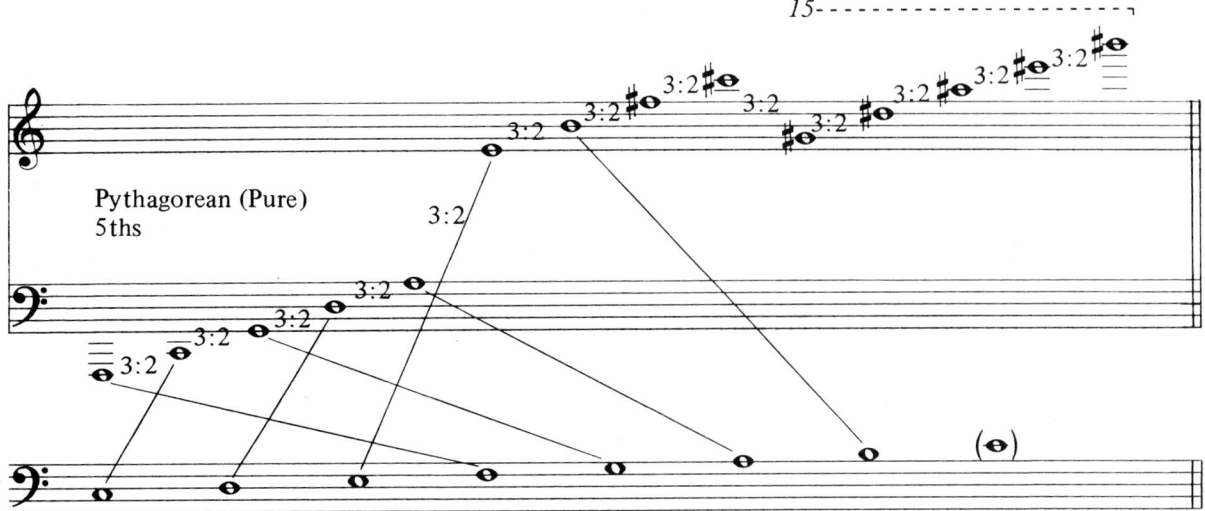

C major scale derived from Pythagorean tuning

On the surface, it would appear that the Pythagorean system of tuning is ideal because it provides the pure fifth (3:2). However, if the octaves at a ratio of 2:1 were extended from the same pitch up to the same octave as that of the 3:2 fifth, the B-sharp derived by the fifths is higher than the C derived by the 2:1 octaves.

By starting both series at the pitch of 33 vibrations per second for CC, the final pitch of c^5 derived by octaves is 4224 cycles per second (cps) while that of the same note derived by fifths is 4282 cycles per second.

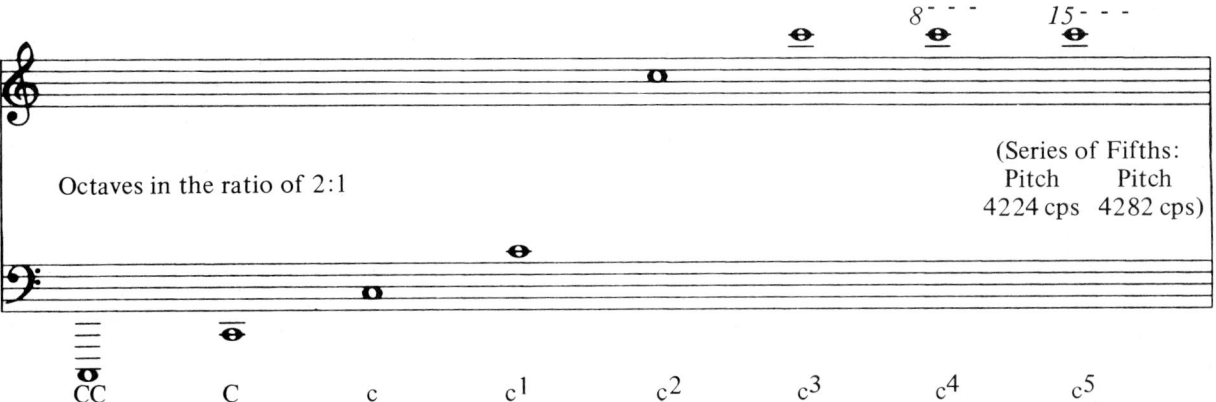

Mean-Tone Tuning

In addition to the Pythagorean method, musicians employed a variety of tuning systems. By the early sixteenth century, *mean-tone tuning* gained considerable acceptance. This system made the pure fifth slightly smaller, but retained the *pure third* (fourth to fifth partial) as illustrated on page 6.

Musicians continued to experiment with tuning. The mean-tone system survived to the early part of the nineteenth century when it was superseded by equal temperament.

Equal Temperament Tuning

Equal temperament was discussed as early as 1518. It divides the octave into twelve equal half steps, thus compromising both the pure fifths and thirds but preserving the 2:1 octave. Among its supporters was J. S. Bach who wrote the first volume of the *Well-Tempered Clavier* somewhere between 1717 and 1723. In this work, Bach sought to demonstrate the superiority of equal temperament tuning over the accepted mean-tone system. He composed a prelude and a fugue in each of the twenty-four possible keys (twelve major and twelve minor) beginning with C major and concluding with B minor. In mean-tone temperament, the out-of-tune quality of Bach's *Prelude and Fugue in G-flat Major* would have been intolerable to most musicians!

ASSIGNMENT 1
1. Write the scales requested—ascending only.
2. When the melodic minor scale is requested, include the first three notes of the descending form.
3. Write the accidentals as they occur in the scale—not as a key signature.

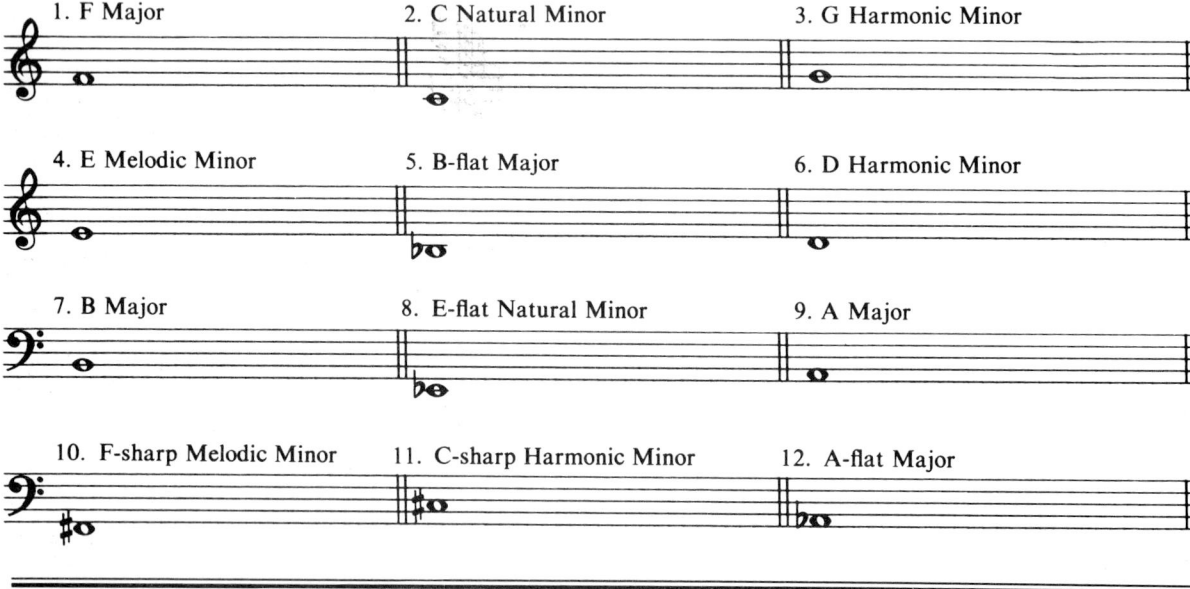

ASSIGNMENT 2
1. Below are groups of four successive notes of major scales.
2. Most of these tetrachords (stepwise series of four tones) are part of two major scales, but three examples are part of only one.
3. Indicate the scales of which each example is a part.

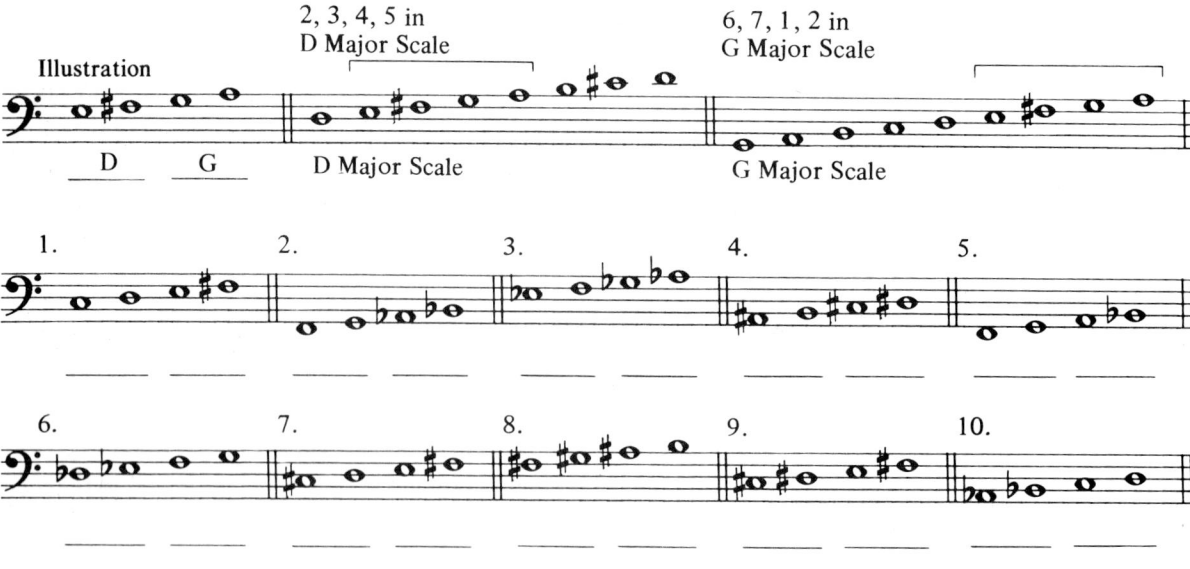

36 Scales, Modes, Intervals, Tonality, Key

ASSIGNMENT 3 Each tetrachord is part of a harmonic minor scale. Name only one application.

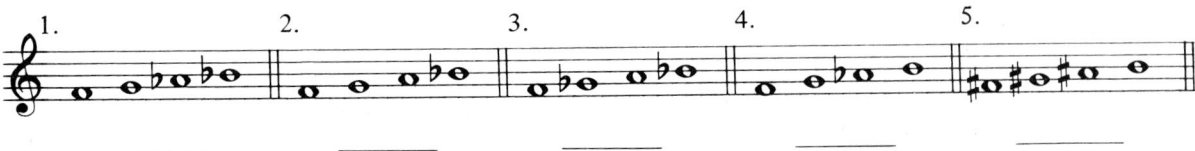

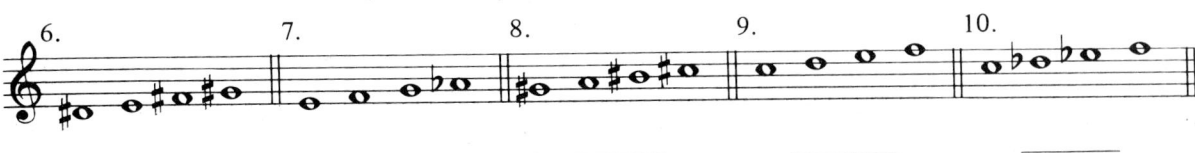

SCALE RELATIONSHIPS

It is important on occasion to associate and compare the patterns of major and minor scales. Two relationships often apply—the relative and the parallel.

Relative Relationship

Major and minor scales that have the same key signatures are in a *relative* relationship. To find the *relative minor* of any major scale, proceed to the sixth degree of that scale. This tone is the tonic of the relative minor.

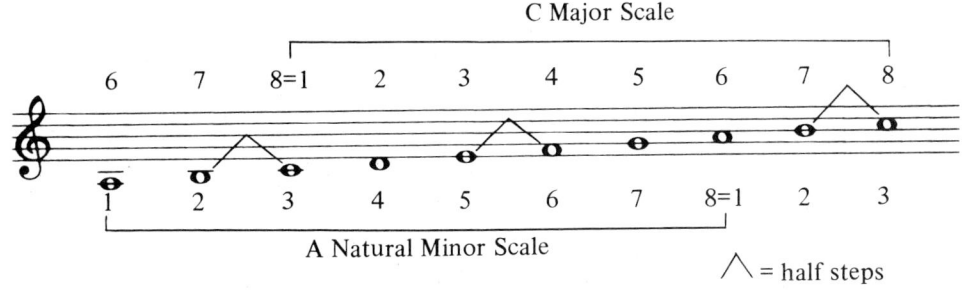

To find the *relative major* of a minor key, proceed to the third degree of the minor scale. This tone is the tonic of the relative major key.

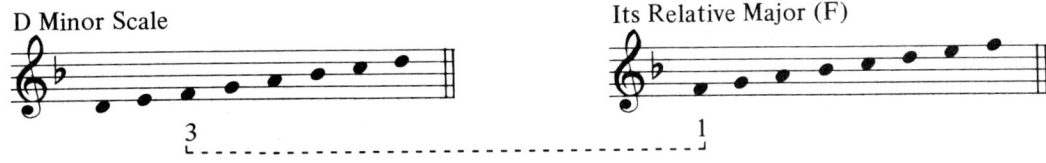

Scales, Modes, Intervals, Tonality, Key 37

MAJOR-RELATIVE MINOR RELATIONSHIPS

MAJOR SCALE	RELATIVE MINOR SCALE	NUMBER OF SHARPS OR FLATS	KEY SIGNATURES AND KEY NOTES (MAJOR AND MINOR)
C	a	NONE	
G	e	1 SHARP	
D	b	2 SHARPS	
A	f♯	3 SHARPS	
E	c♯	4 SHARPS	
B = C♭	g♯ = a♭	5 SHARPS / 7 FLATS	
F♯ = G♭	d♯ = e♭	6 SHARPS / 6 FLATS	
C♯ = D♭	a♯ = b♭	7 SHARPS / 5 FLATS	
A♭	f	4 FLATS	
E♭	c	3 FLATS	
B♭	g	2 FLATS	
F♭	d	1 FLAT	

Scales, Modes, Intervals, Tonality, Key

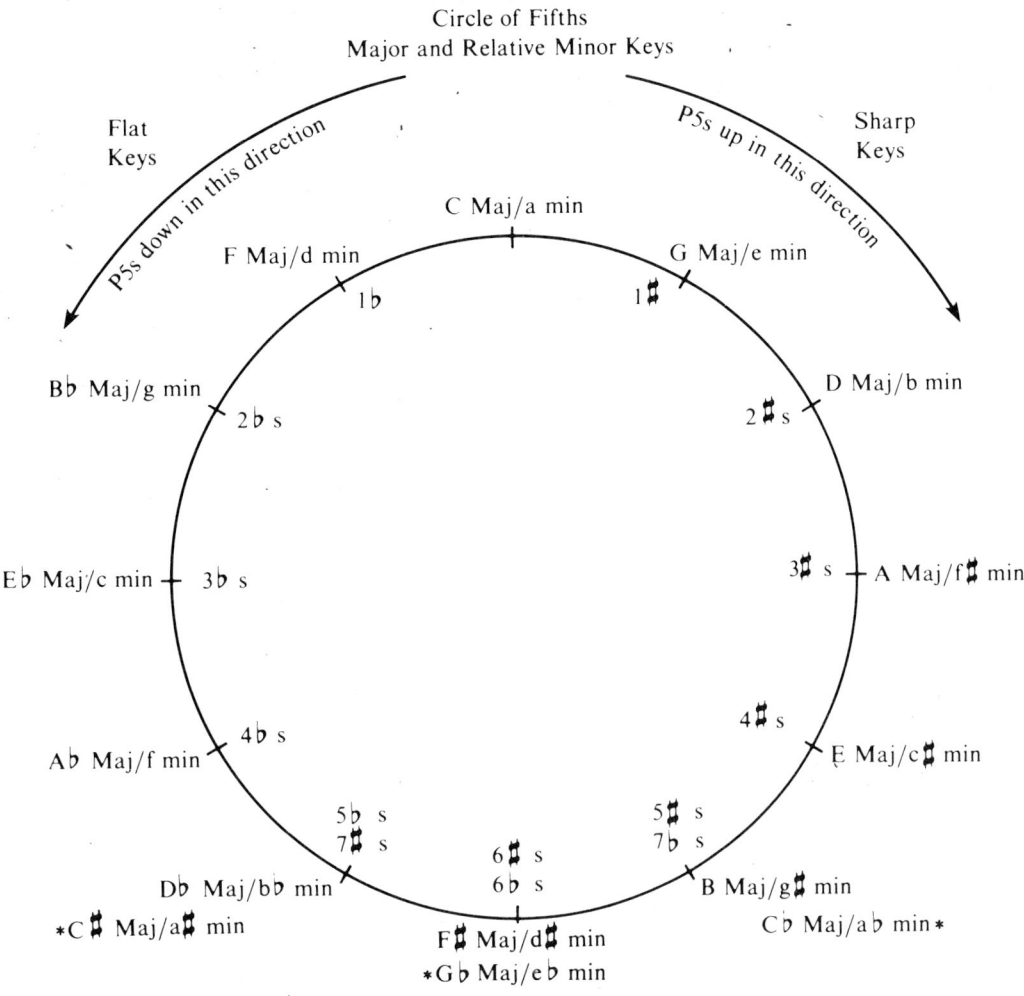

Parallel Relationship	Major and minor scales that have the same tonic note have a *parallel* relationship. In the following example using C as the tonic, the major scale is written without accidentals. Using C as the tonic of the natural minor scale requires accidentals to produce the required sequence of whole and half steps. The accidentals required for this change become the key signature for C minor.

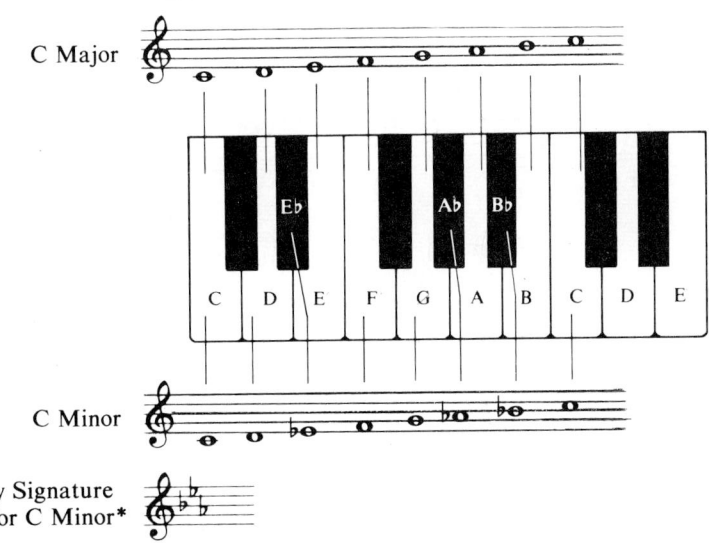

*The C minor key signature is the same as that of its relative major, E-flat.

Scales, Modes, Intervals, Tonality, Key

The process may be seen in reverse by using A natural minor as a point of reference:

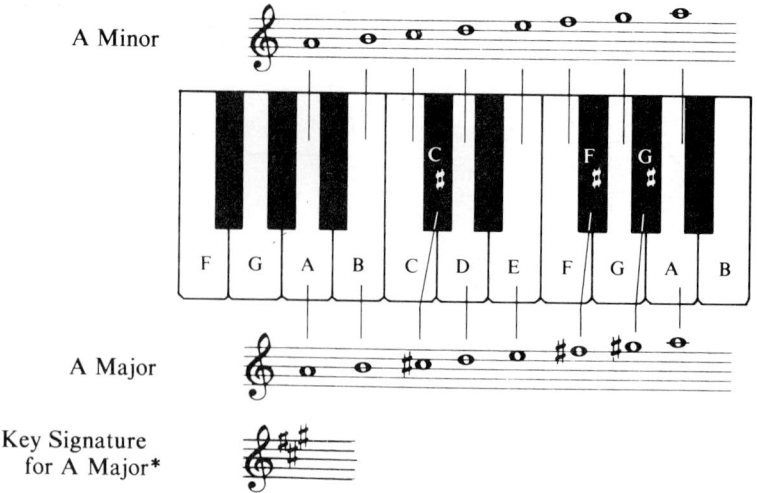

The following illustration shows the D major scale and the scale degrees affected in the parallel natural, harmonic, and melodic minor scales:

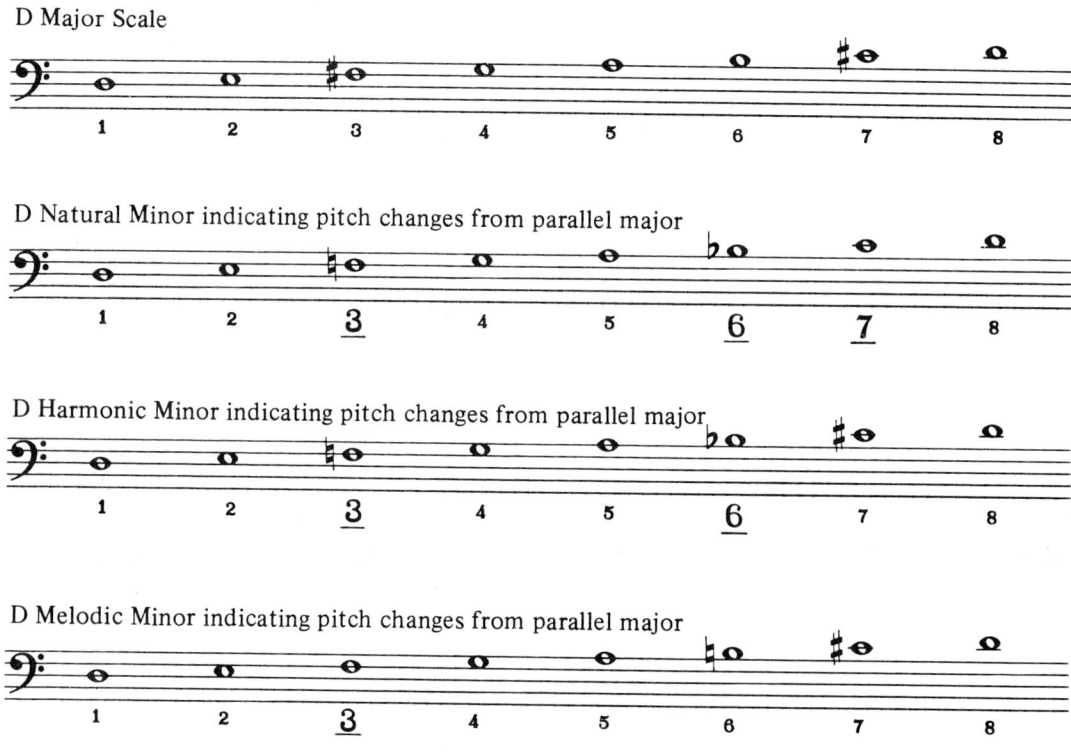

By the same reasoning, the *parallel major* of D minor is D major.

*The A major key signature is the same as that of its relative minor, F-sharp.

40 Scales, Modes, Intervals, Tonality, Key

OTHER SCALES

While the major scale and the three forms of the minor scale represent by far the largest percentage of music written from the seventeenth century to the end of the nineteenth century, a number of other scale formations are found now and then. Some of these are listed below.

Pentatonic Scale

As its name suggests, the *pentatonic scale* is a five-tone scale. It is an example of a gapped scale, one that contains interval gaps of more than a whole step between adjacent pitches.

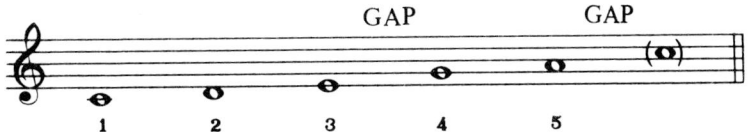

Other arrangements of gaps are also found in music:

The sequence of black keys on the keyboard coincides with the interval relationships of the pentatonic scale. A singularly brilliant exploitation of the pentatonic scale occurs in the right-hand melodic line of Chopin's *Étude in G-flat Major* op. 10 no. 5, the popular *"Black Key" Étude.*

Ravel also utilized pentatonic material:

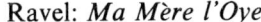
Ravel: *Ma Mère l'Oye*

Examples of the use of pentatonic scales are often found in folk tunes:

Swiss Folk Tune

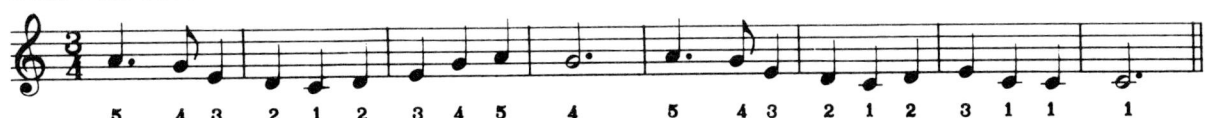

Some familiar tunes are based on pentatonic scales:

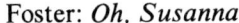
Foster: *Oh, Susanna*

The pentatonic scale is used in the traditional music of China, Japan, other Far Eastern countries, and of Africa. The tuning of pentatonic scales differs from culture to culture, and some are nearly equal-tempered five-tone scales (five tones to the octave).

NONDIATONIC SCALES
Chromatic Scale

A *nondiatonic scale* is a scale that has no identifiable tonal center (tonic).

A *chromatic scale* consists entirely of half-step intervals. Since each tone of the scale is equidistant from the next, it has no tonic and is basically a nondiatonic scale.

Sometimes, however, a melody based on a regular diatonic scale (major or minor) is laced with many accidentals, and although all twelve tones of the chromatic scale may appear, the tonal characteristics of the diatonic scale are maintained. The following excerpt from Purcell's *Dido and Aeneas* demonstrates this use of chromatic half steps by including eleven of the twelve tones in its gradual descent:

Purcell: "Thy Hand, Belinda" from *Dido and Aeneas*   Opera

*Asterisks mark the gradual chromatic descent.

42   Scales, Modes, Intervals, Tonality, Key

Whole Tone Scale   A *whole tone scale* is a six-tone scale made up entirely of whole steps between adjacent degrees of the scale.

Examples of whole tone material are found in music from the late Romantic and Impressionistic periods:

Debussy: *Voiles* (Sails)   Copyright 1910, Durand et Cie. Used by permission of the publisher. Elkan-Vogel, Inc. sole representative, United States.

ASSIGNMENT 4   Each of the following six melodies is based on one of the following scales:

Pentatonic   Chromatic   Melodic Minor
Whole Tone   Natural Minor

Determine the scale upon which each melody is based and place the name in the blank provided.

Scales, Modes, Intervals, Tonality, Key   43

ASSIGNMENT 4 (continued)

THE MODES

A *mode* is a series of pitches within the octave that comprise the basic material of a composition. Upon first investigation, it would seem that the terms "mode" and "scale" are entirely synonymous, but in certain instances, especially in medieval church music, the modes are directly related to idiomatic melodic expressions and thus transcend the usual pitch material definitions of scale patterns. However, for all practical purposes at the moment, the modes may be conveniently classified as scale forms. Two different modal systems will be discussed: *Greek* and *church*.

Greek Modes

The modal systems of the ancient Greeks were fully developed by the fourth century B.C., but because of the decline of early Greek civilization, few of their traditions have been handed down to us. Because of the tuning differences, it is impossible to notate the Greek modes accurately using our present semitone system. Nevertheless, we know that they consisted of a variety of arrangements of *tetrachords* (series of four notes) and were conceived as progressing downward rather than upward (as we usually illustrate our scales). Although the intervals are quite inaccurate, the following is a rough approximation of the Greek *Dorian* mode:

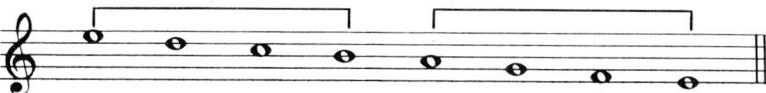

Church Modes

From roughly 800 to 1500, the church modes formed the basis for nearly all Western music. Since the music of this period was primarily vocal, the modes reflect the many influences and accommodations of this medium of expression. Notice in the following illustration that the church modes are divided by range, and that the beginning tone is called the *final* rather than the *tonic* as in the diatonic scales.

44 Scales, Modes, Intervals, Tonality, Key

NAME	NUMBER	RANGE	FINAL	HALF STEPS BETWEEN	COMPARES TO
DORIAN	I			2–3, 6–7	Natural minor scale with raised sixth degree
PHRYGIAN	III			1–2, 5–6	Natural minor scale with lowered second degree
LYDIAN	V			4–5, 7–8	Major scale with raised fourth degree
MIXOLYDIAN	VII			3–4, 6–7	Major scale with lowered seventh degree

Modes I, III, V, and VII are called *authentic* because the final is at the bottom of the range. Modes II, IV, VI, and VIII are called *plagal* (each mode is given the prefix *hypo-*) and contain the same pattern of half and whole steps except that their range surrounds the final (o = final):

Early in the Renaissance (1450 to 1600), four other modes were acknowledged. The *Aeolian* is the same as the natural minor scale, and the *Ionian* is the same as the major scale.

NAME	NUMBER	RANGE	FINAL	HALF STEPS BETWEEN	COMPARES TO
AEOLIAN	IX			2–3, 5–6	Same as natural minor scale
IONIAN	XI			3–4, 7–8	Same as major scale

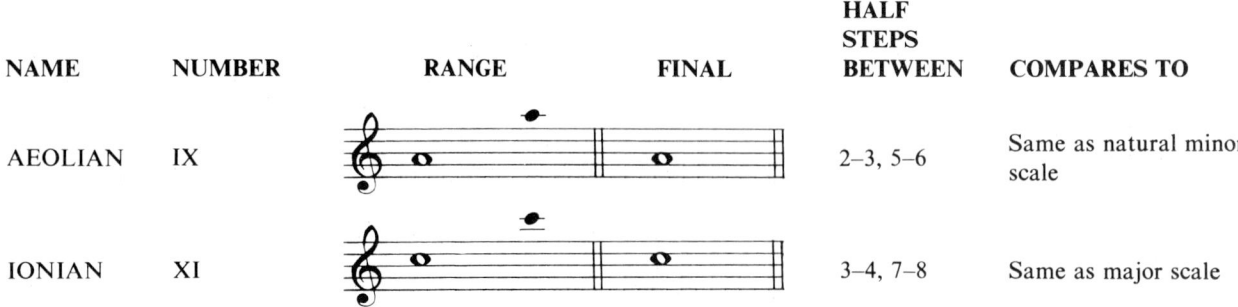

AUTHENTIC

IX
AEOLIAN

PLAGAL

X
HYPOAEOLIAN

XI
IONIAN

XII
HYPOIONIAN

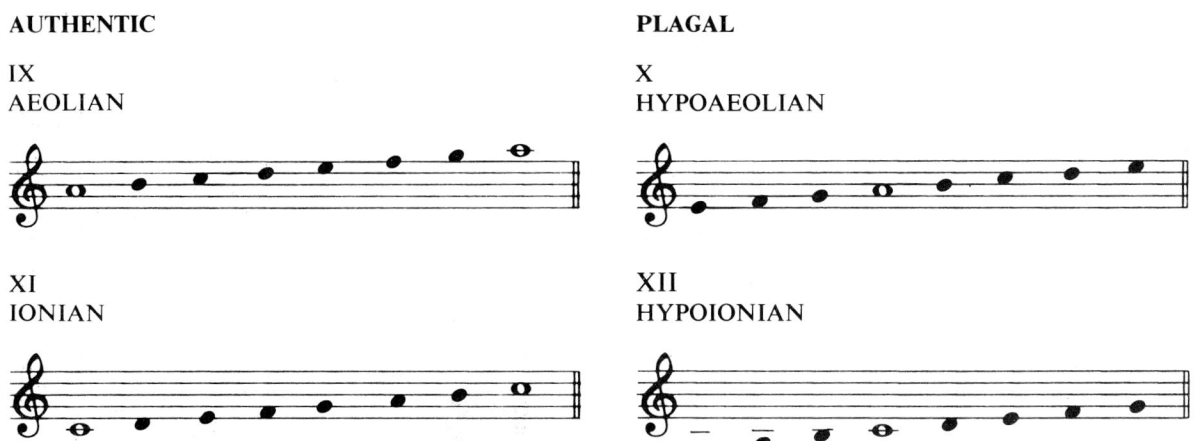

As with the major and minor scales, the modes may begin on any tone as long as the arrangements of half and whole steps remain the same.

Since the final of each transposed mode lies in the same relationship to the tonic of the major scale with the same key signature, the identity of a transposed mode can be quickly determined—

1. The final of the *Dorian* mode is always the *second* degree of a major scale.
2. The final of the *Phrygian* mode is always the *third* degree of a major scale.
3. The final of the *Lydian* mode is always the *fourth* degree of a major scale.
4. The final of the *Mixolydian* mode is always the *fifth* degree of a major scale.
5. The final of the *Aeolian* mode is always the *sixth* degree of a major scale.
6. The final of the *Ionian* mode is always the *first* degree of a major scale.

To illustrate:

Final of nontransposed Dorian is second degree of C major scale

Dorian Mode

C Major Scale

Final of Dorian transposed to F is second degree of E-flat major scale

Dorian Mode (same melody as above)

E-flat Major Scale

ASSIGNMENT 5
1. Below are six modal melodies. All are authentic modes.
2. Write the name of each mode in the blank provided.

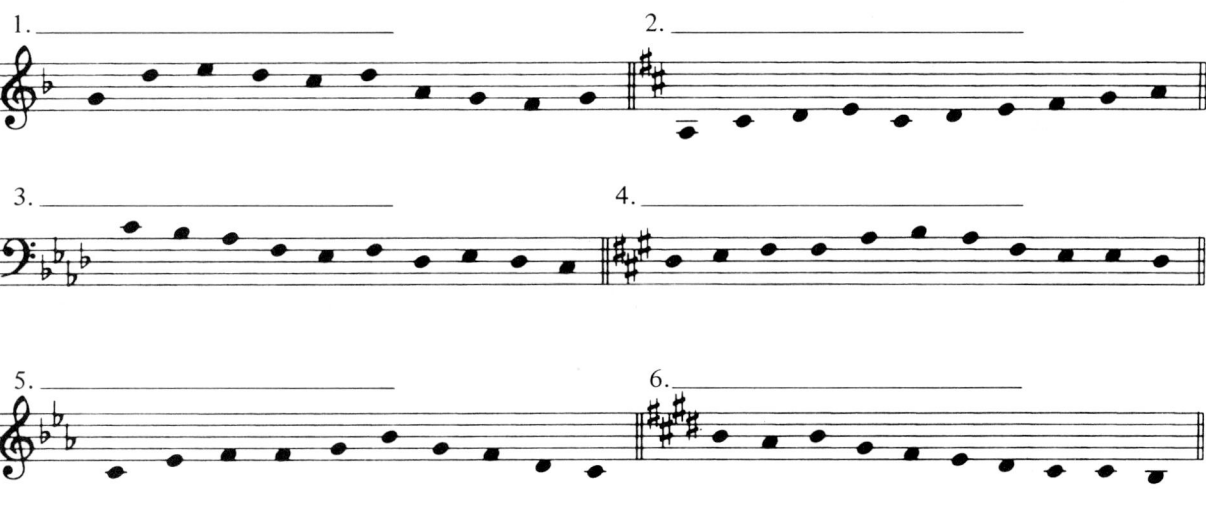

INTERVALS An *interval* is the difference in pitch between two tones.

Major, Minor, and Perfect Intervals Major, minor, and perfect intervals are illustrated in the following chart:

NAME	ILLUSTRATION	NUMBER OF STEPS	CONVENIENT EXAMPLE FOR QUICK RECALL
PERFECT UNISON (ALSO PRIME)		NONE	
MINOR 2ND (m2)		½	Leading tone to tonic of major scale
MAJOR 2ND (M2)		1	Tonic to supertonic of major scale
MINOR 3RD (m3)		1½	Tonic to mediant of minor scale
MAJOR 3RD (M3)		2	Tonic to mediant of major scale
PERFECT 4TH (P4)		2½	Tonic to subdominant of a major or minor scale
PERFECT 5TH (P5)	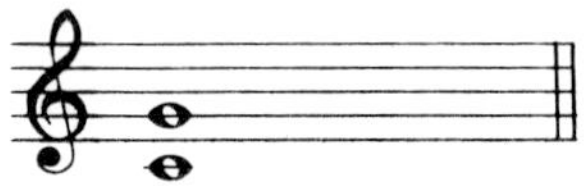	3½	Tonic to dominant of a major or minor scale
MINOR 6TH (m6)		4	Tonic up to submediant of a minor scale
MAJOR 6TH (M6)		4½	Tonic up to submediant of a major scale
MINOR 7TH (m7)	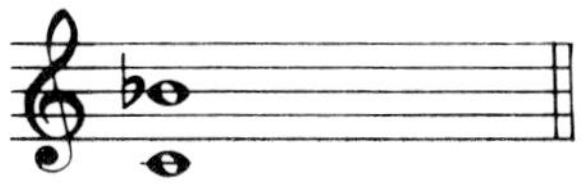	5	Tonic up to subtonic of the natural minor scale
MAJOR 7TH (M7)	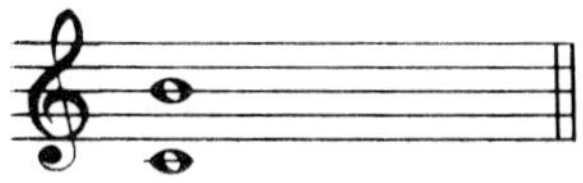	5½	Tonic up to leading tone of a major scale

Only seconds, thirds, sixths, and sevenths are referred to as *major* and *minor*. Only fourths, fifths, octaves, and unisons are referred to as *perfect*.

Augmented and Diminished Intervals

An *augmented interval* is a half step larger than either a major or perfect interval, but it retains the same letter name. A *diminished interval* is a half step smaller than either a minor or perfect interval, but it retains the same letter name.

The order in which a perfect interval is augmented or diminished is:

1. Perfect—interval as is
2. Diminished—a half step smaller than the perfect interval
3. Augmented—a half step larger than the perfect interval

The following chart illustrates augmented or diminished perfect intervals.

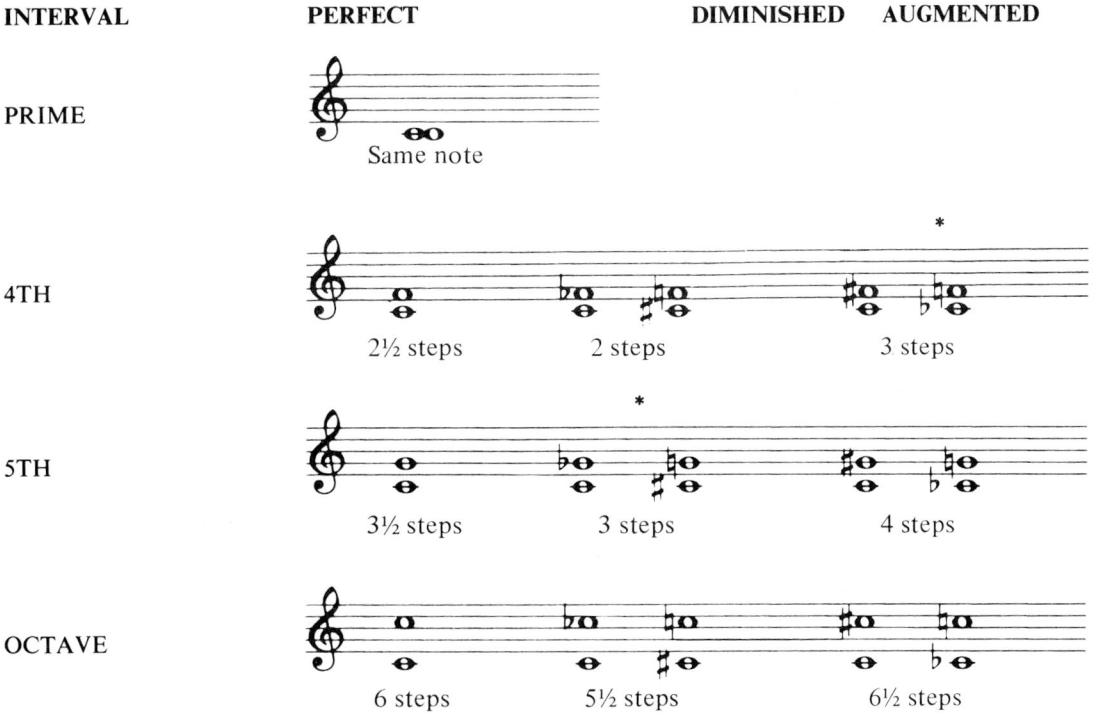

The order in which a major or minor interval is augmented or diminished appears here:

1. Major—interval as is
2. Minor—a half step smaller than a major interval
3. Diminished—a half step smaller than a minor interval
4. Augmented—a half step larger than a major interval

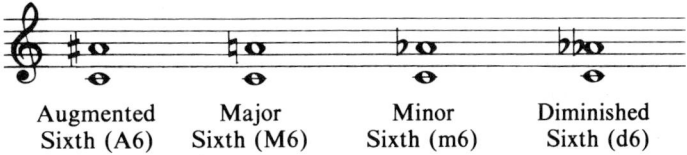

*Another term for an A4 or a d5 is *tritone*.

The following chart illustrates augmented and diminished major or minor intervals.

Enharmonic Intervals

Enharmonic tones have the same pitch but are notated with different letter names. All of the notes below have the same pitch but are spelled differently:

G-flat   F-sharp   E-double sharp

Enharmonic intervals also have the same quality (sound) but are spelled differently. Such intervals result, of course, from enharmonic tones. All of the intervals below have the same sound but are spelled differently:

Minor Sixth (m6)   Minor Sixth (m6)   Augmented Fifth (A5)

Care must be taken in spelling intervals. If a specific interval is requested, the enharmonic-equivalent spelling is not correct.

Thus, if a major third above E-flat is called for, a diminished fourth above D-sharp is not correct even though the sound is the same:

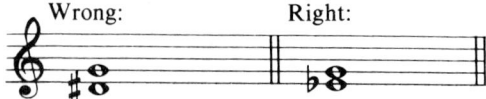

50   Scales, Modes, Intervals, Tonality, Key

Inversion of Intervals   The inversion of an interval means that the lower tone of an interval becomes the higher tone or the higher tone becomes the lower tone. Literally the interval is turned upside down:

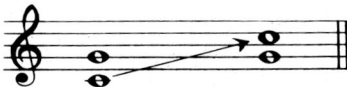

The following table shows various intervals and their inversions:

INTERVAL NAME	WHEN INVERTED BECOMES
PERFECT	PERFECT
MAJOR	MINOR
MINOR	MAJOR
DIMINISHED	AUGMENTED
AUGMENTED	DIMINISHED
UNISONS	OCTAVES
2NDS	7THS
3RDS	6THS
4THS	5THS
5THS	4THS
6THS	3RDS
7THS	2NDS
OCTAVES	UNISONS

Illustrated are some typical intervals and their inversions:

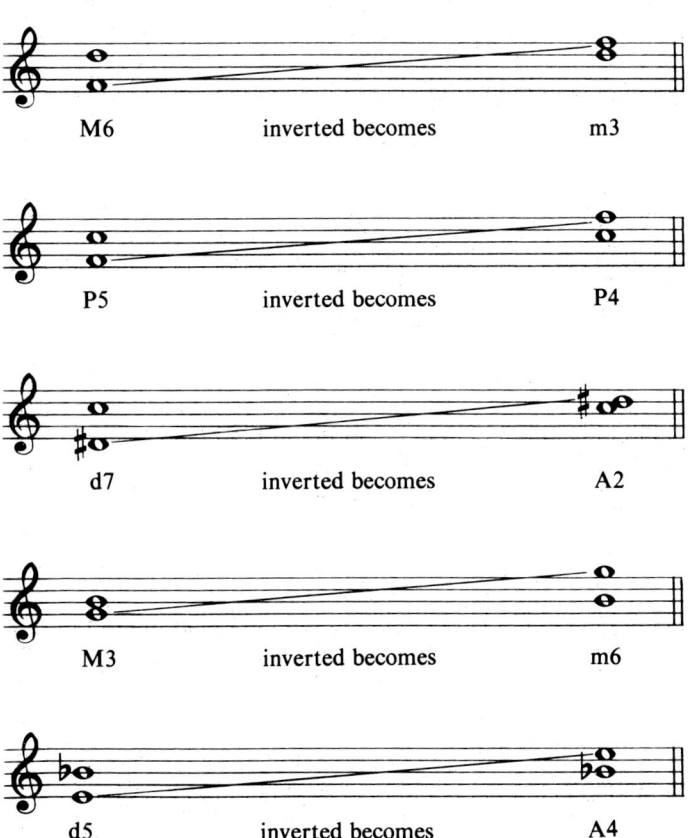

Scales, Modes, Intervals, Tonality, Key

The following is an excerpt of a two-voice composition from music literature. In the second version, the same excerpt is inverted.

Bach: *The Art of Fugue, Contrapunctus VIII*

The same excerpt inverted

ASSIGNMENT 6 Write the interval requested *above* the given note.

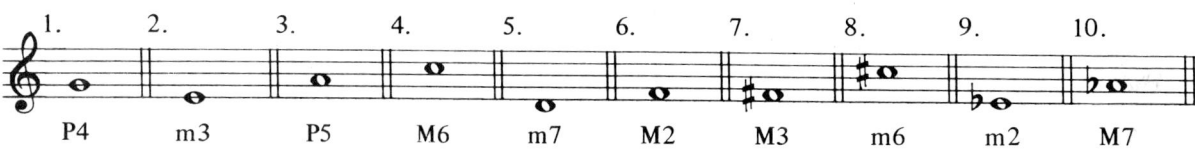

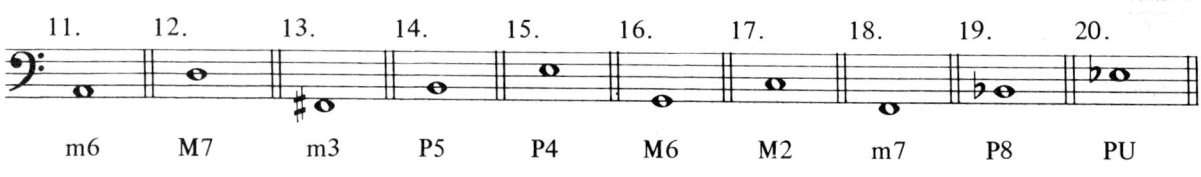

ASSIGNMENT 7 Write the interval requested *below* the given tone.

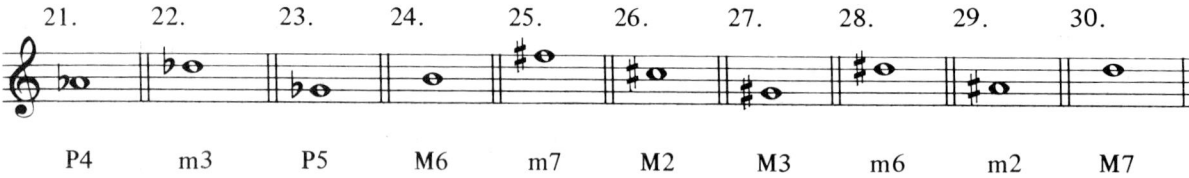

52 Scales, Modes, Intervals, Tonality, Key

ASSIGNMENT 7 (continued)

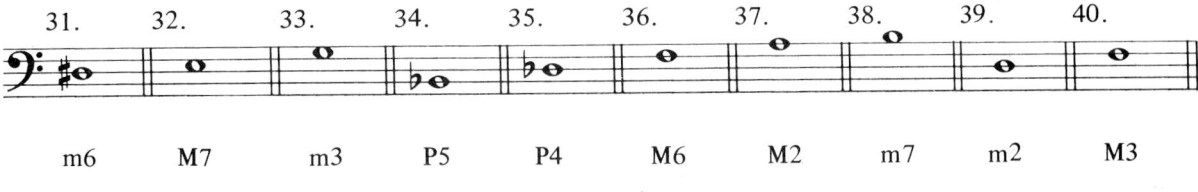

ASSIGNMENT 8

1. Indicate the intervals between the two voices of this canon.*
2. Predict (by interval inversion) the intervals that will be produced if the upper voice were placed an octave lower and the lower voice placed an octave higher (inversion at the double octave).
3. Then, write out the canon in inversion to show the intervals as inverted.

Strict canon, invertible at the double octave

ASSIGNMENT 9

Match the column at right with the column at left. The left column refers to key signatures. No. 1 is worked correctly for you.

	KEY SIGNATURE		KEY
H	1.	1 sharp	A. Relative Major of D Minor
____	2.	4 sharps	B. Relative Major of B-flat Minor
____	3.	2 flats	C. Parallel Minor of C-sharp Major
____	4.	5 sharps	D. Parallel Minor of F Major
____	5.	1 flat	E. Relative Major of E-flat Minor

*A *canon* is a contrapuntal composition of two or more parts, each part consisting of the same melodic line, but starting at different times.

Scales, Modes, Intervals, Tonality, Key

ASSIGNMENT 9 (continued)

_____ 6. 2 sharps   F. Parallel Major of A Minor

_____ 7. 6 flats   G. Relative Minor of B-flat Major

_____ 8. 3 sharps   H. Relative Minor of G Major

_____ 9. 5 flats   I. Parallel Major of B Minor

_____ 10. 4 flats   J. Parallel Minor of B Major

TONALITY

Tonality refers to a system of tones (example: the tones of a major or a minor scale) used in such a way that one tone becomes central (*tonal center*) and the remaining tones modify and relate to it.

Although most musicians consider the meaning obvious, the exact definition of tonality is difficult to draft because the term describes a subjective perception that differs from person to person. For the moment, the above definition will suffice.

Key

A *key* is a system of tones all of which are related to a central tone or tonic. It is limited to those combinations of tones that make up diatonic scales. For all practical purposes, *key* and *tonality* are synonymous when used in connection with diatonic major and minor systems. To understand the contents of Volume 1 of this text the above statements will suffice, but in Volume 2, when twentieth-century music is discussed, a small but important difference between the two terms will be explained and illustrated in detail.

Pitch Inventory

A *pitch inventory* is a scalewise list of the tones used in a composition or a section of the composition. For purposes of organization, the pitch inventories in this text always begin with A. A pitch inventory is useful in that it permits a quick assessment of the selected pitches without prejudice to key or tonality.

The selection of a pitch inventory is helpful for those who have had little experience in analyzing music. Reducing the notes of a melody to a scalewise list of the different pitches consolidates the task of determining the key.

As soon as competency in analysis is developed, and the ability to scan a melody or harmony accurately and quickly is acquired, this step (the first step) in the analytical procedure can be abandoned.

The following illustration provides a melody, its pitch inventory, and finally its scale.

Dvořák: Symphony in E Minor op. 95 no. 5 (from *The New World*)

54 Scales, Modes, Intervals, Tonality, Key

ASSIGNMENT 10   On the blank staff below each melody on the following page, write:

1. The pitch inventory beginning on A (or A-flat, or A-sharp)
2. The scale, with the tonic as the first note.

Suggested procedure:

1. Sing each melody over enough times to be familiar with it.
2. Look carefully at the pitch inventory to determine the number of sharps or flats.
3. Reconstruct the key signature if possible. Remember that the raised seventh degree in the harmonic minor might throw you off.
4. When you think you have the correct key signature, you should then try to determine whether the melody is major or minor.
5. Go back to the melody itself, and sing it over again. Your ear can be a great help. Sometimes (but not always), the first and last note will be a clue. If this fails, try to find outlined triads in the melody line—such outlined triads are often either tonic or dominant.
6. When you have decided the key signature and the tonality (whether major or minor), write the scale on the blank staff.

1.
Haydn: *Symphony no. 28*

2.
D. Scarlatti: *Sonata Longo 261*

3.
Mozart: *Eine kleine Nachtmusik K 525*

Scales, Modes, Intervals, Tonality, Key 55

ASSIGNMENT 10 (continued)

4.
Franck: *Quintet for Piano and Strings*

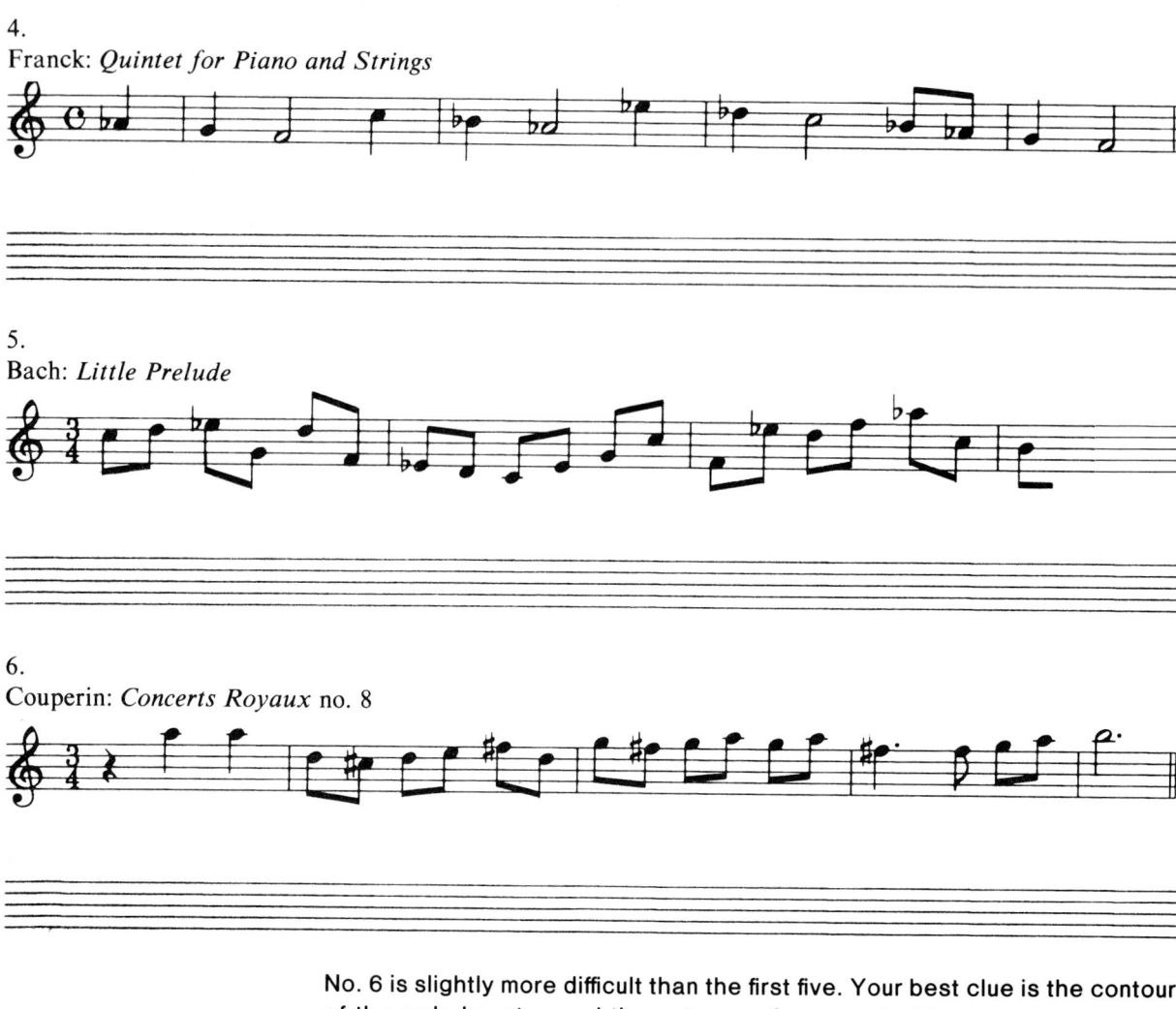

5.
Bach: *Little Prelude*

6.
Couperin: *Concerts Royaux* no. 8

No. 6 is slightly more difficult than the first five. Your best clue is the contour of the melody notes and the notes on the accented beats.

3 The Anatomy of Harmony

Chord
Major Triad
Minor Triad
Diminished Triad
Augmented Triad
Triad Roots
Scale Degree Names
Triad Stability

Triad Inversion
Triad Analysis Symbols
Figured Bass Symbols
*Perfect Authentic
    Cadence*
*Imperfect Authentic
    Cadence*

Half Cadence
Plagal Cadence
Deceptive Cadence
Nonharmonic Tones
Passing Tones
Neighboring Tone
Escape Tone

Appoggiatura
Suspension
Anticipation
Retardation
Pedal Tone
Changing Tone
Harmonic Rhythm

HARMONY

Harmony is the study of simultaneously sounding tones. Whereas in the study of melody the linear aspect of music is paramount, in the study of harmony the vertical dimension is the subject of discussion.

Harmony began to emerge during the thirteenth century. Prior to that, *organum,* a rather simple form of *counterpoint* (the study of melody against melody, i.e., two or more simultaneous melodies), found extensive use. Organum began as a succession of parallel fourths and fifths, but soon developed into two semi-independent lines. By the mid-fourteenth century, the barest outlines of harmony were beginning to show in the multivoiced compositions of the times. These continued through the sixteenth century, the great age of polyphony. In 1722 Jean-Philippe Rameau wrote a treatise, *Traité de l'Harmonie* (Treatise on Harmony), and in 1726 another, *Nouveau Système de Musique Théorique* (New System of Music Theory), in which he discussed the invertibility of triads and the relationships of successive chords.

CHORD

A *chord* is a harmonic unit of a minimum of three different tones sounding simultaneously. The term includes all possible sonorities.

Triad

Strictly speaking, a *triad* is any three-tone chord. However, since Western music of the seventeenth through nineteenth centuries is *tertian* (chords are a superposition of harmonic thirds), the term has come to mean a three-note chord built in superposed thirds. Four types of triads are in common use.

57

Major Triad   A *major triad* consists of a major third and a perfect fifth.

Minor Triad   A *minor triad* consists of a minor third and a perfect fifth.

Diminished Triad   A *diminished triad* consists of a minor third and a diminished fifth.

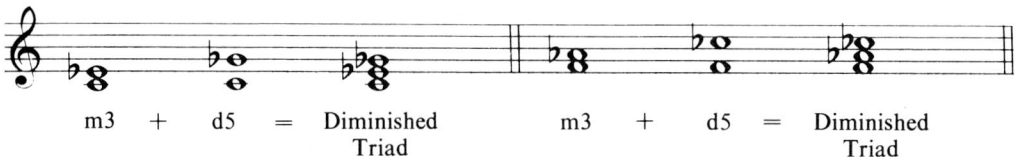

Augmented Triad   An *augmented triad* consists of a major third and an augmented fifth.

The following illustration demonstrates how each of the four types of triads may be constructed on any tone.

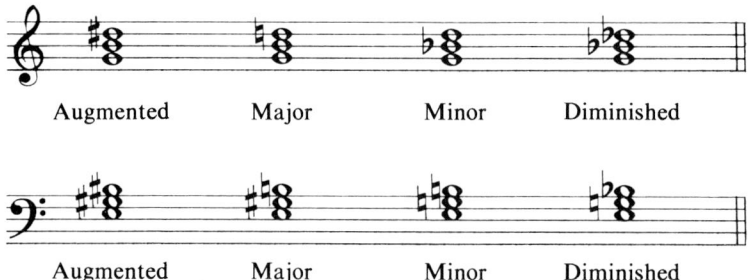

Triad Roots   The *chord root* is the lowest pitch of the most stable interval in the chord. All intervals have roots that are determined by *combination* tones created by the interaction of directly produced tones. Although too complex to explain here, curious students are encouraged to consult sections of the book by Paul Hindemith, *Craft of Musical Composition.**

*Paul Hindemith, *Craft of Musical Composition* (New York: Associated Music Publishers, Inc., 1937)

Some intervals have considerable strength and stability while others seem to portend restlessness and lack finality. The following is a list of interval strengths from strongest to weakest:

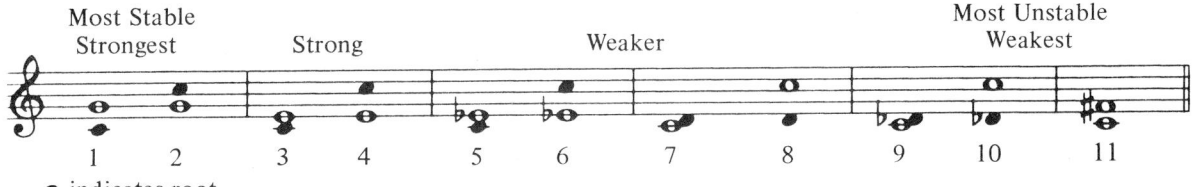

• indicates root

Since triads are chords, they too have roots that are determined by the root of the most stable interval in their makeup. The root of any triad (no matter what the arrangement) is the root of its lowest and most stable interval. The root of a major triad is its lowest tone.

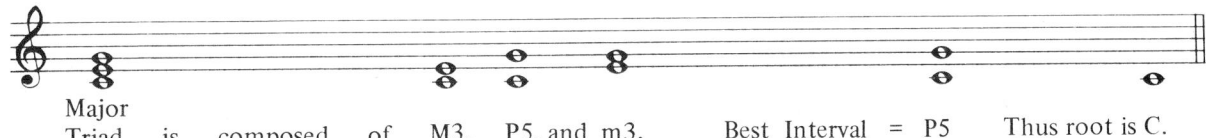

Major Triad is composed of M3, P5, and m3.   Best Interval = P5   Thus root is C.

The root of a minor triad is its lowest tone.

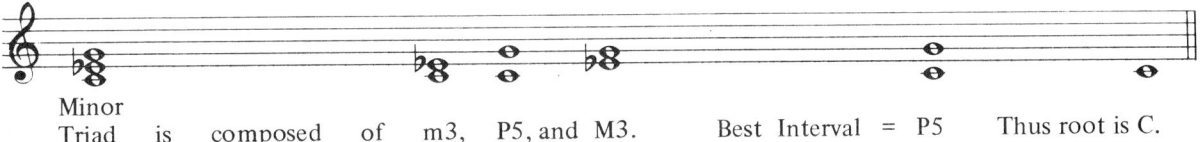

Minor Triad is composed of m3, P5, and M3.   Best Interval = P5   Thus root is C.

The root of a diminished triad is its lowest tone.

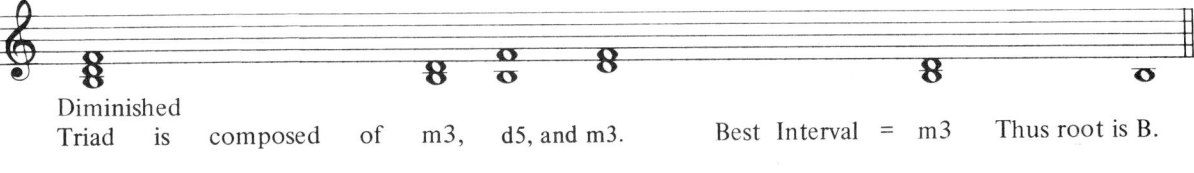

Diminished Triad is composed of m3, d5, and m3.   Best Interval = m3   Thus root is B.

The root of an augmented triad is its lowest tone.

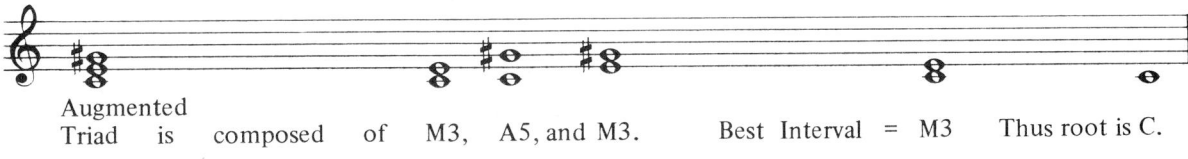

Augmented Triad is composed of M3, A5, and M3.   Best Interval = M3   Thus root is C.

ASSIGNMENT 1   Write the requested triad above each given note as shown in the example.

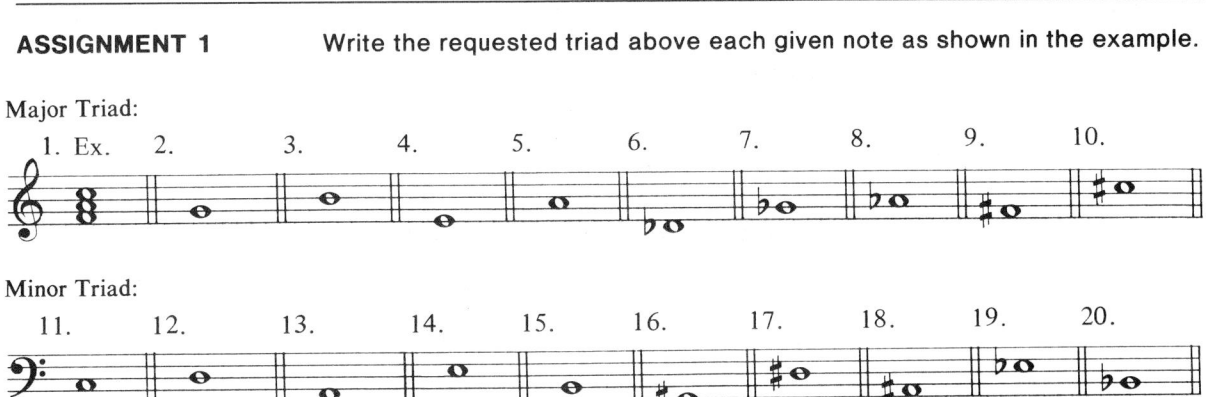

The Anatomy of Harmony   59

ASSIGNMENT 1 (continued)

Diminished Triad:

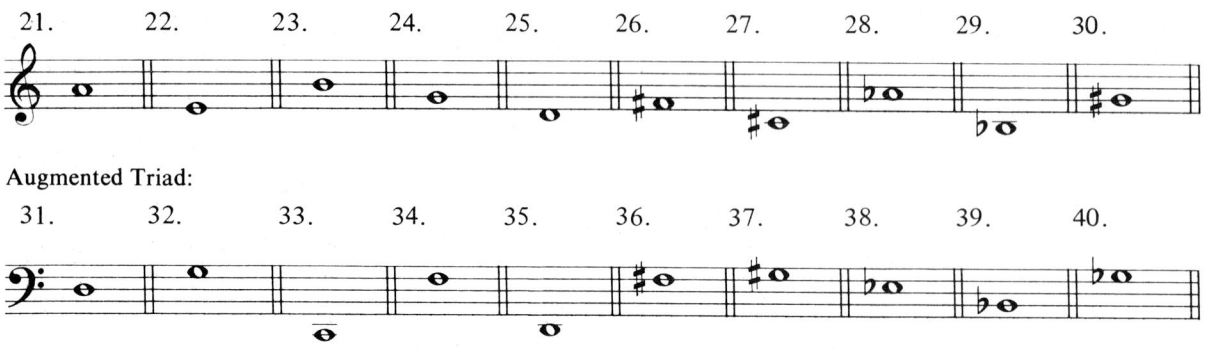

Augmented Triad:

SCALE DEGREE NAMES

Each degree of the seven-tone diatonic scale has a name that relates to its function. Thus, the major scale and all three forms of the minor scale share these terms.

SCALE DEGREE	NAME	MEANING
1ST	TONIC	Tonal center—the final resolution tone
2ND	SUPERTONIC	One step above the tonic
3RD	MEDIANT	Midway between tonic and dominant
4TH	SUBDOMINANT	The lower dominant—the fifth tone down from the tonic (also the fourth tone up from the tonic)
5TH	DOMINANT	So called because its function is next in importance to the tonic
6TH	SUBMEDIANT	The lower mediant. Halfway between tonic and lower dominant (subdominant). The third tone down from the tonic (also the sixth tone up from the tonic)
7TH	LEADING TONE	Strong affinity for and leads melodically to the tonic
7TH	SUBTONIC	Used only to designate the seventh degree of the natural minor scale (a whole step below the tonic)

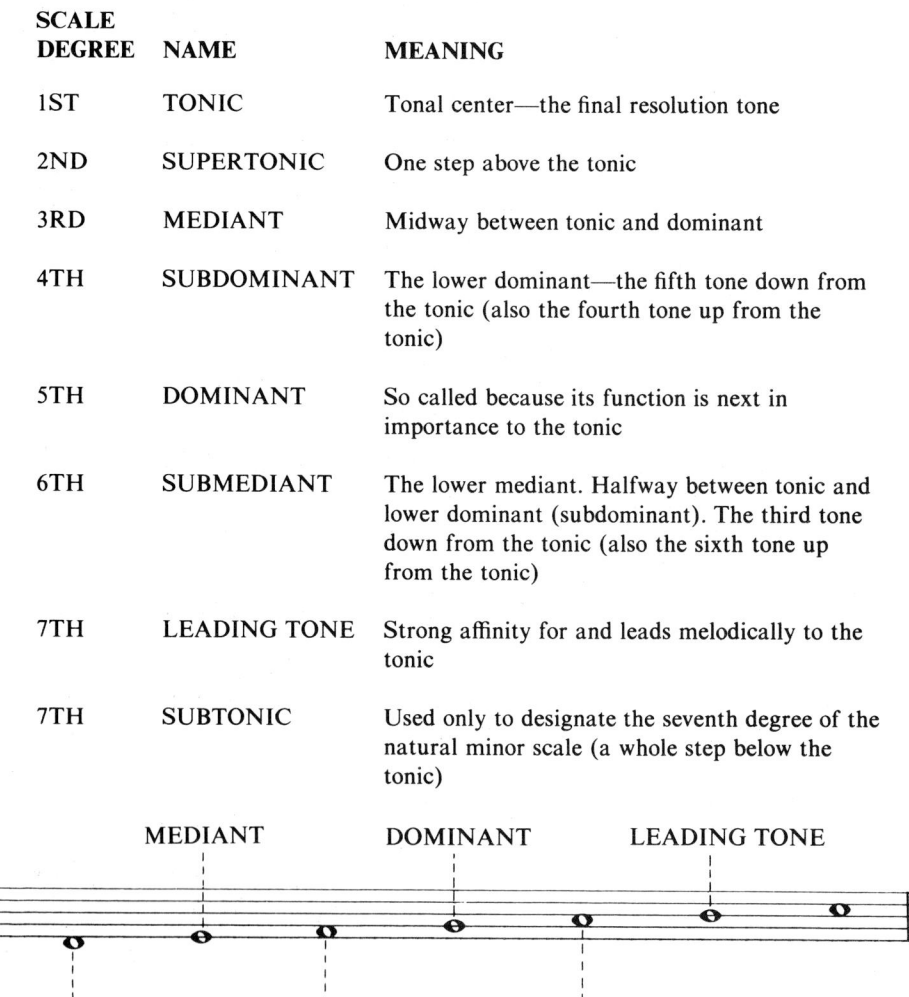

60 The Anatomy of Harmony

ASSIGNMENT 2 The key, mode, and scale degree are given, but the letter name of the note is missing. Fill in the letter name.

	KEY		SCALE DEGREE NAME	LETTER NAME		KEY		SCALE DEGREE NAME	LETTER NAME
1	G	Har Min	Submediant	_____	6	C♯	Har Min	Dominant	_____
2	B	Maj	Supertonic	_____	7	G♯	Mel Min	Submediant	_____
3	B♭	Nat Min	Subdominant	_____	8	D	Maj	Mediant	_____
4	F♯	Mel Min	Submediant	_____	9	F	Nat Min	Subtonic	_____
5	E♭	Maj	Leading Tone	_____	10	D♯	Har Min	Subdominant	_____

Triads on Scale Tones   A triad may be constructed on any pitch. Memorize the type of triads that appear on each tone of the major scale and the three forms of the minor scale.

In analysis, Roman numerals are used for triads (to distinguish triads based on scale degrees from scale degrees alone). Arabic numerals are used for scale degrees themselves.

Uppercase Roman numerals	I IV V = *Major* triads
Lowercase Roman numerals	ii iii vi = *Minor* triads
Lowercase Roman numerals with °	vii° = *Diminished* triads
Uppercase Roman numerals with +	III+ = *Augmented* triads

In the major scale:

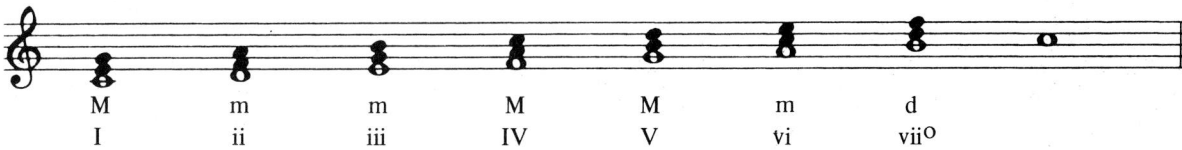

M m m M M m d
I ii iii IV V vi vii°

In the natural minor scale:

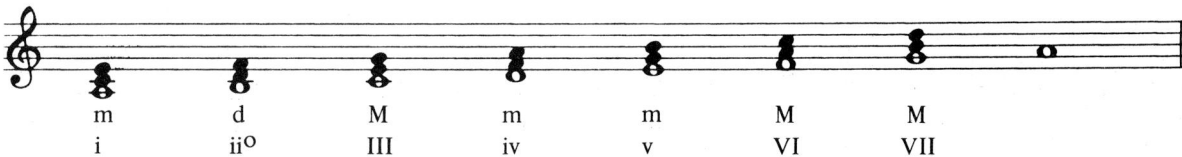

m d M m m M M
i ii° III iv v VI VII

In the harmonic minor scale:

m d A m M M d
i ii° III+ iv V VI vii°

In the melodic minor scale:

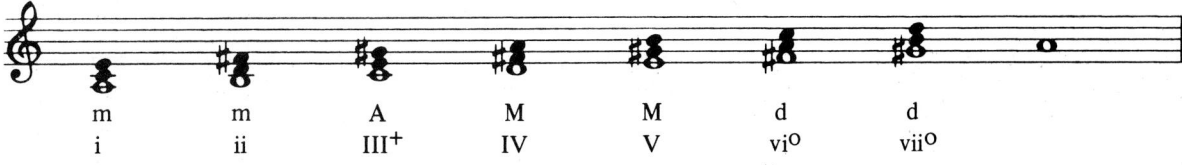

m m A M M d d
i ii III+ IV V vi° vii°

The Anatomy of Harmony   61

The following chart is a summary of triad types in the diatonic scales:

SCALE	MAJOR TRIADS ON	MINOR TRIADS ON	DIMINISHED TRIADS ON	AUGMENTED TRIADS ON
MAJOR	I, IV, V	ii, iii, vi	vii°	NONE
NATURAL MINOR	III, VI, VII	*i, iv, v	ii°	NONE
HARMONIC MINOR	V, VI	*i, iv	ii°, vii°	III+
MELODIC MINOR	IV, V	*i, ii	vi°, vii°	III+

*On occasion a major tonic triad is found at the end of a composition in minor. This is known as a *picardy third*.

ASSIGNMENT 3

1. Below is a series of major triads.
2. Write the three major keys and two harmonic minor keys in which each triad is diatonic. The example is worked correctly for you.

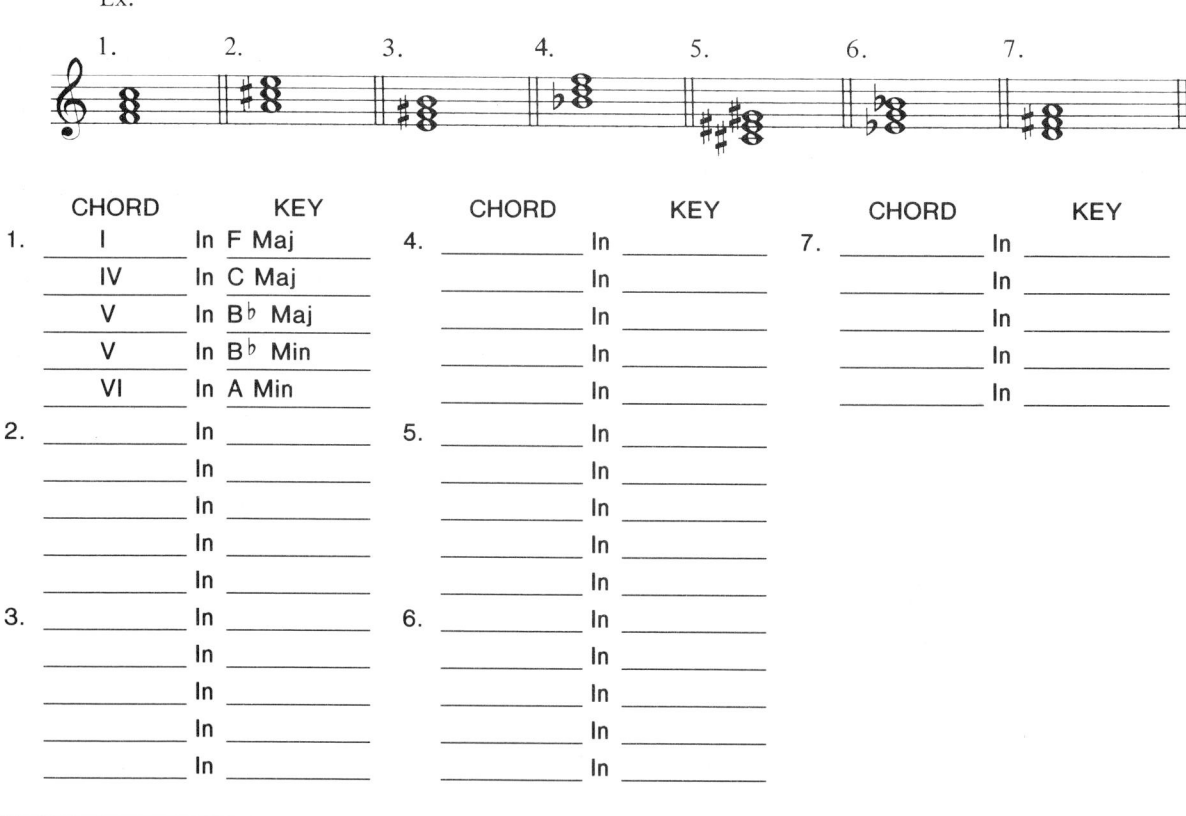

	CHORD	KEY			CHORD	KEY			CHORD	KEY
1.	I	In F Maj	4.	___	In ___	7.	___	In ___
	IV	In C Maj		___	In ___		___	In ___
	V	In B♭ Maj		___	In ___		___	In ___
	V	In B♭ Min		___	In ___		___	In ___
	VI	In A Min		___	In ___		___	In ___
2.	___	In ___	5.	___	In ___			
	___	In ___		___	In ___			
	___	In ___		___	In ___			
	___	In ___		___	In ___			
	___	In ___		___	In ___			
3.	___	In ___	6.	___	In ___			
	___	In ___		___	In ___			
	___	In ___		___	In ___			
	___	In ___		___	In ___			
	___	In ___		___	In ___			

ASSIGNMENT 4

1. On the next page is a series of minor triads.
2. Write the three major keys and two harmonic minor keys in which each triad is diatonic. The example is worked correctly for you.

The Anatomy of Harmony

Ex.

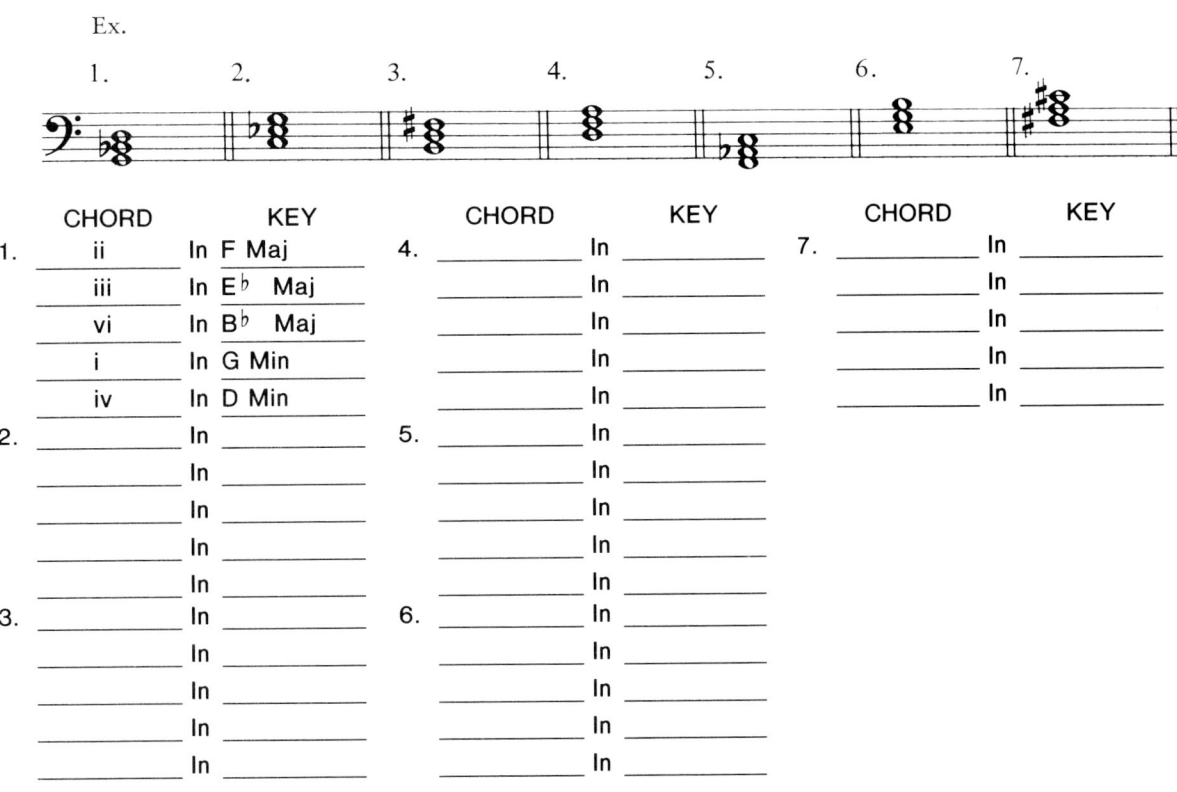

	CHORD	KEY		CHORD	KEY		CHORD	KEY
1.	ii	In F Maj	4.	___	In ___	7.	___	In ___
	iii	In E♭ Maj		___	In ___		___	In ___
	vi	In B♭ Maj		___	In ___		___	In ___
	i	In G Min		___	In ___		___	In ___
	iv	In D Min		___	In ___		___	In ___
2.	___	In ___	5.	___	In ___			
	___	In ___		___	In ___			
	___	In ___		___	In ___			
	___	In ___		___	In ___			
	___	In ___		___	In ___			
3.	___	In ___	6.	___	In ___			
	___	In ___		___	In ___			
	___	In ___		___	In ___			
	___	In ___		___	In ___			
	___	In ___		___	In ___			

ASSIGNMENT 5

1. Below is a series of diminished triads.
2. Write the one major key, two harmonic minor keys, and two melodic minor keys in which each triad is diatonic.

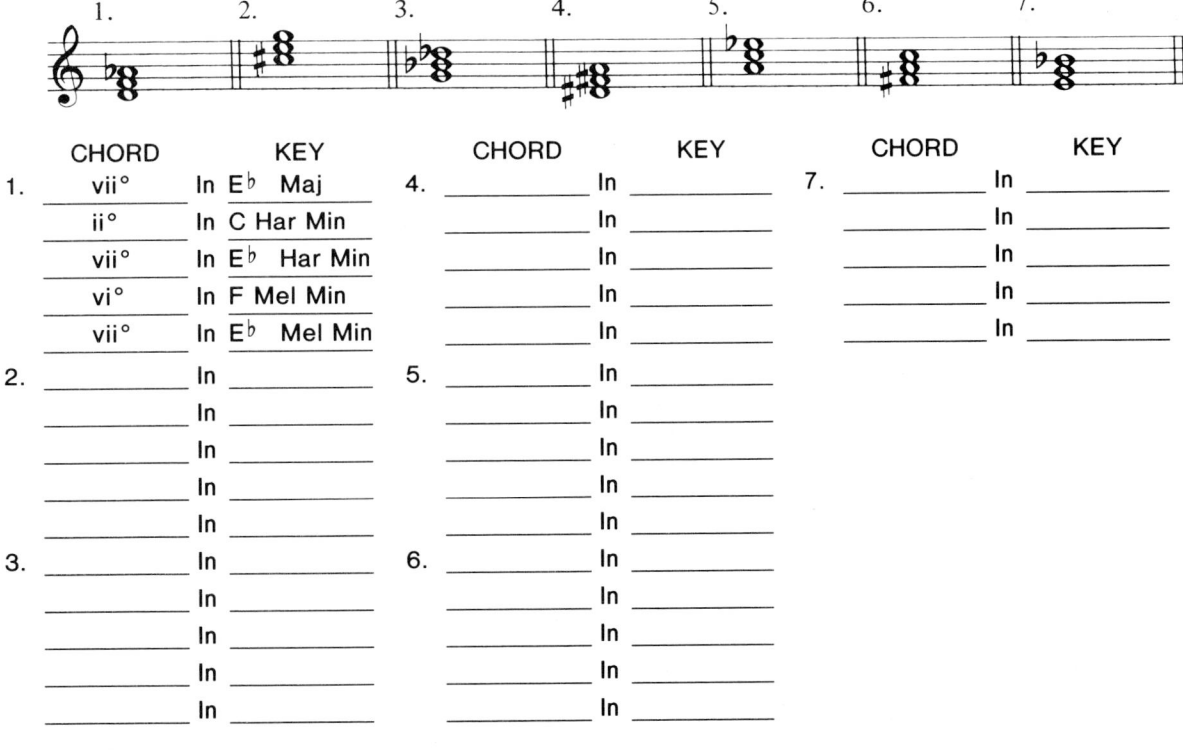

	CHORD	KEY		CHORD	KEY		CHORD	KEY
1.	vii°	In E♭ Maj	4.	___	In ___	7.	___	In ___
	ii°	In C Har Min		___	In ___		___	In ___
	vii°	In E♭ Har Min		___	In ___		___	In ___
	vi°	In F Mel Min		___	In ___		___	In ___
	vii°	In E♭ Mel Min		___	In ___		___	In ___
2.	___	In ___	5.	___	In ___			
	___	In ___		___	In ___			
	___	In ___		___	In ___			
	___	In ___		___	In ___			
	___	In ___		___	In ___			
3.	___	In ___	6.	___	In ___			
	___	In ___		___	In ___			
	___	In ___		___	In ___			
	___	In ___		___	In ___			
	___	In ___		___	In ___			

The Anatomy of Harmony 63

Triad Stability   A triad that is a combination of the strongest intervals is the most stable.

> Strongest and most stable   Major triad
> Strong and quite stable   Minor triad
> Weak and unstable   Diminished triad
> Weak and unstable   Augmented triad

Triad Inversion   An *inversion* of a triad occurs when the root (the lowest pitch forming the triad) is placed higher than another factor. The root is not the lowest sounding pitch.

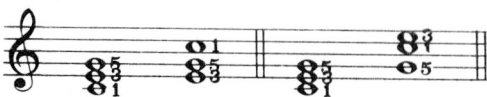

In chapter 8 of his *Treatise on Harmony, Book One* (1722),* Rameau discusses the inversion of chords, a concept that profoundly influenced later theoretical writing.

Triad Position   *Triad position* identifies the note of the chord that appears as the lowest sounding pitch of the harmony. Any of the three notes of the triad may appear as the lowest sounding pitch.

Root Position   No matter what the arrangement of the third and fifth factors is, the triad is in *root position* if the root is the lowest sounding pitch.

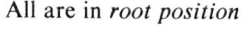

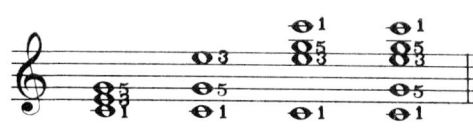 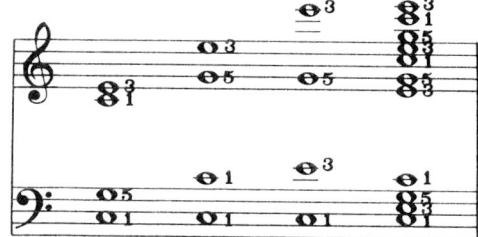

First Inversion   No matter what the arrangement of the root and fifth factors, the triad is in *first inversion* if the third of the triad is the lowest sounding pitch.

All are in *first inversion*

 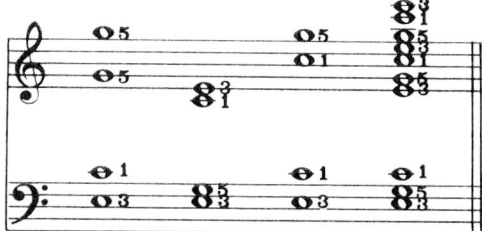

Second Inversion   No matter what the arrangement of the root and third factor, the triad is in *second inversion*, if the fifth factor is the lowest sounding pitch.

All are in *second inversion*

 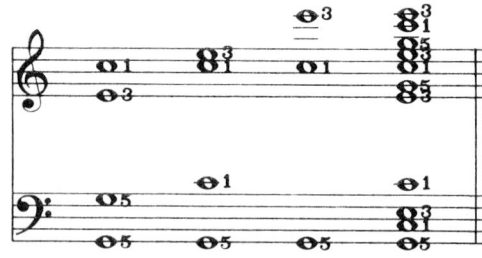

*Jean-Philippe Rameau, *Treatise on Harmony*, trans. Philip Gossett (New York: Dover, 1900)

TRIAD ANALYSIS SYMBOLS

Root position triads are without additional symbols.

First inversion triads are indicated with a small superscript ^{6} to the right of the roman numeral.

Second inversion triads are indicated with a superscript $^6_4$ to the right of the roman numeral.

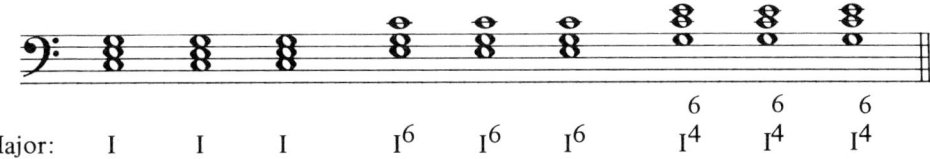

ASSIGNMENT 6

1. Below are ten triads, in various positions and of various types, arranged in four-part harmony (soprano, alto, tenor, and bass).
2. Complete the blanks as requested. The example is worked correctly for you.

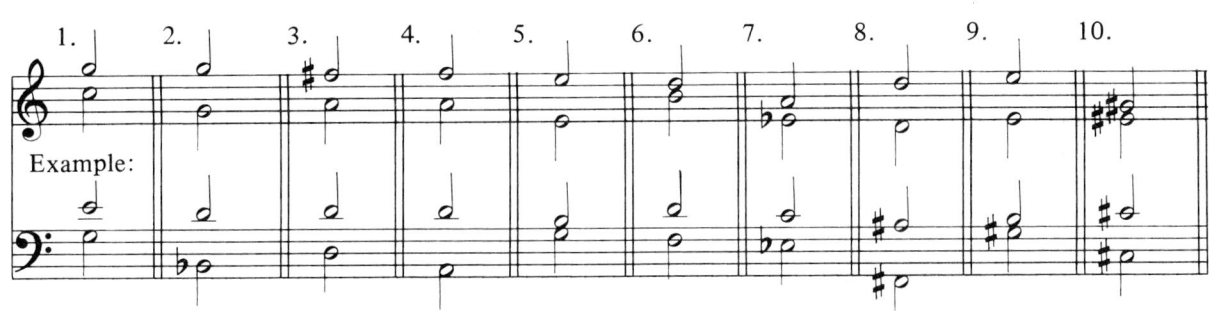

	ROOT	POSITION	TYPE	ANALYSIS SYMBOL
Chord No. 1:	C	2nd Inversion	Major	in G Major: IV^6_4
Chord No. 2:	___	___	___	in F Major: ___
Chord No. 3:	___	___	___	in A Major: ___
Chord No. 4:	___	___	___	in F Major: ___
Chord No. 5:	___	___	___	in B Har Minor ___
Chord No. 6:	___	___	___	in A Nat Minor ___
Chord No. 7:	___	___	___	In B♭ Har Minor ___
Chord No. 8:	___	___	___	in B Har Minor ___
Chord No. 9:	___	___	___	in G♯ Har Minor ___
Chord No. 10:	___	___	___	in F♯ Major ___

FIGURED BASS   *Figured bass* consists essentially of a bass part (single line) with figures (numbers) below to indicate the type of harmony. It is a shorthand method of showing the harmony without the drudgery of writing out the remainder of each chord. This method saved time, and was employed throughout the Baroque period (1600 to 1750) for keyboard accompaniments and keyboard parts for solo songs, solo instrumental compositions, and small and large ensembles.

Continuo   *Continuo* refers to the bass melody plus the figures beneath. According to Baroque performance practice, the bass melody itself was played by both a *viola da gamba* (a stringed instrument with a range similar to that of the cello) and a keyboard instrument (usually a harpsichord or organ) while at the same time the keyboard player *realized* (filled in) the harmony according to the meaning of the figures. Practical editions of the present day are generally printed with the figured bass already realized.

The following excerpt is from a Baroque composition as it appeared originally:

The following is an excerpt from the same Baroque composition as it appears in a modern edition:

In some respects the figured bass of the Baroque era is similar to the popular music symbols presently in use by composers and arrangers.

Figured Bass Symbols   Some standard figured bass symbols along with their realizations are:

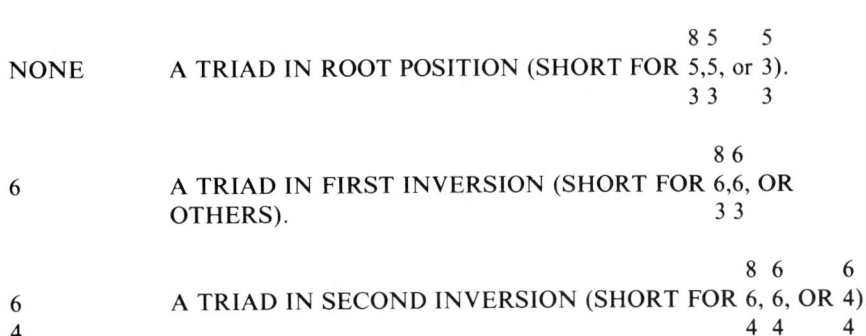

SYMBOL	MEANING
NONE	A TRIAD IN ROOT POSITION (SHORT FOR 5,5, or 3).
6	A TRIAD IN FIRST INVERSION (SHORT FOR 6,6, OR OTHERS).
6 4	A TRIAD IN SECOND INVERSION (SHORT FOR 6, 6, OR 4).

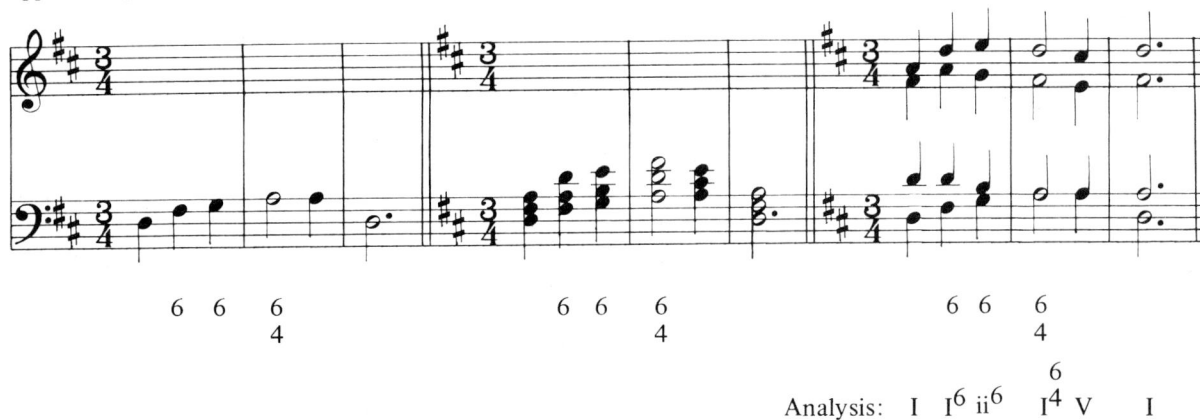

Analysis: I   I⁶   ii⁶   I$_4^6$ V   I

The numbers 6 and 4 refer to intervals above the bass tone, but they only imply others and do not denote specific arrangements. Composers of the Baroque period could have indicated all intended notes above the bass tone—including octaves, thirds, and doublings where they occur—in actual practice, they used only those figures that would specifically denote the arrangement of intervals above the bass note. Thus, they simplified the system and adopted 6 as a symbol of first inversion triads and the $_4^6$ as a symbol of second inversion triads.

The Anatomy of Harmony

The same figured bass as it might be realized: The same figured bass realized correctly also but with different arrangement of chord factors above the bass notes:

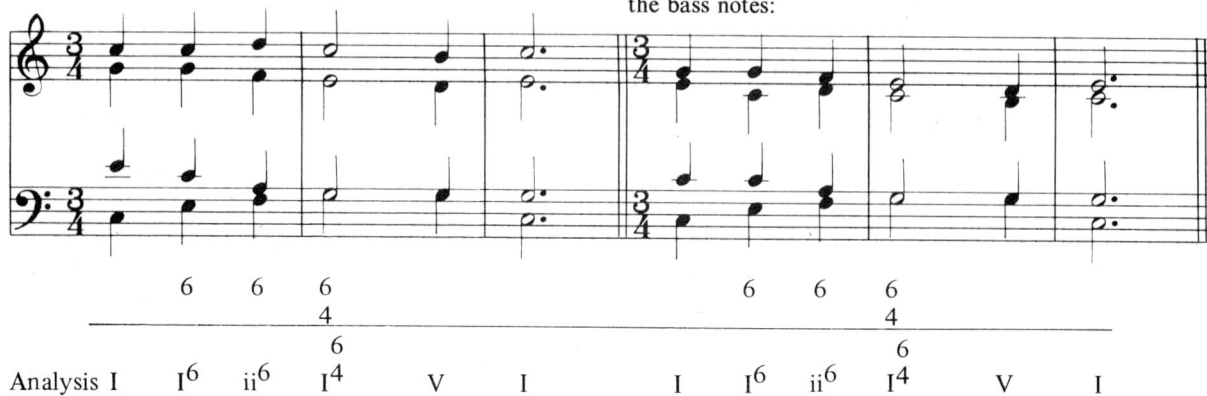

Analysis I I⁶ ii⁶ I⁶₄ V I   I I⁶ ii⁶ I⁶₄ V I

Sometimes it is necessary to indicate sharps, flats, or naturals above the bass note. These are shown in the following manner:

SYMBOL	MEANING
♯, ♭, or ♮	A sharp, flat, or natural alone beneath a bass note indicates a triad in root position with the third interval above the bass note sharped, flatted, or naturaled.
6, 6, or 6 ♯ ♭ ♮	A sharp, flat, or natural below a 6 indicates a first inversion triad with the third interval above the bass note sharped, flatted, or naturaled.
♯6, ♭6, ♮6, ♯6 4 ♭4 or other	Any sharp, flat, or natural sign on either side of a number indicates that this interval above the bass note should be sharped, flatted, or naturaled depending on the symbol. Some composers placed the accidentals to the left of the number while others placed them to the right. Remember that accidentals beside numbers do not change the original intent of the numbers themselves.
⌀, ⌀, 4+	A slash mark through a number indicates that this interval above the bass note should be raised a half step. It means the same as a sharp sign beside the number and was employed by some composers instead of the sharp sign.

Figured bass: Figured bass as realized:

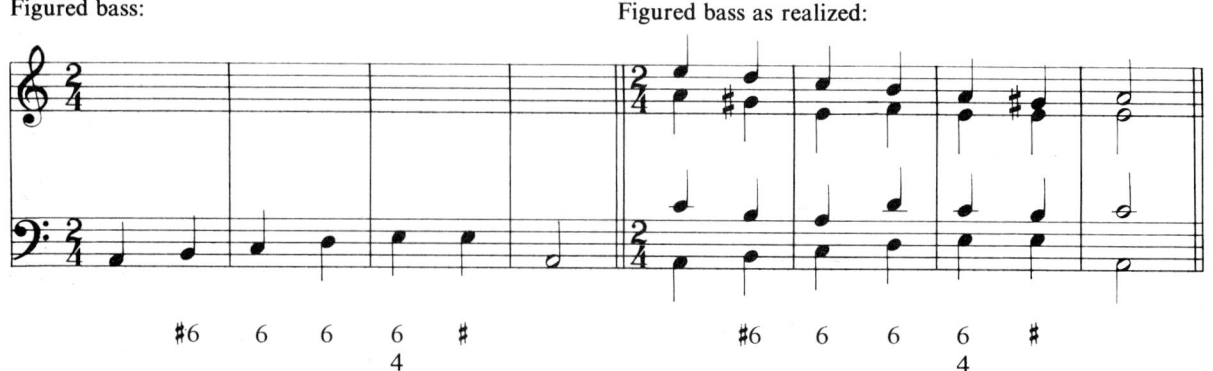

♯6 6 6 6 ♯   ♯6 6 6 6 ♯
         4   4

68   The Anatomy of Harmony

To summarize, any figured bass that contains a 6 but *not* a 4 means first inversion:

All mean first inversion:
```
         8 6 6
6 6 6 3 6 6 etc.
         3 3 3 3 6
```

Any figured bass that contains a 6 *and* a 4 means second inversion:

All mean second inversion:
```
        8 6 6
6 6 6 4 etc.
        4 4 4 4
```

All of these arrangements are correct:

Intervals, such as 6, may be realized in any octave above the bass note.

ASSIGNMENT 7   The following are examples from music literature.

1. Write the chords in simple position on the blank staves provided. Each successive chord is bracketed for convenience.
2. Certain notes have been circled. These are not to be considered as part of the chords.
3. Write the Roman numeral analysis of each chord and indicate the position—6 if in first inversion, $^6_4$ if in second inversion, and no numbers if in root position.
4. The first chord of each illustration is analyzed correctly.
5. Each chord is numbered for convenience in class discussions.

Schumann: *Volksliedchen*
(Little Folk Song)

The Anatomy of Harmony   69

ASSIGNMENT 7 (continued)

70 The Anatomy of Harmony

ASSIGNMENT 7 (continued)

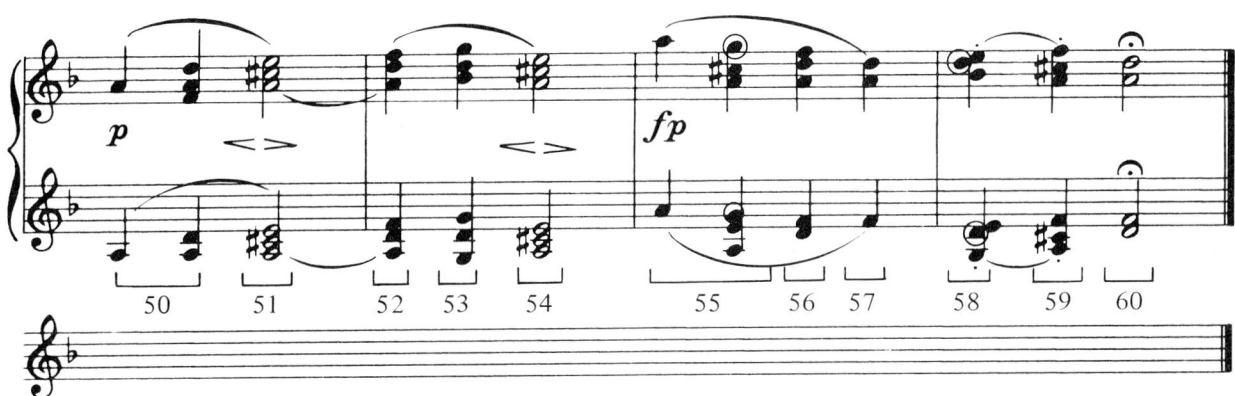

ASSIGNMENT 8 Below are four-part chorale phrases harmonized by J. S. Bach.

1. The embellishing tones have been omitted.
2. Under the staves, indicate the figured bass symbols that would be used to obtain the chords written by Bach.
3. This assignment is designed to help you learn figured bass symbols. In selecting chords that require a variety of symbols, some chords have been included that are not intended for analysis at this time. So, supply only figured bass symbols and *not* analysis symbols.
4. The example illustrates the correct procedure.
5. One figured bass symbol (in no. 1) has been supplied for you.

Example

Bach: *Von Gott will ich nicht lassen*
(I Will Not Leave God)

1. Bach: *Das neugeborne Kinderlein*
   (The Newborn Child)

ASSIGNMENT 8 (continued)

2. Bach: *Seelen—Bräutigam*
(Bridegroom of the Soul)

etc.

3. Bach: *Schwing' dich auf zu deinem Gott*
(Soar Upwards to Thy God)

4. Bach: *Warum sollt' ich mich denn gramen*
(Why Should I Grieve Then)

CADENCE

Cadences function as musical punctuation. For the periods from the Baroque (1600–1750) through the Romantic (1825–1900), and as related to harmony, a cadence consists of two chords signaling the completion of a composition or sections thereof.

Cadences punctuate music in much the same way as periods, commas, colons, and semicolons punctuate our written language. Thus, in music, as in language, thoughts and ideas are separated to avoid confusion. In traditional Western music of the seventeenth through nineteenth centuries, four basic types of harmonic cadences occur:

Authentic Cadence In an *authentic cadence*, the harmonic progression is dominant to tonic.

Perfect Authentic Cadence In a *perfect authentic cadence*, the tonic tone appears in the upper voice of the final tonic chord, and both the dominant and tonic are in root position.

72 The Anatomy of Harmony

Imperfect Authentic Cadence | In an *imperfect authentic cadence,* the third or fifth factor of the tonic chord appears in the upper voice of the final chord of the phrase or one of the two chords, dominant or tonic, is not in root position. Occasionally the vii° triad in first inversion is substituted for the dominant.

Perfect Authentic: Imperfect Authentic: (Rare)

V I   V I   V I   V I   V⁶ I   V I⁶   vii°⁶ I

Half Cadence | In a *half cadence,* the harmonic progression is tonic to dominant, subdominant to dominant, supertonic to dominant, or even submediant to dominant. This cadence usually ends on the dominant.

Half:

IV V   ii V   I V

Plagal Cadence | In a *plagal cadence,* the harmonic progression is from subdominant to tonic (the "Amen" cadence). Less often, the harmonic progression is supertonic (sometimes in first inversion) to tonic (ii⁶ to I).

IV I   IV I   IV I

The Anatomy of Harmony   73

Deceptive Cadence

In a *deceptive cadence,* the harmonic progression is from dominant to submediant. The term "deceptive" refers to the dominant harmony that leads to some harmony other than the expected tonic harmony. In most cases this is the submediant, but others such as the supertonic or mediant are possible.

V vi V vi

NONHARMONIC TONES

Nonharmonic tones are the nonchord tones that occur simultaneously with the harmony and in some manner embellish one or more chord tones. Nonharmonic tones may be regarded as "embellishing tones" when referring to melody, and as "nonharmonic tones" when combined with harmony.

Some characteristics of nonharmonic tones:

1. Basically, all such tones are calculated between two voices only. Most often the two voices are the upper voice that contains the nonharmonic tone and the lowest sounding voice:

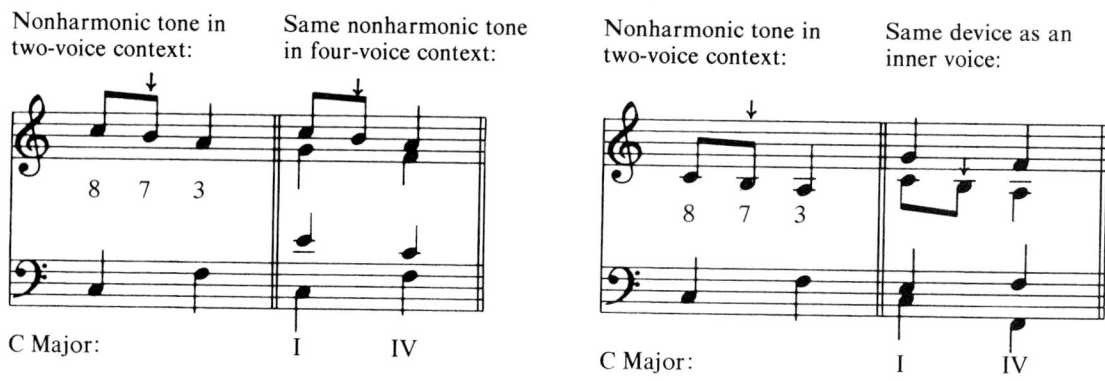

2. Besides being dissonant with the harmony of the moment, nonharmonic tones most often form a dissonant interval with the lowest sounding voice—incidentally with other voices also.

3. For all nonharmonic tones—except the pedal tone, changing tone, and successive passing tones described on page 80—the melody tones immediately preceding and following the nonharmonic tone are consonant, thus forming a pattern:

Consonant	**Dissonant**	**Consonant**
PRECEDING TONE	NONHARMONIC TONE	FOLLOWING TONE

Nonharmonic Tones showing the Consonance-Dissonance-Consonance Pattern:

4. The dissonances created by nonharmonic tones are:
   Major and minor seconds
   Major and minor sevenths
   Perfect fourths
   Augmented and diminished intervals
5. On occasion the intervals of a P5 and M6 or m6 may be considered as nonharmonic tones if they clash with tones of the chord other than the lowest or are of such weak rhythmic strength that they do not create the effect of a chord change:

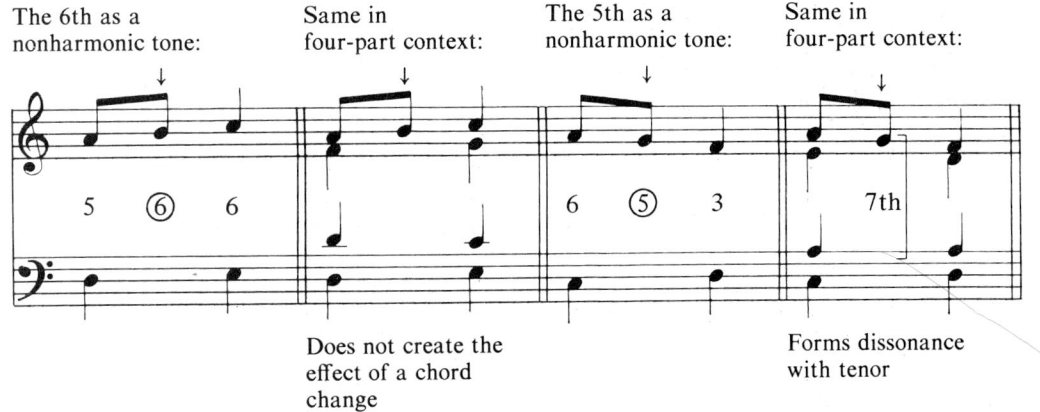

The Anatomy of Harmony 75

Nonharmonic Tone Types

Passing Tone

A *passing tone* is a nonchord tone leading by step from one chord tone to another of different pitch. The passing tone may occur as accented or unaccented.

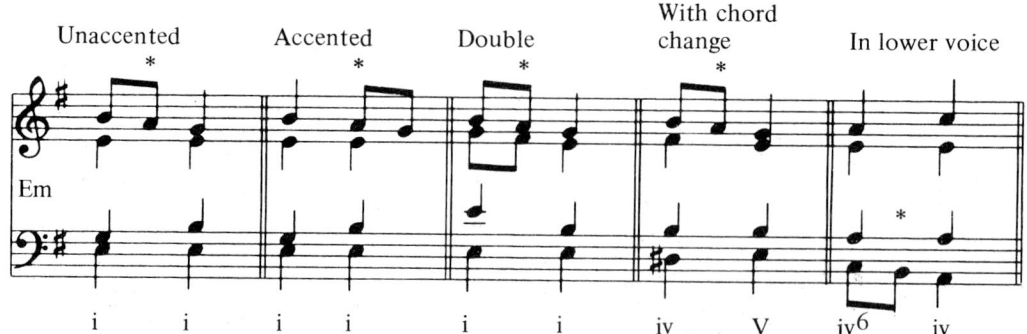

Neighboring Tone

A *neighboring tone* is a nonchord tone that leads by step from one chord tone to another of the same pitch. Neighboring tones may occur as accented or unaccented.

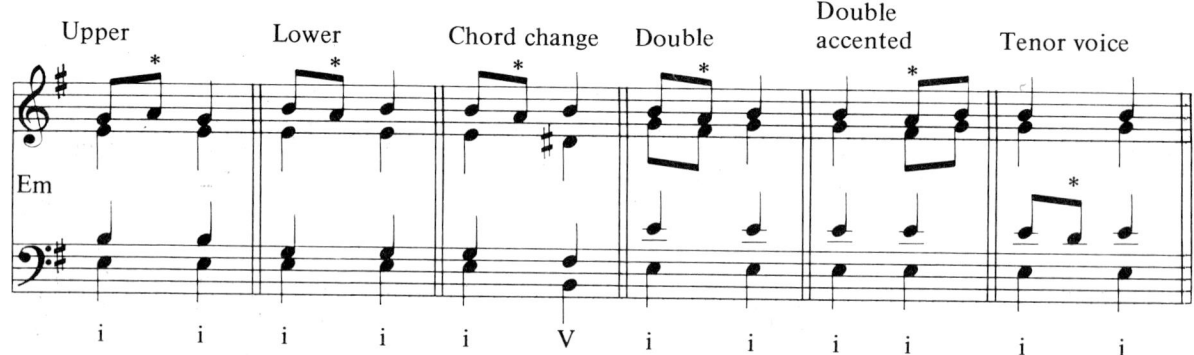

Escape Tone

An *escape tone* is a nonchord tone that leads by step from a chord tone and then leaps to another of different pitch. The escape tone of the eighteenth century is a step above the preceding chord tone and leaps down a third. The escape tone usually occurs as unaccented.

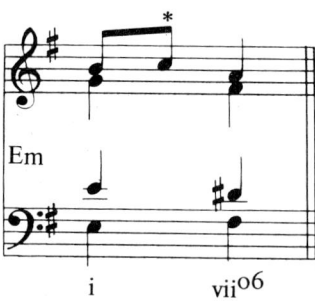

*Indicates the nonharmonic tone.

76 The Anatomy of Harmony

Appoggiatura The *appoggiatura* is a nonchord tone that is approached by leap and resolved by step. It is generally found on a beat or a portion of a beat that is metrically stronger than its resolution.

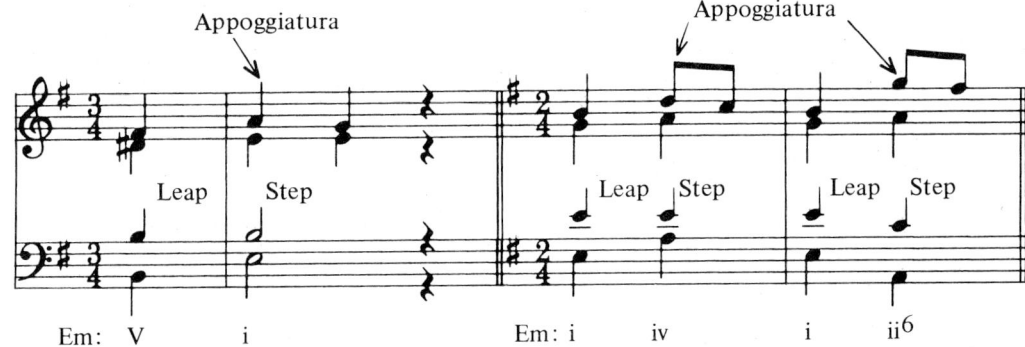

Suspension A *suspension* is a nonchord tone that includes a prepared dissonance and resolution. Suspensions are almost always stressed metrically in relation to their resolutions.

Suspensions are the most complex and the most difficult of all nonharmonic tones to understand. The following will help to explain some of their intricacies:

1. To form a suspension, three melodic notes in succession are required.
2. The melodic pattern of the suspension figure is always as follows:

3. The middle (repeated) note of the suspension figure is the suspended tone. Suspensions contain three phases:

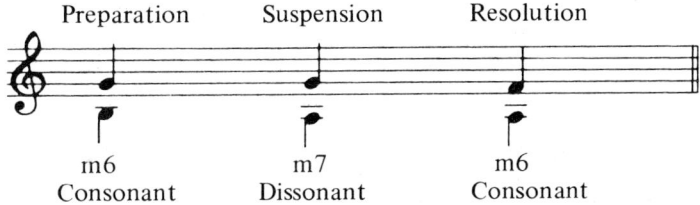

4. The suspended tone (the middle tone of the figure) is always dissonant. Suspensions are of the following types, designated by the interval forming the suspended tone and resolution with the lowest sounding voice (usually the bass voice):

TYPE	SUSPENDED TONE	RESOLUTION
9–8	9TH	8TH
7–6	7TH	6TH
4–3	4TH	3RD

The Anatomy of Harmony

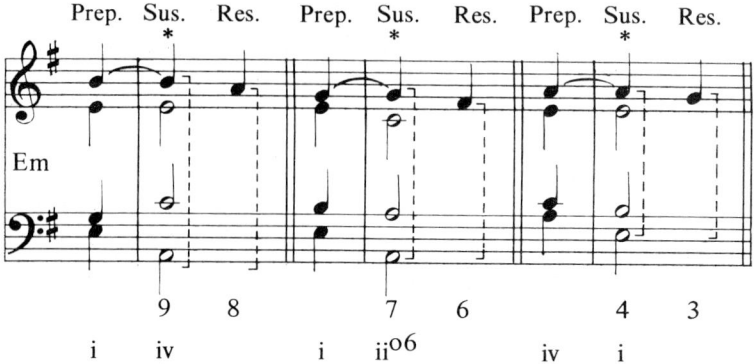

*Indicates the nonharmonic tone.

5. There is one other type of suspension—the 2–3. Whereas, the suspension figure (note, same note, one step lower) is in one of the upper voices in all of the previously described suspension types, in the 2–3 suspension the suspended tone is in the lowest voice.

TYPE	SUSPENDED TONE	RESOLUTION
2–3	2ND	3RD

2–3 suspension showing suspension figure in lower voice.

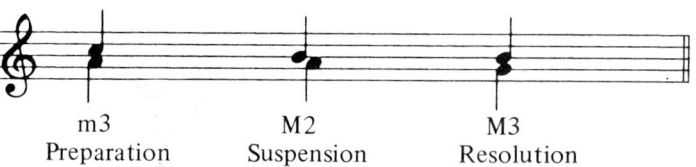

6. The other voice (not containing the suspension figure) may move in almost any way so long as it provides the necessary preparation, suspension, and resolution phases for the suspension figure.

7. Remember that suspensions occur between only two voices—even in four-voice writing. The other voices do not take part and for the present moment may be ignored. The following are suspensions (between only two voices) found in a four-voice setting.

Bach: *Freu' dich sehr, o meine Seele*   Bach: *Was Gott tut, das ist wohlgetan*
(Rejoice, O My Soul)   (What God Does Is Well Done)

8. Suspensions may occur in pairs simultaneously, have decorated resolutions, and occur in chains.

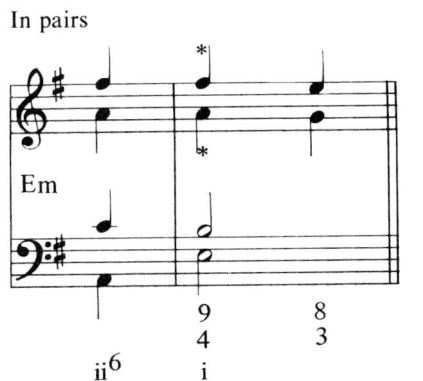

Anticipation

An *anticipation* is a nonchord tone that anticipates a tone of the following chord. It departs by step from a chord tone and progresses by repetition to a chord tone. Occasionally it is approached by leap.

*Indicates the nonharmonic tone.

Retardation
: A *retardation* is a nonchord tone similar to a suspension except that the resolution is upward instead of downward as in the suspension.

Pedal Tone
: A *pedal tone* (pedal point) is a held or repeated note, usually in the lowest voice, that alternates between consonance and dissonance with the chord structures above it. When a pedal tone occurs above other voices or chord structures, it is called an *inverted pedal tone*.

Changing Tone
: A *changing tone* is actually two successive nonharmonic tones. It leads by step from a chord tone, leaps to another nonharmonic tone, and then leads by step to a chord tone.

*Indicates the nonharmonic tone.

Other Nonharmonic Tones in Pairs
: There are times when nonharmonic tones that usually occur singly are found in pairs. The following illustration shows but one of the less frequent occasions.

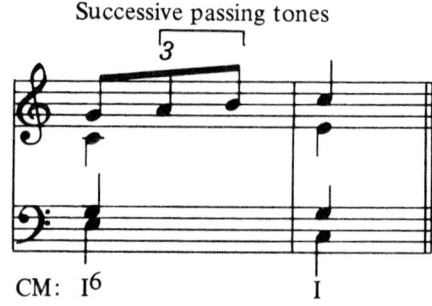

80   The Anatomy of Harmony

ASSIGNMENT 9 Below are nonharmonic tones excerpted from music literature.

1. Circle the nonharmonic tone or tones.
2. Write the name of the type of nonharmonic tone in the blank provided beneath the staves.

ASSIGNMENT 10 Following are three excerpts from music literature.

1. Write the chords in simple position on the blank staves provided.
2. Analyze each chord with Roman numerals indicating also its position. Some chords are provided to help you understand the procedure.
3. Circle and indicate the type of each nonharmonic tone.
4. For convenience use the following abbreviations or initials:

    UPT = Unaccented passing tone
    APT = Accented passing tone
    UNT = Unaccented neighboring tone
    ANT = Accented neighboring tone
    ET = Escape tone
    SUS = Suspension

5. In numbers 1 and 2, the chords change every quarter note. In no. 3 (Corelli), the chords are bracketed—one chord per bracket.

The Anatomy of Harmony   81

ASSIGNMENT 10 (continued)

1. Bach: *Als Jesus Christus in der Nacht*
(When Jesus Christ in the Night)

FM: vi   II$^6_5$
                       mm

2. Bach: *Ach bleib bei uns, Herr Jesu Christ*
(Ah, Stay With Us, Lord Jesus Christ)

AM:

AM: vi

To help you complete the analysis of the excerpt by Corelli the following hints will help.

1. The analysis for three of the chords is provided. The chord at no. 1 is given to help you get started, the chord at no. 9 is one not yet explained in the test—ignore it for the moment. The analysis at no. 12 is also given.
2. The chords at no. 6 and 7 are incomplete. Each requires another note to complete the triad. These are called *implied* harmonies meaning that the missing note is suggested but not stated.
   Hint for chord 6—the missing triad note is suggested in chord 5. Which note of chord 5 would fill out the triad in chord 6?
   Hint for chord 7—the missing triad tone is suggested in chord 8. Which note of chord 8 would fill out the triad in chord 7?
3. The answer to the analysis of the C in chord 7 is found on page 79.
4. The remainder of the analysis you can discover for yourself.

*Not yet explained in text. Ignore for the moment.

ASSIGNMENT 10 (continued)

3. Corelli: *Sonata in F* op. 3 no. 1 for two violins and continuo
on Tändeln und Scherzen by Süssmayr

HARMONIC RHYTHM

Harmonic rhythm is the frequency of harmonic change in a composition. In some compositions each successive melody tone is harmonized with a different chord. Thus, the harmonic rhythm is that of one chord per melody tone.

Bach: *Wer nur den lieben Gott lasst walten*
(If We Will But Let God Guide Us)

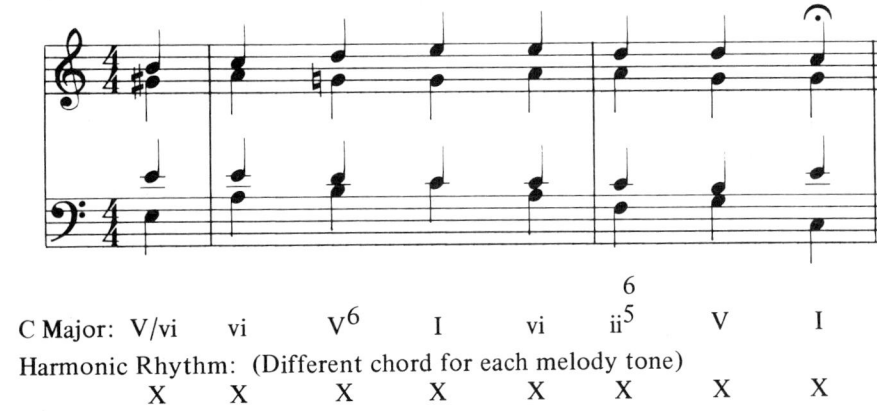

C Major: V/vi   vi   V^6 I   vi   ii$^6_5$ V   I
Harmonic Rhythm: (Different chord for each melody tone)
         X   X   X   X   X   X   X   X

Other compositions may exhibit a very slow harmonic rhythm even though the tempo is fast and the rate of change in melody tones is very rapid.

The Anatomy of Harmony 83

Fast moving melody tones with slow harmonic rhythm:

La Cucaracha
(The Cockroach)

Folk Song

On occasion a single melody tone may be harmonized with several different chords:

Schumann; *Papillons* op. 2 no. 12

Fast harmonic rhythm—harmony changes on each successive melody tone (12 changes in all):

Medium harmonic rhythm—same melody with only half as many harmony changes (7 changes in all):

C Major: I   IV   I   V   ii   I   V   I
Harmonic Rhythm:
              X   X   X   X   X   X   X   X

Slow harmonic rhythm—same melody harmonized with only one chord per measure (4 changes in all):

C Major: I   ii   V   I
Harmonic Rhythm:
              X   X   X   X

ASSIGNMENT 11 In the two compositions that follow:

1. Indicate the harmonic rhythm by placing an "X" under each new harmony.
2. Discuss:
    a. Harmonic rhythm in relation to the phrases.
    b. Use of rhythmic figures in the melody.

Beethoven: *Eight Variations* (theme and first variation)

The Anatomy of Harmony   85

ASSIGNMENT 11 (continued)

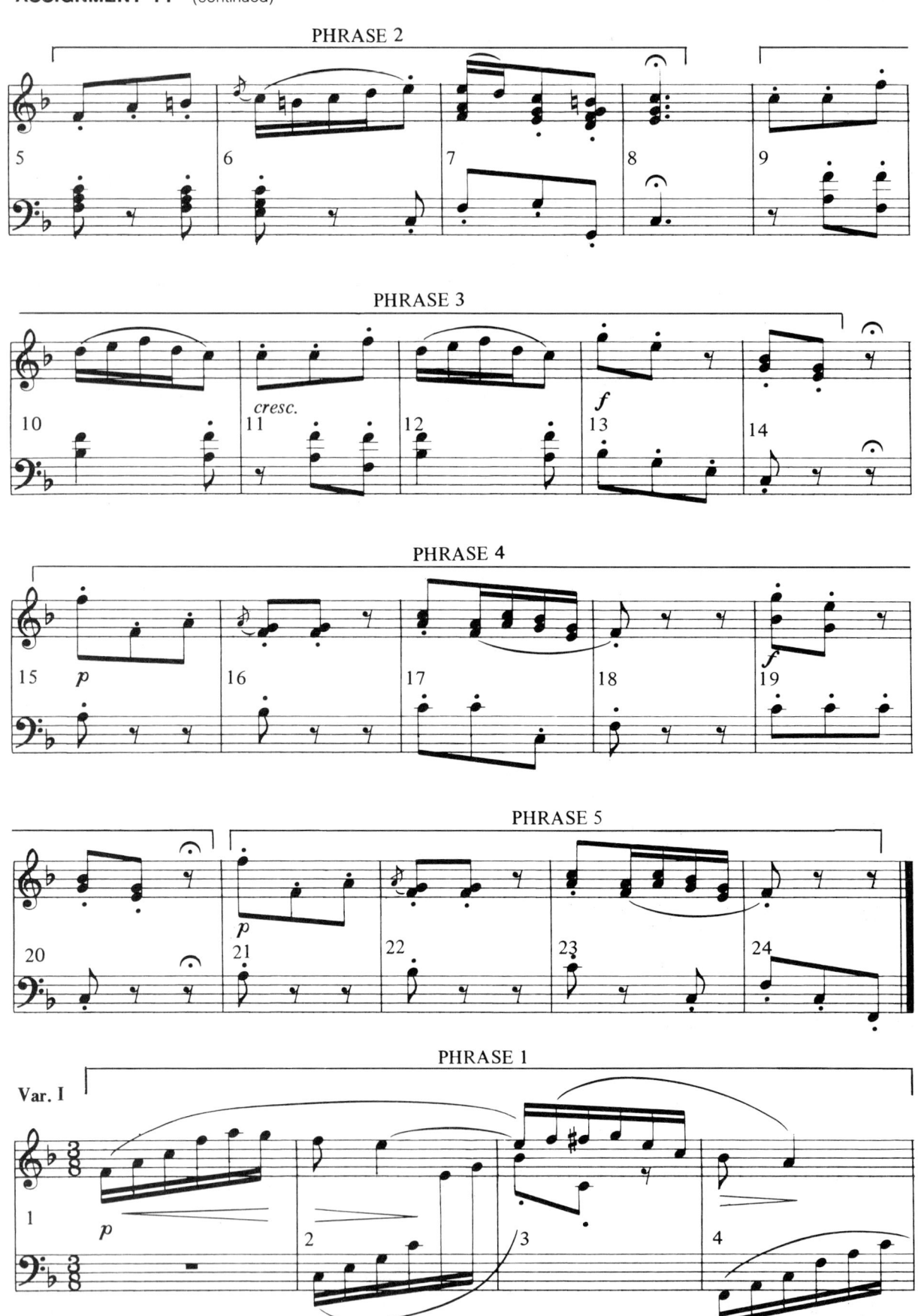

86 The Anatomy of Harmony

ASSIGNMENT 11 (continued)

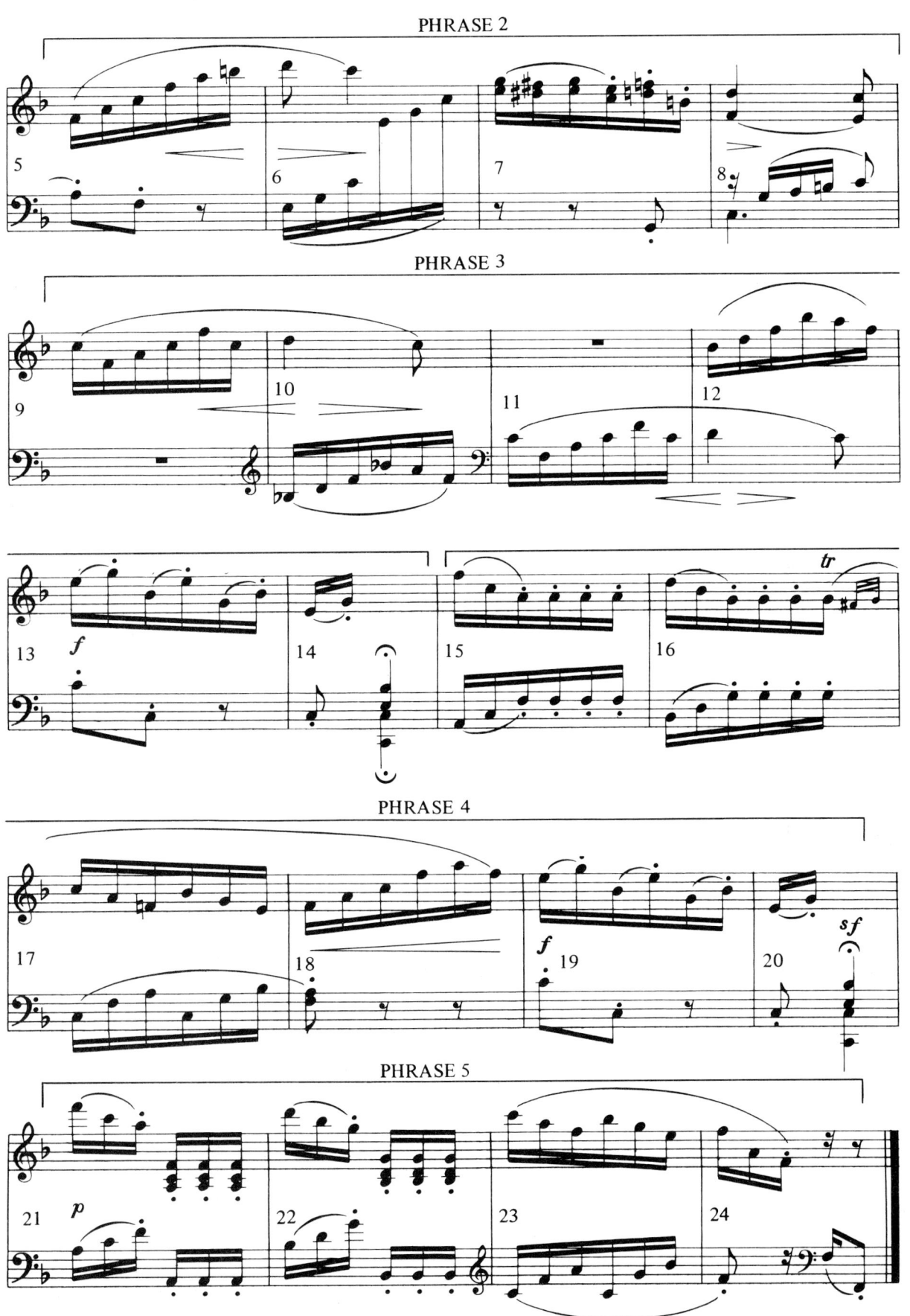

ASSIGNMENT 11 (continued)

Schubert: *Mit dem grünen Lautenbande* op. 25 no. 7
(With the Green Lute Ribbon)

88   The Anatomy of Harmony

ASSIGNMENT 11 (continued)

ASSIGNMENT 11 (continued)

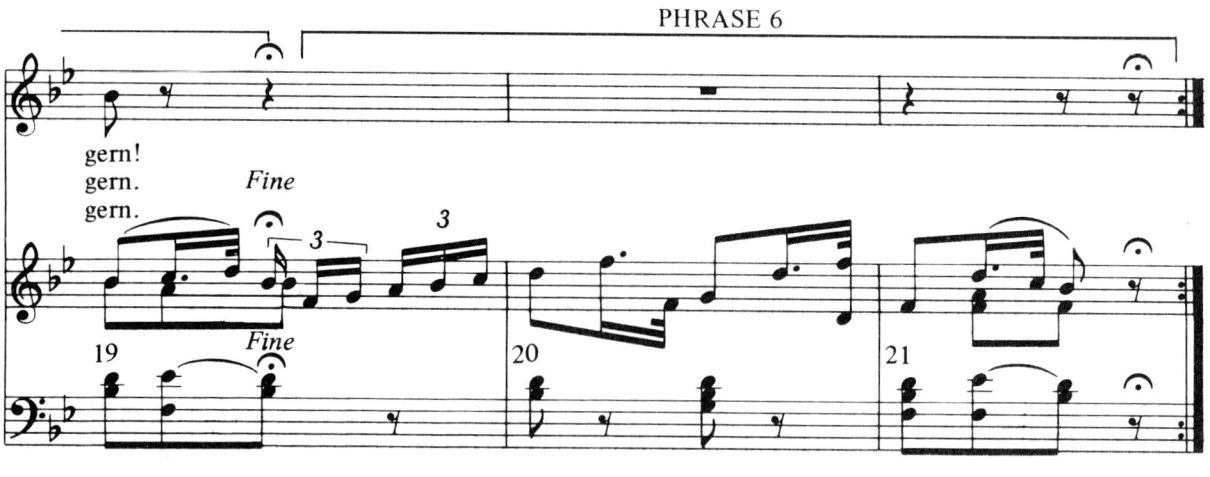

ASSIGNMENT 12

1. Following are three well-known folk song melodies.
2. Sing each melody to refresh your memory.
3. Above each melody are the triads to be used in the harmonization. Use only these chords.
4. After you have sung the melody over a few times, decide:
   a. Which triad (harmony) is best for a particular section of the melody.
   b. How long each triad should sound before another takes over (harmonic rhythm). Hopefully you won't try to harmonize each successive melody note with a different triad.
5. Indicate your choices by writing each chord symbol (G, C, D, etc.) above the melody note where that particular harmony should begin.
6. Then, circle each nonharmonic tone and name it (below the staff).
7. Have each class member play his or her harmonization in class.
8. Hold a contest. Each class member votes on the most musical harmonization.

1. Harmonize only with these triads

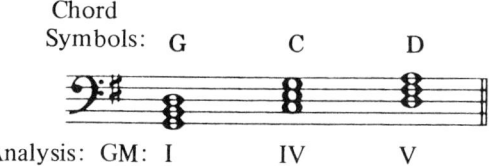

Little Brown Jug
Folk Song

90   The Anatomy of Harmony

ASSIGNMENT 12 (continued)

2. Harmonize only with these triads

   Chord Symbols: G   D

   GM: I   V

   Down in the Valley   Folk Song

3. Harmonize only with these triads

   Chord Symbols: Am   Dm   E

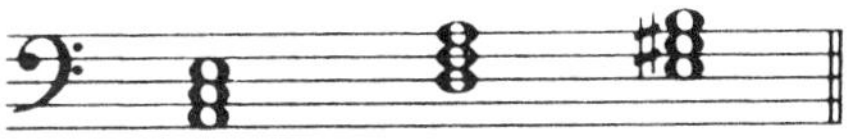

   Am: i   iv   V

   Charlie Is My Darling   Folk Song

4 The Anatomy of Melody

Step Progression *Embellishing Tone* *Escape Tone* *Retardation*
Structural Tone *Passing Tone* *Appoggiatura* *Changing Tone*
Secondary Tone *Neighboring Tone* *Anticipation* *Pedal Tone*

MELODY *Melody* is an organized succession of tones. Distinguished from harmony, which comprises tones in simultaneity (tones sounding together), it is the linear aspect of music. Three of the four properties of sound—pitch, duration, and intensity—govern the flow of melody, and the ways in which these interact constitute a vital component of the art of music. Many important forces organize and direct melody, and some of these are discussed in this chapter.

Step Progression A *step progression* consists of selected tones (usually not adjacent) moving by step and giving the melody direction.

Step Progression

The Pig Got Up Folk Song

Two conditions are vital in the formation of step progressions:

1. The adjacent components move by step (half or whole step).
2. The step progression is in one direction only (up or down). On occasion, a step progression in one direction may follow immediately after another in the opposite direction.

Other factors relating to step progressions:

1. Step progressions may be of any length, spanning a phrase of four to six measures, or ordering a single measure or an entire movement.
2. There is no limit to the number of tones in a step progression. Many step progressions contain as many as eight or ten tones while others contain only two.
3. The importance of a step progression depends upon the importance of the tones that make it up. Some step progressions made up of incidental tones are of only minor consequence, but others formed by vital melodic tones are of major significance to the melody.
4. More than one step progression may occur simultaneously in a melody (see unaccompanied suites and sonatas for stringed instruments by Bach).

A seven-tone step progression:

Handel: *Concerto Grosso in D Minor* op. 6 no. 10

A two-tone step progression:

Dvořák: *Slavonic Dances* op. 46 no. 1

Two simultaneous step progressions:

Handel: *Fantasia in C*

HIERARCHY OF MELODIC COMPONENTS

Inherent in almost all melodies are—

1. tones that receive particular stress.
2. tones that are repeated more often than others.
3. tones that have longer duration than others.

Along with these tones are others that serve in a secondary role and provide subtle decorations and enhancements of the more important highlights. Three strata of musical importance exist in the tones of a melody:

Structural Tone

A *structural tone* is a melody tone of maximum importance. A structural tone stands out as part of the framework upon which the other tones are distributed and can be heard as a focal point for that section of the melody. There are, of course, no rules regarding the number of structural tones that may be present in a melody, and in addition their closeness or sparseness cannot be categorized.

Several elements exist that produce structural tones. In some instances a structural tone results from a single element, if that element exerts sufficient influence, but often two or more elements combine to place a tone in the structural category. For example:

1. *The first and last tones of a phrase.* Since they initiate and conclude the melodic activity, these tones have a built-in importance that the ear tends to class as significant.
2. *The highest and lowest tones.* The highest and lowest tones in a melodic group have a tendency to predominate and thus are sometimes interpreted as structural by the ear.
3. *Stressed (dynamic) tones.* Tones that receive heavy dynamic accents stand out in importance and thus are influenced to become structural tones.
4. *Tones of longer duration.* Tones that dominate the time span of a melody or melodic group are good candidates for structural tones. Their durational quality is in direct relationship to their importance in the phrase.
5. *Repeated tones.* Although each separate tone may be of short duration, repeated tones tend to receive attention, and in this sense exert the same influence as long duration tones.

Relationship of Structural Tones to Step Progressions

The strongest step progressions are those that contain the largest number of structural tones. Most step progressions contain essentially structural tones. In the following illustration, the step progression is made up exclusively of structural tones:

J. Strauss: *Emperor Waltzes*

Structural Tones:

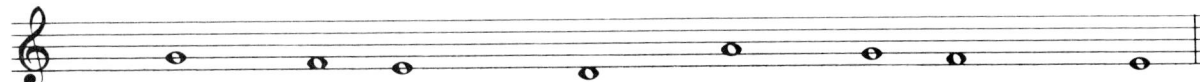

In the following example, a structural tone is elaborated for four measures. The melody returns to the first (structural) tone four times after its original appearance:

Prokofieff: *Symphony no. 5.*

© Copyright 1946, renewed 1974 by MCA Music, A Division of MCA, Inc. Used by permission. All rights reserved.

Structural Tones:

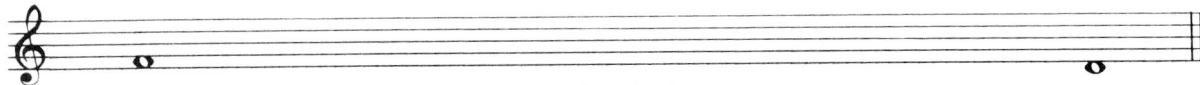

(Octave displacement does not eliminate structural relationships.)

In the next example, structural tones are produced through high pitch:

Bach: *Three-Part Invention in D Major*

Structural Tones:

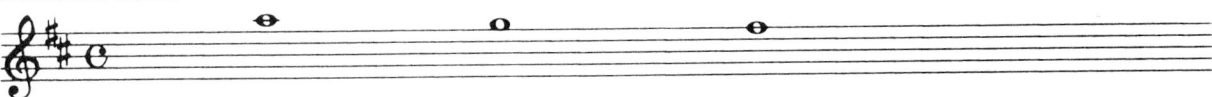

The Anatomy of Melody 95

Structural tones may be produced by repeated notes:

Haydn: *Quartet in G Minor* op. 74 no. 3

Structural Tones:

It must be remembered that the selection of structural tones is not entirely an objective procedure. Two tones of almost equal importance may on occasion compete for the title of "structural tone." Listeners will differ in their opinions concerning the proper selection, and individuals must rely on their own dictates—providing these are substantiated by logic and sound reasoning.

In the following example, there are two instances where individual preferences may differ. The notes given as structural tones may be the first choice, but the notes suggested in dotted lines may also be a logical choice.

Tchaikovsky: *Concerto in B-flat for Piano and Orchestra*

Structural Tones:

The following examples are two analytical interpretations of the same melody. Each has a different set of dynamic markings. The change in accents alters the selection of structural tones.

Structural Tones:

Structural Tones:

96   The Anatomy of Melody

The following example is an excerpt from an American folk song that has been rewritten to show that structural pitches are not intrinsic to a particular sequence of tones and may change when durations and intensity are altered.

Out on the Plains Folk Song

Secondary Tone

A *secondary tone* is a tone that elaborates a structural tone. Often outlining chords, secondary tones lie at intervals larger than a step from the structural tones they embellish. Secondary tones are spaced close enough to the structural tone to support and heighten the dominating effect of the structural tone.

In the diatonic (key-related) music of the seventeenth through nineteenth centuries, secondary tones relate to structural tones by harmonic implication, usually outlining chords. Although this harmonic implication of the secondary tone exists also in twentieth-century music, its clarity and function is sometimes clouded by the more complex contemporary harmony.

The following melodies from music literature have been analyzed for both structural and secondary tones.

In the analysis the following symbols are used:

o = Structural Tones

♩ = Secondary Tones

Ties = Repeated Structural Tones

Beethoven: *Symphony no. 3 (Eroica)*

Structural and Secondary Tones:

The Anatomy of Melody   97

Beethoven: *Symphony no. 5*

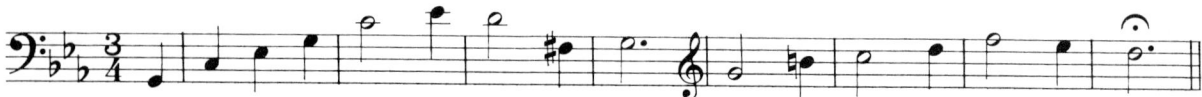

Structural and Secondary Tones:

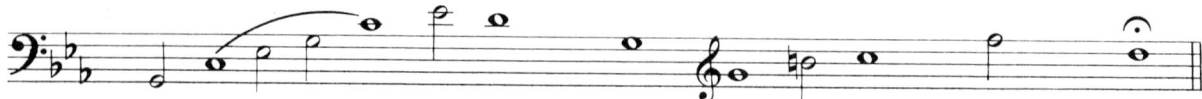

Stravinsky: *Petrouchka*

Structural and Secondary Tones:

Embellishing Tone

An *embellishing tone* is the decoration or ornament to the structural tone and the secondary tone. In relation to harmony, embellishing tones are the nonharmonic tones. They are generally of shorter value and less conspicuous metrically than either structural or secondary tones.

In the preceding chapter, these same tones are discussed in relation to the chords with which they appear. Now the focus is centered on the melodic setting in which these tones occur.

Whether spoken of as embellishing or nonharmonic, these tones fall into the following categories:

Passing tone	Anticipation
Neighboring tone	Retardation
Escape tone	Changing tone
Appoggiatura	Pedal tone

Definitions of embellishing tones as *nonharmonic tones* are found in the preceding chapter, "Anatomy of Harmony," and will not be repeated here. In the following examples, embellishing tones are illustrated to show how they relate to structural and secondary tones. The following symbols are used:

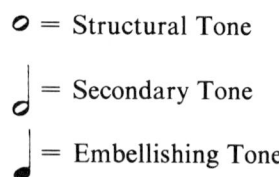

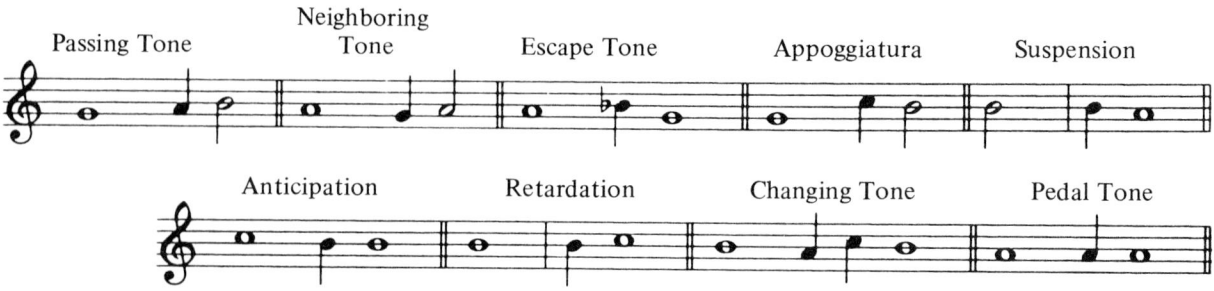

98   The Anatomy of Melody

The following melodies have a melodic analysis directly below each. Chord symbols are added to show the interaction of melody with harmony. In these examples:

1. All structural tones are one of the factors (1, 3, or 5) of the supporting chord.
2. Secondary tones are also factors of the existing harmony.
3. Embellishing tones, besides being nonharmonic, are decorations of either structural or secondary tones.

The Anatomy of Melody

Brahms: *Deutsche Volkslieder*
(German Folk Song)

ASSIGNMENT 1

1. On the blank staff provided under each melody, write the structural, secondary, and embellishing tones.
2. Circle all notes that are a part of important step progressions.
3. Some melodies include chord symbols. Adjust your selection of structural, secondary, and embellishing tones to conform to the chords listed.
4. Other melodies are without chord symbols. Play or sing these several times. Then, decide on the selection of structural, secondary, and embellishing tones as you determine the chord symbols. Sing the melody and play your chord symbols when you are finished. When you are satisfied with your selection, write the chord symbols above the staves.

The Muffin Man
Folk Song

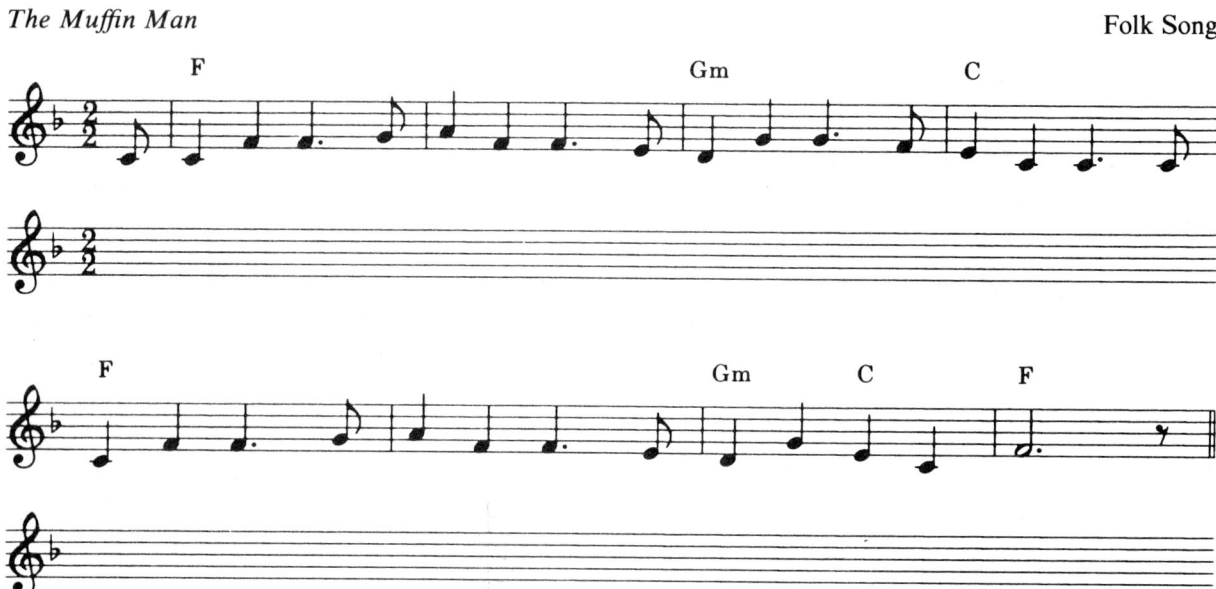

100   The Anatomy of Melody

ASSIGNMENT 1 (continued)

Schubert: *Täuschung*
(Delusion)

The Hero of Hoosierdom

ASSIGNMENT 1 (continued)

Lord Lovelle
Folk Song

102 The Anatomy of Melody

5 Melodic Organization

Motive
Phrase Member
Phrase
Period
Repeated Phrases

Parallel Phrases
Contrasting Phrases
Three-Part Period
Double Period

Song Form
Extension of a Phrase
Phrase Mutation
Exact Sequence

Diatonic Sequence
Modified Sequence
Modulating Sequence
False Sequence

THE ORGANIZATION OF MELODIC THOUGHT

In the previous chapter, the function of melodic tones, the interaction of structural, secondary, and embellishing tones with step progressions, and the basic point and direction of melody were discussed. This chapter discusses the organization of melodic thought and the ways in which musical units are combined into larger and larger sections. In much the same way as written language is made meaningful through the grouping of sentences and paragraphs, melody is grouped into convenient and meaningful units or sections.

The Motive

The *motive* is the smallest of all musical units. It may consist of as few as two tones or as many as seven or eight. Frequently, larger units are constructed through successive statements, sometimes modified slightly, of the same motive.

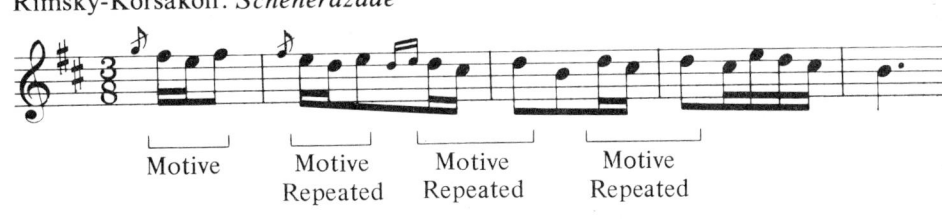

Rimsky-Korsakoff: *Scheherazade*

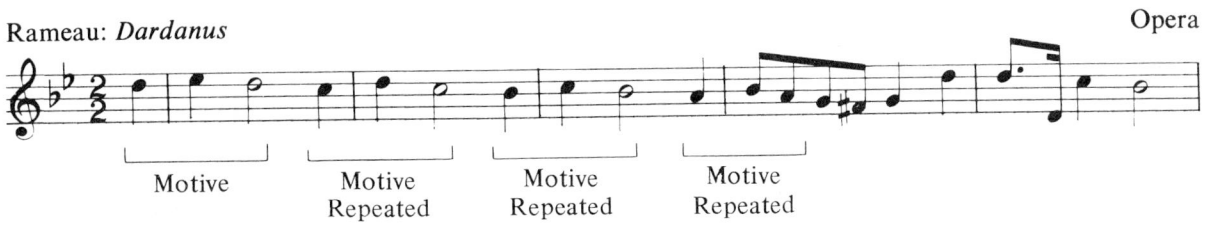

Rameau: *Dardanus*   Opera

Lalo: *Concerto Russe* op. 29

103

Phrase Member A *phrase member* is a musical unit often larger than a motive and generally two measures long. Phrase members when combined give rise to larger units called *phrases*.

Haydn: *Symphony in C (Toy)*

Haydn: *Trio no. 1 in G Major*

Haydn: *Symphony in B-flat Major* no. 102

Phrase A *phrase* is a substantial musical thought ending with a cadence. Its length and cadence usually distinguish the phrase from a motive, but only length distinguishes it from a phrase member. Phrases are frequently four measures long, but they may be of any length so long as they contain a complete (though sometimes dependent) musical thought and end with some kind of cadential implication.

Lennon and McCartney: *I Want to Hold Your Hand*

Words and music by John Lennon and Paul McCartney. © Copyright 1963 by Modern Songs Limited. London W.C. 2, England. Sole selling agent Duchess Music Corporation, 445 Park Avenue, New York, N.Y. 10022. Used by permission. All rights reserved.

Period A *period* is a combination of two phrases (sometimes three) that are in some way related so that this new and larger, complete musical unit is formed.

Repeated Phrases Although *repeated phrases* are not typically regarded as period structures, since the first phrase is self-contained and not dependent upon the second for completion, they may resemble and even function as periods since the time span involved corresponds with that of a period.

Modified Repeated Phrases

With *modified repeated phrases*, the second phrase is somewhat altered but still contains the same contour of the first. Modifications most often consist of the embellishment of melody tones, altered rhythm, or deleted melody tones. The cadences are usually of the same type. Occasionally the two phrases function in the "question/answer" relationship generally referred to as "antecedent/consequent."

The excerpt below from the light opera, *The Fortune Teller,* illustrates how the melody from the first phrase is modified in the second.

Herbert: *Gypsy Love Song*

PHRASE 1

PHRASE 2 - MODIFIED REPEATED

Parallel Phrases

Parallel phrases combine to form a period in which the first portion of both phrases is the same or at least similar. In parallel construction, the phrases function in the antecedent/consequent relationship. Most common is a half cadence at the end of the antecedent phrase and a more conclusive authentic cadence at the end of the consequent phrase.

Foster: *Camptown Races*

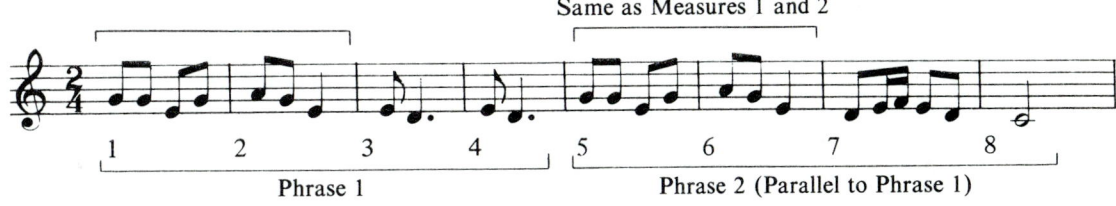

Cockles and Mussels   Irish Folk Song

Occasionally the similarity between the two phrases may be less or more than the first two measures of each. The following example shows only the final three notes of the second phrase to be different from the first. Note also that the second phrase ends with an authentic cadence—stronger than the half cadence of the first phrase.

Melodic Organization 105

Schubert: *Impromptu* op. 90 no. 1

The following parallel phrases by Mozart begin in D major but end in A major. Only the first measure of each phrase is the same.

Mozart: *Piano Sonata*, K 284 (third movement)

In the following example by Grieg, the repeated section of the second phrase is transposed up one letter name.

Grieg: *The Last Spring* op. 34 no. 2

Notes of 1st Phrase transposed up one letter name

106   Melodic Organization

Contrasting Phrases

Contrasting phrases in a period structure are characterized by a dissimilar melodic content while maintaining an antecedent/consequent relationship. As with parallel construction, the antecedent phrase ends with a half cadence and the consequent phrase with a more definitive authentic cadence.

In this type of construction the contrast (in the second phrase) occurs primarily in subtle features such as melodic shaping and direction. Severe changes in general style, or bold differences such as the sudden introduction of markedly different rhythms or motives, are seldom a part of contrasting construction.

In the following example, no new rhythmic values (except the final cadence note) are introduced. Measures 2, 4, 6, and 7 contain the same rhythm while measure 5 duplicates that of 3. The second phrase, however, reaches a new low pitch (B-flat) not found in the first phrase. Otherwise, the melodic direction of the two phrases is analogous.

Ash Grove — Folk Song

2nd Phrase contrasting to the 1st in both pitch and rhythm

Thus, in the three types of phrases described, it is possible to see in period structure a gamut of phrase relationships ranging from similarity (modified repeated phrases) through the various mixtures (parallel phrases) to a high degree of contrast (contrasting phrases).

Three-Part Period

Most periods are composed of just two phrases, but *three-part,* or three-phrase, *periods* do occur. Such periods consist generally of phrases with an A B A or A B B relationship.

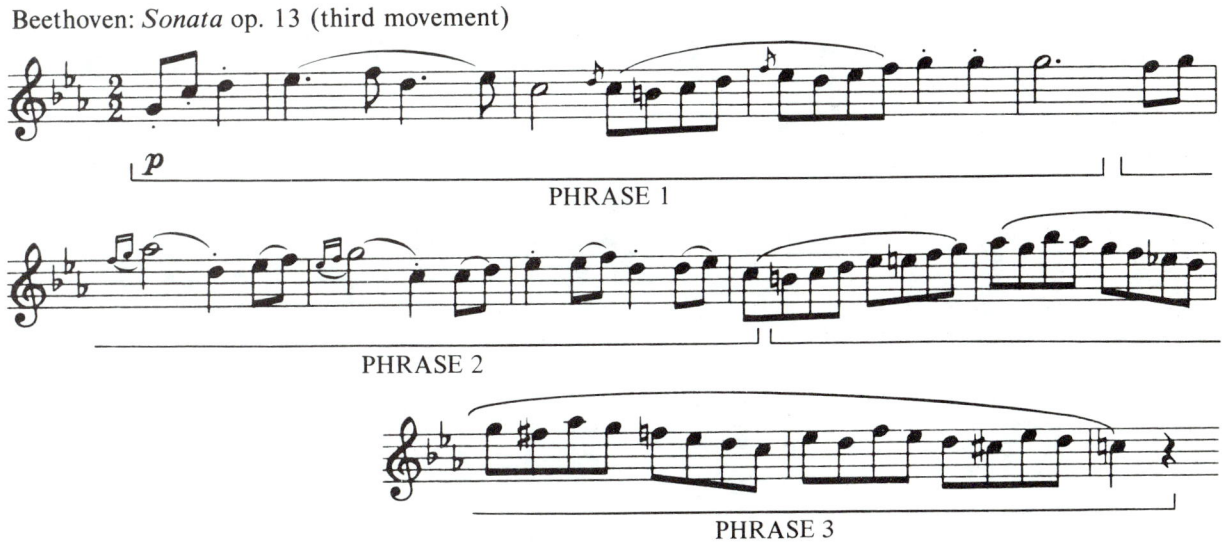

Beethoven: *Sonata* op. 13 (third movement)

Frequently 12-bar blues melodies are three-part periods. Note the example on page 336, *Sweet Home Chicago,* in A A B form.

Melodic Organization 107

ASSIGNMENT 1

You are to use the following seven phrases from music literature as a basis for period construction.

On a separate sheet of score paper:

1. Write an additional phrase for each in parallel construction.
2. Write an additional phrase for each in contrasting construction.
3. Select two of the melodies and complete them to a three-part period.
4. Discuss the analysis of each phrase—structural, secondary, and embellishing tones as well as step progressions.

1. Haydn: *Piano Sonata in G Major* Hob. XVI/40

G Major:

2. Bizet: *Carmen*

B-flat Major:

3. Sullivan: *When Britain Really Ruled the Waves*

A Major:

4. Couperin: *La Bandoline*

A Minor:

5. Brahms: *Waltzes* op. 39 no. 2

E Major:

6. Weber: *Concertstuck* op. 79

F Minor:

7. Schubert: *Piano Sonata* op. 78

B Minor:

108   Melodic Organization

Double Period

A *double period* typically includes a series of four phrases where each of the first three phrases is punctuated by a relatively weak cadence and the fourth by a stronger authentic cadence. The following phrase analysis of the Chopin *Prelude in A Major* op. 28 no. 7 shows how phrases combine to form a double period.

Measures:	1 2 3 4	5 6 7 8	9 10 11 12	13 14 15 16
Phrases:	Phrase 1	Phrase 2	Phrase 3	Phrase 4
Relation:	Phrase	Contrasting Phrase	Phrase 1 Modified	Phrase 2 Modified
Letters:	A	B	A′	B′
	Period: Contrasting Phrases		Period: Contrasting Phrases	
	Modified Repeated Period			

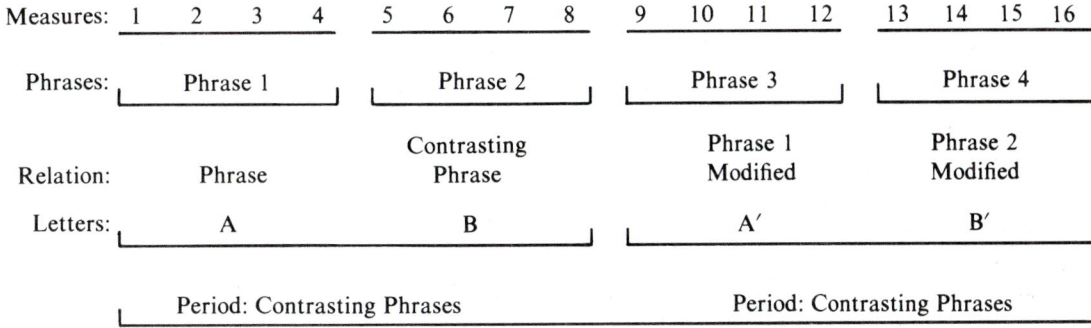

Other examples of double periods may be found in the following excerpts:

Mozart: *Piano Sonata in C Major* K. 309 (second movement)

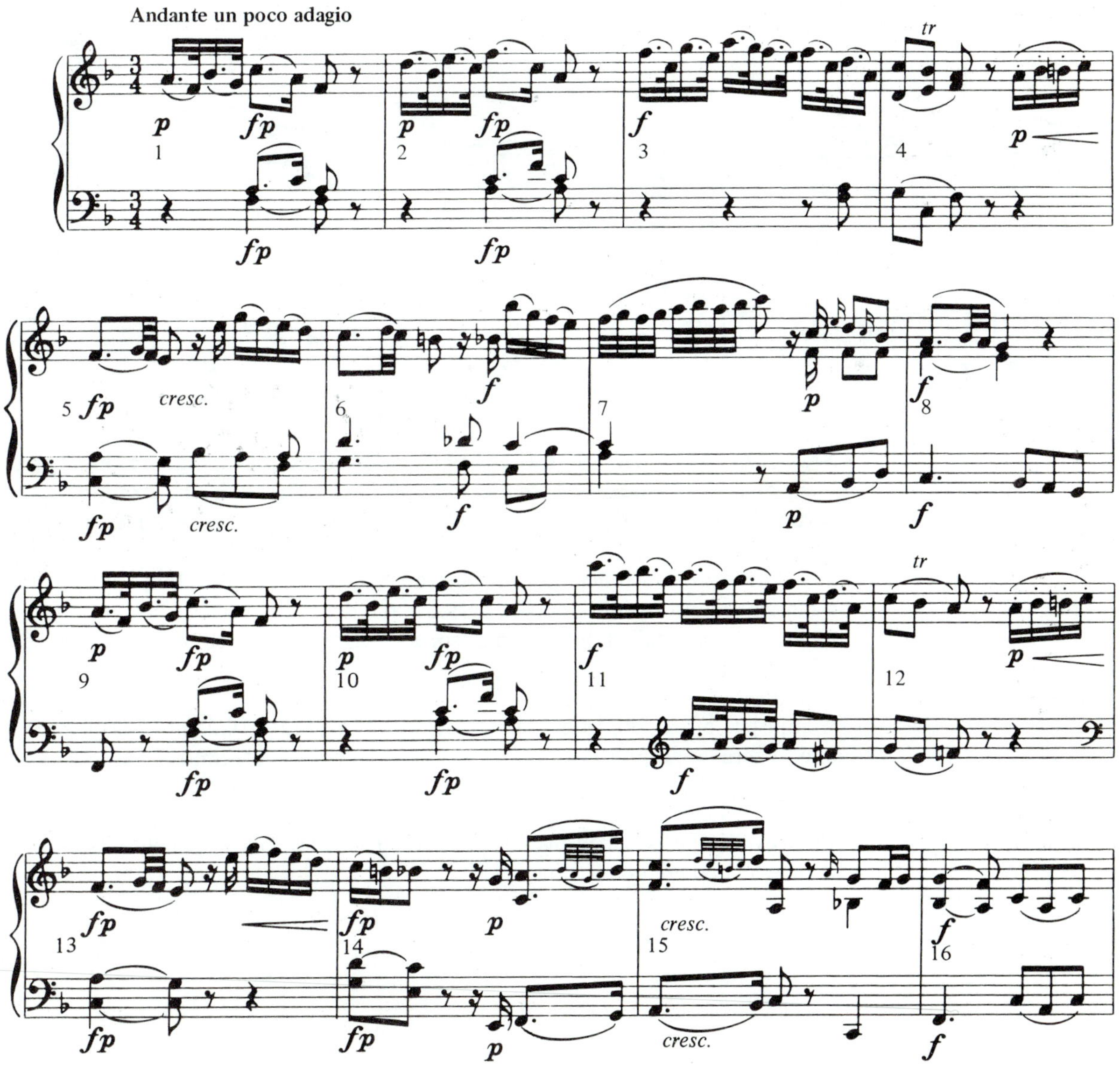

Chopin: *Mazurka* op. 33 no. 3

| **Song Form** | *Song form* is a broad and misleading term often used to designate three-part form and less frequently homophonic two-part form. It is the combining of period or double period structures to form a large, but still related, musical unit. |

The term is included here to illustrate the growth process that begins with a motive and grows into phrases, periods, and double periods to produce a song form. A more detailed discussion of song forms will be taken up in chapter 16, "Three-Part Form."

Modifications of the Phrase — Composers often seek to modify the length of a phrase. This provides variety, and where appropriate, eliminates the dullness of continued, same-length phrases.

Extension of a Phrase — Phrases may be extended by half again their normal length without destroying their essential characteristics.

Extension near the Beginning of a Phrase
Phrases may be extended near the beginning by repeating or sequencing a few opening tones.

Haydn: *Symphony in D no. 104*

Internal Extension
A small melodic group or groups may be repeated in the middle of the phrase to extend its length.

Haydn: *Symphony in D no. 101 (Clock)*

Cadential Extension
Elaborating or repeating a cadence, a cadence figure, or individual cadence chords is an effective way in which to extend a phrase.

Mendelssohn: *Songs Without Words* op. 85 no. 6

Phrase Mutation

Phrase mutation modifies a phrase by a change of mode from major to parallel minor or vice versa.

Smetana: *The Moldau* from the symphonic cycle *My Country*

Melodic Organization 111

Other Melodic Organization

Repetition
Repetition refers to the immediate reiteration of a melodic figure or group in the same voice.

Sequence
Sequence is the immediate restatement of a melodic figure in the same instrumental or vocal part at a higher or lower pitch so that the structure of the figure is maintained. Each separate unit of the sequence is called a *section* or *leg*. It is one of the most common and basic methods of melodic elaboration found in the eighteenth and nineteenth centuries. Some characteristics of sequences follow:

1. In order to be classed as a sequence at least two legs must be present.
2. Musical dictates will determine the number of legs in a sequence, but tedium usually prevents more than three or four in any one set.
3. The legs of a sequence usually proceed in a continuous downward or continuous upward movement. Seldom do the legs move upward (or downward) and then change directions.
4. The intervallic distances between the legs of a sequence are usually consistent throughout a particular sequence. For instance, if the second leg is one diatonic step above the first, the third will also be a diatonic step above the second.
5. Almost any intervallic distance may be found between the legs of a sequence, but as stated in no. 4 above, once that interval is determined in any specific instance between the first and the second leg, the others usually proceed by the same interval.

Exact Sequence
In an *exact sequence*, the transposition of every tone is by exactly the same intervallic distance:

Beethoven: *Symphony no. 9 in D Minor*

Diatonic Sequence
In a *diatonic sequence*, the transposition accommodates the diatonic scale, so that occasionally a half step is sequenced as a whole step and vice versa:

Sibelius: *Symphony no. 5 in E-flat Major* op. 82

By Jan Sibelius. Copyright 1915 by Wilhelm Hansen Musik-Forlag. Copyright renewed. Used by permission.

Tchaikovsky: *Symphony no. 5 in E Minor*

Sequence Leg 1   Sequence Leg 2

Modified Sequence
In a *modified sequence,* a sequenced melodic group is elaborated or embellished in a way that does not destroy its original character:

C.P.E. Bach: *Sonata for Violin and Piano*

Modulating Sequence
A *modulating sequence* leads from one tonal center to another. Sometimes each leg of the sequence is in a different key:

Beethoven: *Piano Sonata* op. 13 (third movement)

Leg 1 – Cm   Leg 2 – E♭M   Leg 3 – GM?

False Sequence
A *false sequence* repeats part of the figure and states the remainder in sequence or vice versa:

Beethoven: *Trio in B-flat Major* op. 11

Rep.   Sequence   Rep.   Sequence

Schubert: *Symphony no. 5 in B-flat Major*

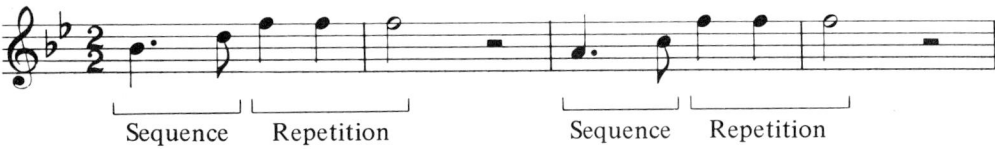

Sequence   Repetition   Sequence   Repetition

Melodic Organization   113

ASSIGNMENT 2 Example 1:

1. Have a class member play the excerpt provided from the *Sonata* K 331.
2. Then, answer the following questions. For the purpose of these questions, be concerned only with the melody (highest sounding tones):
   a. A period made up of parallel phrases occurs at _____.
   (measure numbers)
   b. A sequence occurs at _____.
   (measure numbers)
   c. Including the repeat marks, a repeated period occurs at _____.
   (measure numbers)
   d. A phrase extension occurs at _____.
   (measure numbers)
   e. The phrase (see d. above) is extended in _____.
   (part of the phrase)
   f. A phrase that is contrasting to all other phrases occurs at _____.
   (measure numbers)

Mozart: *Sonata for Piano* K. 331

114   Melodic Organization

ASSIGNMENT 2   (continued)

Example 2:

1. An excerpt from Schubert's *Impromptu* op. 142 follows.
2. The following chart analyzes the structure of the first sixteen measures.
3. On a separate piece of paper, chart the remainder of the composition.
4. For the purpose of this chart, be concerned only with the melody (highest sounding tones).

MEASURES	PHRASE NUMBER	PHRASE RELATIONSHIP	PERIOD NUMBER	PERIOD RELATIONSHIP
1–4	1	PHRASE 1	1	PERIOD 1
5–8	2	CONTRASTING TO PHRASE 1		
9–12	3	PHRASE 1 MODIFIED	2	PERIOD 1 MODIFIED
13–16	4	PHRASE 2 MODIFIED		

Schubert: *Impromptu* op. 142 no. 4

ASSIGNMENT 2 (continued)

ASSIGNMENT 3

1. Write a four-measure melody in A major and include a diatonic sequence of two legs.

2. Write a four-measure melody in B harmonic minor and include a diatonic sequence of three legs.

3. Write a four-measure melody in B-flat major and include a false sequence of two legs.

4. Write a four-measure melody starting in E harmonic minor and include an exact sequence of two legs.

5. Write a four-measure melody in E-flat major and include a modified diatonic sequence of two legs.

ASSIGNMENT 4

1. Write a four-measure phrase of music in G harmonic minor. Then, rewrite it with an extension at the beginning.

2. Write a four-measure phrase of music in A-flat major. Then, rewrite it with an extension in the interior of the phrase.

3. Write a four-measure phrase of music in F major. Then, rewrite it with an extension at the end of the phrase.

ASSIGNMENT 4 (continued)

6. Write a four-measure phrase of music in F-sharp harmonic minor and follow it with the same phrase in mutation.

118 Melodic Organization

6 Instruments and Voices

Voice Ranges
Instrumental Ranges

Nontransposing
Instruments

Transposing Instruments
Tessitura

VOICE RANGES

In vocal and choral writing, four general voice ranges are given. In the following illustration, whole notes indicate the best usable ranges. Black notes represent pitch ranges that should be used sparingly.

INSTRUMENTAL RANGES

A knowledge of instrumental ranges, transpositions, tone colors or timbres, and general characteristics is important for every musician. The study of timbre is fascinating. The results of various combinations of instruments is often unpredictable, and it is difficult to obtain objective information that will be constant under all conditions.

In the charts on the following pages, the instruments are of two types.

Nontransposing Instruments

Nontransposing instruments produce a pitch that is the same as the written pitch. In the chart, the nontransposing instruments are those whose actual sound is "as written."

Transposing Instruments

Transposing instruments produce a pitch other than the written pitch. In the following chart, the actual transposition is given for instruments of this type. Most transposing instruments developed from traditions of the past, and to convert these instruments to nontransposing instruments would be extremely difficult at this time.

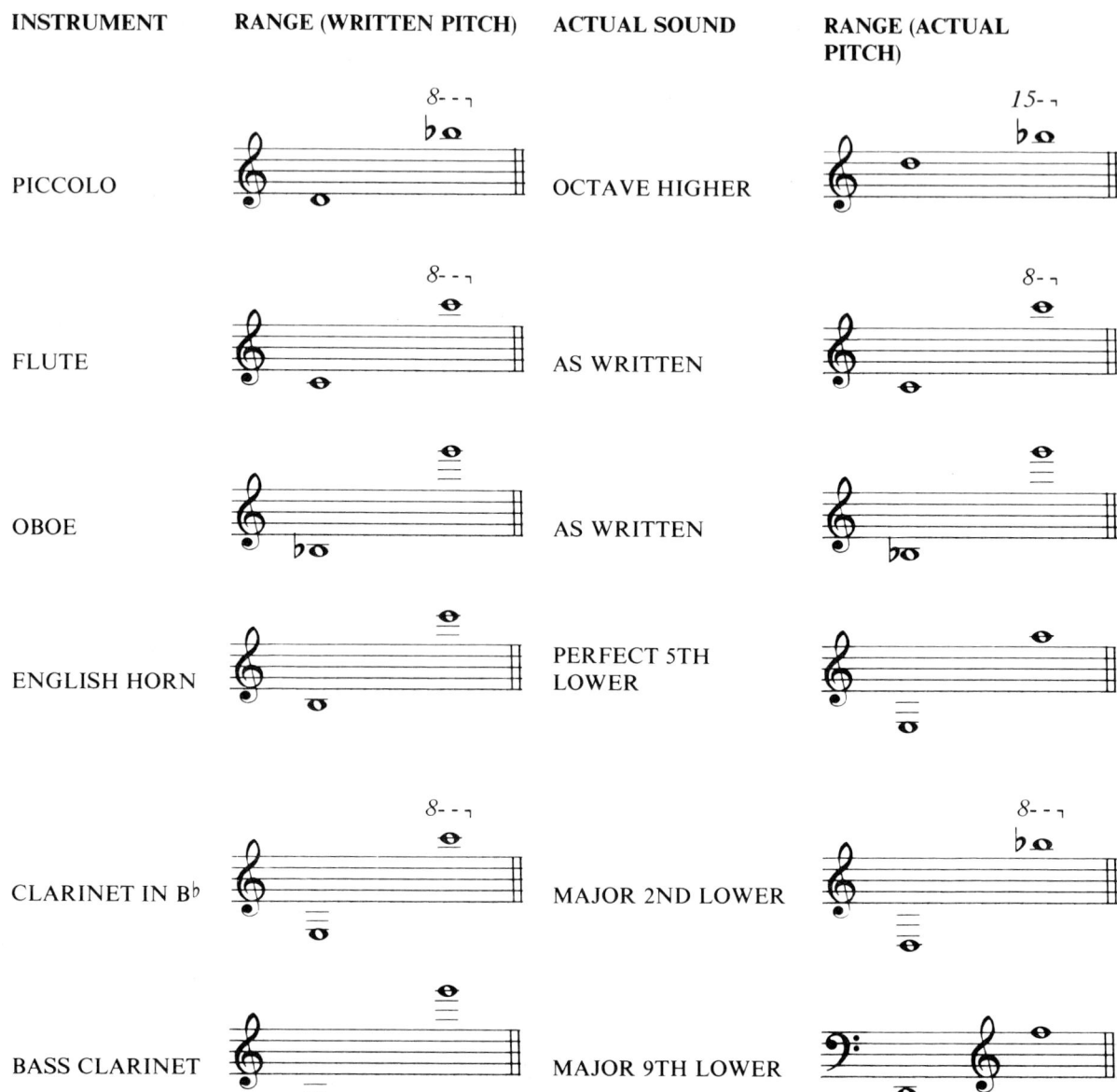

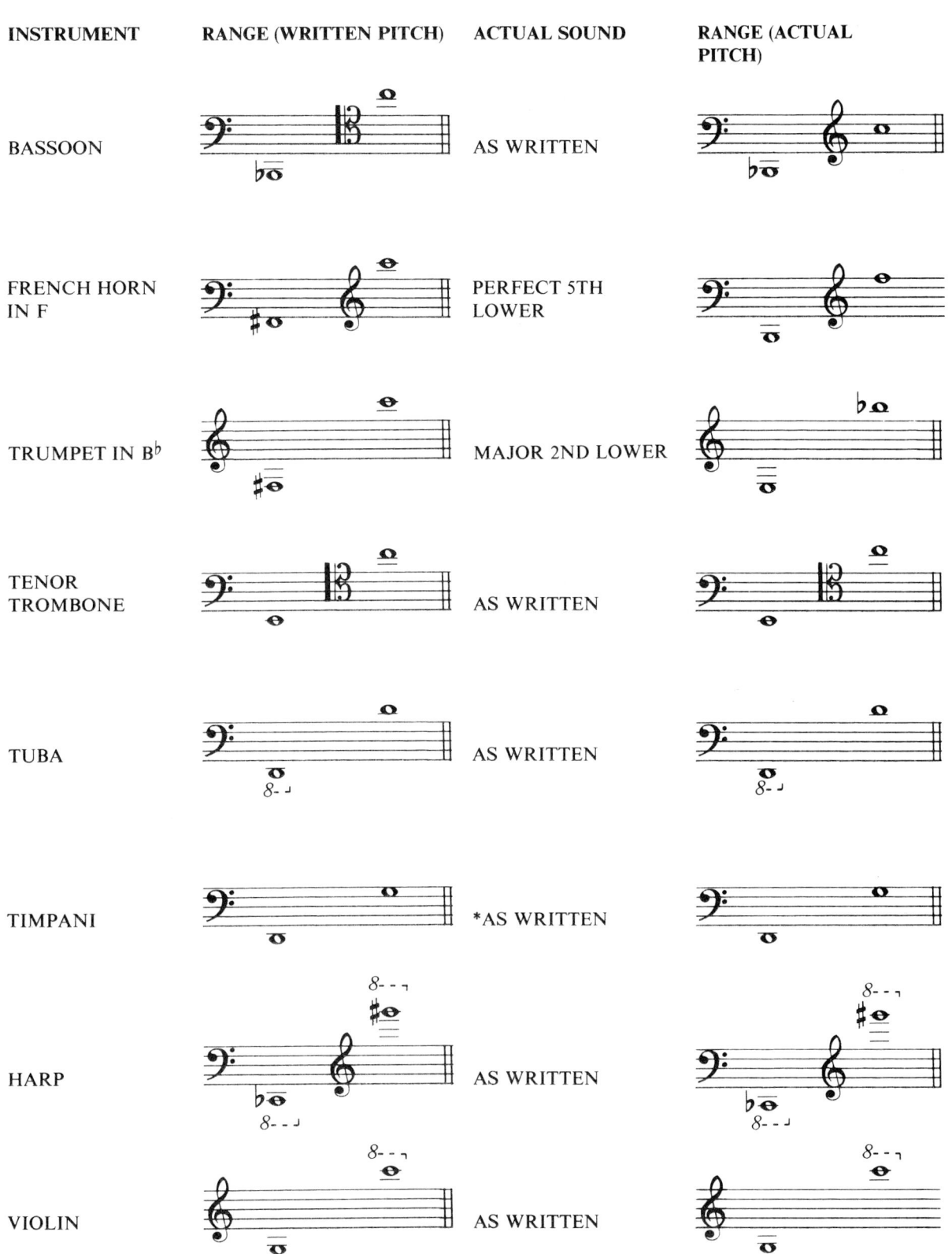

*Very early scores included the timpani as transposing instruments with directions for the actual tuning.

Instruments and Voices

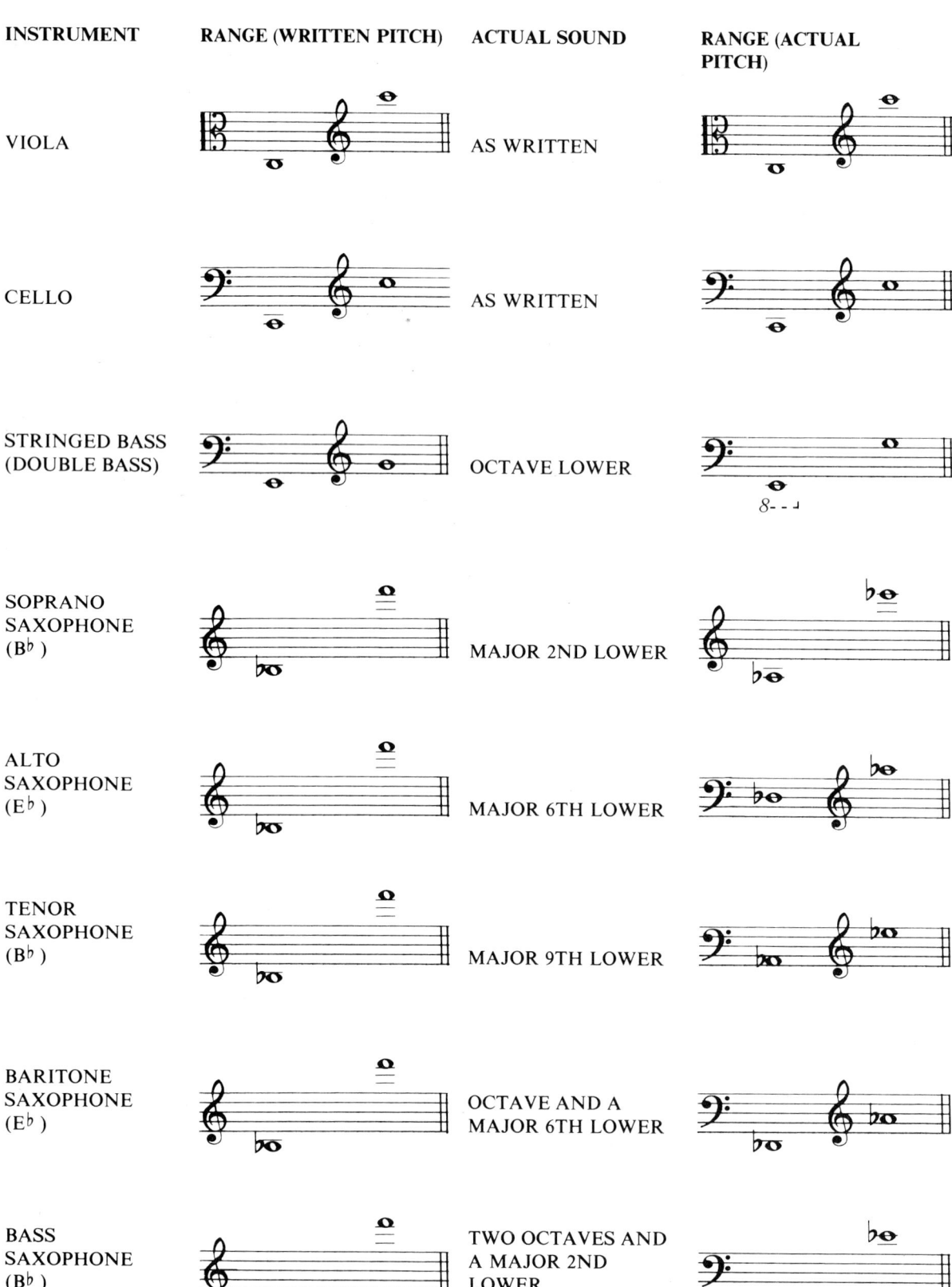

TESSITURA

Tessitura is the general pitch compass of a particular instrument or voice in a composition or a section of a composition:

Trumpet in B Flat: High Tessitura

Trumpet in B Flat: Low Tessitura

The ranges listed for most of the instruments are extensive and provide both the lowest and highest possible tones. Scoring consistently at the extremes of the range for any instrument is not wise, since facility and mobility are often restricted at the low and high ends. For most instrumental writing, it is advisable to remain in the middle tessitura, thus avoiding forced tones and allowing the performer to use the instrument to best advantage.

The following excerpt would prove difficult except for the more accomplished performer:

Oboe: Fast passage in the low range

ASSIGNMENT 1

The beginning of each staff contains a measure of music that represents actual pitch.

1. Rewrite this measure for the instruments indicated so that each will play the same pitches as given.
2. It may be necessary on occasion to change the clef sign to one most often used by a particular instrument.
3. The example illustrates the correct procedure.

Instruments and Voices 123

ASSIGNMENT 1 (continued)

ASSIGNMENT 2

At the beginning of each staff is a key signature representing a composition at actual pitch.

1. Write the key signature for each instrument so it will be in the same key (actual pitch) as that given.
2. It may be necessary on occasion to change the clef sign to the one most often used by a particular instrument.
3. The example illustrates the correct procedure.

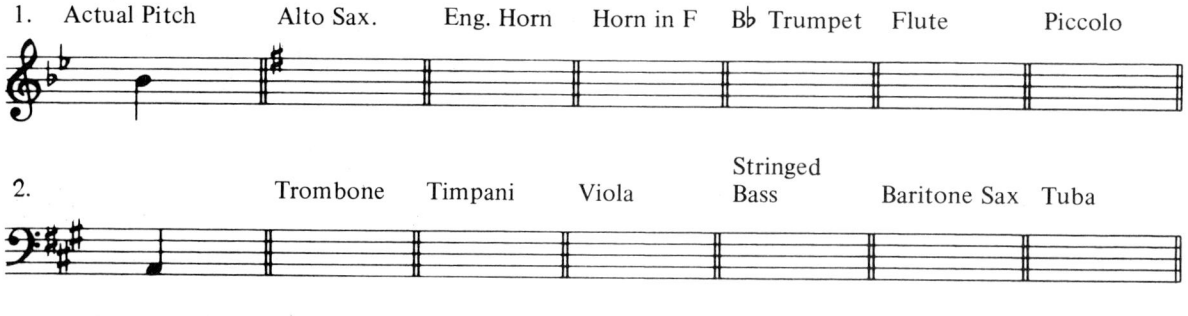

124 Instruments and Voices

ASSIGNMENT 3 Following is an excerpt from a string quartet by Mozart.

1. On a separate sheet of score paper, arrange the eight measures for one or more of the following groups of instruments:

   a. 2 alto saxophones   b. 1 flute   c. 1 B-flat trumpet
      1 tenor saxophone   2 clarinets   2 french horns in F
      1 baritone saxophone   1 bassoon   1 tuba

2. If none of the above combinations is available in your class, write for four instruments that are available.
3. Write a separate staff for each instrument.
4. Perform the arrangement in class.

Mozart: *String Quartet* K.464 (*Menuetto*)

Instruments and Voices   125

7 Voice Leading in Four-Part Chorale Writing— Model Analysis

Chorale
Parallel Fifths
Parallel Octaves

Parallel Unisons
Uneven Fifths
Common Tones

Doubling
Spacing

Modulation
Voice-Leading Procedures

CHORALE BY JOHANNES CRÜGER

The analysis of the chorale by Johannes Crüger, *Herr, ich habe missgehandelt* (Lord, I Have Transgressed), is included in this chapter for several reasons:

1. It provides an in-depth study of the principles of voice leading observed in a single four-part chorale.
2. Four-part writing demonstrates in an embryonic and uncomplicated fashion the principles upon which composers of functional harmony have based the application of their style. It is important, of course, to study music written in a variety of media (orchestral, choral, ensemble, solo, etc.), but the basic principles that govern chord progression and voice leading in all media are inherent in four-part writing, and these can be viewed simply and without the confusion resulting from the study of large scale works, which may involve transposing instruments, thick textures, and multi-voiced doublings that are difficult to assess quickly.
3. Since an exhaustive study of many chorales is not within the scope of this text, a thorough analysis of this single chorale will help to identify many of the basic idioms of the Baroque style. During this period, musical patterns of previous centuries were consolidated to form a style of writing based on the principle of chord progression.
4. The careful analysis of music can never provide an exact formula for the composition of music or fully explain the charismatic qualities of a particular composer, but the approximation afforded by this approach offers more insights than any other approach yet discovered.

A *chorale* is a hymn of the Lutheran church. These melodies were derived from (1) adaptations of Latin hymns already in use in the Catholic church, (2) adaptations of pre-Reformation popular hymns in German, (3) adaptations of popular songs (secular, not sacred) of the time, and (4) some original hymns composed by Lutheran church musicians.

The chorale was meant to be sung by the entire congregation in order to provide increased participation and involvement in the church service. Since music printing (or any kind of printing for that matter) was expensive, few churches could afford to provide hymnals. Thus, before singing, the melody (with harmonization) was repeated several times by the church organist to familiarize the congregation with the tune. The melody remained standard, but the harmonization was generally the product of the local church musician. The Protestant chorale became a favorite basis for compositions by the composers of the times since their audiences knew many of the melodies from singing them in the service.

Johannes Crüger (1598–1662) was one of the earlier Baroque composers. He was both a music theorist and composer. Many of his settings of chorales have remained in use to the present day.

The chorale, *Herr, ich habe missgehandelt* (Oh Lord, I Have Transgressed) was one of those in common use at the time, and was also harmonized twice by Bach. This is Crüger's harmonization of the chorale tune:

Crüger: *Herr, ich habe missgehandelt*
(Lord, I Have Transgressed)

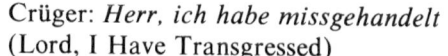

128 Voice Leading in Four-Part Chorale Writing—Model Analysis

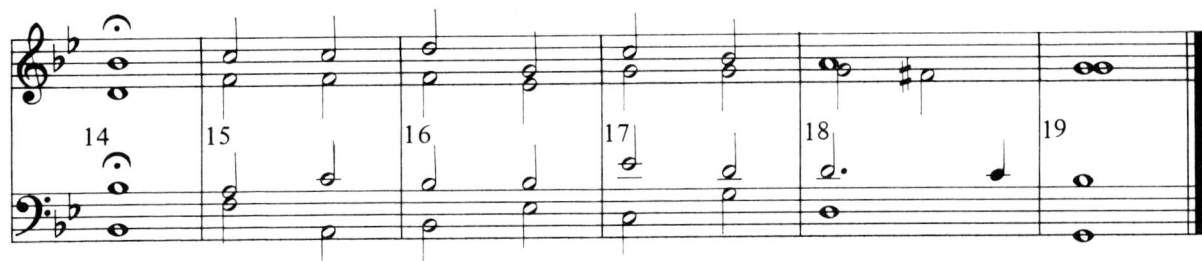

I	V	V⁶	I	IV	ii	i	V ⁴—³	i
					G Minor: iv			

ANALYSIS OF THE CHORALE

Because no individual composition is a complete summation of period style, knowledge gained from the analysis of this chorale should be compared with studies of many similar works and corrected to insure accuracy in relation to the entire period.

Pitch Inventory

MEASURE	PITCH
MEASURES 1–10 and 17–19	A B♭ C D E♭ F♯ G
MEASURES 11–16	A B♭ C D E♭ F G

Scale

MEASURE	SCALE
MEASURES 1–10 and 17–19	G A B♭ C D E♭ F♯ G
MEASURES 11–16	B♭ C D E♭ F G A B♭

Key

MEASURE	KEY
MEASURES 1–10 and 17–19	G HARMONIC MINOR
MEASURES 11–16	B-FLAT MAJOR

Justification of B-flat major lies in the change from F-sharp (measures 9) to F-natural (measures 11), the strong root relationships of F and B-flat, and the forceful cadence on B-flat in measures 13 and 14.

Melody
Tones

TYPE	NUMBER
STRUCTURAL TONES	19
SECONDARY TONES	2
EMBELLISHING TONES	8

Although an analysis of the melody alone reveals a distribution of structural, secondary, and embellishing tones, chorale melodies are traditionally harmonized so that a chord change most often occurs with each succeeding melody note. Thus, in the harmonization, the intrinsic strength of structural tones is diminished while the normally weak embellishing tones are given added emphasis.

Step Progressions

The first two phrases contain ascending step progressions, the second two phrases incorporate descending step progressions, and the step progression in phrase 4 is a sequence of that in phrase 3. This arrangement forms a symmetry that provides the entire composition with a directional logic that is simply organized but very effective.

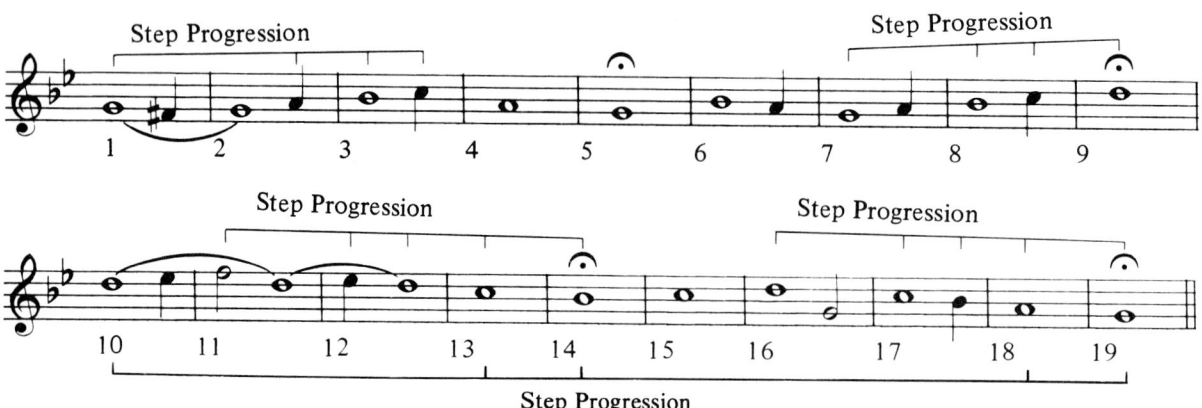

Form of the Melody

PHRASE	MEASURES	PHRASE RELATIONSHIPS
1	1–5	
2	6–9	CONTRASTING WITH PHRASE 1
3	10–14	CONTRASTING WITH PHRASE 2
4	15–19	CONTRASTING WITH PHRASE 3

This composition is based on a chorale melody that is normally treated with one syllable per melody note.

The length of phrases in chorales is dictated by the words of the text, which accounts for the five-measure phrases.

The contrasting nature of all phrases confirms the general nature of chorale melody construction. Parallel and repeated phrase relationships are in the minority. The *fermatas* (pauses) that signal the end of each phrase clearly define each line of the text.

Harmony

Harmonic Vocabulary

CHORD	NUMBER OF OCCURRENCES
i or I	15
V	11
iv or IV	4
vii°6	1
iii	1
ii	1

The composition strays very little from the tonic and dominant. The primary triads (tonic, dominant, and subdominant) account for eighty-four percent of the harmony in this work, which signifies a very strong key feeling.

Harmonic Progression	CHORD PROGRESSION	NUMBER OF OCCURRENCES	RELATIONSHIPS
	DESCENDING P5 OR ASCENDING P4	10	V–i, i–iv
	ASCENDING P5 OR DESCENDING P4	9	i–V, iv–i
	ASCENDING 2ND	4	iv–V
	DESCENDING 3RD	2	i–VI, IV–ii
	DESCENDING 2ND	2	I–vii°6, ii–I

Seventy percent of the root movement is by P5 either up or down. In addition, the tonic-dominant polarity is very prominent—a trademark of this period of composition.

Harmonic Cadence	PHRASE	MEASURES	CADENCE CHORDS	CADENCE TYPES
	1	4–5	V–I (Gm)	PERFECT AUTHENTIC
	2	8–9	iv6–V (Gm)	HALF
	3	13–14	V–I (B♭M)	PERFECT AUTHENTIC
	4	18–19	V–I (Gm)	PERFECT AUTHENTIC

The strongest possible cadences are in the majority here and provide the composition with considerable tonal stability.

Harmonic Rhythm — Except for two cadence measures in each phrase, there is an almost steady stream of chord changes. All chord changes occur on either beat 1 or 3. The harmonic rhythm is virtually metric since the periodicity of harmonic change is so regular. This type of steady and regular harmonic change is very common to the chorale and hymn. An examination of many chorales and hymns corroborate the steady rate of chord change.

Rhythm — Because of the steady and measured harmonic movement, there is little variation derived from the rhythm in this composition. Again, such regularity of harmonic rhythm is common in most chorale and hymn harmonizations.

Texture — There is a very simple four-part harmony throughout with no interruptions.

VOICE LEADING

1. *No two voices move in parallel perfect fifths (P5s), parallel perfect eighths (P8s), or parallel perfect unisons (PUs).* Uneven fifths (P5 to d5, d5 to P5) are used occasionally. Perfect fifth (P5) to diminished fifth (d5) does not appear in this composition, but one instance of diminished fifth (d5) to perfect fifth (P5) occurs in measure 12. Also not found are perfect fifths (P5s), perfect octaves (P8s), or perfect unisons (PUs) by contrary motion.

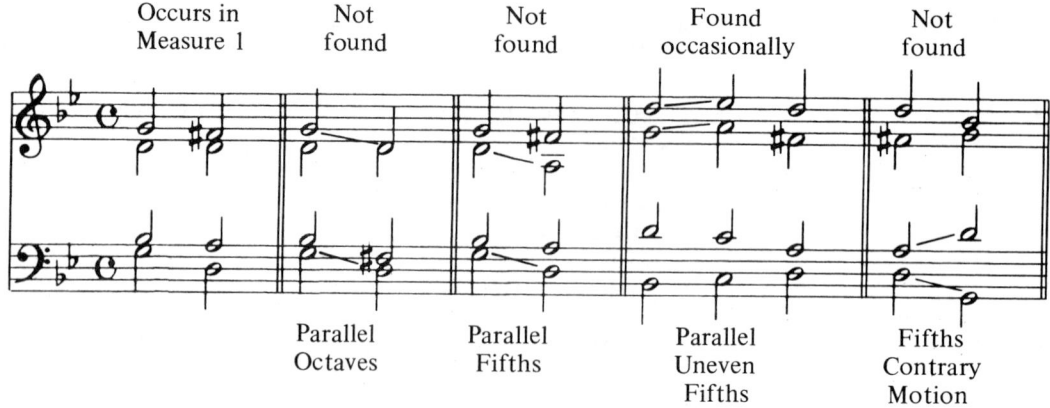

2. *In leading from one triad to the next, the voices generally move in the most nearly conjunct (stepwise) manner possible.*
   Only one example in this composition shows all four voices moving by disjunct (leaps) motion.

3. *If common tones exist between two adjacent triads, they are usually maintained in the same voice.*
   a. *Triads whose roots are a fourth or a fifth apart have one tone in common.* The following are the most frequently found ways of connecting such chords. These examples are arranged to make comparisons easier. The first and third types are found in the Crüger chorale. The second is used less often.

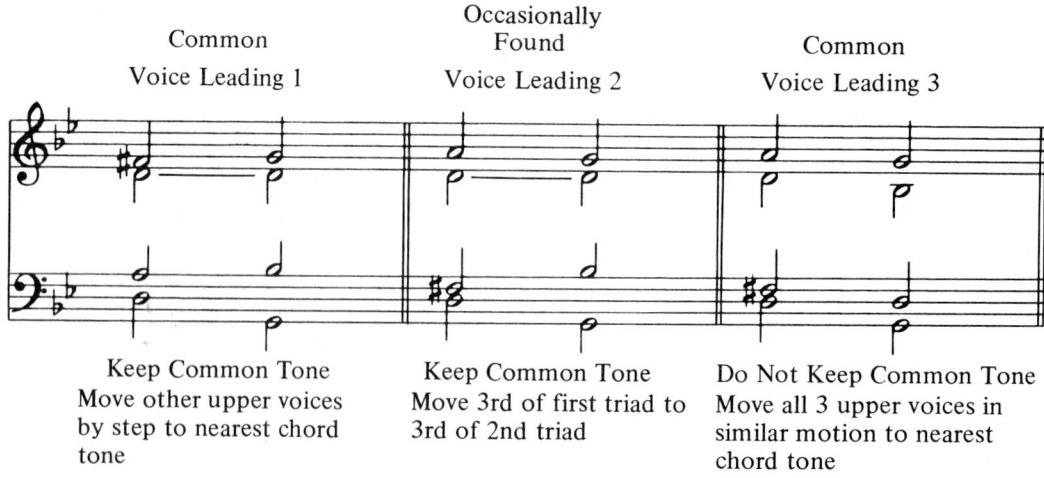

132   Voice Leading in Four-Part Chorale Writing—Model Analysis

b. *Triads whose roots lie a third or a sixth apart have two common tones.* When possible these are maintained in the same voice. Occasionally, when melody tones of a chorale are given, it is not possible to keep the two tones in the same voice.

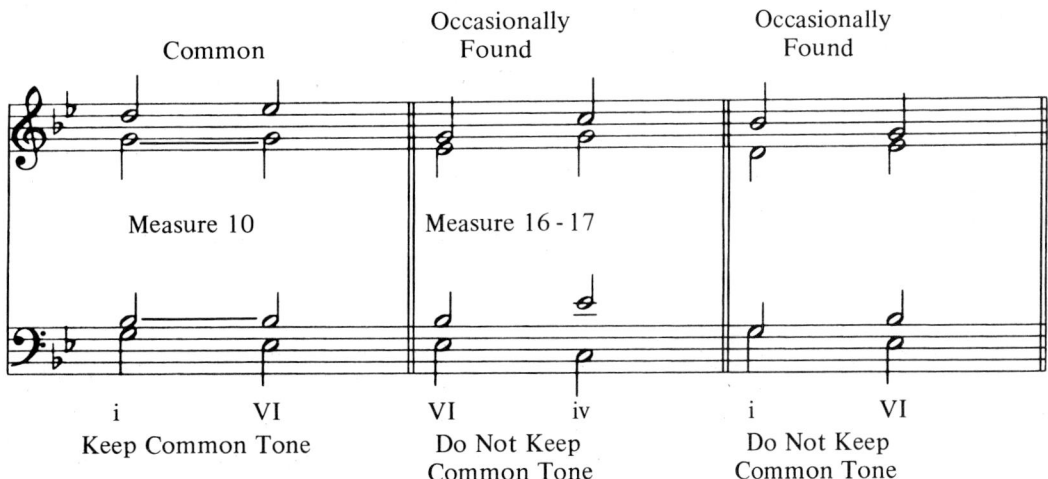

c. *Triads whose roots lie a second apart have no tones in common.* The voices utilize as much contrary motion as possible. The progression IV to V is a frequent example, and when both chords are in root position the upper voices move contrary to the bass.

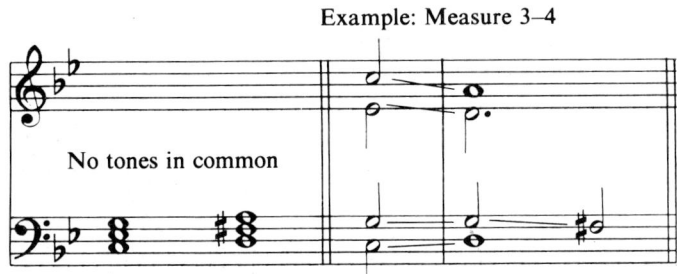

4. *In the leading of the individual voices, augmented and diminished intervals are not found.* Such intervals were considered difficult for the average singer. The augmented second (A2) and augmented fourth (A4) lie within the diatonic systems and are awkward intervals to sing.

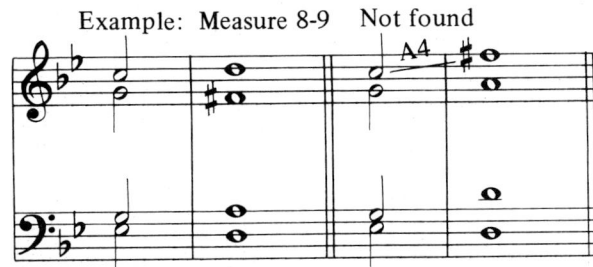

Voice Leading in Four-Part Chorale Writing—Model Analysis

Doubling Since this composition contains four voices and a triad contains but three, it is always necessary to *double* (duplicate) one of the tones in the vertical sonority. Conclusions from this composition indicate:

Triads In
Root Position

DOUBLED TONE	NUMBER
ROOT	22
THIRD	1
FIFTH	0

The root is doubled almost exclusively.

Triads In
First Inversion

DOUBLED TONE	NUMBER
BASS NOTE	4
SOPRANO	3
INNER VOICE	1

Bass or soprano tones are doubled almost exclusively. In the chorales harmonized by Bach, the soprano voice is more consistently doubled than the bass. The soprano note is usually the root, or fifth, of the chord.

Triads In
Second Inversion

There are no second inversions in this composition. In the chorales harmonized by Bach, however, the bass note (fifth of the chord) is almost exclusively doubled.

Diminished Triad

The bass tone (third of the triad) is doubled. In this composition, as well as in the music of other composers, the *leading tone is never doubled*.

Spacing Some chords are in *open position* (the gap between tenor and soprano is greater than an octave). Others are in *close position* (the gap between tenor and soprano is less than an octave). At the octave itself the position is neutral.

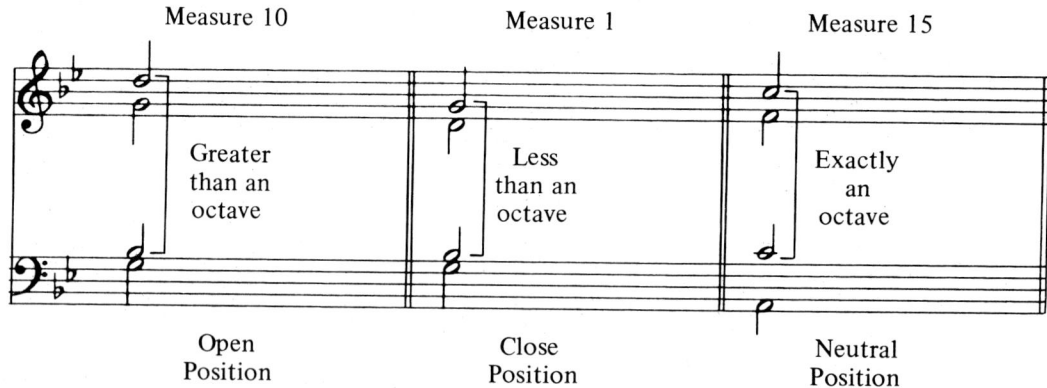

The space between the bass and tenor may be less or greater than an octave. The Crüger chorale contains four examples where the gap is larger than an octave. Open position and close position are not affected by the interval between bass and tenor.

Example:
Measure 15

There are no instances where the gap between any two adjacent voices (except bass and tenor) is larger than an octave.

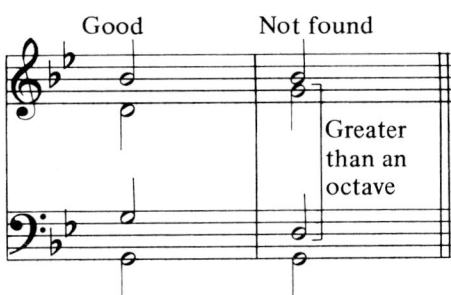

Modulation

Measures 11 through 16 contain a *modulation* (change of key on which the tonal center shifts, in this case, from G minor to B-flat major). Modulation will be discussed thoroughly in a later chapter, so this aspect will be observed here but not dealt with at length.

Most important, at the moment, is the recognition that as a new key is introduced the analysis immediately drops the functions of the previous key and takes on the functions in the new key to reflect the change of tonal center.

Example: Measures 10–11   Example: Measures 16–17

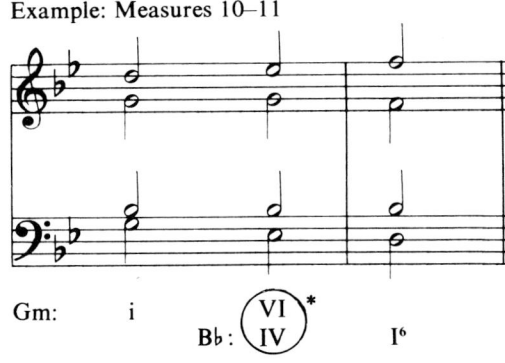 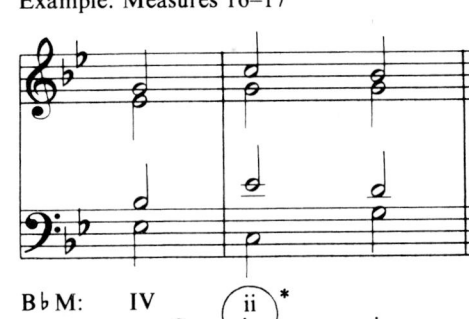

*These chords, which are common to both keys in the modulation, are called *pivot chords*.

SUMMARY

The following list is a summary of part-writing procedures based on practices followed by eighteenth-century composers of chorale harmonizations.

Fixed Practices

There are no exceptions to these practices:

1. *Avoid parallel perfect octaves (P8s), perfect fifths (P5s), or perfect unisons (PUs or P1s). Such successive intervals, which remain on the same pitch, are not considered parallel.*
2. *Never double the leading tone of the scale.*
3. *Keep the four voices within their ranges.*
4. *Avoid the augmented second (A2) and the augmented fourth (A4) in the melodic line of any of the four voices.*

Preferred Practices These practices should be carefully observed unless a particular situation permits no other alternative:

5. First choice: *Double the root in root position major and minor triads.*
   Second choice: Double the first, fourth, or fifth degree of the scale (if first choice is impossible).

6. First choice: *Double the soprano note in first inversion major and minor triads.*
   Second choice: Double the bass note. In a series of first inversions, double the soprano and the bass alternately.

7. *In second inversion, the triads double the bass note (fifth factor).*

8. First choice: *Double the bass note (third factor) in the first inversion of diminished triads.* The root positions of diminished triads are seldom used.
   Second choice: Double the fifth factor (fourth degree of the scale). For the ii°6 in minor, double the root or the third.

9. *All factors of triads should be present.* The exception is the final chord of a phrase or section—it may contain a tripled root and a single third.

10. *Avoid large melodic leaps—a sixth or more.* The exceptions are octave leaps in the bass voice or rearrangements of the same chord.

11. *Do not overlap the voices from one chord to the next.* Overlapping occurs between adjacent chords when one voice leaps above (or below) the pitch of an adjacent voice. This is best explained by the following illustration:

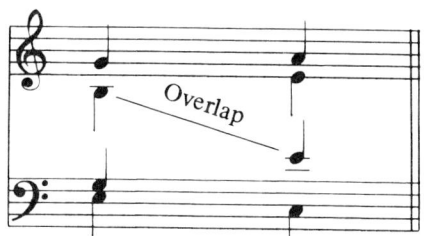

Tenor G leaps up to E, which is higher than the alto B in the previous chord.

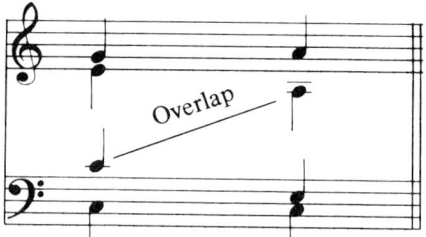

Alto E leaps down to A, which is lower than the previous tenor note C.

*Half-step overlap used on occasion

Bass D leaps to G which is above the previous tenor F-sharp

*Overlaps of a half or whole step are occasionally found and may be used with discretion.

12. *In the outer voices, do not leap in the same direction to perfect intervals (P8s, P5s, P1s).*

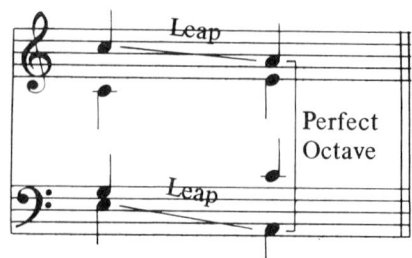

136 Voice Leading in Four-Part Chorale Writing—Model Analysis

13. *Maintain regular order of voices.* The bass is lowest, next is the tenor, then the alto, and the highest is the soprano.
14. *Maintain an octave or less (harmonic interval) between the soprano and the alto and between the alto and the tenor.* More than an octave frequently occurs between the tenor and the bass.
15. Although augmented seconds (A2s) and augmented fourths (A4s) are always avoided, leaps downward of a diminished fifth (d5) and a diminished fourth (d4) occur occasionally.

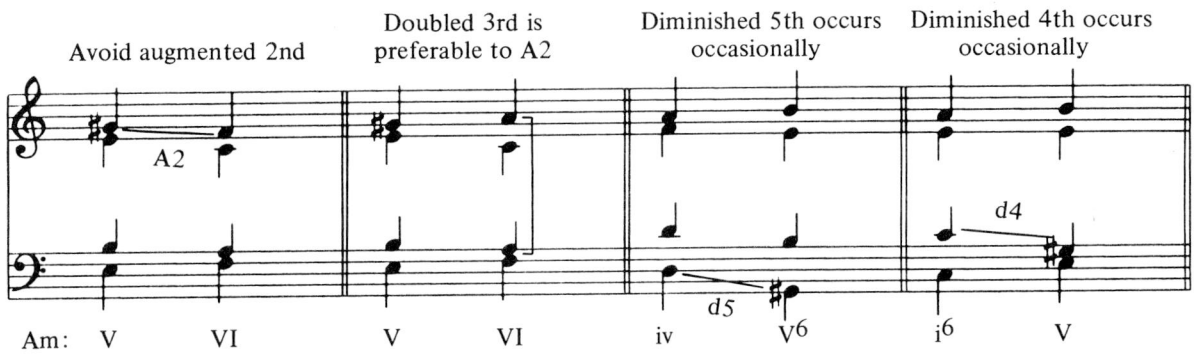

ASSIGNMENT 1

1. Following are four-part chorale phrases with the tenor and the alto omitted in most instances.
2. Add the tenor and the alto where they are missing using the part-writing procedures discussed in this chapter.
3. In the first four chorale phrases, all triads are in root position. Review pages 131 through 135 for part-writing procedures and item 5 of the summary starting on page 135 before beginning.

ASSIGNMENT 1 (continued)

ASSIGNMENT 2

1. The six chorale phrases contain first inversion triads and second inversion triads.
2. Add the tenor and the alto where they are missing.
3. In connecting triads in first and second inversion, no categorized part-writing procedures can be applied because of the great number of possibilities.
4. Follow the "Summary of Part-writing Procedures" listed on **pages 135 through 137, especially items 5 through 8.**
5. The numbers above the chorales refer to the item numbers in the "Summary of Part-writing Procedures." If you have difficulty, reread the summary items—they will help.

ASSIGNMENT 2   (continued)

2.
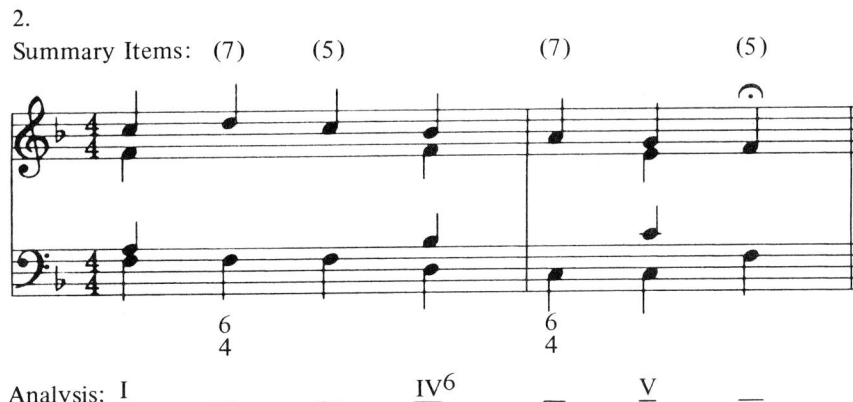

3.
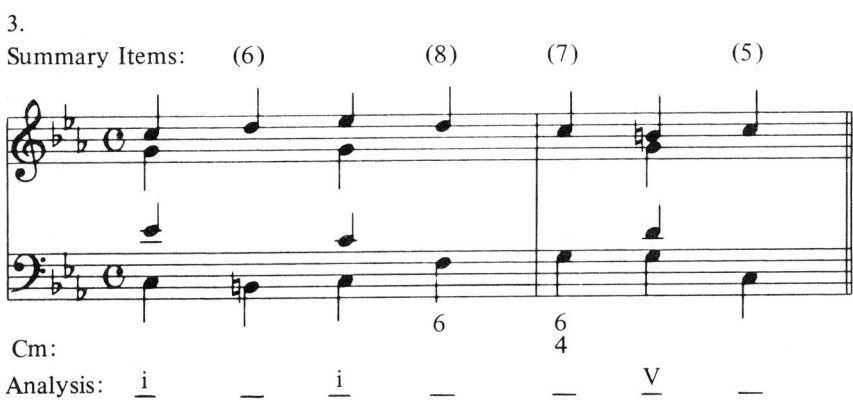

4.
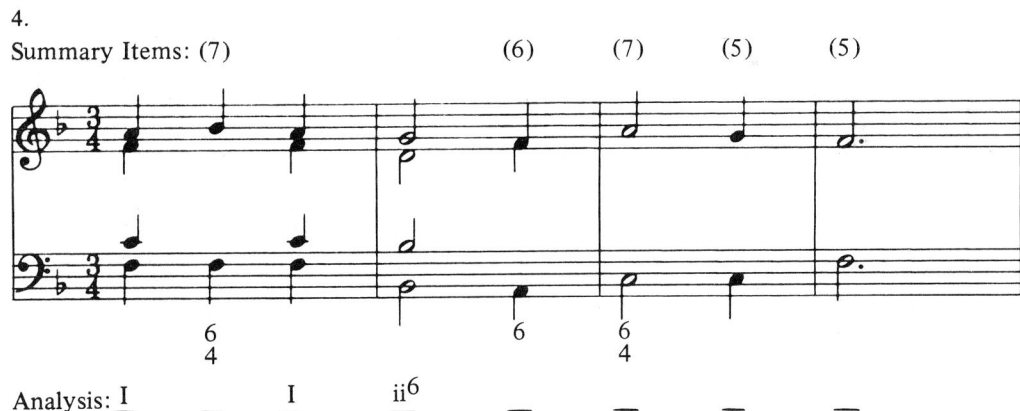

ASSIGNMENT 2 (continued)

140 Voice Leading in Four-Part Chorale Writing—Model Analysis

8 Harmonic Progression

Root Relationships *Ascending Fifth* *Ascending Third* *⁶₄ Chords*
Chord Progressions *Ascending Second* *Descending Second* *Chord Selection*
Descending Fifth *Descending Third*

Up to this point, attention has been focused on the vertical aspects as well as the connecting voice-leading of harmony. Now, the study will concentrate on chord progressions—the way in which chords are selected to succeed each other in a section of music.

THE RELATIONSHIP OF CHORDS

From the Baroque through the Classical and Romantic periods, composers employed the relationship of chords as a principal organizing force. The movement of one chord to another provides an additional impetus to music and contributes a stimulus not found in melody or rhythm alone. Throughout the entire gamut of music involving functional harmony, the shape of a composition is to a large extent determined or at least influenced by the design and fashioning of the chord progressions.

In tonal music, the tonic chord (I) is the most stable of all. Chords that move away from the tonic tend to create tension, while those that progress toward the tonic give fulfillment and relax the tension caused by the departure.

Thus, complete compositions invariably end with the tonic triad and more often than not begin with that same chord. Tonal music employing functional harmony is simply a movement away from the tonic (tension) or toward the tonic (stability)—rather like musical respiration.

Root Relationships

Two forces govern the relationship of chords in succession. Together, they help to provide tonal organization for phrases, periods, sections, and other musical units. These two forces are:

1. *The relationship of each chord root to the tonic of the scale.*

The diatonic tones of a scale upon which triads are constructed all relate to the tonic, but a hierarchy exists that emphasizes some tones as more important than others. Those chords whose roots lie in strong intervallic relationship to the tonic naturally have greater affinity for it while other tones with less stable status have a weaker association.

Tones of the diatonic scale and their relationship to the tonic irrespective of other implications:*

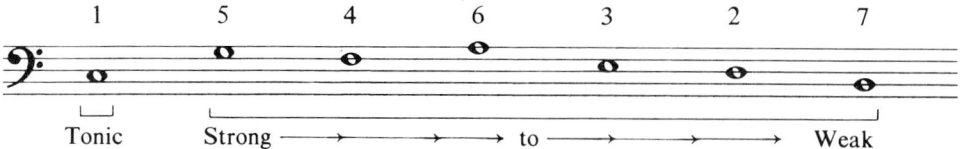

2. *The intervals formed by the roots of adjacent chords.*

Along with the relationship of each chord root to the tonic is the affinity of one chord root for the next. All chord progressions eventually seek the tonic as a final goal, but the chord-by-chord advance depends upon the relationship of each to the succeeding one. The interval that separates the roots has much to do with the attraction of a chord for the one that follows it. We find, for instance, that the dominant triad (V) progresses most naturally to the tonic (I) because the roots lie in a relationship of a descending perfect fifth (P5). The supertonic triad (ii) progresses to the dominant triad (V) most often since the roots again lie in a relationship of a descending perfect fifth (P5).

The stronger to weaker progressions are shown here:

Progression types (based on the interval between adjacent chord roots):

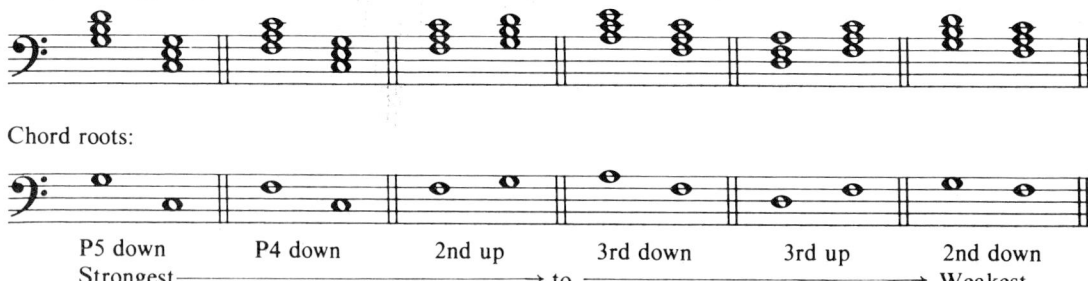

Since these two interacting forces are heard by the listener as a single effort, the effect is a single cohesive design that operates throughout most extant music containing functional harmony.

CHORD PROGRESSIONS

In planning the movement of chord progressions, the whole musical unit—a phrase, a period, and so forth—must be taken into consideration. The chord-to-chord progression is of course important, but the goal of any phrase must be unity, and the fluctuation between tonic and nontonic chords must be carefully calculated. Each single progression must be examined in its relation to the entire phrase or musical unit. For instance, if a particular phrase is to begin and end with a tonic chord, the chords leading from the opening tonic toward the closing tonic must be fashioned in such a manner that appropriate motion is exerted to produce the desired unity. Maximum motion to the tonic may be obtained by one series of chords but if less attraction to the tonic is desired, another series of chords may be selected.

Progression Patterns

Throughout the period of functional harmony, certain conventional patterns of progression occur. Sometimes these patterns concern a single progression only, but more often than not the pattern extends to two or more progressions, and patterns including four or five progressions are not uncommon.

*Hindemith, *Craft of Musical Composition*, p. 53.

Circle Progression: Undoubtedly the most common and the strongest of all harmonic progressions
Descending Perfect is the circle progression—chord roots in a descending perfect fifth (P5) pattern.
Fifth
    This progression has the capability, more than any other, to determine a tonality, to give direction and thrust, and to provide order in a section or phrase of music. It is indeed the basis of all harmonic progression.

    Some phrases consist almost entirely of circle progressions:

    Note that ascending P4s may be used in place of descending P5s and descending P4s may be used in place of ascending P5s.

ASSIGNMENT 1

1. Below are short phrases of melody.
2. The first two chords of each phrase are given.
3. Harmonize the remaining melody notes exclusively with descending P5 progressions. End with the tonic triad.
4. Placing all triads in root position (the root is the bass note), sketch in the bass voice as prescribed by the brackets.
5. Then, part-write the alto and tenor voices using procedures found in number 3.a. on page 132 (connecting chords whose roots lie a descending P5 apart).
6. After completion each harmonization should be sung by the entire class.

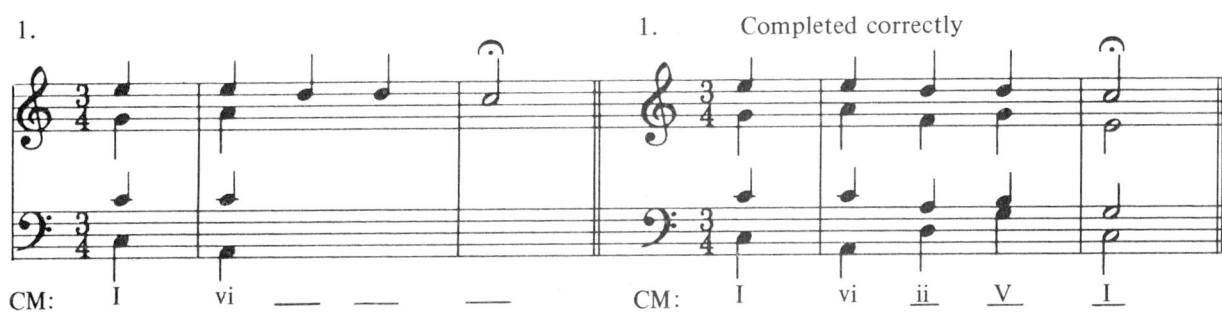

Harmonic Progression   143

ASSIGNMENT 1 (continued)

Ascending Perfect Fifth

Compared to the pattern of descending P5s, the ascending P5s tend to create a feeling of tension and instability as the progression moves away from the tonic. The most frequent application is the progression from the tonic to the dominant harmony.

Since the root of the P5 is its lowest note, the progression of root relationships up and away from the root of the interval (as in the ascending P5 progression) may be regarded as a digression from strength.

While the progression of tonic to dominant is the most popular, the ascending P5 may occur between chord roots on any scale degrees. The half cadence (I to V), which appears often, is an example of this type of movement.

ASSIGNMENT 2

1. Following are short phrases of melody.
2. The first and occasionally other chords are written out.
3. Above the melody notes are brackets that indicate which pattern of progression (descending P5s or ascending P5s) to use in harmonizing.
4. Placing all triads in root position (the root is the bass note), sketch in the bass voice as prescribed by the brackets.
5. Then, part-write the alto and tenor voices using procedures found in number 3.a. on page 132 (connecting chords whose roots lie a descending P5 apart).

ASSIGNMENT 2 (continued)

6. After completion, each harmonization should be sung by the entire class. Try singing a few exercises backwards (from last chord to first). If they sound just as good backwards as forwards, drop the course.

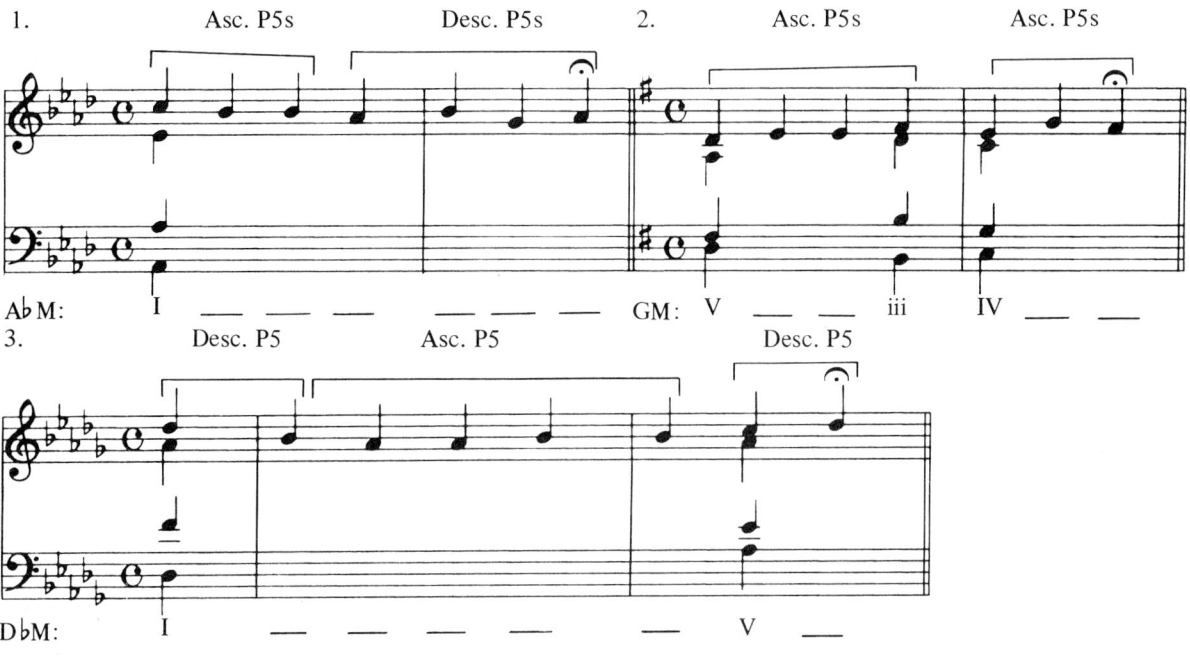

Ascending Second (M2 or m2)

Adjacent chords whose roots lie in the relationship of an ascending second (major or minor) perform a most important function even though they are not as abundant as those related by a descending P5.

Ascending seconds are not found in succession as often as descending P5s, but do provide a very important function—that of allowing a shift from one descending P5 pattern to another. This illustration shows the ascending-second progression placed between two single descending P5 progressions. Tonic-sub-dominant-dominant-tonic is one of the most prevailing progressions in all of music.

Ascending 2nd progression between descending P5 progressions:

Harmonic Progression 145

In the following excerpt from music literature, the ascending-second progressions occur between descending P5 patterns and permit the harmonic flow of the phrase to switch from one series to another.

Ascending 2nds between descending P5 patterns (nonharmonic tones circled):

Bach: *Lobt Gott, ihr Christen, allzugleich*
(Praise God, Ye Christians, All Together)

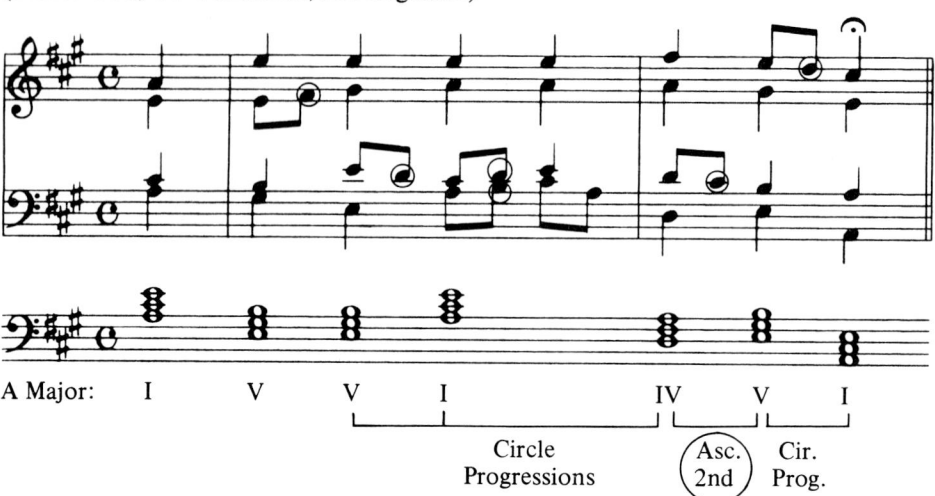

The deceptive cadence (V to vi or VI) is another application of the ascending-second progression:

Bach: *O Gott, du frommer Gott*
(O God, Thou Gentle God)

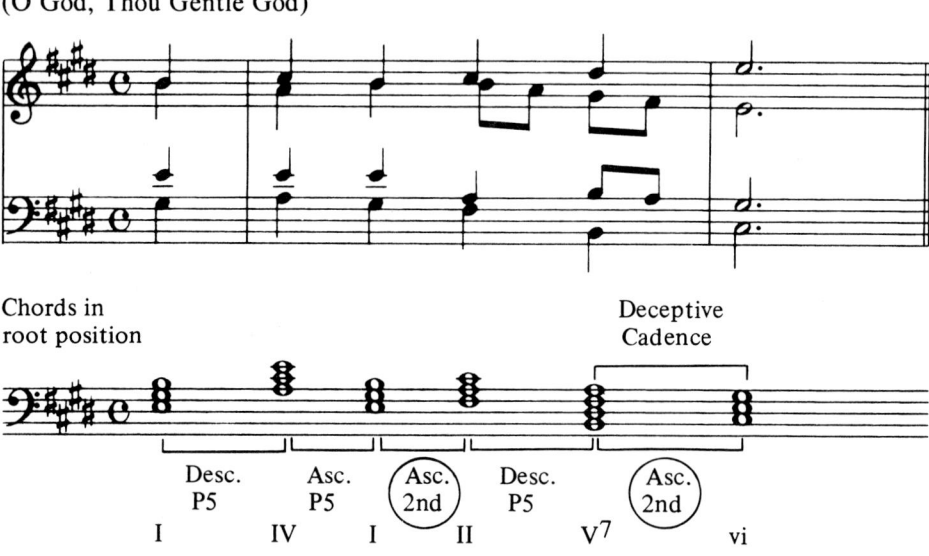

In this phrase, Tchaikovsky uses the ascending-second pattern as a means to repeat part of the descending P5 pattern. The descending P5 pattern (chord roots A D) is reiterated and expanded (chord roots E A D) at the cadence of the phrase.

146 Harmonic Progression

Ascending 2nd used between repetitions of descending P5 patterns:

Tchaikovsky: *Symphony no. 5 op. 64*

The ascending second (root relationship) is employed in other capacities, one of which involves the leading tone (vii°) triad or seventh chord. Leading tone harmony is most often considered dominant harmony since the triad contains the third, fifth, and seventh factors of the dominant seventh chord. For this reason the vii° triad usually progresses to the tonic in an ascending-second relationship although it is heard by many as a descending P5 progression similar to that of V to I.

Ascending 2nd in the vii° to I progression:

Beethoven: *Piano Sonata* op. 49 no. 1

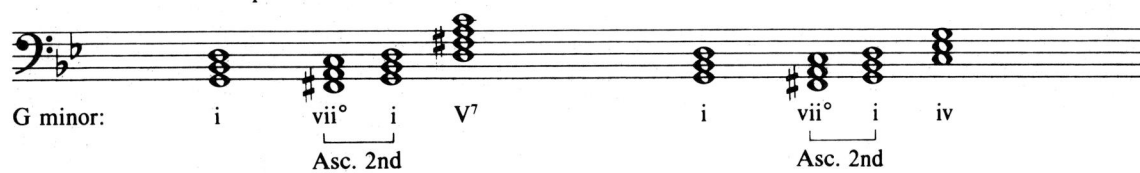

*7th chords: The added factor does not affect their function or the root movement described above.

Harmonic Progression 147

ASSIGNMENT 3

1. Below are short phrases of melody.
2. The first and occasionally other chords are written out.
3. Above the melody notes are brackets that indicate which pattern of progression (descending P5s, ascending P5s, or ascending seconds) to use in harmonizing.
4. Placing all triads in root position (the root is the bass note), sketch in the bass voice as prescribed by the brackets.
5. Then, part-write the alto and tenor voices using procedures found in numbers 3.a. and 3.c. on pages 132-33 (connecting chords whose roots lie a descending P5 apart and an ascending second apart).
6. After completion, each harmonization should be sung by the entire class.

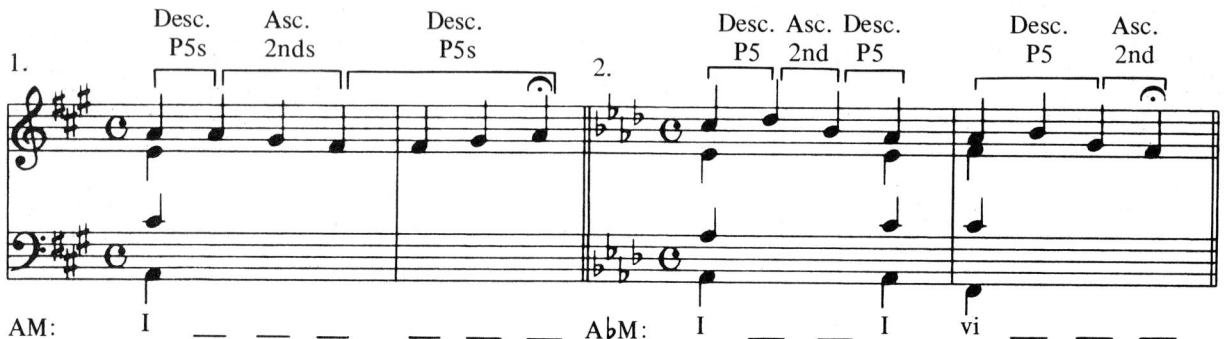

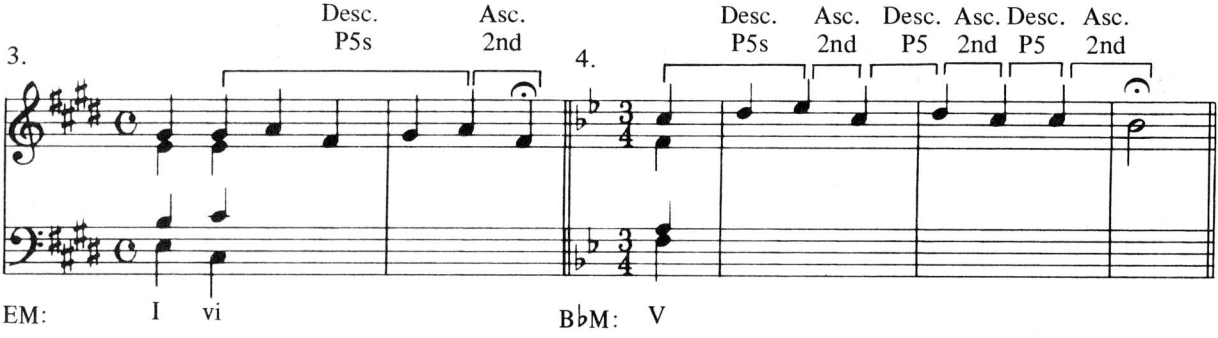

| Descending Third (M3 or m3) | Chord roots that lie in a relationship of descending thirds appear systematically throughout the period of functional harmony. Their prevalence is notably less than that of the descending P5, which dominates the period, but they serve a definite function in that they provide contrast. Furthermore, they act as a shift to convert from one descending P5 series to another as is the case with the ascending second described above.

Medtner's *Novelette*, which is excerpted here, illustrates the use of the descending third to switch from one descending P5 series to another.

Descending 3rd between two descending P5 patterns:

Medtner: *Novelette* op. 17 no. 1

Although the descending-third pattern does not occur as often in succession as does the descending P5, examples are available from almost every style period from the Baroque through the Romantic periods. In this grouping of three successive such progressions, nearly an octave is spanned.

Descending 3rds in series:

Bach: *Der Tag der ist so Freudenreich*
(This Glorious Day is Filled with Joy)

Descending 3rds in series

Harmonic Progression

ASSIGNMENT 4 Using the same directions as in assignment 3, complete the following.

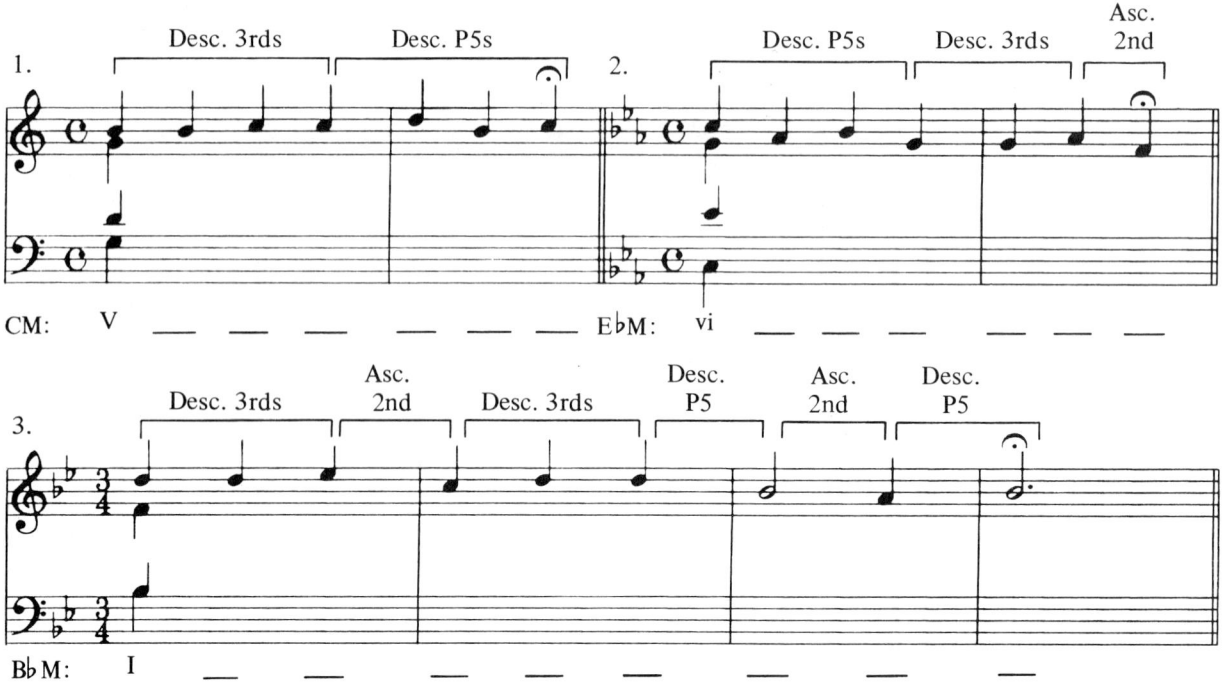

| Ascending Third (M3 or m3) | Since the lowest tone of the third is its root, chord roots in descending fashion lead *toward* the root of the interval. However, when the chord roots ascend by thirds, the motion is *away* from the root of the interval. Thus, ascending thirds, like the ascending P5 progression, are backward or retrogressive. |

Chord roots in ascending thirds are less often found than any of the previously described patterns of progression. Tonality is weakened by ascending-third progressions; consequently, when it is the intent of the composer to diminish the effect of tonality (as in the Impressionistic period) such progressions are more prevalent.

During the period of functional harmony, the ascending third is sometimes used in the same manner as the descending third—to convert from one descending P5 pattern to another.

The pattern tonic-mediant-subdominant (I iii IV), containing the ascending third from tonic, occurs especially when a softer, less urgent effect is desired.

The first phrase of the old Welsh tune *All Through the Night* is shown here harmonized in two ways. First, the melody is harmonized with a majority of descending P5s and second, with ascending thirds and descending seconds. The second harmonization is often found in preference to the first.

Descending Second (M2 or m2)

As with the ascending P5 and ascending third, the descending second is retrogressive because its highest tone is the root, and the progression is away from that strength.

Only a very small percentage of progressions are of the descending-second pattern. This pattern occasionally functions as a shifting point between descending P5 patterns.

In this excerpt from a Bach *Chorale,* the descending second occurs between phrases.

*7th chords do not affect the root movement described.

Harmonic Progression

Descending 2nd between two descending P5 progressions:

Bach: *Weltlich Ehr und Zeitlich Gut*
(Earth's Frail Pomp and Vanities)

Chords reduced to root position:

Descending 2nd between
two descending P5 progressions

$^6_4$ CHORDS

The second inversion of any triad should be used with extreme caution because of its unstable nature. The chord contains the interval of a fourth (considered a dissonance to be resolved) above the bass and cannot be used in the functional way that typifies both root position and first inversion triads. The $^6_4$ position of the tonic is very common, but other triads are seldom found in second inversion. All $^6_4$ chords and in particular the tonic $^6_4$ should be employed in one of the following ways **only:**

Cadential—the tonic $^6_4$ chord "resolves" to the V chord at the cadence. It is often preceded by the ii, ii⁶, IV, IV⁶, vi, I, or I⁶ (in either major or minor keys). The fifth (bass tone) is doubled.

Passing bass—the lowest tone (usually the bass) acts as a passing tone between a triad and its inversion or vice versa. The fifth (bass tone) is doubled. The passing bass is sometimes referred to as passing $^6_4$.

Arpeggiated bass—the lowest tone (usually bass) participates in an arpeggiation of the chord. Again, the lowest tone is doubled.

Neighboring tone (also called static or stationary bass)—the lowest tone (usually the bass) is preceded and followed by the same tone and is interspersed between two root positions of the same triad.

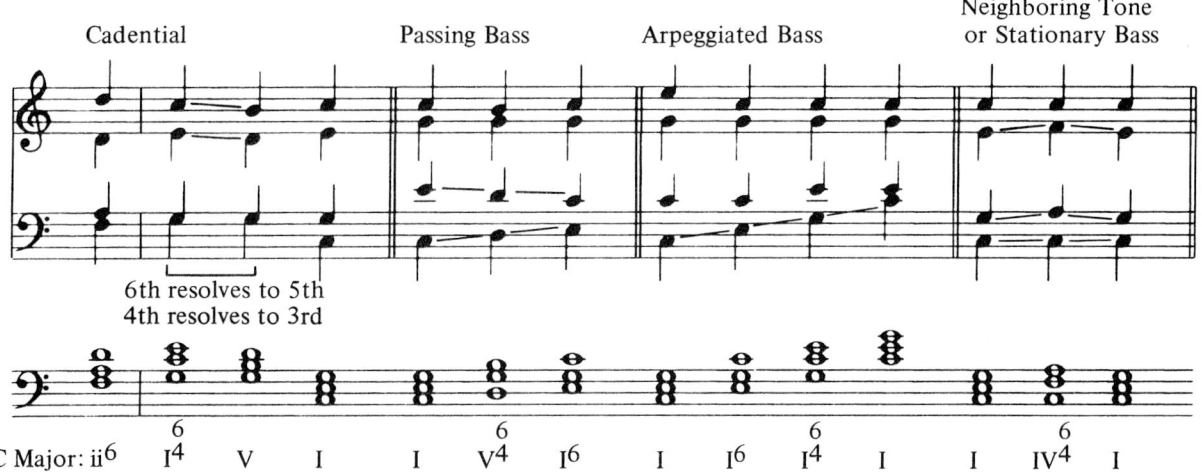

CHORD SELECTION

As mentioned earlier, each chord chosen to accompany a melodic phrase must be selected with regard for its position and role in the root movement of the entire phrase and not as an isolated progression unrelated to its surroundings. Such harmony must proceed consistently and logically from the beginning tone to the cadence.

A step-by-step procedure for harmonizing a melody is presented below. Thus, beginning with the melody itself, this logical plan yields a number of possible harmonizations, demonstrates each step in the approach, and contributes a methodical access to this most important technique.

1. Determine the harmonic rhythm—the number and placement of the triads. Play or sing the melody several times at the correct tempo and decide whether the chord changes should take place every beat, every two beats, once per measure, or irregularly throughout. Then, mark off the points at which chord changes should take place.

2. In a column under each change of harmony write the letter name (designating the root) or chord symbol for all possible triads that could be used to harmonize the melody tone. Each melody tone may be harmonized as the root, third, or fifth of a triad. When there are several melody tones within a single chord function, make sure you list only those triads that will accommodate all the melody tones.

3. Indicate obvious nonharmonic tones (passing tones, neighboring tones, etc.). These tones need not agree with the basic triads you select.

The following phrase, selected from a Schubert song, will help to illustrate these first three steps. At this point, the marked phrase should look like this:

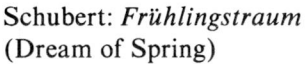

Schubert: *Frühlingstraum*
(Dream of Spring)

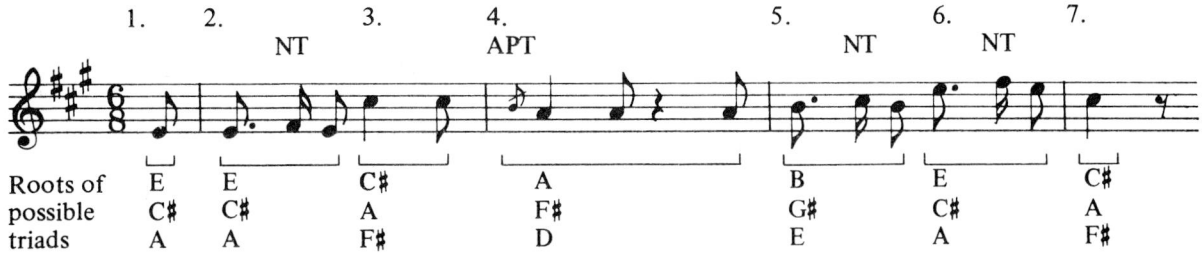

Harmonic Progression   153

4. Select the cadence chords. Using the three possible harmonizations for each melody tone, experiment with the two cadence chords. Remember that the last two chords of the phrase form the cadence and that the cadence should be one of the four types: authentic, half, plagal, or deceptive. After sufficient investigation, write in the cadence chords you have chosen.

5. Draw a line between all adjacent chords whose roots form a descending P5 progression (the strongest of all progressions). The phrase from the Schubert song yields the following analysis:

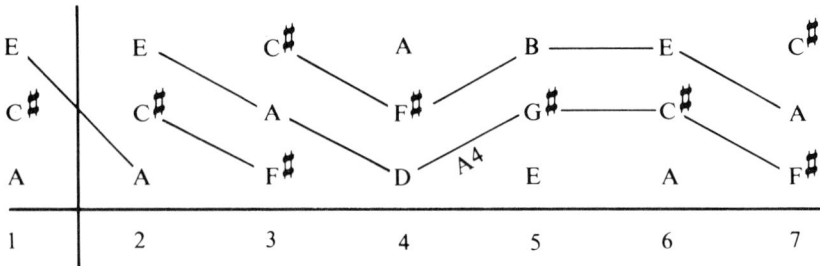

6. Chart three or four possible harmonizations using a majority of descending P5 progressions while separating the series with a descending third or an ascending second as described earlier in this chapter. Also, investigate the possibility of repeating the same triad in two adjacent harmonic areas. Bear in mind that the tonic, dominant, and subdominant are important in tonality and should not be neglected.

The following four possibilities are selected from the Schubert song:

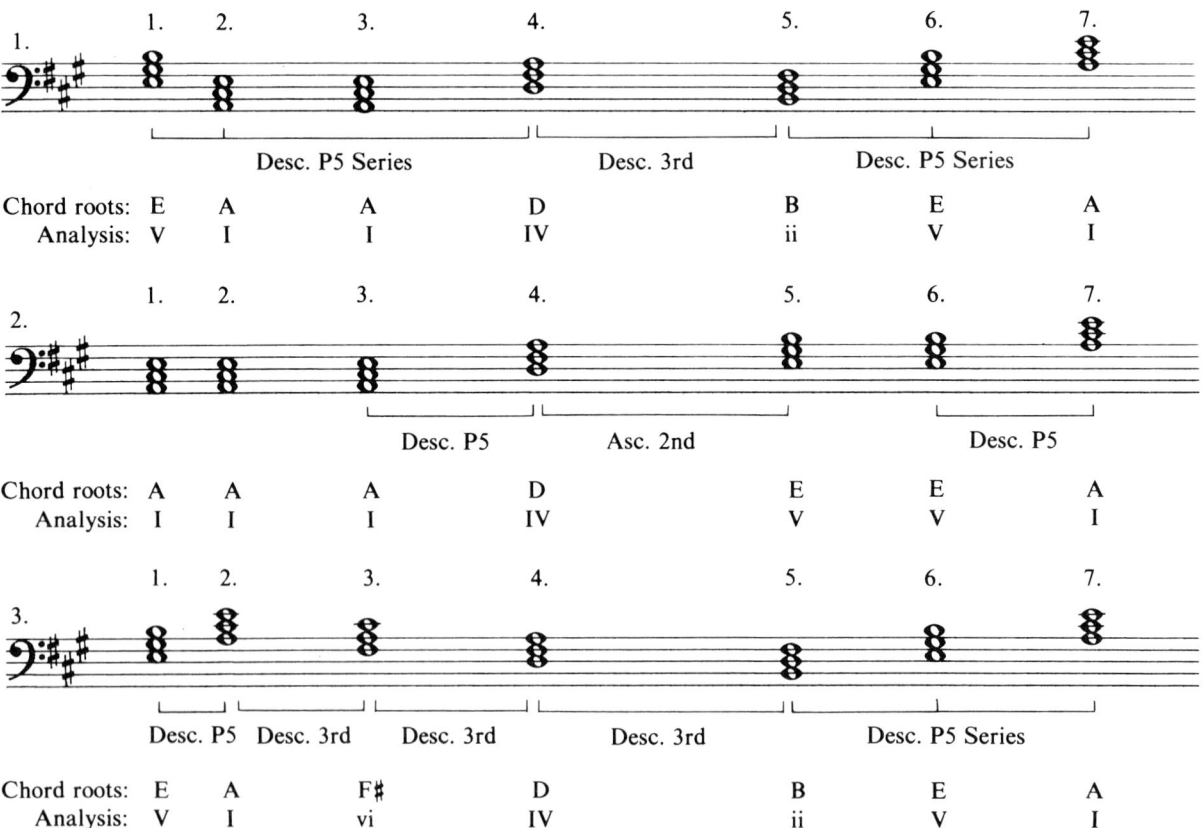

154   Harmonic Progression

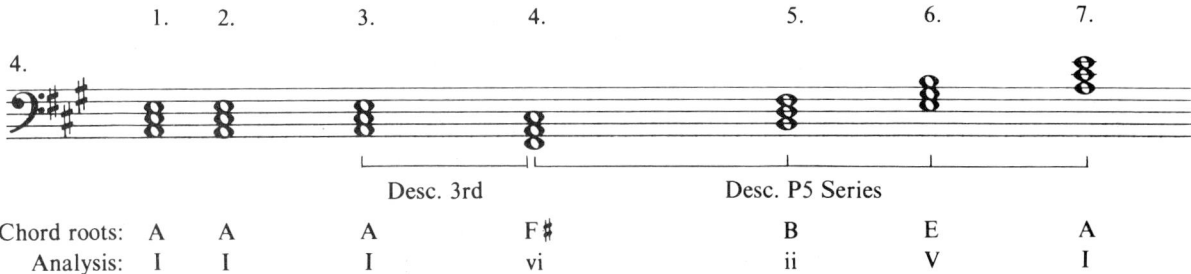

7. Sing or play the melody, and accompany it on the piano with each of your proposed harmonic solutions. If your pianistic accomplishments are somewhat limited, play each triad in its simplest (three-tone) root position with the left hand. Try to determine which supports and reinforces the melody best and at the same time substantiates the tonality and the tonic-nontonic distribution.

8. Select the most satisfying version and arrange it to fit the medium and style of the composition. As an illustration, the Schubert melody includes piano accompaniment, so the harmonization is arranged with a pianistic idiom in mind.

Although the four versions illustrated in no. 6 are acceptable and would support the melody well, *the fourth harmonization was composed by Schubert*. This particular harmonization is the only one of the four that contains a pattern of three successive descending P5 progressions.

The complete phrase as composed by Schubert is:

Schubert: *Frühlingstraum*
(Dream of Spring)

Harmonic Progression 155

The other harmonizations in no. 6 would render quite satisfactory results also. The first harmonization, for instance, is arranged for comparison in the same pianistic idiom as that of Schubert:

Schubert melody with first harmonization:

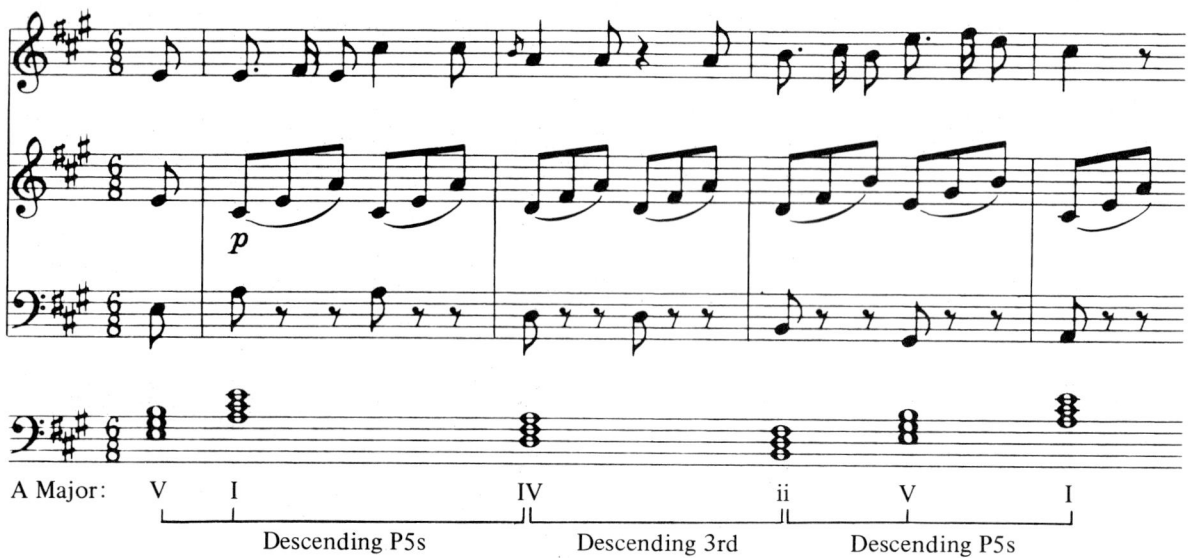

As a further demonstration of the procedure for harmonizing a melody, the first phrase of the chorale *Jesu, meine Freude* (Jesus, My Joy), harmonized by Bach in five different ways, is illustrated here. The five different harmonizations are listed below the melody. Note that the first, fourth, sixth, and seventh chords are the same in all versions. Descending P5 progressions are marked in heavy lines. For present purposes consider seventh chords (IV^7, etc.) as if they were triads. Seventh chords will be discussed later.

Five melody harmonizations by Bach:

Bach: *Jesu, meine Freude*
(Jesus, My Joy)

Version 1:

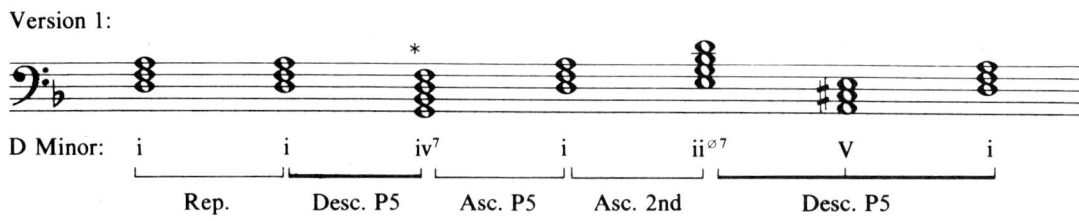

*7th chords do not affect the root movement described.

156   Harmonic Progression

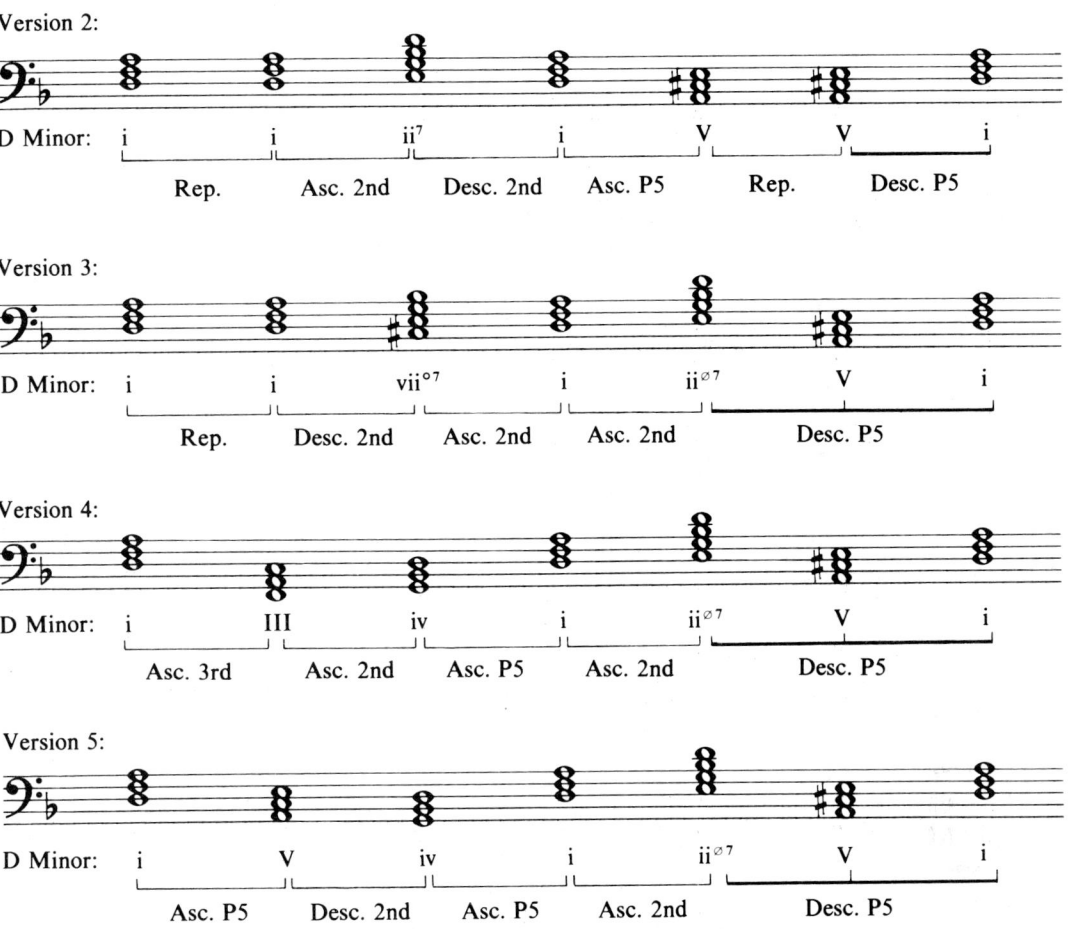

The following chart indicates the frequency of the various types of progressions and the prevalence of the primary triads (I, IV, and V) in the phrase from *Jesu, meine Freude*. Note the following:

a. In all five versions, the descending P5 progression is used more often than any other type of progression.
b. The tonic, dominant, or subdominant triads account for eighty percent of all harmony in the five versions.

TYPES OF PROGRESSIONS

VERSION	DESCENDING P5	ASCENDING P5	ASCENDING 2NDS	DESCENDING 3RDS	ASCENDING 3RDS	DESCENDING 2NDS	REPETITIONS	APPEARANCE OF TONIC, SUBDOMINANT, OR DOMINANT
1	50%	17%	17%	0%	0%	17%	17%	86%
2	17%	17%	17%	0%	0%	17%	33%	83%
3	33%	0%	33%	0%	0%	17%	17%	71%
4	33%	17%	33%	0%	17%	0%	0%	71%
5	33%	33%	17%	0%	0%	17%	0%	86%
TOTAL:	33%	17%	23%	0%	3%	14%	13%	80%

Harmonic Progression

Version 2 of the first phrase of *Jesu, meine Freude* is illustrated here to show the adaptation of basic harmony to four-part chorale writing:

Bach: *Jesu, meine Freude*
(Jesus, My Joy)

D Minor: i   i   ii⌀7   i   V   V   i

9. Alternate analysis of leading tone (vii°) harmony. In calculating the movement of roots, the vii° triad may be classified as dominant harmony. Conditions that substantiate this analysis are:

   a. The vii° triad contains two tones of the V triad:

   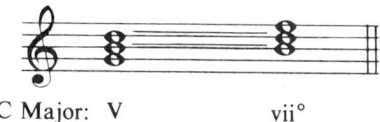

   C Major: V   vii°

   b. One of the most frequent types of dominant harmony is the V⁷ chord (contains an additional third above the fifth factor). The vii° triad is comprised of three of the four tones of that seventh chord:

   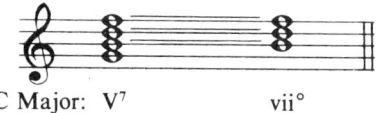

   C Major: V⁷   vii°

   c. The vii° triad (in major and harmonic minor) contains a tritone (d5) that resolves most naturally to two tones of the tonic triad:

   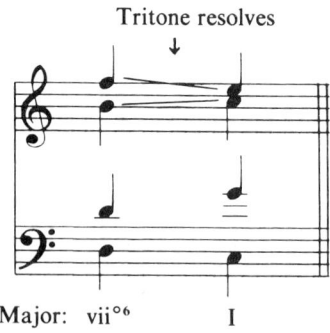

   C Major: vii°⁶   I

   d. In practice, composers treat the vii° triad as if it were dominant harmony. The following illustration is made up entirely of tonic and dominant harmony with the vii° triad functioning as a dominant.

Bach: *Vater unser in Himmelreich*
(Our Father in Heaven Above)

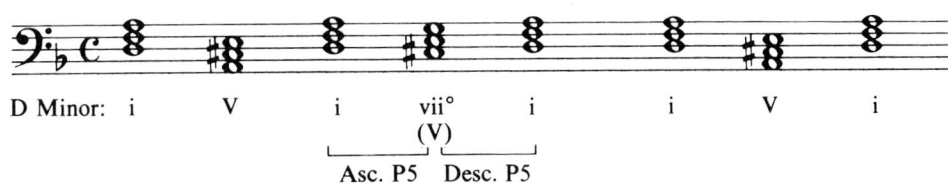

Thus, although the harmonic analysis of the vii° triad may remain vii°, the reckoning of the root movement for purposes of harmonic progression can reflect the strong dominant tendencies of the chord.

At the cadence of the following chorale phrase, Bach uses the vii° triad in an authentic cadence as a substitute for the dominant:

Bach: *Ach Gott und Herr*
(Alas! My God)

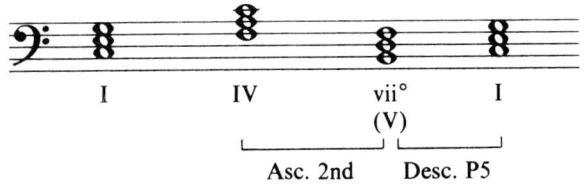

10. Analyze the cadential I$_4^6$ chord in harmonic progressions. The cadential I$_4^6$ chord for purposes of harmonic progression may be analyzed as a part of the V or V^7 that follows it. Hence, the I$_4^6$ may be omitted in considering chord roots when it appears immediately before the V or V^7 at the cadence.

Harmonic Progression

In the following excerpt from Beethoven's *Symphony no. 1*, the two successive descending P5 progressions are not interrupted by the second inversion tonic:

The sixth and fourth of the I$^6_4$ act as decorations to the fifth and third of the V chord and as a consequence the two chords may be treated as one when calculating root movement.

SUMMARY

The following chart shows each triad and the chord to which it progresses in each category. The chords are categorized as follows:

ⓘⓥ = most common   V = common   iii = less common

DESC. P5 TRIAD	PROGRESSION BY DESC. P5 TO:	PROGRESSION BY ASC. P5 TO:	PROGRESSION BY ASC. 2ND TO:	PROGRESSION BY DESC. 3RD TO:	PROGRESSION BY ASC. 3RD TO:	PROGRESSION BY DESC. 2ND TO:
I	Ⓘⓥ	V	ii	vi	iii	vii°
ii	Ⓥ	vi	iii	vii°	IV	I
iii	ⓥⓘ	vii°	IV	I	V	ii
IV	A4 ONLY TO: vii°	I	Ⓥ	ii	vi	iii
V	Ⓘ	ii	vi	iii	vii°	IV
vi	ⓘⓘ	iii	vii°	IV	I	V
vii°	iii	d5 ONLY TO: IV	Ⓘ	V	ii	vi

A few observations:

1. Progressions by descending P5s are most common for all triads except IV (no diatonic P5 exists) and vii° (a diminished triad closely related to V that tends to resolve to i as does the V triad).

2. Since the tonic triad appears often in literature, the chords leading from it occur frequently as well. Thus, although the I to IV chord is a favorite progression, I to any of three other chords is also prevalent.
3. Since the IV is deprived of a descending P5 resolution, it spreads the chords following it among the I, V, and ii.
4. The pull from dominant to tonic is so strong that it allows for little variety in progressions.

The harmonization of a melody as described in this chapter is a very subtle and sophisticated procedure. No little amount of creative insight is needed for successful results. Following the steps set forth here will assist considerably in the sorting and selection of suitable harmonizations, but will in no way insure that the results will be artistic accomplishments. Those will be forever within the domain of the individual seeking aesthetic realization.

ASSIGNMENT 5

1. Following are four folk tunes.
2. Harmonize each melody first with block chords (chords in simple position).
3. When you have arrived at a musically satisfying harmonization, then change the block chords to an accompaniment figure or pattern for the piano or harpsichord. Any of the patterns suggested can be used if you cannot think of an interesting one yourself. (Use only one pattern consistently throughout a single melody.)
4. Play at least one of each student's harmonizations in class and have the class members determine which they find most appropriate.

Suggested accompaniment patterns:

These contain a nonharmonic tone or two

The brackets above the notes in nos. 1 and 2 indicate the harmonic rhythm (one chord per bracket).

1.
Ash Grove   Folk Song

Harmonic Rhythm: One chord per bracket

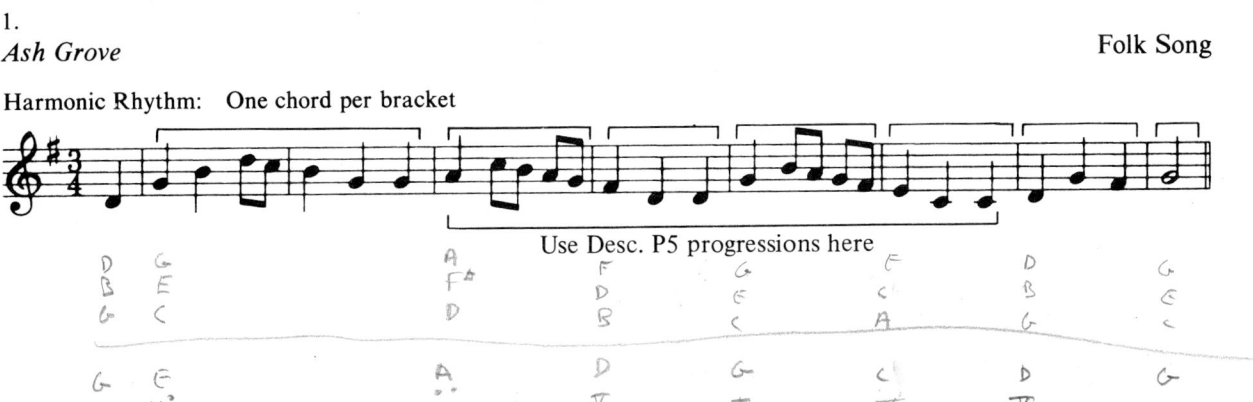

Use Desc. P5 progressions here

Harmonic Progression   161

ASSIGNMENT 5 (continued)

2.
Tell Me Why — Folk Song

In harmonizing no. 3, use (1) at least one uninterrupted string of three descending P5 progressions, (2) make sure that the entire composition contains a majority of descending P5 progressions, and (3) use only half and authentic cadences.

3.
The Sailor — Folk Song

In harmonizing this composition, choose from among the following triads: I, IV, and V. One measure will require three different triads. Which measure?

4.
Las Mananitas — Folk Song

ASSIGNMENT 6	1. Below are two typical chorale phrases.
	2. Using principles discussed in this chapter, harmonize each phrase.
	3. First, make the basic chord selection. In the first phrase, limit your selection of chords to: I, V, IV, and ii and inversions.
	4. Place the roots of the chords on the staff.
	5. If the bass line seems too angular (too many leaps), consider placing some of the chords in first inversion.
	6. When the bass line is satisfactory, add the alto and tenor voices.
	7. Finally, include a few nonharmonic tones.
	8. All members should play their harmonizations in class.
	9. Discuss the merits of each.

Bach: *Herzlich lieb hab ich dich, O Herr*
(Dearly I Love Thee, O Lord)

Bach: *Herr Jesu Christ, du höchstes Gut*
(Lord Jesus Christ, Thou Highest Good)

ASSIGNMENT 7	1. Following are two chorale melodies with figured bass.
	2. Add alto and tenor voices according to the figured bass symbols.
	3. Make sure your part-writing conforms to recommended practice.
	4. Analyze each chord.
	5. Play your harmonization in class.

Bach: *So wünsch ich mir zu gutter*
(Thus at Last I Wish to Die in Peace)

Analysis: ___ ___ ___ ___ ___ ___ ___ ___

Harmonic Progression

ASSIGNMENT 7 (continued)

Bach: *Jesu, meine Freude*
(Jesus, My Joy)

*In these two chords, double the root (E).

9 Style Periods

Renaissance *Classical* *Post-Romantic and*
Baroque *Romantic* *Impressionistic*
          Contemporary

STYLE Music theory is approached through musical style. Music is a means of communication—artistic communication. Music comes into existence when musical material is organized in such a manner that it establishes communication among human beings.

At any one time in the enormous span of musical existence, a particular aspect of the material is manipulated in a particular way, and much of the music of that time has particular and salient characteristics in common—a style.

Musical style combines a group of elements or characteristics that relate a composition to a particular period of time, a particular function, a particular composer, or a particular country. Thus, style allows a composition of music to be scrutinized with respect to its elements or characteristics and to be classified by its historical location.

A style period is best described as a period of time in which certain elements prevail over the sound and shape of the music then being composed. Thus, style periods yield a convenient and identifiable framework on which theorists can tack the large-scale generalizations they need to assess the mass of material that they encounter. In providing titles for style periods, theorists often borrow from literature, painting, and architecture since the same eras frequently apply to music as well.

The style periods are indeed broad and general. Within each of these wide spans there are many small and more detailed subsections. For instance, the Renaissance can easily be divided into the Early Renaissance and the Late Renaissance, the Rococo period falls mainly into the larger title of Baroque, and the Neoclassical style is but one phase of the Contemporary period. No other style period comprises as many different and divergent styles as the Contemporary period.

Here, then, are the general style periods.

STYLE PERIOD	APPROXIMATE DATES
RENAISSANCE	1450–1600
BAROQUE	1600–1750
CLASSICAL	1750–1825
ROMANTIC	1825–1900
POST-ROMANTIC AND IMPRESSIONISTIC	1875–1920
CONTEMPORARY	1920–Present

Renaissance Period (1450–1600)

The term "Renaissance" refers historically to the era of the rebirth of culture and intellectual curiosity that followed the Dark Ages. It began (1450) about the time that Christopher Columbus (1446–1506) was a child; its middle period saw the rise of the Protestant Reformation movement spurred by Martin Luther. It reached its zenith about the time of Shakespeare (1564–1616). The overriding function of music in the Renaissance period was sacred; that is, to contribute to worship. Although greatly overshadowed by the sacred music of the period, secular works did exist and were an important part of the literature at that time.

By volume, vocal music far outweighed instrumental music, and it was during this period that choral music became fully established. Choruses came into being shortly before the beginning of the Renaissance, but did not reach full flower until well into the era. Choruses of the time were usually small groups of perhaps twelve to fifteen singers, whereas today a chorus may include several hundred. Through much of history, the choral group has been divided into four parts—the familiar soprano, alto, tenor, and bass—and referred to as a "mixed" chorus. Late Renaissance music often required a fifth part, either a second soprano or a second tenor. Works for six-, eight-, and even sixteen-part choruses were not exceptional. Choruses were frequently accompanied by instrumental groups that usually doubled the voice parts. Most often in chapels, however, the groups sang *a cappella*, or unaccompanied.

Baroque Period (1600–1750)

The Baroque was a period of many changes. Baroque composers arranged for the words of sung texts to be more easily heard. They preferred new tonality systems to the modality of the Renaissance. Instrumental music came of age and began to assume more importance than vocal music for the first time in history.

Rameau, in his *Traité de L'Harmonie* (1722), sought to prove the invertibility of chords and designed an entire system of harmony that recognized the progression of triads and other sonorities. Furthermore, the older systems of tuning (just and meantone) found a new competitor in equal temperament, a system that allowed more freedom for modulation and a method of tuning that would eventually supersede all others in the ensuing century. These are some of the radical changes that took place in the Baroque period and were in direct contrast to the established practices of the Renaissance.

The Baroque period paralleled the rise of our own country from a wilderness to an established system of colonies. Shakespeare was still alive at the period's beginning and George Washington (1732–1799) was a young man at its close.

Classical Period (1750–1825)

This period encompassed the lives of many of our best-known composers whose works are still performed regularly in concert halls throughout the world. Haydn, Mozart, Schubert, and Beethoven, giants of the music world, were included in this artistically wealthy period. The balance shifted even more in favor of instrumental music although operas, sacred and secular, continued to be written. Chamber music, orchestral, and other instrumental works gained the ascendancy. The sonata and sonata-allegro form developed during the Classical period, and the string quartet took the place of the older trio sonata. Figured bass suffered a considerable decline, and the piano-forte (our modern piano), invented about 1710 by Christofori, became a popular household instrument. The improvisatory attitude toward performance died out, except in instances like the cadenzas in concertos, and the woodwind quintet became a stable medium. As the Baroque period gave way to the Classical and the orchestral literature grew in size and importance, the orchestra itself acquired more color and flexibility. Clarinets became permanent fixtures along with flutes, oboes, and bassoons.

In the configuration of history, the early Classical period saw the American Revolution and the formation of the United States. The Napoleonic wars and the general cultural disorder in Europe were symptoms of Romanticism.

Romantic Period (1825–1900)

In the United States, the Romantic period began with the presidency of Andrew Jackson and ended with that of McKinley. A wrenching civil war tore at the basic fibers of the country, most of the states west of the Mississippi were admitted to the union, railroads spanned the country, and big business became a dominant force in our country for the first time.

Music of this period was dominated by a wider range of emotional expression, more personal and individual styles, and more subjectivity. Musical forms, such as the sonata and symphony, became longer and more involved, but shorter forms, especially piano compositions were also numerous. Harmony and orchestration expanded, as did sonorities in general. Homophonic texture still prevailed.

The most substantial achievement of the Romantic period was the development of harmonic technique and instrumental color. The increased use of chords, chromatic melody, tonal vagueness, the freer use of nonharmonic tones, modulation to distant keys, and the increasing tendency to avoid strong cadences, all operated to extend and eventually to blur the outlines of tonality. Romantic harmony as a means of boundless expression resulted in an ever-expanding gamut of color.

As against the classic ideals of organization, symmetry, control, and perfection within acknowledged limits, Romanticism sought independence, movement, passion, and pursued the mysterious or exotic because its ideals could not be obtained. Romantic art was troubled by the spirit of longing and seeking after an unattainable goal.

Post-Romantic and Impressionistic (1875–1920)

This period in the United States began with the reconstruction days after the Civil War, and ended about the time of World War I. Jazz music was becoming established throughout the nation, the Spanish-American War (1898) was fought, and Teddy Roosevelt (1901–1909) and Woodrow Wilson (1913–1921) took turns as president.

Musically, the sturdy bastion of harmonic progression (first discussed by Rameau in the Baroque era and which continued undaunted through the Classical and Romantic period) gave way to the parallel movement of chords, more emphasis on the ostinato and pedal point, and an even greater departure from the clear and strongly demarcated tonality of the Late Romantic period.

Triadic harmony continued into the period, free tonality developed, and a new array of fragile and deceptively well-organized forms came into being. The tone poem surged to new heights, and most of the old ideas of Romanticism faded into oblivion.

As a movement among French painters, *Impressionism* sought to eliminate the heroic subjects, the obsession with realistic detail, and the representational quality of Romantic painting. In essence, the impressionist painter hoped to capture the impression a subject or object made on him rather than to paint its literal representation. So too, in music, composers such as Debussy aspired to renounce the squarecut antecedent-consequent phrase, the plodding harmony of the past, and replace them with a hint of the melody and an allusion to harmony in a way that was very effective but not at all similar to that of the Romantic style. The composer abandoned traditional thematic development and became more concerned with the color or mood of a particular moment. Bits of thematic material separated by other contrasting material returns periodically so that form is reinforced, but the effect of the whole is colorful, whimsical, and unpredictable.

Contemporary Period (1910–Present)

A veritable flood of new styles invaded the world of music during the period from 1910 to the present. The revolt against traditional tonality brought forth the comparatively conservative style known as *free tonality* (preserves the idea of a tonal center but discards the diatonic key systems). Another offshoot of this revolution was that of *atonality* (complete absence of tonality) as witnessed in composers such as Schoenberg, Berg, and Webern. Not only was tonality negated, but a whole new system of musical organization known as the serial technique was developed.

Other composers experimented with new methods of scale construction, and as a result several new *microtonal* (less than the traditional half-step) scales were developed including one that utilized the quarter tone and doubled the number of pitches in the octave scale. Alois Haba, a leading proponent of this style, wrote a number of compositions for keyboard and other instruments.

Musique concrète is a term used to denote musical compositions that employ sounds produced either by musical instruments or from nature but are processed through a tape recorder or other electronic means. Thus, additional freedom in composition was accomplished since combinations of sound could be generated that would have been impossible by direct methods.

The electronic sound generator (electronic synthesizer) also became a tool for composers who sought new and different ways to produce music. This device differs from that of *musique concrète* in that the tones are created by the oscillation of electrical waves rather than being generated in nature and then processed. More often than not, compositions prepared through this means are recorded directly on tape recorders rather than performed live for an audience.

Aleatoric (chance) music developed in the twentieth century, but it has its roots in the distant past when composers and performers were one and the same. Improvisation has been with us for many centuries, and indeterminacy has been controlled in various ways. Aleatoric music provides yet another path for allowing performers unusual freedom in the performance of music.

Jazz, an indigenous product of the United States, has undergone many changes and interpretations in its brief history. Its acceptance as a substantive art form has at last been accomplished.

ASSIGNMENT 1

Listed are the names of composers who represent the following style periods:

Renaissance	1450-1600	Romantic	1825-1900
Baroque	1600-1750	Post-Romantic and	1875-1920
Classical	1750-1825	Impressionistic	
		Contemporary	1920-Present

1. Look over the following names of composers, and place a check mark beside those whose music you have played or heard.
2. For each name you have checked, list the musical period the composer represents. Not all composers fall neatly into a single period, so some may require two.
3. In class, compare your list with those of other class members, and ask the instructor to comment on the less well-known composers.

Hindemith	_____	Lully	_____
Bach	_____	Puccini	_____
Brahms	_____	Ibert	_____
Ravel	_____	Palestrina	_____
Mel Powell	_____	Mahler	_____
De Lassus	_____	Chopin	_____

ASSIGNMENT 1 (continued)

Tchaikovsky	_____	Buxtehude	_____
Haydn	_____	Schubert	_____
Victoria	_____	Prokofieff	_____
Stephen Foster	_____	D. Scarlatti	_____
Von Weber	_____	Copland	_____
Schoenberg	_____	Handel	_____
Rimsky-Korsakov	_____	Beethoven	_____
Delius	_____	Debussy	_____
Purcell	_____	R. Schumann	_____
Wagner	_____	Barber	_____
Elgar	_____	MacDowell	_____
Mussorgsky	_____	Mozart	_____
Berlioz	_____	Vivaldi	_____
Foss	_____	Dvořák	_____

10 Approach to Style Analysis

Analysis
Analytical Procedure
Style Analysis
Pitch Inventory
Scale

Key and Mode
Tonality
Melody
Harmony
Rhythm

Texture
Form
Contrapuntal
   Applications

ANALYSIS

Two ways exist in which an understanding of music can be gained. One is through *analysis* (the taking apart of a composition), and the other is through *synthesis* (the putting together of a composition). In this instance, the study will be confined to analysis.

Analytical Procedure

The analytical approach is composed of two interrelated procedures:

1. Gathering statistical information.
2. Drawing conclusions from all the available factual information.

Little is gained from the task of collecting statistical information if the processor does not learn from it. Thus, the conclusions constitute the real test of any analytical procedure. The true value of analysis is the meaning gleaned from the collected information. Fact gathering is of no consequence in itself. The statistics are *not* to be memorized or used in any other way except as a basis for logical judgment and studied conclusions.

In order to assemble the statistical information and draw isolated facts into a meaningful whole, it is necessary to establish a procedure that can be used regularly and that will not become a burden.

The outline provided in this chapter will serve as a reminder of the separate items to observe in a composition. Through its continued use, the sequence of information gathering will become familiar and the efficiency and speed of the analysis will increase.

Some of the items in the outline will not apply to all compositions since no two compositions are alike. However, as a reminder of the wide gamut of possibilities, the outline will also be valuable in comparing one composition with another.

STYLE ANALYSIS

Style is the total effect of all interacting aspects of a musical composition. Through observation, it is possible to determine the characteristic dimensions of the activity and the controlling elements that produce individual movement and shape in a composition. Some of the factors that produce style and should be considered in analysis are:

Pitch Inventory The pitch inventory—those pitches selected for use in a composition.

Scale The scale—the pitch inventory arranged within one octave so that the beginning tone is also the tonal center.

Key or Mode The key or mode—the term "key" applies only if the composition utilizes a diatonic scale such as the major scale or one of the three forms of the minor. The term "mode" may be substituted for "key" when applicable.

Tonality Tonality—the term "tonality" may apply to diatonic systems, but it also applies to any music in which a tonal center exists (whether the pitch selection of a diatonic scale is followed or not). When tonality is not synonymous with key, it is sometimes referred to as free tonality.

Melody The melody of a composition includes:

1. The way in which structural, secondary, and embellishing tones are combined.
2. The importance, length, duration, and number of step progressions.
3. The formal way in which melodic units are connected in the length of musical thoughts, repetition, imitation, sequences, etc.

Harmony The harmony of a composition includes:

1. Harmonic patterns—the types of vertical structures found.
2. Harmonic progression—the patterns of chord change.
3. Harmonic rhythm—the rate of harmonic change, the number of changes per unit of music, the patterns of harmonic duration.
4. Harmonic elaboration—the ways in which harmony is sustained. A chord is generally considered as a simultaneous combination of tones. Yet, composers have developed different techniques for continuing the effect of a single chord over a span of time. Among these are:
   a. Repeated note patterns
   b. Arpeggiation
   c. Sustained chords
   d. The use of pedal tones, embellishing tones, etc.
   e. The use of scale lines.

Rhythm The rhythm of a composition includes:

1. The nature of rhythmic activity—patterned or unpatterned, regular or irregular, simple or complex, repetitive or nonrepetitive, sustained or sporadic.
2. Tempo and tempo changes—consistent or inconsistent, fast or slow, many changes or few changes, etc.
3. Other rhythmic activity—any unusual features such as rhythmic canon, etc.

Texture Texture—a broad term that refers in music to the dimensions and characteristics of sound combinations in a composition:

1. Thick texture—many voices, many chord factors, complex sonority.
2. Thin texture—few voices, few chord factors, simple sonority.

3. Wide texture—gap between lowest and highest tone is considerable.
4. Narrow texture—gap between lowest and highest tone is very close.
5. Contrapuntal texture—a generally linear writing with emphasis on the simultaneous use of independent melodies.
6. Homophonic texture—a single line of melody with supporting accompaniment.

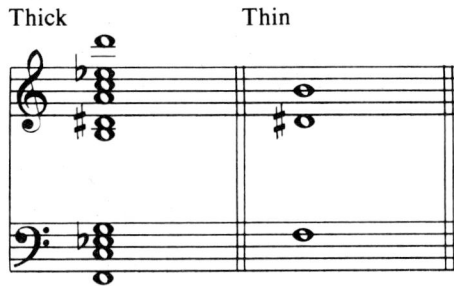

Contrapuntal

Homophonic

Form

Form—the *macro* (larger) aspects of the composition. These include the relationships of the larger units such as phrases, periods, double periods, song forms, sonata-allegro form, etc. This should also include such items as key relationships, modulations, melodic and harmonic continuity, etc.

Contrapuntal Applications

Contrapuntal applications—the linear aspects of composition or counterpoint, the relationship of one line to another, the interaction of simultaneous melodies.

11 The Major-Minor Dominant Seventh Chord

Symbols for Seventh
  Chords
Major Keys
Minor Keys
Major-Minor Dominant
  Seventh Chord
Inversions of Seventh
  Chords
Progressions of Seventh
  Chords
Resolution of Seventh
  Chord
Circle Progressions
  (Descending Fifth)
Noncircle Progressions
Nonresolution
Part-writing

THE SEVENTH CHORD IN GENERAL

The seventh chord—a triad with an added factor a third degree above the fifth factor—is so named because in root position it has a characteristic interval of a seventh degree between the root and the added factor.

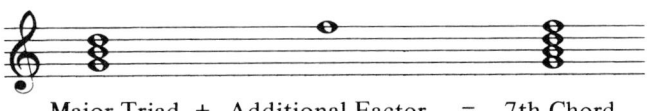

Major Triad + Additional Factor = 7th Chord

History

The seventh chord developed in the sixteenth century as a result of "frozen" nonharmonic tones that gradually assumed the importance of a chord tone.

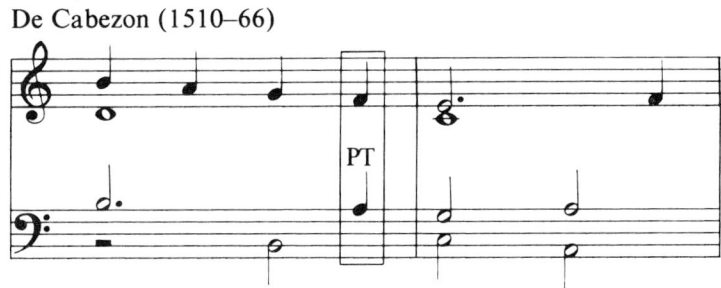

De Cabezon (1510–66)

During the seventeenth through nineteenth century, such seventh chords became commonplace although the seventh factor was most often treated as if it were a nonharmonic tone—the seventh resolved down one step in the succeeding chord.

175

J. S. Bach

V   V^7 I

7th   Resolution

Analysis Symbols

The particular sound of a seventh chord is indicated in analysis—

1. By the type of triad—major (M), minor (m), diminished (d), augmented (A).
2. By the type of interval from the root to the seventh factor.

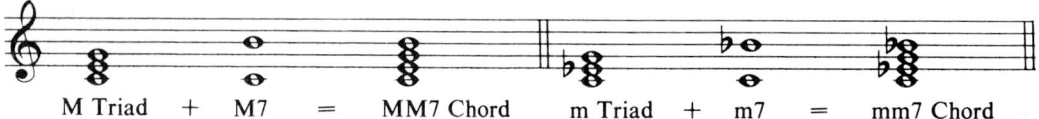

M Triad + M7 = MM7 Chord   m Triad + m7 = mm7 Chord

Follow these steps in writing analysis symbols for seventh chords:

1. First write the symbol indicating the triad.

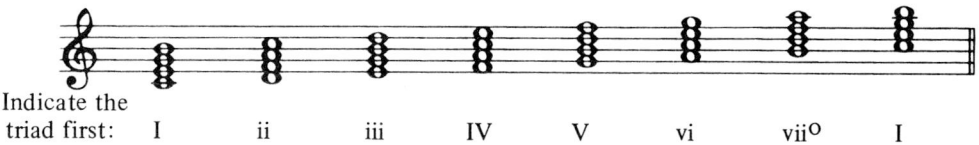

Indicate the triad first: I   ii   iii   IV   V   vi   vii°   I

2. If the interval of the seventh (from root to seventh) is the *same* as the type of triad (i.e., both are major, both are minor, both are diminished, etc.), write only 7 (I^7).
3. If the interval quality of the seventh is *different* from the quality of the triad (i.e., the triad is major and the seventh is minor, etc.), write the quality (M, m) of the seventh below the 7 (I^7_m).
4. *Exceptions:*
   a. Since the dominant seventh (major triad and minor seventh) is so frequently used and so easily recognized, the small m beneath the 7 may be omitted (V^7 instead of V^7_m).
   b. The seventh chord formed by a diminished triad and minor seventh is written as vii^{ø7} instead of vii$^{ø7}_m$.

Some examples:

SYMBOL	TRIAD TYPE	INTERVAL OF SEVENTH	TYPE OF SEVENTH CHORD
I^7	MAJOR	MAJOR	Major-Major seventh chord on first scale degree (tonic)
i^7_M	MINOR	MAJOR	minor-Major seventh chord on first scale degree (tonic)
ii^7	MINOR	MINOR	minor-minor seventh chord on second scale degree (supertonic)
ii^{ø7}	DIMINISHED	MINOR	diminished-minor seventh chord on second scale degree (supertonic)
V^7	MAJOR	MINOR	Major-minor seventh chord on fifth scale degree (dominant)
vii$^{°7}$	DIMINISHED	DIMINISHED	diminished-diminished seventh chord on seventh scale degree (leading tone)

Seventh Chords in Major Keys

Symbols used for seventh chords in major keys (examples are in C major):

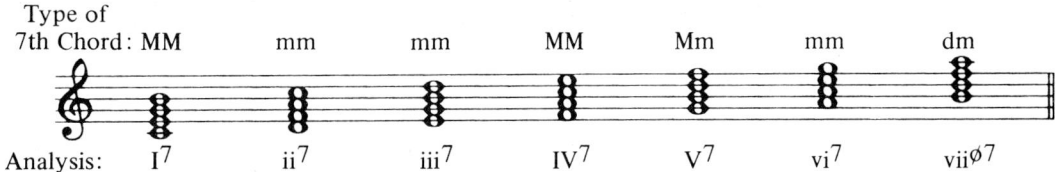

Seventh Chords in Minor Keys

Symbols used for seventh chords in minor keys (examples are in C minor, all forms):

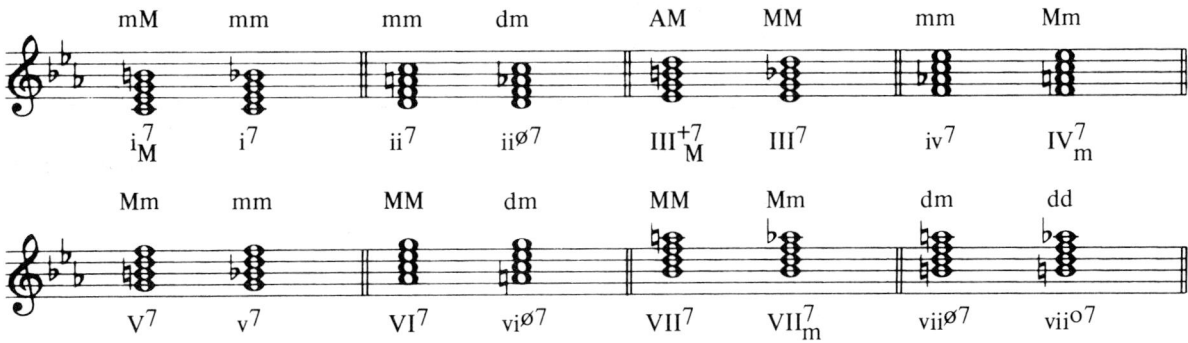

ASSIGNMENT 1

1. To help you practice writing analysis symbols, the following chords are provided.
2. In the first box of each exercise, write the analysis of the triad.
3. In the second box, write the type of interval from the root to the seventh factor.
4. If the seventh interval is the same as the triad write only 7. If it is different from the triad, write the quality of the seventh below the 7. Remember the exceptions described earlier (4a and 4b).
5. No. 1 illustrates the correct procedure.

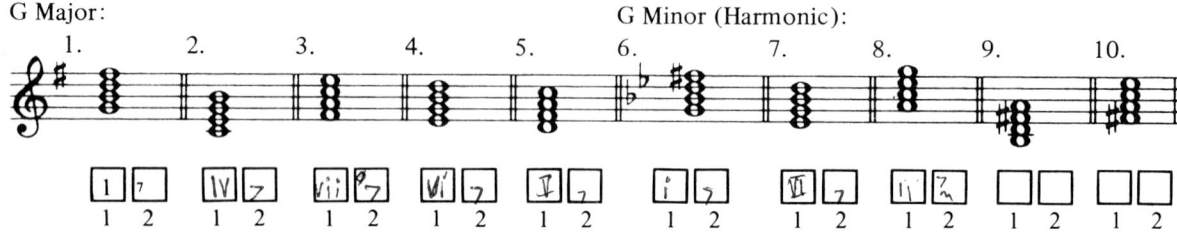

THE MAJOR-MINOR DOMINANT SEVENTH CHORD

The *major-minor dominant seventh chord* is a diatonic seventh chord built on the fifth degree of the major, harmonic minor, and melodic minor scales.

The major-minor sound (major triad and minor seventh from root to seventh) has come to be associated with a dominant function since the same sound appears diatonically in only one other place in the tonal systems—on the fourth degree of the melodic minor scale (IV^7_m). Since its use in this capacity is not common, the uniqueness of the major-minor dominant seventh chord (V^7) is preserved.

The V^7 is found almost as frequently as is the dominant triad. This illustration from a Beethoven concerto is typical of the widespread use of the V^7.

Beethoven: *Piano Concerto no. 2 in B-flat* op. 19

Chords reduced to simple position

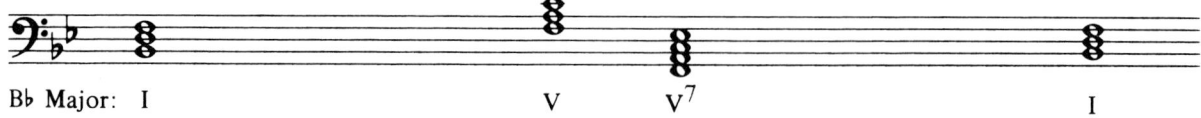

B♭ Major: I   V V^7 I

INVERSION OF SEVENTH CHORDS

The seventh chords, including the V^7, can be inverted in the same manner as triads.

Positions

The various positions of the seventh chord are illustrated in the following chart. The numbers used in analysis to designate the various positions of the chord are derived from the intervals above the bass note, but, as with triads, conventional practice eliminates some.

POSITION	ANALYSIS SHOWING ALL INTERVALS ABOVE THE BASS TONE	ANALYSIS AS SIMPLIFIED FOR CONVENTIONAL USE
ROOT POSITION	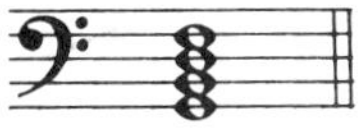 $V^{7}_{5_{3}}$	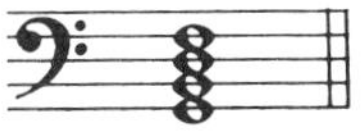 V^7
1ST INVERSION	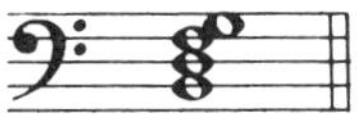 $V^{6}_{5_{3}}$	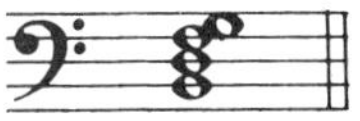 V^{6}_{5}
2ND INVERSION	 $V^{6}_{4_{3}}$	 V^{4}_{3}
3RD INVERSION	 $V^{6}_{4_{2}}$	 V^{4}_{2} or V^2

RESOLUTION OF SEVENTH CHORDS

Unlike major and minor triads, the seventh chord contains a dissonance—the seventh factor. Thus, although major and minor triads are comparatively free to move about from one to another, seventh chords are restricted by the added factor.

Musical style is much affected by the way in which the seventh factor of the seventh chord is treated. From its emergence in the sixteenth century until the Post-Romantic and Impressionistic periods, composers routinely resolved the dissonant seventh factor downward by step in the succeeding chord and followed the V^7 with the tonic triad. Although this was the common practice, it by no means represents the only possible technique, and it is therefore important to investigate the V^7 in its broader treatment.

The V^7 in particular and seventh chords in general are treated by composers as three general types.

Circle Progression

Type 1.
The circle progression (descending P5s), as mentioned on page 143 of chapter 8, "Harmonic Progressions," is the basis of all harmonic progressions. The statement holds true for the V^7 as well as other seventh chords. Certainly, one of the most common progressions in all of music is that of V^7 proceeding to I.

Such a relationship of chord roots provides not only the strongest type of progression but also permits the seventh factor of the seventh chord to resolve downward by step.

The Major-Minor Dominant Seventh Chord

Composers of the Baroque, Classical, and Romantic periods observed the following two conditions:

1. The chord roots lie in a descending P5 (or ascending P4) relationship. When both the V^7 and I are in root position, the root of the V^7 progresses to the root of the tonic, but in inversions, the roots of the two chords are seldom in the same voice.
2. The seventh factor of the V^7 resolves one scale degree down to the third of the tonic triad.

    In traditional four-part writing, this resolution usually occurs in the same voice, but, in piano or other broken styles, the resolution of the seventh may be shifted to another voice.

    V^7 appears in any position (V^7 V^6_5 V^4_3 V^4_2), and all may be succeeded by the tonic chord to produce a circle progression with resolution of the dissonant seventh.

Some examples of circle progressions in different positions:

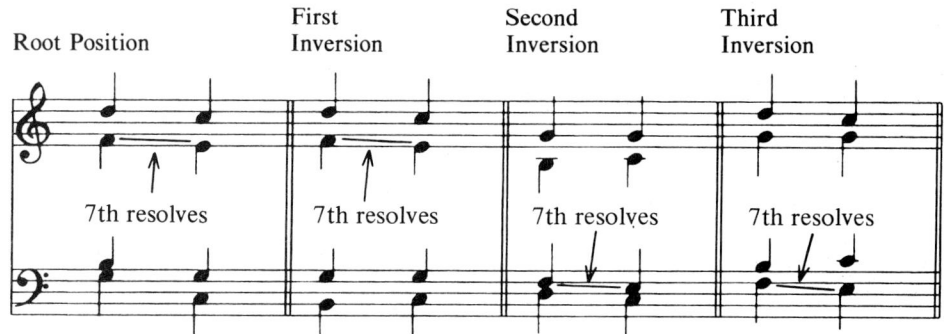

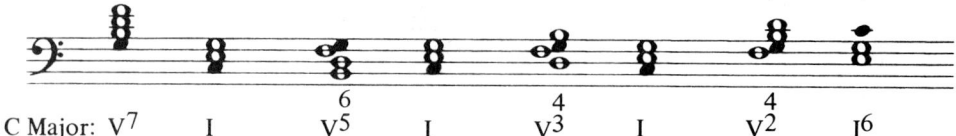

The following illustrations are typical of circle resolutions for the V^7:

Bach: *Es ist Genug*
(It is Enough)

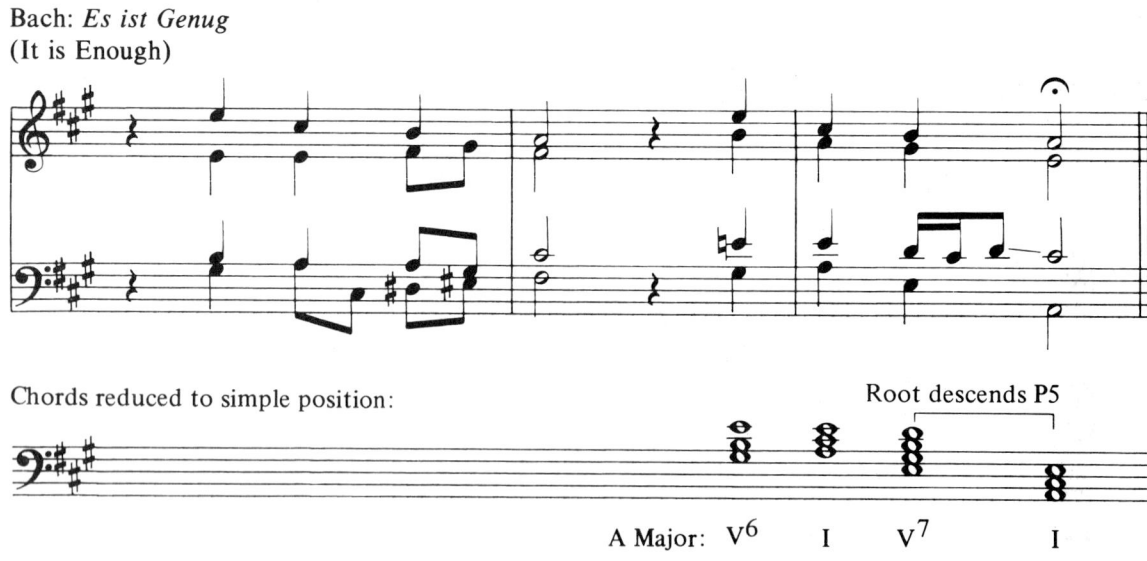

180   The Major-Minor Dominant Seventh Chord

Noncircle Progression with Resolution

Type 2.

Sometimes the seventh factor of the seventh chord resolves, but the roots of the two chords involved lie a second or third apart. This happens most often with the V⁷ chord when it progresses up a step to the vi (or VI in minor). Thus, the two conditions required for noncircle progression with resolution are:

1. V⁷ proceeds to a chord whose root lies a second degree above or a third degree below it.

    The deceptive cadence V to vi (or VI in minor) is the most common of this type for the V⁷ chord.

2. The seventh factor of the V⁷ resolves one scale degree down to a factor of the following chord.

    In the deceptive cadence, the seventh factor of V⁷ resolves to the fifth factor of vi (or VI in minor).

Type 2 resolutions

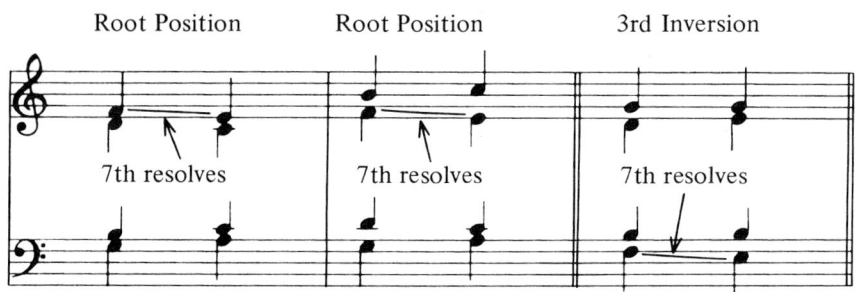

Chords reduced to simple position:

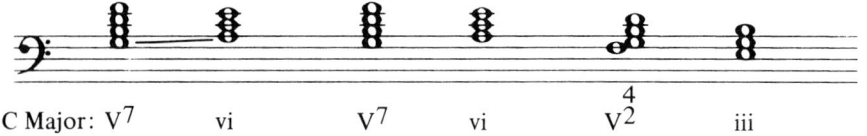

Roots progress either by 2nd or 3rd.

Typical type 2 progressions from music literature follow:

Bach: *O Herre Gott, dein gottlichs Wort*
(O God, Our Lord, Thy Holy Word)

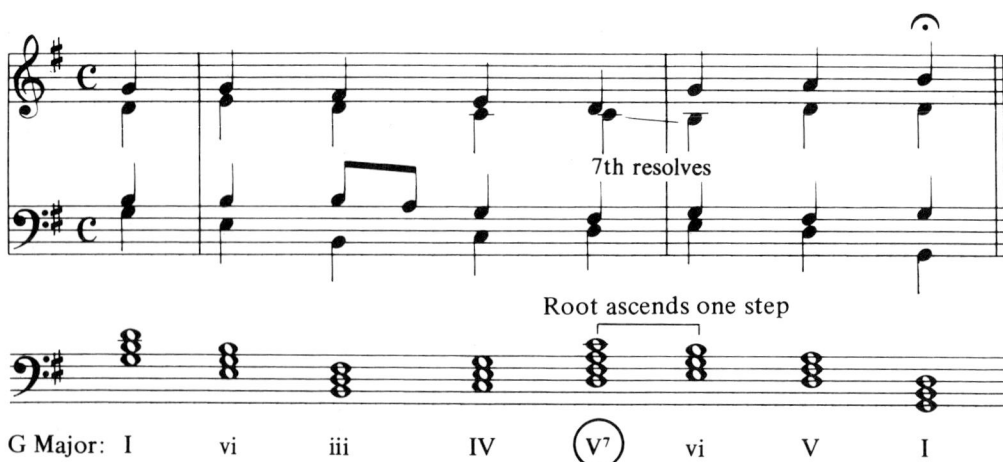

182   The Major-Minor Dominant Seventh Chord

Mozart: *Quintet in A Major* K. 581

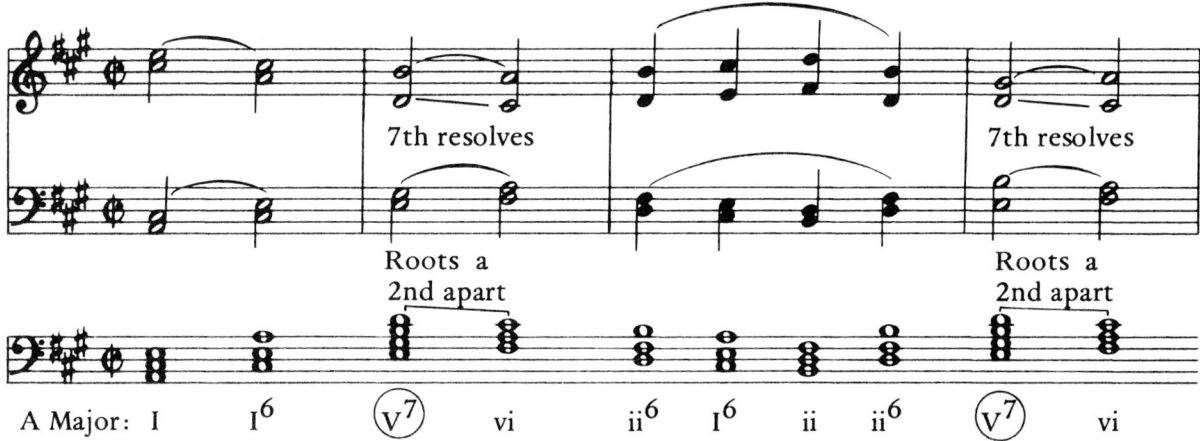

Mendelssohn: *Sonata for Cello and Piano* op. 45

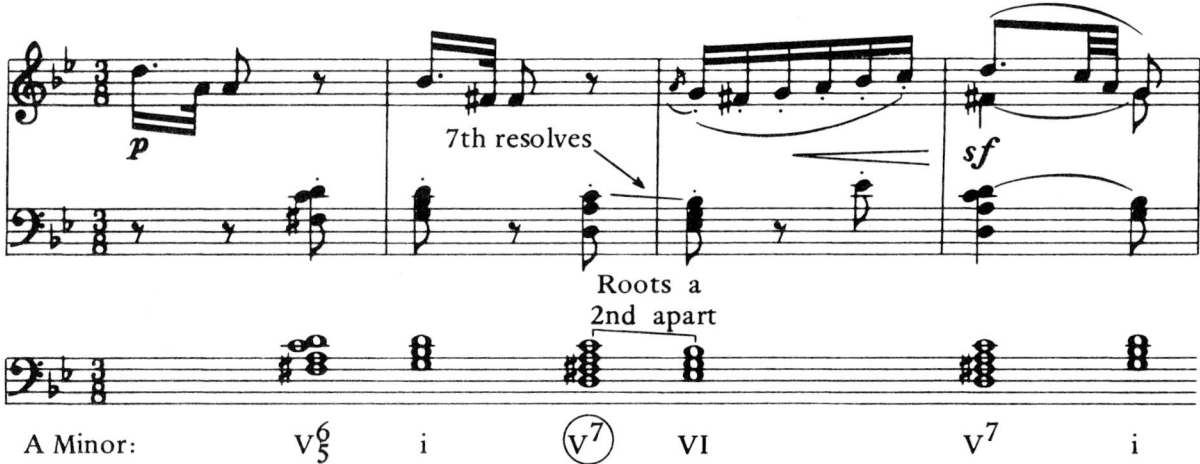

Nonresolution

Type 3.

On occasion, the dissonant seventh of a seventh chord cannot be resolved in the ensuing chord. This nonresolvable seventh chord occurs when the resolution note (down one scale degree from the seventh) is not a part of the succeeding chord.

In most instances, however, the resolution of the seventh is only delayed and eventually occurs in the appropriate manner after a few intervening chords.

The two conditions needed for type 3 seventh chords are:

1. A circle progression from type 1 is not present. In other words, the V^7 is not followed by the tonic.
2. The resolution note (down a scale step from the seventh) is not present in the following chord.

Composers sometimes preferred the nonresolution as a contrast to the more common circle of P5 progressions with the seventh resolved.

Type 3

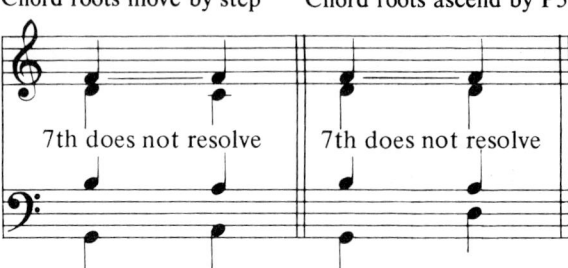

Chords reduced to simple position:

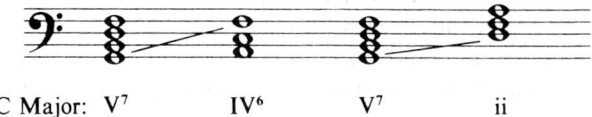

C Major: V⁷   IV⁶   V⁷   ii

The following illustration by Mozart shows the iv⁶ triad as an embellishment of the V⁷.

Mozart: *Sonata for Violin and Piano* K. 379

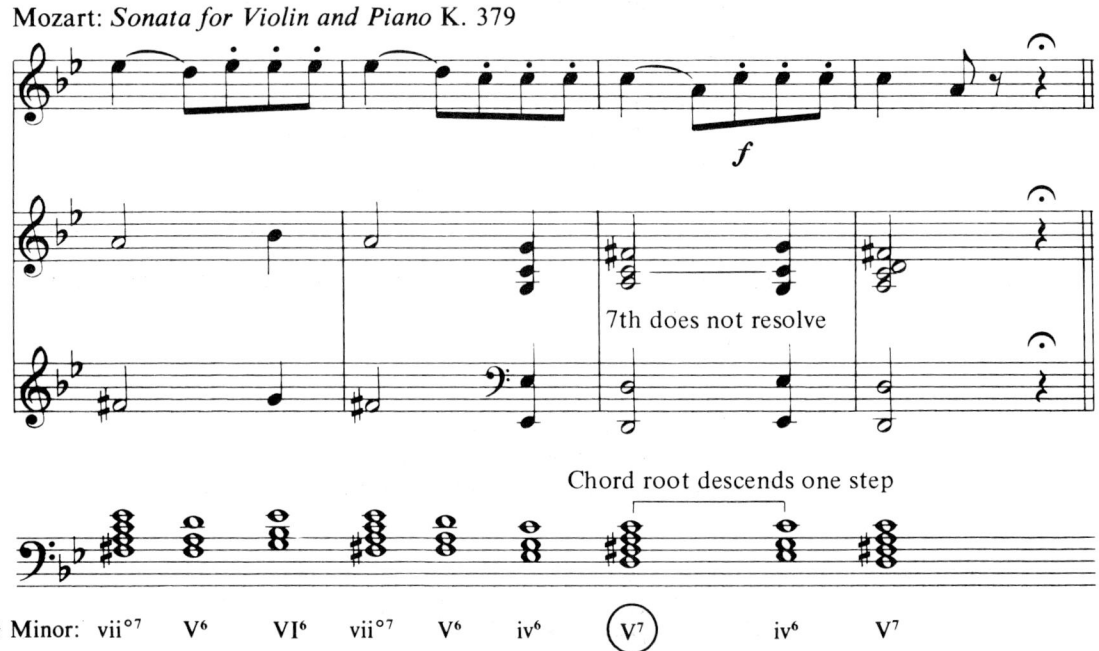

G Minor: vii°⁷ V⁶ VI⁶ vii°⁷ V⁶ iv⁶ (V⁷) iv⁶ V⁷

Late in the Romantic period, composers such as Wagner developed a stylistic idiom in which both alternate resolution and nonresolution of the V⁷ became the rule rather than the exception.

The following chart summarizes the three types of progressions from seventh chords.

	CIRCLE OF P5S	SEVENTH RESOLVES?	IN REGARD TO V⁷ CHORDS
TYPE 1	YES	YES	One of the most common progressions in all of music—V⁷ to I
TYPE 2	NO	YES	Most common usage is the deceptive cadence, V⁷ to vi (VI in minor)
TYPE 3	NO	NO	Not often found

Remember that for types 1 and 2 in four-part chorale style, the seventh factor of the seventh chord should always resolve down one scale degree in the same voice. In broken style, (such as in assignment 2 following), the seventh factor of the seventh chord is sometimes resolved in another voice.

PART-WRITING PROCEDURES FOR V⁷

(These three rules continue the list begun on p. 135.)

16. *Resolve the seventh of the V⁷ chord in the same voice except when the resolution tone (one scale step down from the seventh factor) is not present in the following chord.*
17. *The V⁷ usually contains all four factors, but on occasion, for smoothness in part-writing, the root is doubled and the fifth omitted.*
18. *Omit the fifth (triple the root) following the V⁷ on occasion to avoid parallel fifths.*

ASSIGNMENT 2

Each exercise consists of two chords, the first of which is a major-minor dominant seventh chord.
Indicate:

1. The key.
2. The analysis of both chords.
3. The type of resolution—1, 2, or 3
4. The example illustrates the correct procedure.

ASSIGNMENT 2 (continued)

	KEY	CHORD ANALYSIS	TYPE
1.	G Major	V^6_5 I	1
2.			
3.			
4.			
5.			
6.			
7.			
8.			
9.			
10.			

ASSIGNMENT 3   Following are transcriptions from Haydn symphonies.

1. Write the chords in simple position on the blank staff.
2. Make a complete harmonic analysis.
3. Circle nonharmonic tones and name them (passing tone, suspension, etc.).
4. Beneath the analysis indicate whether each V^7 is of type 1, 2, or 3.
5. On a separate sheet of paper, make a complete analysis of the melody showing the structural, secondary, and embellishing tones.
6. Discuss the number of phrases and the relationships thereof.
7. Discuss other composition aspects such as sequence, phrase extension, rhythmic repetition, etc.
8. Get a recording of each of these works from your music library and listen to each movement in its entirety.

ASSIGNMENT 3 (continued)

Haydn: *Symphony no. 98 in B-flat Major* (second movement)

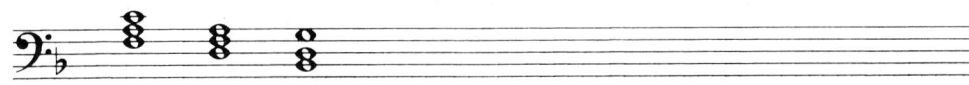

F Major: I   vi   ii⁶

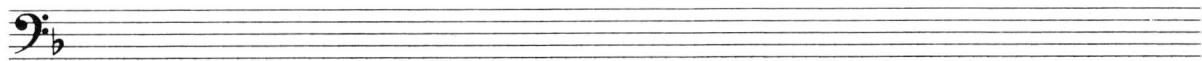

*V$^6_5$/IV

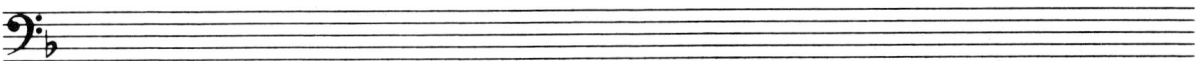

*This is a secondary dominant chord described in chapter 15. For the moment complete only item 4 of the assignment.

ASSIGNMENT 3 (continued)

Haydn: *Symphony no. 97 in C Major* (third movement)

*These are secondary dominant chords described in chapter 15. For the moment complete only item 4 of the assignment.

188   The Major-Minor Dominant Seventh Chord

ASSIGNMENT 3 (continued)

Haydn: *Symphony no. 97 in C Major* (first movement, second theme)

GM:

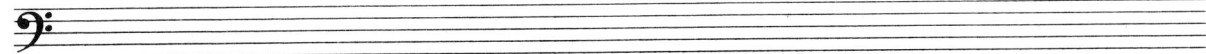

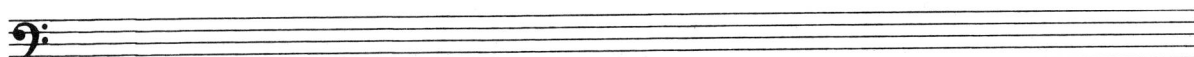

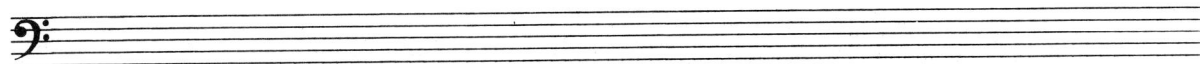

ASSIGNMENT 3 (continued)

ASSIGNMENT 4

1. Add the alto and the tenor to the following chorale-style harmonizations.
2. Analyze each chord using Roman numerals.
3. Observe all part-writing procedures found on pages 135, 136, and 137.
4. Additional procedures printed on p. 185 apply especially to the V^7 chord. Follow these as well.
5. The numbers above the staves indicate the part-writing procedures that apply especially to the chord beneath them.

190 The Major-Minor Dominant Seventh Chord

ASSIGNMENT 4 (continued)

ASSIGNMENT 5

1. Harmonize the following folksong.
2. Select no more than one chord per measure. Occasionally, a single chord will harmonize more than one measure.
3. Use only the following chords:

   E♭ = I
   Fm = ii
   A♭ = IV
   B♭7 = V⁷
   Cm = vi

ASSIGNMENT 5 (continued)

4. Make up your own accompaniment figure or select one of those shown below.
5. When you have decided on the harmony and placed it in the accompaniment pattern, write out the two parts (melody and accompaniment).
6. All of the arrangements should be played in class. Discuss the merits of each.

If you cannot think of a good accompaniment figure yourself, choose one of these. Each example shows how the pattern can be fit into the tonic and dominant seventh chord. Other chords will require other treatment.

Accompaniment Figures

The Sailor — Folk Song

12 The vii^{ø7} and vii$^{°7}$ Chords

Dominant Tendencies *Part-writing* *Historical Use*
Resolution

DOMINANT TENDENCIES

Both the vii^{ø7} and the vii$^{°7}$ have strong dominant tendencies since both contain all tones of the V^9 chord except the root:

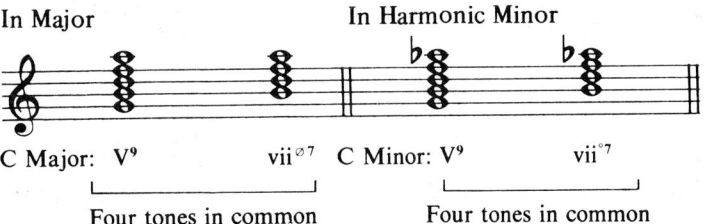

Both the iii^7 and I^9 contain the V triad, but both lack the tritone contained in the vii^{ø7} or the two tritones in the vii$^{°7}$. The resolution of the tritone (or two tritones) is most important as will be seen in the ensuing paragraphs.

Composers frequently substituted the leading tone seventh for the dominant itself to lend variety and diversification. In the following illustration, Beethoven mixes the V^6 and vii$^{°6}$ and the vii$^{°7}$ freely to represent dominant harmony.

Beethoven: *Piano Sonata* op. 10 no. 1

Progressions from vii^{ø7} and vii^{o7}

Unlike the V^7 chord that follows a circle progression (type I), the vii^{ø7} and vii^{o7} seek a type 2 resolution (seventh resolves but circle progression is missing) most often. The reason involves the tritone.

Since diminished intervals naturally resolve inward by half steps, both the half-diminished (vii^{ø7}) and diminished (vii^{o7}) seventh chords allow this resolution when followed by the tonic but not when progressing by circle progression to the mediant. Such a resolution to the tonic also permits the seventh to descend one scale degree.

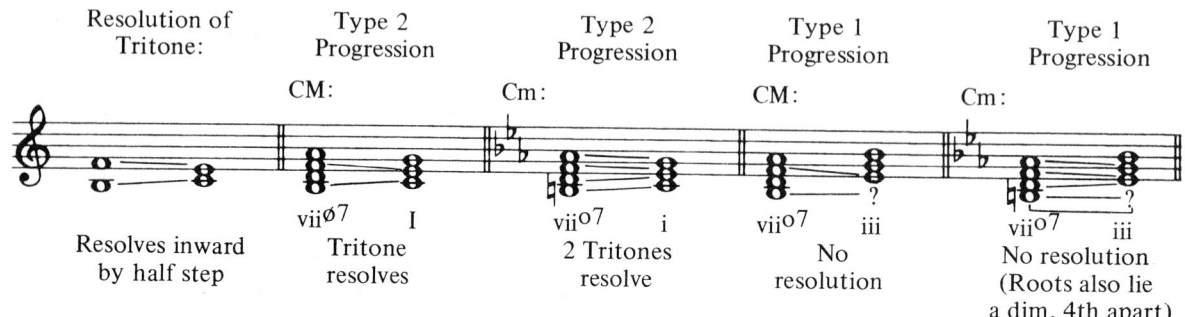

The seventh resolves down one scale degree and the root of the chord resolves up a half step to the tonic:

Mozart: *Don Giovanni*   Opera

Part-writing the vii^{ø7}

These rules continue the list on pages 135–37 and 185.

19. *Resolve the seventh of the vii^{ø7} in the ensuing chord (tonic).*
20. *Resolution of the tritone (inward if a d5 and outward if an A4) in the same two voices is desirable but not always possible.*

Some possible arrangements:

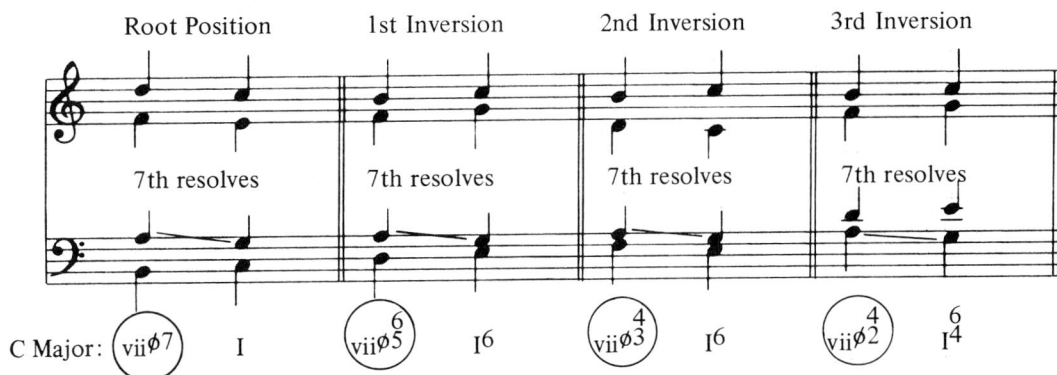

Part-writing the vii°7

This chord, in comparison with the vii⌀7, is fairly plentiful.

21. *Resolve the seventh of the vii°7 in the ensuing chord (tonic).*
22. *Resolve at least the lower tritone (root to fifth) whenever possible.* Music literature reveals a variety of part-writing procedures in the progression vii°7 to i. Parallel uneven fifths (d5 to P5) are observed in literature but are comparatively rare.

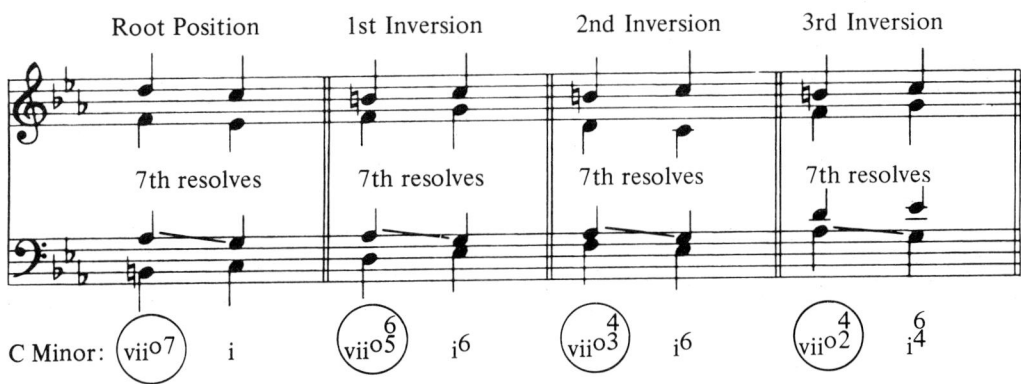

ASSIGNMENT 1

1. Add the alto and the tenor to the following figured bass phrases according to suggestions on pages 135–37, 185, and 194–95. (A complete list of all part-writing suggestions can also be found in Appendix 2.)
2. Make a harmonic analysis of each chord.
3. When this is completed in the above manner, add the appropriate nonharmonic tones.
4. Divide the class into four sections (soprano, alto, tenor, and bass), and sing the completed phrases.
5. The numbers above the chords in the first exercise represent part-writing procedures particularly applicable to that chord.

ASSIGNMENT 1 (continued)

1. *Herzliebster Jesu, was hast du* (Dearest Jesus, How Hast Thou Transgressed) — Chorale

Part-writing Procedure Numbers: 5   5   6   5   16 17   6   8   5   5   21 22   5   5

Figured Bass: 6   ♯   ♯4 2   6   ♯6   7   ♯

Analysis: Gm: __ __ __ __ __ __ __ __ __ __ __ __ __

2. *Jesu, meine Freude* (Jesus, My Joy) — Chorale

6   7   6   ♯

Analysis: __ __ __ __ __ __

3. *Hilf, Herr Jesu, lass gelingen* (Help, Lord Jesus, Send Good Speed) — Chorale

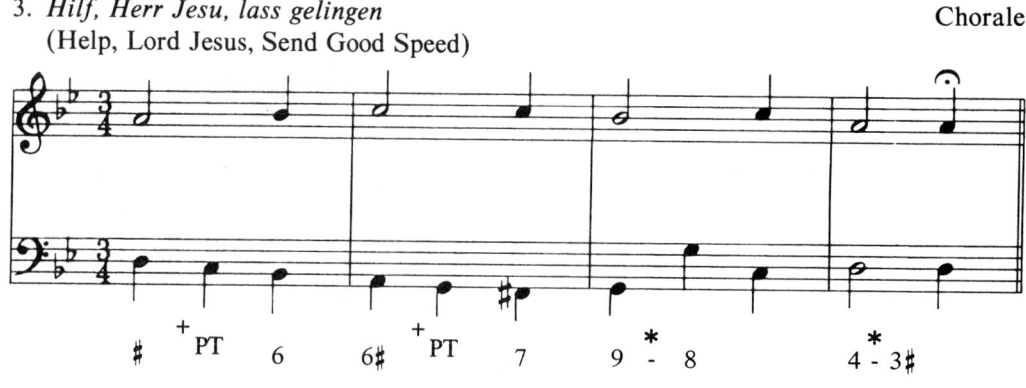

♯   +PT   6   6♯   +PT   7   9 - 8*   4 - 3♯*

Analysis: Gm: __ __ __ __ __ __ __ __

Each of the above chorale melodies was harmonized by Bach. When you have completed your harmonization look up the phrases (by title) in any competent edition of the 371 Bach Chorale Harmonizations. Compare your results with those of Bach.

+ These are passing tones. Do not harmonize them.

* These are suspensions—ninth to octave above the bass note and fourth to third above the bass note.

ASSIGNMENT 2

The waltz melody shown below is typical of those written during the late eighteenth century and much of the nineteenth century.

1. Determine the harmonic rhythm.
2. Make a list of possible harmonizations for the melody using procedures outlined in chapter 8, "Harmonic Progressions."
3. Answer the questions immediately beneath the printed melody.
4. Compose a harmonization of the melody using block chords.
5. From the block chords, fashion an accompaniment that will accentuate the waltz characteristics of the melody.
6. Write for piano and/or any group of instruments (or voices) that are played by members of the class.
7. Be sure to include at least one or two leading tone seventh chords.
8. Avoid $^6_4$ chords except the cadential I$^6_4$.

Before answering the following questions, play this melody over several times at the tempo suggested.

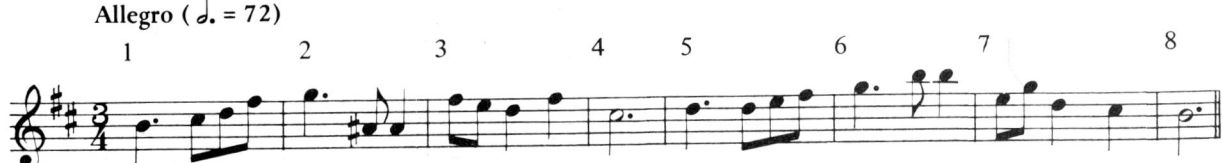

Questions concerning the preceding melody:

1. In a majority of measures, the obvious harmonic rhythm is (a) one chord per beat (b) one chord per measure (c) two chords per measure (d) one chord per two measures (e) two chords per beat.
2. The most obvious and natural harmonization for this melody is in the key of (a) D major (b) B minor modulating to G major (c) D major modulating to B minor (d) D Dorian mode (e) B minor.
3. Among the possibilities for the cadence ending the first phrase are *two* of the following *five*. Underline the two.
   a. Deceptive in B minor   d. Authentic in B minor
   b. Plagal in D major   e. Half in B minor
   c. Half in D major
4. Among the possibilities for the cadence ending the final (second) phrase are *three* of the following *five*. Underline the three.
   a. Authentic in D major
   b. Half in D major
   c. Deceptive in D major
   d. Deceptive in B minor
   e. Authentic in B minor
5. A vii°7 could be accommodated best in measure (a) 4 (b) 3 (c) 1 (d) 5 (e) 2.

ASSIGNMENT 3   Harmonize the following waltz melodies using the same procedure described in assignment 2. Employ a harmonic rhythm of one chord per measure. One or two exceptions can be made.

1. Allegro ($\dot{\fbox{}} = 72$)

2. Allegro ($\dot{\fbox{}} = 72$)

ASSIGNMENT 4   Write a composition.

1. Sixteen measures consisting of four, four-measure phrases.
2. Make the first and third phrases the same.
3. Second and fourth phrases may be of any relationship to the others.
4. Write in 9/8 meter and B-flat minor.
5. Include at least two or three leading tone seventh chords.
6. Write for piano or any group of instruments that are played by class members.

ASSIGNMENT 5   Write an original composition of any form you wish and for any combination of instruments you choose. The only restriction is that you demonstrate the conventional use of leading tone seventh chords.

HISTORICAL USE   The vii^{ø7} and the vii$^{°7}$ were treated in the various style periods as follows:

Renaissance   Both the vii^{ø7} and vii$^{°7}$ were so rare as to be virtually nonexistent in the Renaissance period.

Baroque   With the development of equal tempered tuning and the ascendency of the major and minor key systems, the leading tone seventh chords took their place as a basic part of the harmonic vocabulary of the Baroque period.

     The following excerpt is typical of the use of the vii$^{°7}$ during the middle and late Baroque. Types 1 and 3 were infrequent. Type 2 resolution prevailed.

Bach: *Wir Christenleut*
(We Christian People)

Chords reduced to simple position:

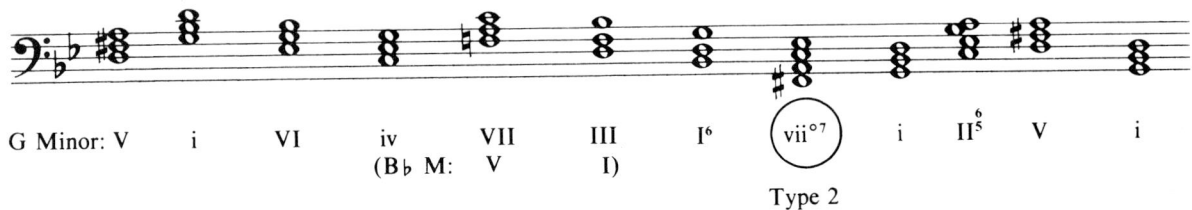

G Minor: V   i   VI   iv   VII   III   I⁶   vii°⁷   i   II⁶₅   V   i
              (B♭ M: V   I)   Type 2

Classical   The Classical period continued the use of the leading tone seventh chords with little change in stylistic application. The illustrations from Mozart and Beethoven are representative of the general treatment given these chords.

Mozart: *Piano Sonata in D Major* K. 284 (third movement)

D Major: I⁶₄   I   IV⁶₄   IV   vii⌀⁷   I   ii⁶   I⁶₄   V   I
                                   Type 2

The vii⌀⁷ and vii°⁷ Chords   199

Beethoven: *Piano Sonata* op. 13 (third movement)

C Minor: V⁷   vii°⁴₃
             Type 2

i⁶   *Gr⁶   i⁶₄   V   i

Romantic

The Romantic period saw a more relaxed and somewhat freer use of the leading tone seventh chords. Although more traditional and conservative applications continued in the majority, one of the more frequent nonresolutions involves successive diminished seventh chords.

The following example by Brahms illustrates three consecutive diminished seventh chords. Although the analysis symbols may not be understood for the present, the concept of nonresolution (type 3—the resolution note for the seventh of the chord is not present in the succeeding chord) is quite clear. Play the excerpt (or at least the reduced chords) on the piano, and note the tension that is not resolved until the final chord (V).

* German augmented sixth chord. Augmented sixth chords are included in chapter 11, volume 2.

Brahms: *Capriccio* op. 116 no. 7

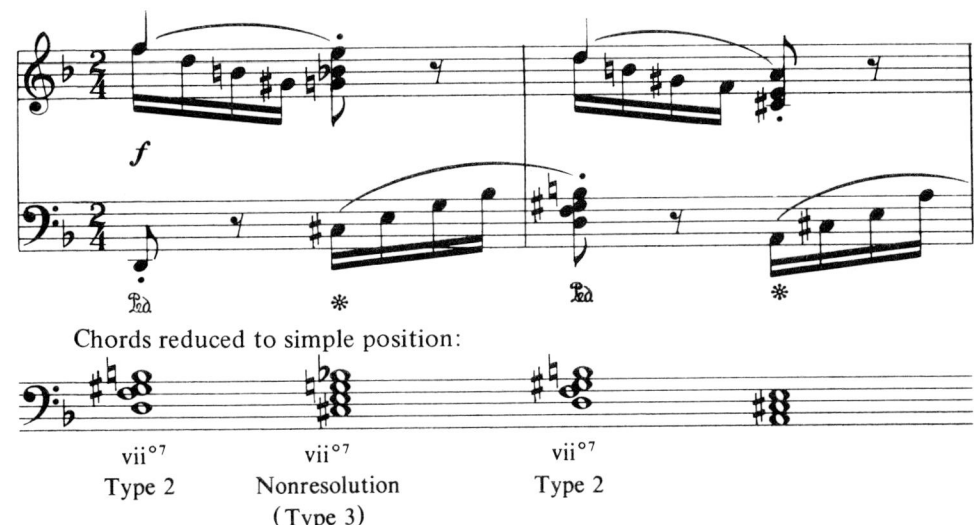

This excerpt illustrates the use of the vii°7 in major keys. The chord is borrowed from the parallel minor key.

Brahms: *Ballade* op. 10 no. 4

Post-Romantic and Impressionistic

The Post-Romantic and Impressionistic period saw continued free use of the leading tone seventh chords. During this period, the gradual abandonment of functional harmony brought about the end of the leading tone seventh chords although half-diminished and fully diminished seventh chords continued as sonorities (nonfunctional), and tertian harmony, organized in a new and different way, prevailed into the twentieth century.

The following excerpt by Debussy illustrates the use of the half-diminished seventh chord, substituting for dominant harmony, as part of the final cadence in an extended work. One plausible explanation considers the half-diminished seventh chord as a secondary dominant of V while the dominant chord itself is elided (passed over); thus, the progression vii⌀7/V to I.

Debussy: *Prélude a l'Après-midi d'un faune*

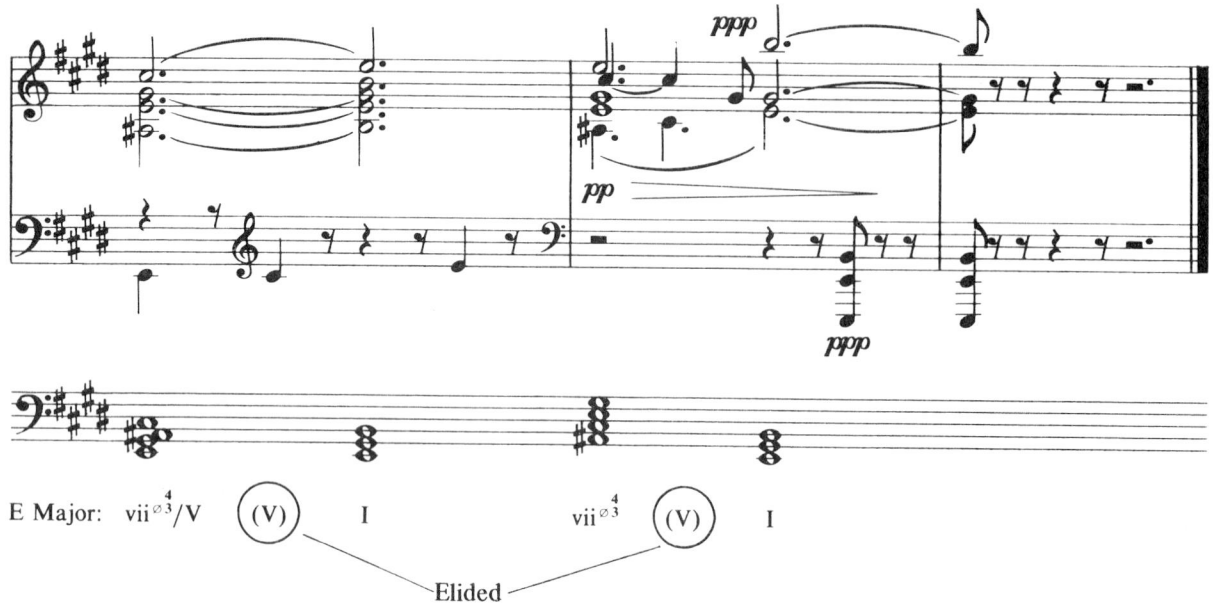

Miscellaneous   Although popular songs and jazz make a limited use of the leading tone seventh chords, ragtime, a popular style of the early twentieth century, employed such chords in greater frequency.

In this example, the leading tone seventh chord is a secondary dominant. In this style, most of the leading tone sevenths were of that type.

Johnson: *A Black Smoke Rag*

Copyright 1973. Published by Dover Publications, Inc., New York, N.Y. Used with permission.

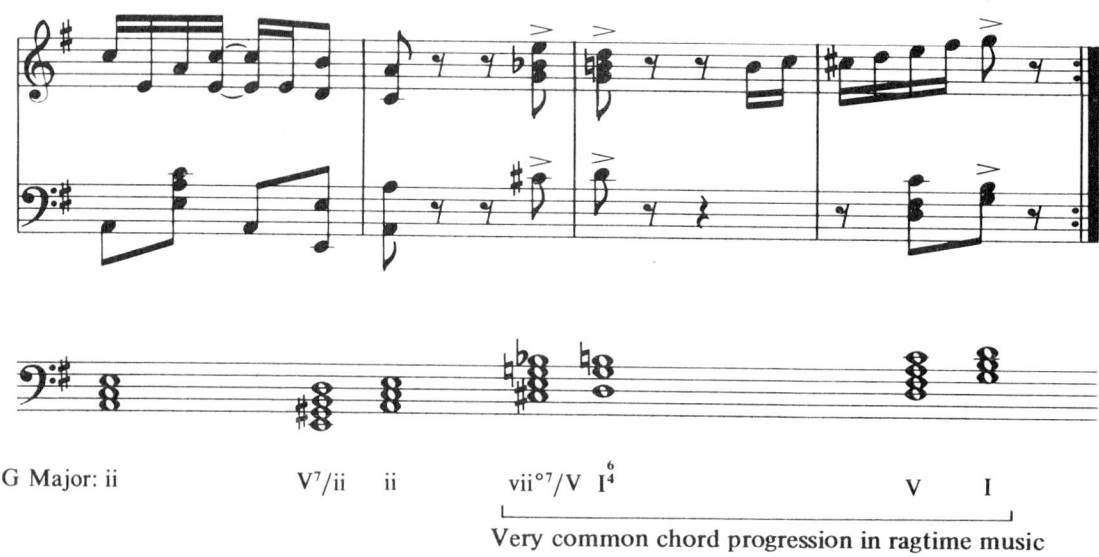

202   The vii$^{\o 7}$ and vii$^{\circ 7}$ Chords

13 Modulation

Modulation
*Common Chord
  Modulation*
Pivot Chord

Closely Related Keys
Static Modulation
Chromatic Modulation

Enharmonic Modulation
*Harmonizing Melodies
  that Modulate*

MODULATION

Modulation is a process by which a shift of tonal center is achieved. The term is generally related to music of a diatonic (key-centered) nature, but may also be applied to modality. It is applied to the common occurrence where a shift is made from one tonic to another. The first example of common chord modulation that follows, for instance, includes a modulation from C major to G major. The composition begins in C major, but toward the end of the phrase the strong root relationships cause a shift of the tonic to G major. The process of modulation undermines the first key (CM) and establishes a second or new key (GM).

Common Chord Modulation

Common chord modulation takes place through the use of chords that are common to both keys involved. The common chord, often called a *pivot chord,* becomes a sort of middle ground between the two keys.

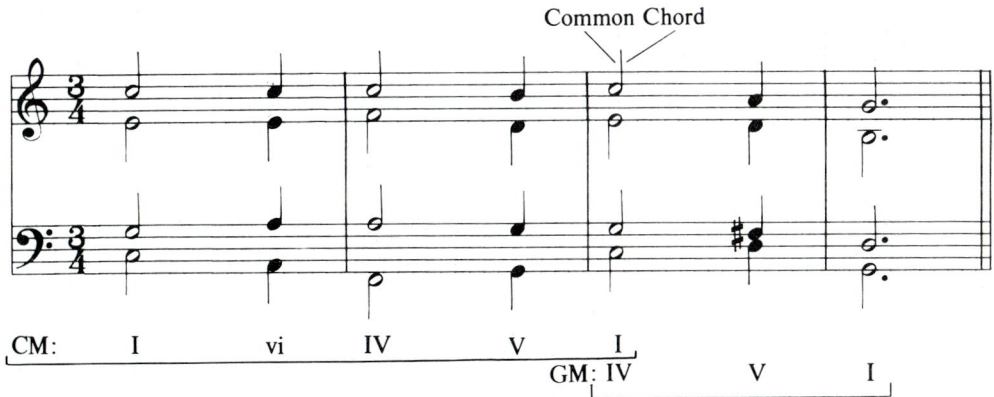

Related Keys
Modulation

Modulation often occurs between a key and any one of the five keys that have the largest number of chords in common with it. These *closely related keys* have either the same signature (relative minor or major) or signatures that contain one accidental (sharp or flat) more or less.

The following diagram shows C major and its closely related keys with the common chords numbered. Each major and minor key has five closely related keys.

203

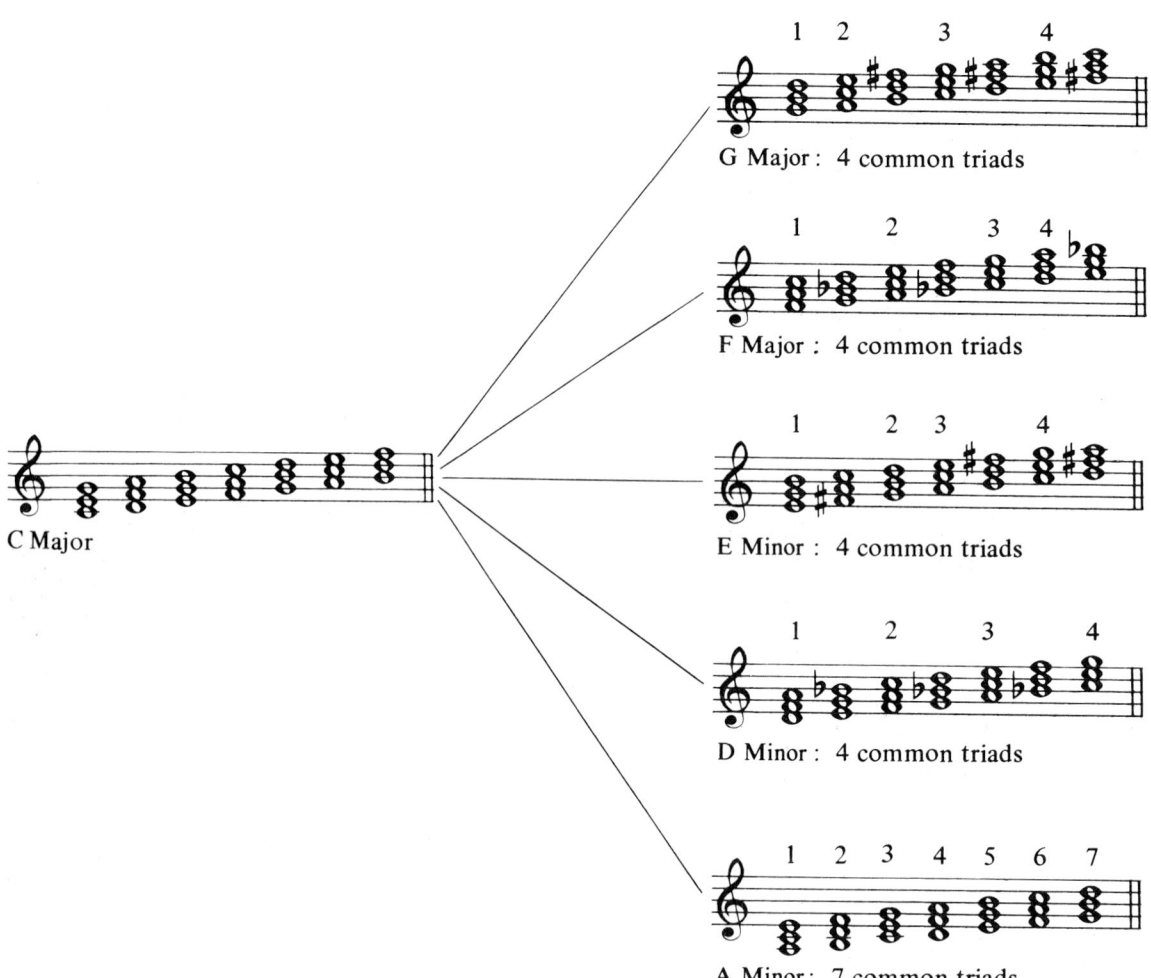

If the key is major, the closely related keys will be the dominant and subdominant and the relative minors of all three major keys. If the key is minor, the closely related keys will be the dominant and subdominant and the relative majors of all three minor keys. In figuring closely related keys, the natural form of the minor scale is used since it is the only one that conforms to the key signature.

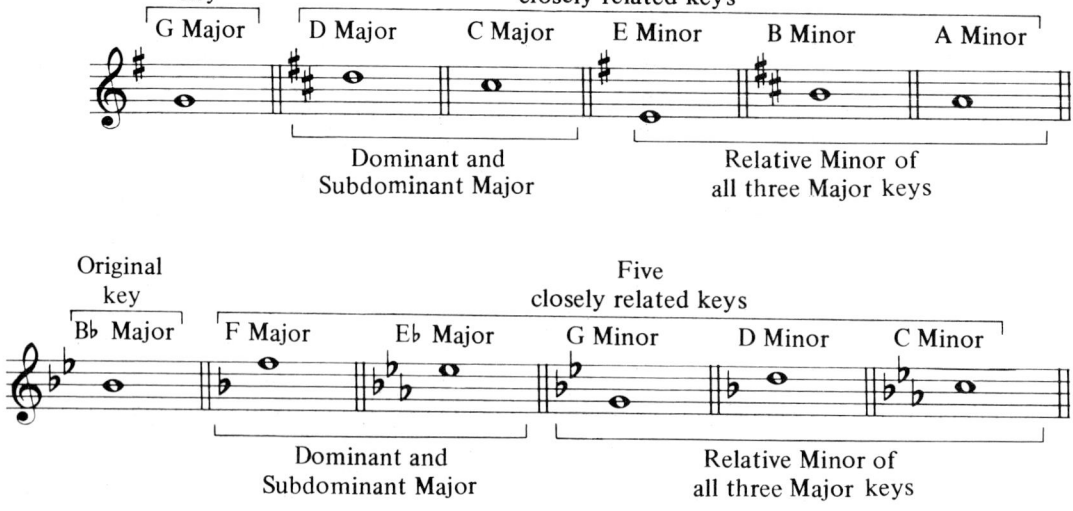

204 Modulation

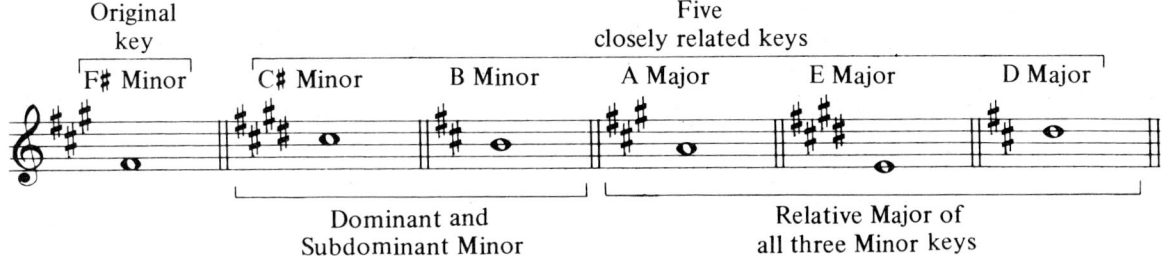

The following excerpt contains a common chord modulation from D major to A major. The triad B D F-sharp in measure 5 occurs diatonically in both keys. In D major it is the vi triad, and in A major it is the ii triad.

Mozart: *Piano Sonata in D Major* K. 284

On the next page is another illustration of a common chord modulation. The triad B D F-sharp in measure 6 is common to both D major and A major.

Modulation 205

Haydn: *Sonata in D Major*

Static Modulation

A *static modulation* takes place between phrases, between sections, or at other musically dormant places in a composition. An example is a phrase that ends in one key and a new phrase that begins in another. In the instance below, a static modulation (from E minor to C major) takes place between the two sections.

Mozart: *Sonata in A Major* K. 331 (third movement)

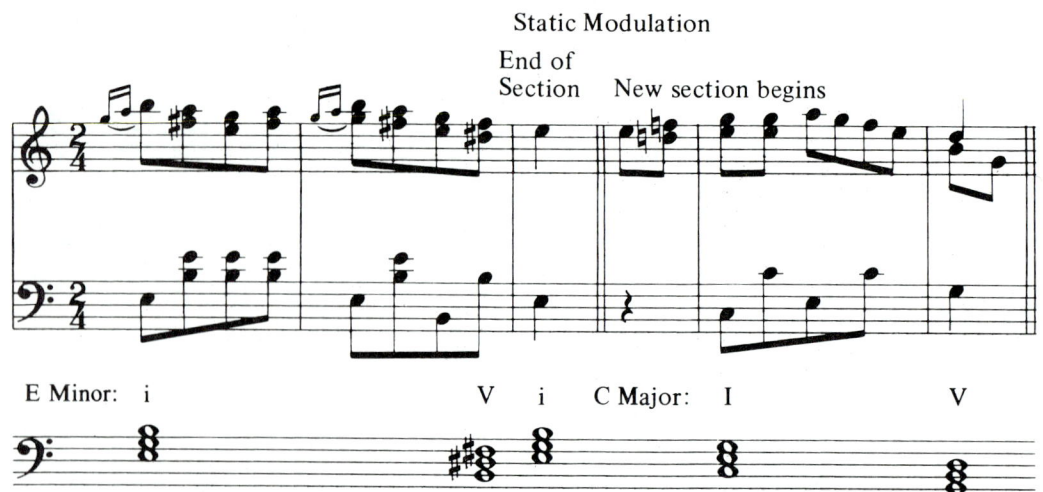

Chromatic Modulation A *chromatic modulation* occurs at the point of a chromatic progression (a progression that involves the chromatic inflection of one of the chord tones). The letter name must remain the same in a chromatic progression—for example, C in the first chord progresses to C-sharp in the next—and this need not always be in the same voice. The following is a simplified example.

Chromatic Progression

An example of a chromatic modulation between F major and D minor follows. As will be noted, there is no possibility of a common chord since the sudden inflection prevents it.

Bach: *Du grosser Schmerzensmann*
(Thou Great Man of Sorrow)

Chromatic Modulation

No Common Chord

The *common chord modulation* is generally smooth and develops so gradually that the listener is most often unaware of a modulation at all. The chromatic modulation, on the other hand, is somewhat less so and on occasion actually calls attention to the fact of modulation. The following excerpt contains a chromatic modulation by Schubert. The D major triad in measure 4 progresses suddenly to an F major triad, which is not its usual inclination.

Schubert: *Waltz* op. 27 no. 12

G Minor: iv   V$^4_3$ i^6 V

B♭ Major: V^7 I   V^7 I

Enharmonic Modulation

Enharmonic modulation is a rare type of modulation in which enharmonic spellings are used to effect a common chord or a chromatic modulation. In the illustration that follows, a diminished seventh chord is spelled enharmonically to effect a modulation to a *foreign* (distant) key.

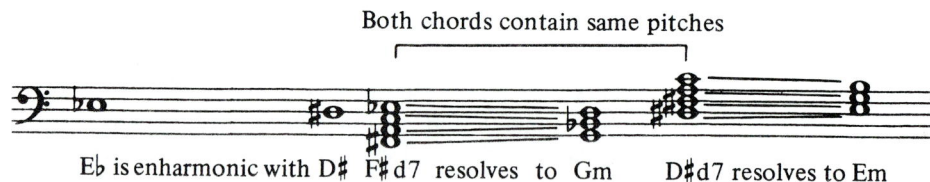

Both chords contain same pitches

E♭ is enharmonic with D♯   F♯d7 resolves to Gm   D♯d7 resolves to Em

Beethoven: *Sonata* op. 13 (*Pathétique*)

Chords reduced to root position:

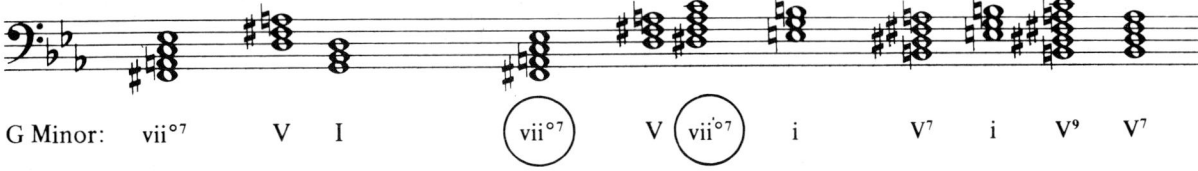

G Minor: vii°7   V   I   vii°7   V   vii°7   i   V7   i   V9   V7

ASSIGNMENT 1   The following six sets of progressions were taken from music literature of the Late Romantic period. All were extracted and reduced to four-part progressions.

1. Write the chords in simple position on the blanks provided.
2. Analyze each chord.
3. Since each set modulates, indicate the following:
   a. The type of modulation:
      (1) common chord
      (2) static
      (3) chromatic
      (4) enharmonic
   b. If the modulation is of the common chord type, circle the common, or pivot, chord and be sure to analyze it in *both* keys.
   c. If it is a chromatic, static, or enharmonic modulation, simply indicate the new key and continue analyzing in the new key.

Modulation 209

ASSIGNMENT 1 (continued)

4. How to spot a modulation:
   a. By all means play the music you are analyzing. Sometimes this is a sufficient way in itself for you to recognize modulations.
   b. Look for accidentals or pitches that are not a part of the established key.
   c. Look for a cadence in a new key. If it can be analyzed as V-I, I-V, IV-V, or some other recognized cadence in a different key (from the established), then trace back to the point of modulation and analyze in the new key from there on.
   d. After you have found enough evidence to support a new key, look back to the first occurrence of a nondiatonic note (one that is not a scale tone in the established key) and determine if the chord preceding it could be analyzed in both keys (the established and the new key). If so, then you have discovered a *common chord* modulation.
   e. If the first nondiatonic note is taken chromatically (has the same letter name but different pitch in the preceding chord), then the modulation is *chromatic*.
   f. If the change of key occurs after the cadence of a section, the modulation is considered *static*.
   g. If a nondiatonic note (in the established key) has the same pitch but a different spelling (such as A-flat = G-sharp), then the modulation is *enharmonic*. Enharmonic modulations often occur through the respelling of a diminished seventh chord.

210   Modulation

ASSIGNMENT 1 (continued)

ASSIGNMENT 2

Following are two short excerpts from music literature.

1. Write the chords in simple position on the blank staves provided.
2. Analyze each chord and indicate the modulations as described in this chapter.
3. See assignment 1 for suggestions about analyzing modulations.
4. Have a class member play each excerpt.
5. Discuss in class the harmonic rhythm and the relationship of the phrases.

Schubert: *Variations on a Theme by Hüttenbrenner* no. 13

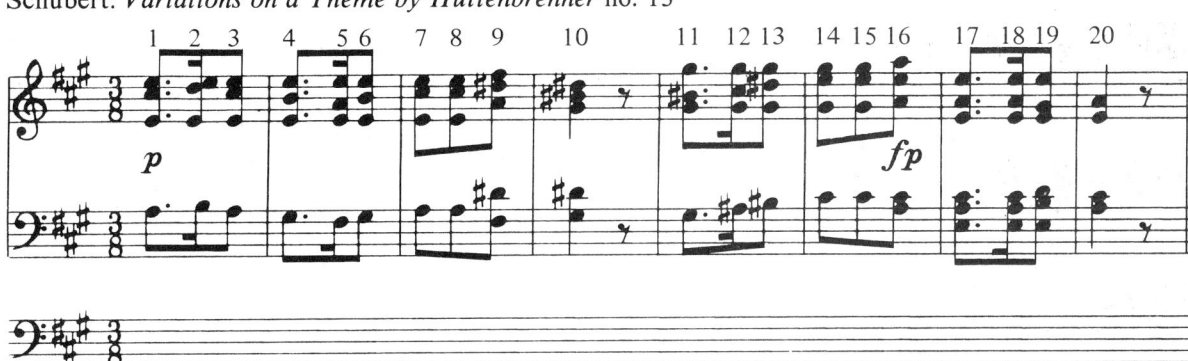

AM:

Schubert: *Impromptu* op. 90 no. 1

Cm: iv^7

*Seventh chord built on fourth scale degree

Modulation   211

ASSIGNMENT 2 (continued)

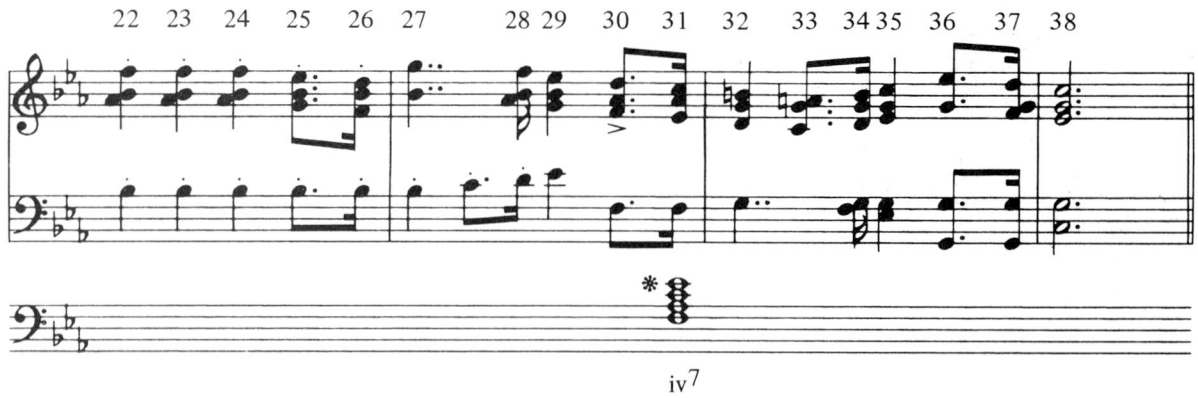

*Seventh chord built on fourth scale degree

ASSIGNMENT 3 Following is a complete chorale harmonization by Bach.

1. Write the chords in simple position on the blank staves provided. A few chords are analyzed for you—some are chords not studied yet.
2. Analyze each chord and indicate modulations as described in this chapter. Some helpful hints are suggested in assignment 1.
3. The phrases in this composition are set off by fermata.
4. Sing the composition in class and have one of the students direct the performance.
5. Discuss the key relationships present.

Bach: *Nun preiset alle Gottes Barmherzigkeit*
(Now Let All Praise God's Mercy)

212 Modulation

ASSIGNMENT 3 (continued)

*Seventh chord built on fourth scale degree

‡ Seventh chord built on second scale degree

ASSIGNMENT 4   On the following page is a complete composition by Schubert. The title *Ecossaise* means a Scottish dance that is rather fast in $\frac{2}{4}$ meter and was popular in Europe during the late eighteenth and early nineteenth century.

1. Write the chords in simple position on the blank staff provided.
2. Measures 9 through 14 and 41 through 44 have been analyzed for you since they contain chords described in chapter 15. For the present, ignore these measures.
3. Analyze each chord and indicate modulations as described in this chapter.
4. Have one of the pianists in the class play the *Ecossaise.*
5. Discuss the key relationships present, and name the types of modulation.

Modulation   213

ASSIGNMENT 4 (continued)

Schubert: *Ecossaise in A-flat*

ASSIGNMENT 4 (continued)

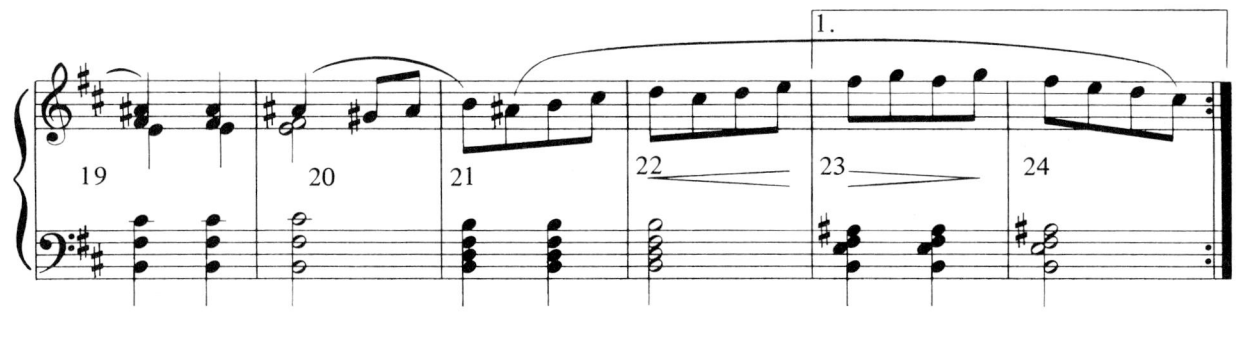

ASSIGNMENT 4 (continued)

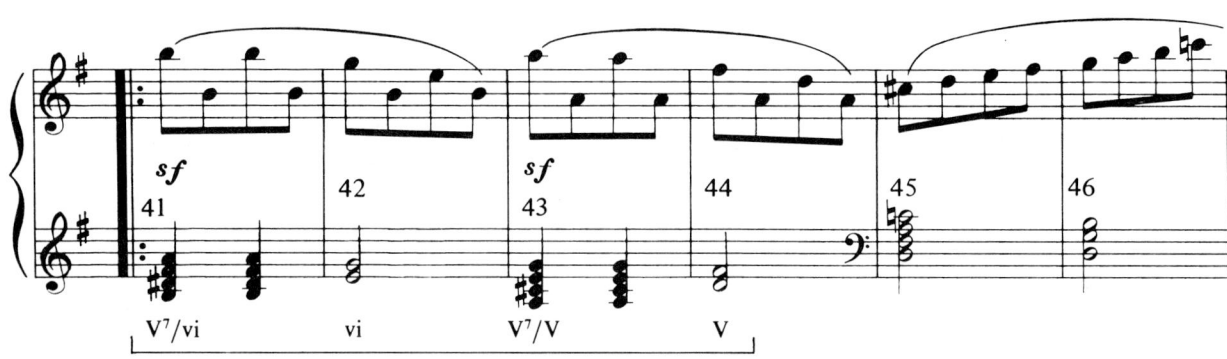

216 Modulation

ASSIGNMENT 4 (continued)

Modulation 217

ASSIGNMENT 4 (continued)

| **HARMONIZING MELODIES THAT MODULATE** | The following suggestions will be helpful in harmonizing melodies that modulate. The same procedure should be followed for melodies that modulate as for those that do not. This procedure is described in chapter 8, "Harmonic Progression." To illustrate the technique, two phrases of the chorale tune, *Keinen hat Gott verlassen* (God Has Forsaken No One), are harmonized here to show each step of the process. |

1. First, determine the harmonic rhythm, and write out the possible harmonizations beneath the melody.
2. Analyze the cadences for all possible formulas (authentic, deceptive, half, and plagal) in all possible keys. Since this is a chorale melody, it lends itself best to modulations of the closely related type. It may be assumed for the moment that the melody could be harmonized in G major, E minor, or a combination of both.

ORIGINAL KEY	CLOSELY RELATED KEYS
G Major	D Major, C Major, E Minor, B Minor, A Minor
E Minor	D Major, C Major, G Major, B Minor, A Minor

218 Modulation

Keinen hat Gott verlassen
(God Has Forsaken No One)

Chorale

The first cadence supports any of the following formulas. It should be pointed out, however, that the cadence in E minor is without the raised seventh and will sound somewhat modal in character. Three possibilities for the first cadence:

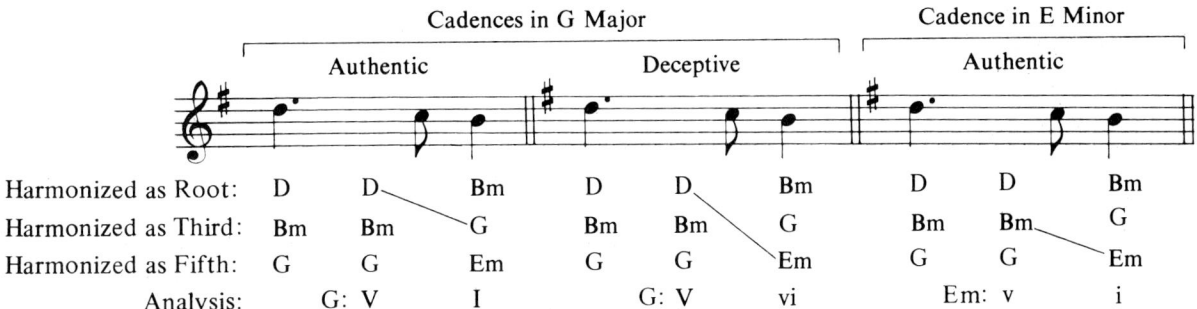

These same cadences in four-part harmony:

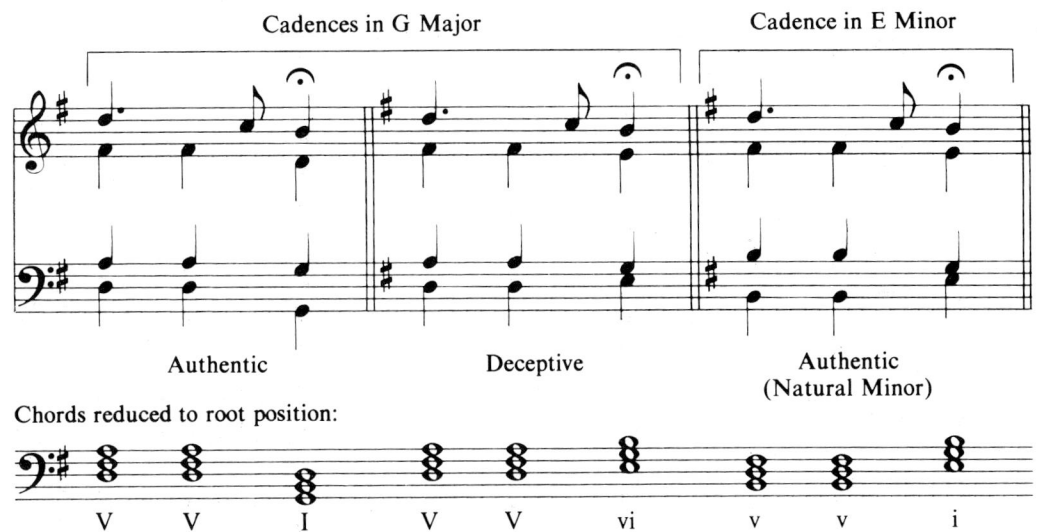

Five possibilities for the second cadence:

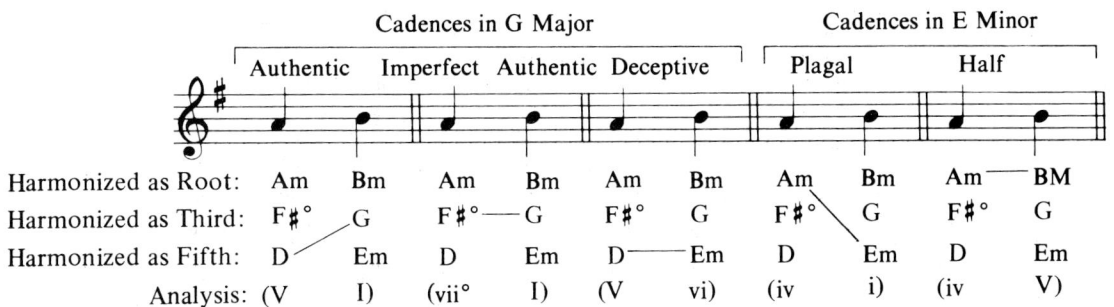

These same cadences in four-part harmony:

Chords reduced to root position:

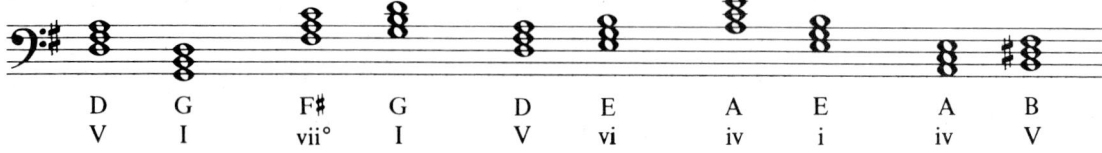

The entire two phrases along with possible harmonizations and circle progressions marked are shown here. The roots of possible triads are expressed in letters first to avoid possible entanglements in key systems. Then, all three possible harmonies for each melody tone are converted to keys of G major and E minor. The following, then, displays the possible chords in two keys and indicates the possibilities for modulation.

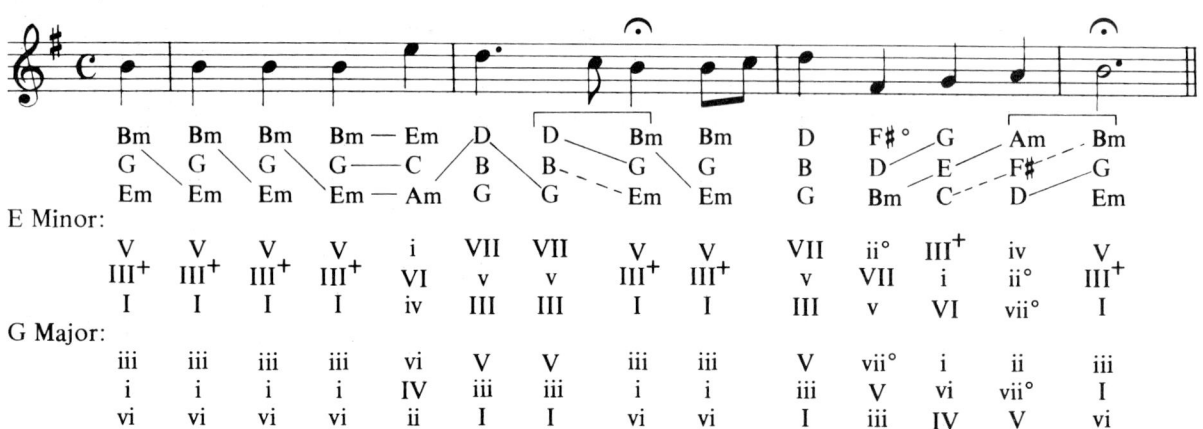

3. Play the chorale melody on the piano and accompany it (using block chords) with several combinations from the above possibilities. When a selection has been made, follow the procedures described in chapter 8, "Harmonic Progression," fashioning a compatible bass line, adding the remaining voices, and finally inserting appropriate nonharmonic tones. The following suggestions will assist in making good choices:
   a. Remember that the descending P5 progression involving dominant and tonic harmony is important in establishing a key and should be included in a set of progressions designed to identify and substantiate a new tonal center.
   b. For the present it is desirable to include at least one chord common to both keys just before the new key is to be initiated.
   c. Start your selection of chords with the cadence and work backwards, if necessary, to establish a smooth set of progressions.

From the previous information, two harmonizations were made by students. The first conceives the entire melody in G major while the second begins in E minor, modulates to G major, then returns to E minor:

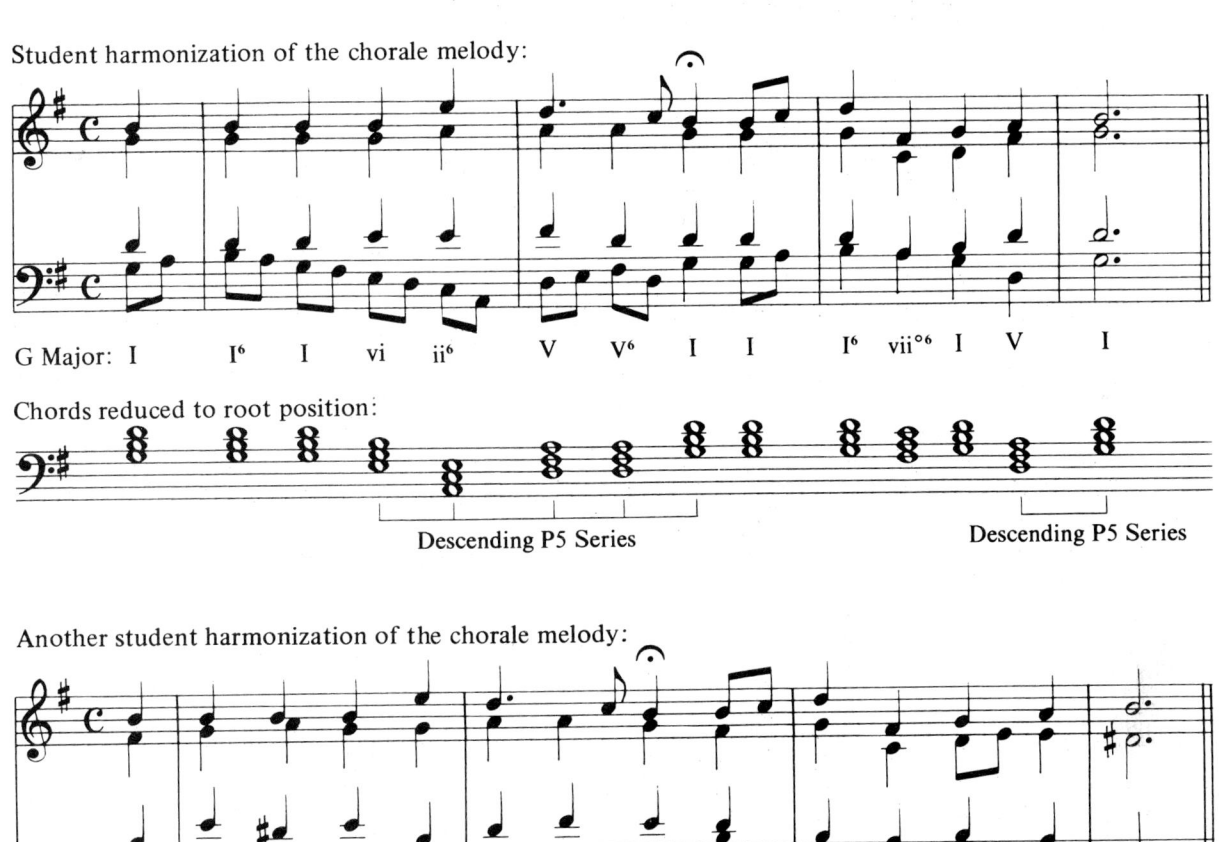

Finally, the harmonization of these two phrases by J. S. Bach is presented for comparison:

Bach harmonization of the same chorale melody:

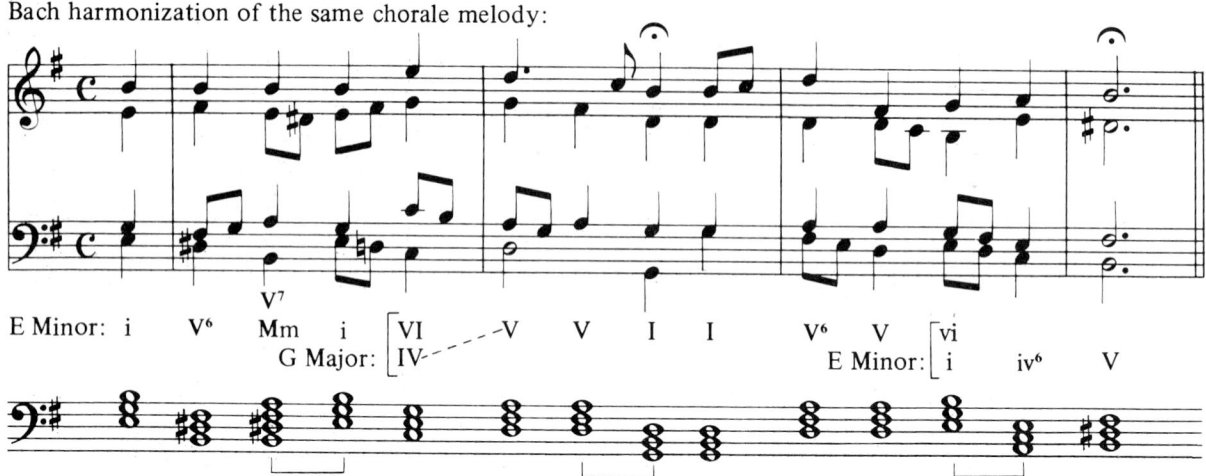

ASSIGNMENT 5 Following are five excerpts from Protestant chorale melodies that were harmonized by J. S. Bach as well as other composers of the Baroque period. Melody notes are numbered for convenience in class discussions.

1. Using the procedures outlined in this chapter, prepare two harmonizations for each of the following excerpts. Make at least one modulation in each.
2. Complete these in four voices (soprano given, alto, tenor, and bass).
3. Select a harmonic rhythm of one chord per beat (quarter note).
4. Play the harmonizations in class. The students should select the most appropriate.
5. Arrange a few of the harmonizations for a quartet of instruments that are played by class members. Perform these in class.

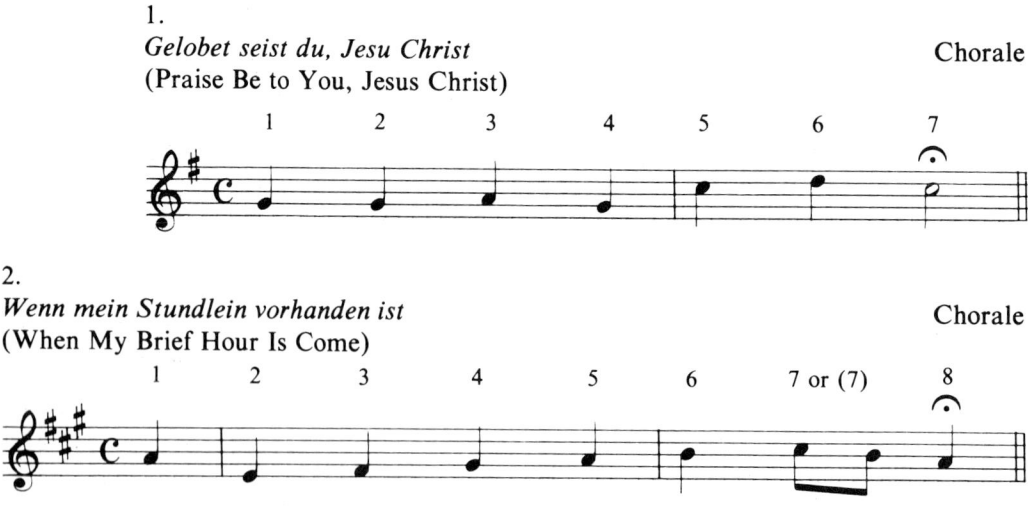

222 Modulation

ASSIGNMENT 5 (continued)

3.
Mit Fried' und Freud' ich fahr' dahin
(With Peace and Joy I Journey Thither) — Chorale

4.
Freu' dich sehr, O meine Seele
(Rejoice, My Soul) — Chorale

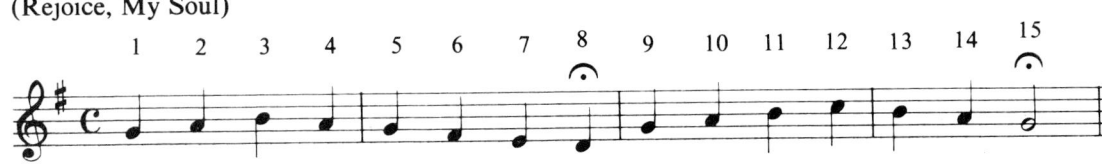

5.
O haupt voll Blut und Wunden
(Oh Head, Bloody and Wounded) — Chorale

ASSIGNMENT 6   Following are four excerpts from instrumental music of the Classical period.

1. Using the procedures outlined in this chapter, prepare two harmonizations for each of the exercises.
2. These may be completed in any texture and for any media you wish. If you are a pianist, write for the piano idiom. If you are an instrumentalist, use the given melody as your solo part and write a piano (or instrumental) accompaniment, etc.
3. Play the melody over several times, and select the harmonic rhythm to suit your taste.
4. Play your completed work in class. The students should select the most appropriate.
5. Be sure to add all interpretation marks, phrasings, tempo indications, etc.

1.

Modulation   223

ASSIGNMENT 6 (continued)

224 Modulation

14 Nondominant Seventh Chords

Seventh Chord Analysis Symbols:
    Major Mode: I^7 ii^7 iii^7 IV^7 vi^7
    Natural Minor Mode: i^7 $ii^{\varnothing 7}$ III^7 iv^7 VI^7
    Harmonic Minor Mode: i^7_M $ii^{\varnothing 7}$ III^{+7}_M iv^7 VI^7
    Melodic Minor Mode: i^7_M ii^7 III^{+7}_M IV^7_m $vi^{\varnothing 7}$

Resolution of Nondominant Seventh Chords
Type 1: Circle Resolution
Type 2: Noncircle Resolution
Type 3: Nonresolution
VI^7 in Minor
Part-writing
Harmonizing a Melody

NONDOMINANT SEVENTH CHORDS

Nondominant seventh chords do not have dominant function. Eliminating only the dominant (V^7) and leading tone seventh chords ($vii^{\varnothing 7}$ and $vii°^7$), the nondominant category includes tonic, supertonic, mediant, subdominant, and submediant sevenths.

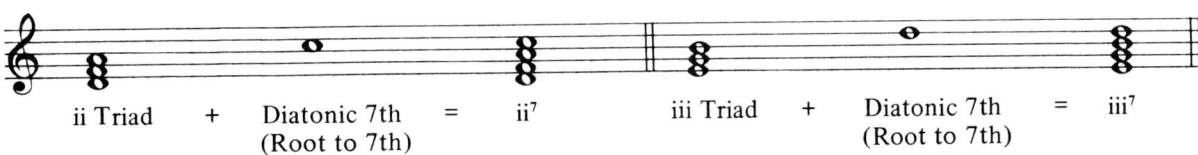

ii Triad + Diatonic 7th = ii^7 iii Triad + Diatonic 7th = iii^7
          (Root to 7th)   (Root to 7th)

Since melodic and rhythmic activity may cause sevenths to appear as nonharmonic tones, it is often difficult to decide whether a dissonant tone is really a member of the chord or merely the result of melodic or rhythmic activity. Duration and accent (importance) are usually the determining factors.

In the excerpt on the following page, for example, is the seventh a chord tone or a nonharmonic tone?

Carissimi: *Sventura, Cuor Mio*
(Misfortune, My Heart)

Analysis Symbols   The directions for writing analysis symbols for seventh chords are found on page 176 of chapter 11, "The Major-Minor Dominant Seventh Chord." The following chart provides all nondominant seventh chord symbols and their meaning:

	SCALE	SOUND
I^7	MAJOR ONLY	MAJOR TRIAD AND MAJOR SEVENTH
i^7	NATURAL MINOR ONLY	MINOR TRIAD AND MINOR SEVENTH
i^7_M	HARMONIC AND MELODIC MINOR	MINOR TRIAD AND MAJOR SEVENTH
ii^7	MAJOR AND MELODIC MINOR	MINOR TRIAD AND MINOR SEVENTH
$ii^{\varnothing 7}$	NATURAL AND HARMONIC MINOR	DIMINISHED TRIAD AND MINOR SEVENTH
iii^7	MAJOR ONLY	MINOR TRIAD AND MINOR SEVENTH
III^7	NATURAL MINOR ONLY	MAJOR TRIAD AND MAJOR SEVENTH
III^{+7}_M	HARMONIC AND MELODIC MINOR	AUGMENTED TRIAD AND MAJOR SEVENTH
IV^7	MAJOR ONLY	MAJOR TRIAD AND MAJOR SEVENTH
iv^7	NATURAL AND HARMONIC MINOR	MINOR TRIAD AND MINOR SEVENTH

	SCALE	SOUND
IV^7_m	MELODIC MINOR	MAJOR TRIAD AND MINOR SEVENTH
vi^7	MAJOR ONLY	MINOR TRIAD AND MINOR SEVENTH
VI^7	NATURAL AND HARMONIC MINOR	MAJOR TRIAD AND MAJOR SEVENTH
$vi^{ø7}$	MELODIC MINOR	DIMINISHED TRIAD AND MINOR SEVENTH

Seventh chord analysis — Major Key

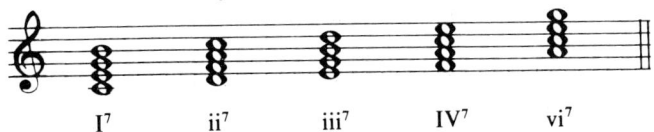

$I^7 \quad ii^7 \quad iii^7 \quad IV^7 \quad vi^7$

Seventh chord analysis — Harmonic Minor Key

$i^7_M \quad ii^{ø7} \quad III^{+7}_M \quad iv^7 \quad VI^7$

Some of the chords in the previous example are found very seldom in music literature. The following chart presents the comparative use of diatonic seventh chords:

SEVENTH CHORD	COMPARATIVE USE
V^7	By far the most frequently found—more than all other seventh chord types combined.
ii^7 AND $ii^{ø7}$	Found often especially in the cadence formula: ii^6_5 to I^6_4 to V to I or $ii^{ø6}_5$ to i^6_4 to V to i
iii^7, III^7, AND III^{+7}_M IV^7, iv^7, AND IV^7_m vi^7, VI^7, AND $vi^{ø7}$	Found only occasionally in the Baroque period except in sequences. Frequency increases during the Romantic and Impressionistic periods.

Resolutions

As with the major-minor dominant seventh chord (V^7), the nondominant sevenths also have three possible treatments.

Circle Progressions

Type 1. Circle progressions with resolution of the seventh:

1. The root of the seventh chord and the root of the chord that follows it lie in descending P5 relationship.
2. The seventh factor of the seventh chord resolves one scale degree down to the third of the following chord. In traditional four-voice writing, this resolution occurs in the same voice as the seventh, but in piano or other broken styles, the resolution of the seventh may be shifted to another voice.

Type 1 (circle) progressions from nondominant seventh chords:

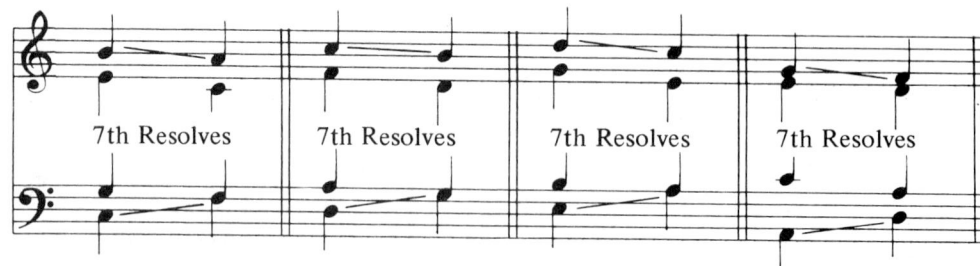

Roots in descending P5 relationships

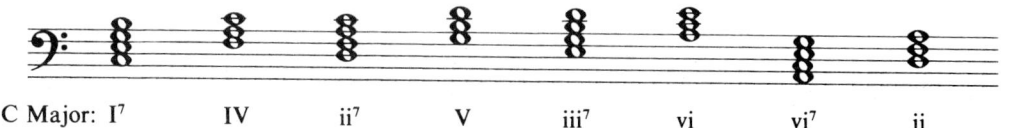

C Major: I⁷   IV   ii⁷   V   iii⁷   vi   vi⁷   ii

The tonic, supertonic, mediant, and submediant seventh chords typically progress according to type 1 specifications.

Type 1 (circle) progressions from inverted nondominant seventh chords:

C Major: ii⁶₅   V   iii⁴₃   vi   vi⁴₂   ii⁶   I⁶₅   IV

Basic: ii⁷   V   iii⁷   vi   vi⁷   ii   I⁷   IV

Pergolesi

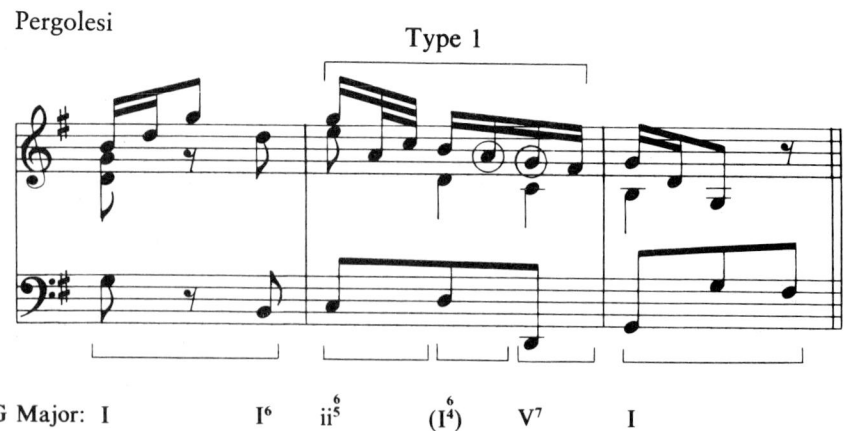

G Major: I   I⁶   ii⁶₅   (I⁶₄)   V⁷   I

Bach

E Minor: i   v⁶   iv⁶   vii°$^4_2$ VI   i$^6_4$ ii$^{{\o}6}_{5}$ V   i

Kuhlau

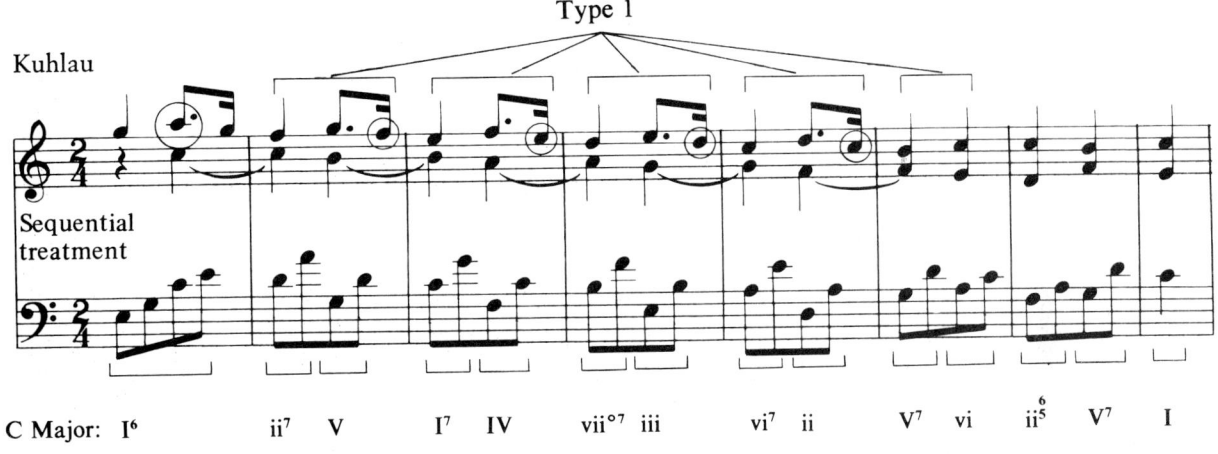

C Major: I⁶   ii⁷   V   I⁷   IV   vii°⁷   iii   vi⁷   ii   V⁷   vi   ii$^6_5$ V⁷   I

ASSIGNMENT 1   Each note is the root of a nondominant seventh chord. Write the chord requested on the staff in simple position. The example illustrates proper procedure.

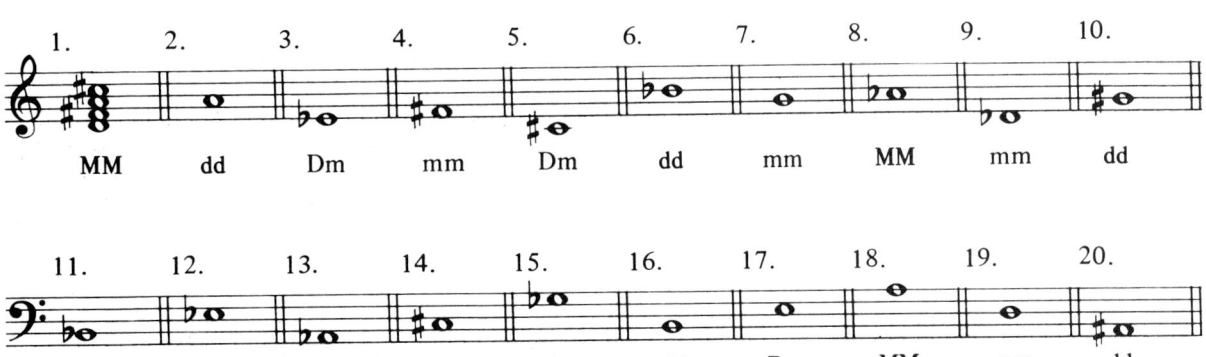

ASSIGNMENT 2   Each given chord is a nondominant seventh in four-part harmony.

1. In the space provided, write the resolution of each given chord on the staff in four parts.
2. Resolve the seventh factor of each seventh chord down one diatonic step to the third of the following chord.

Nondominant Seventh Chords   229

ASSIGNMENT 2 (continued)

3. The root of the second chord should be a descending P5 from the root of the given chord.
4. Observe all part-writing procedures found in Appendix 2.
5. Analyze both chords in each exercise in the key indicated (numbers 1 through 5). Numbers 6 through 10 list no key. From the key signature and the quality of the given seventh chord, you should be able to figure out the key for yourself.
6. The example illustrates correct procedure.

Noncircle Progressions with Resolution

Type 2. Noncircle progressions with resolution:

1. The nondominant seventh chord proceeds to a chord whose root lies a second above or a third below its root.
2. The seventh factor of the seventh chord resolves one scale degree down to a chord tone of the following chord. In traditional four-voice writing, this resolution occurs in the same voice as the seventh, but in piano or other broken styles, the resolution of the seventh may be shifted to another voice.

The subdominant seventh chord (IV^7 or iv^7) is seldom given a type 1 treatment since the resolution chord ($vii°$) is not only a diminished triad but it also lies an A4 above (d5 below). Thus, the IV^7 or iv^7 generally take a type 2 resolution.

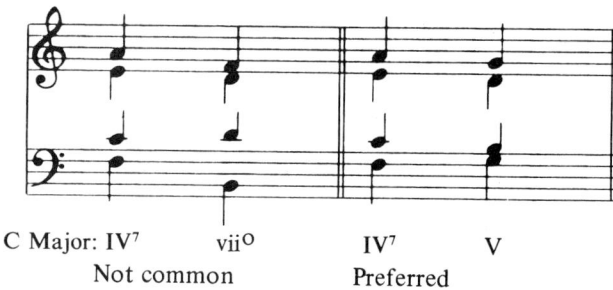

C Major: IV^7 $vii°$ IV^7 V
    Not common   Preferred

230   Nondominant Seventh Chords

ASSIGNMENT 3	Each composition is a phrase of a chorale melody with bass and figured bass added. All were harmonized by Bach.

1. Add the alto and the tenor as required by the figured bass. Remember that figured bass numbers indicate intervals above the bass note.
2. Use the part-writing procedures described in Appendix 2. The three in this chapter appear on pages 233–34.
3. Sing each phrase in class.
4. Arrange the exercises for a quartet of instruments played by class members.

In phrase 1, the second eighth note in each group is a passing tone. Do not harmonize nonharmonic tones. The numbers above the staves represent the part-writing procedures on pages 233 and 234.

1.
Bach: *O Ewigkeit, du Donnerwort*
(O Eternity, Thou Word of Thunder)

2.
Bach: *Herzlich tut mich verlangen*
(I Desire Sincerely a Blessed Ending)

Analysis: __ __ __ __ __ __ __ __ __ __ __ __

3.
Bach: *Allein zu dir, Herr Jesu Christ*
(Only in Thee, Lord Jesus Christ)

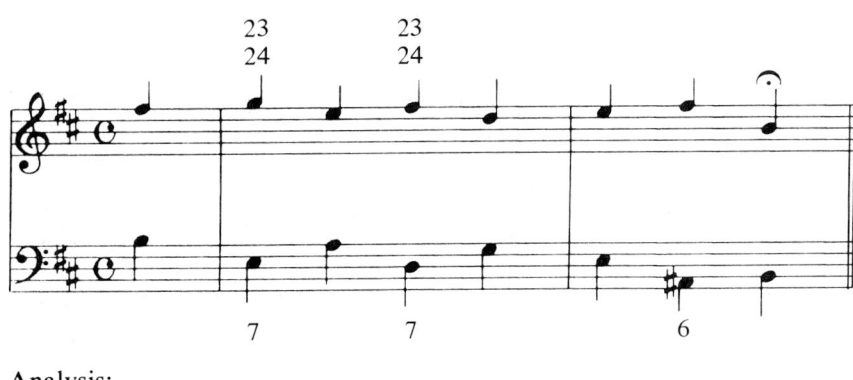

Analysis: __ __ __ __ __ __ __ __

ASSIGNMENT 3 (continued)

Phrase 4 below contains a modulation. Begin in G major. The last figured bass numbers $\begin{smallmatrix}8\\7\\3\end{smallmatrix}$ indicates a seventh chord with the fifth factor missing—a departure from part-writing procedure no. 24. Always include all the factors in seventh chords unless the figured bass decrees otherwise.

4.
Bach: *Meine Seele erhebet den Herrn*
(My Soul Exalts the Lord)

Analysis: __ __ __ __ __ __ __ __ __ __

ASSIGNMENT 4

Following is a complete chorale melody harmonization by Bach.

1. On the blank staff beneath each score, write the chords in simple position. When the chords are in inversion, write the simple position in inversion also.
2. Analyze each chord below the blank staff.
3. Indicate the resolution of each nondominant seventh chord—type 1, 2, or 3.
4. Discuss the modulations. Indicate whether these are common chord, chromatic, enharmonic, or static.
5. Discuss the form of this composition.
6. Enumerate the harmonic vocabulary used in the work.
7. Divide the class into four sections (soprano, alto, tenor, and bass) and sing the chorale. Have a conducting major conduct the performance.
8. Arrange the composition for four instruments that are played by members of the class, and have them perform it.

In measure 7 of the following chorale, the chord results from the use of the melodic minor scale. (See page 227).

236 Nondominant Seventh Chords

ASSIGNMENT 4 (continued)

Bach: *Jesu, du mein liebstes Leben*
(Jesus, Thou, My Dearest Life)

*This major-minor sound is created through the use of the melodic minor scale.

ASSIGNMENT 4 (continued)

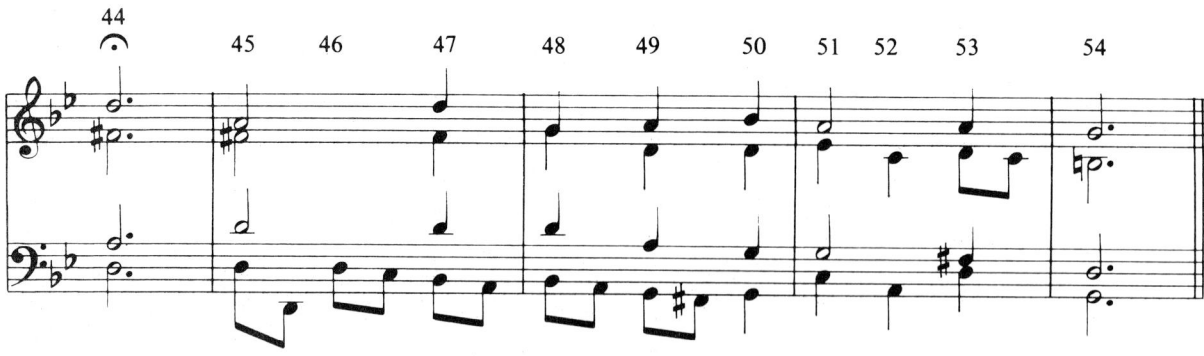

| **Harmonizing Nondominant Seventh Chords** | To harmonize a melody with nondominant seventh chords, simply add the possibilities of a seventh factor to all nondominant triads. To demonstrate the procedure, the first phrase of a chorale melody is harmonized here: |

1. Circled letters indicate tonic or dominant tones in the most obvious key. This does not rule out possibilities for modulation.
2. Solid lines connecting letters indicate descending P5 progressions.
3. Dotted lines connecting letters indicate descending P5 progressions that cannot be used either because the seventh factor of the seventh chord cannot resolve properly into the next chord or because the interval of the descending P5 is diminished.

Bach: *Sei gegrüsset, Jesu gütig*   Chorale
(Hear My Pleading, Holy Jesus)

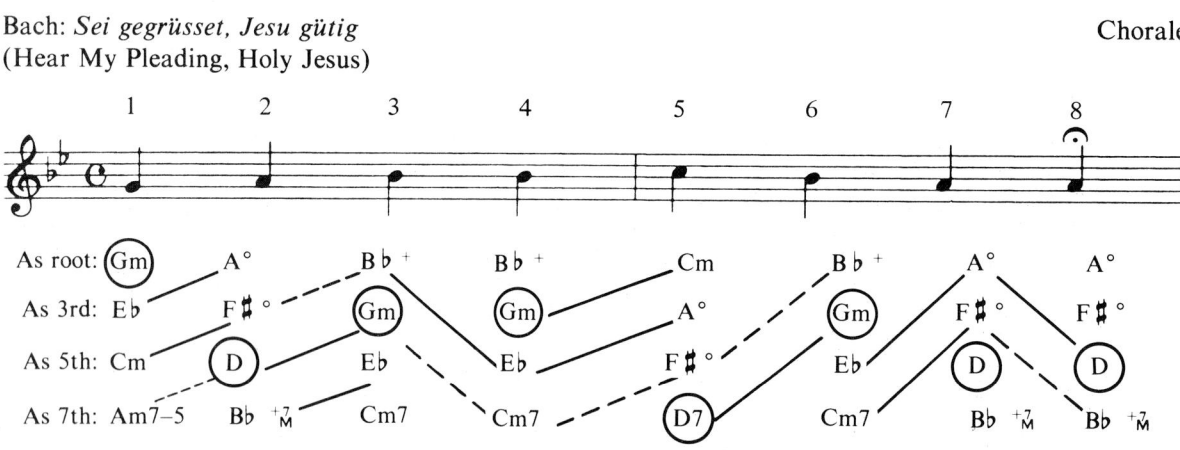

ASSIGNMENT 5

Select a harmonization of the Bach melody, *Sei gegrüsset, Jesu gütig*. Familiarize yourself with the potential chord selections in the previous phrase by answering the following questions.

Considering only the possibilities explored in the phrase of the Bach melody:

1. The melody can be harmonized entirely with (a) descending P5 progressions, (b) major triads, (c) tonic and dominant harmony in G minor, (d) tonic and dominant harmony in C minor, (e) minor triads.

ASSIGNMENT 5 (continued)

2. The two melody tones at the cadence (notes 7 and 8) could support an authentic cadence in (a) C minor (b) E-flat major (c) G minor (d) D minor (e) B-flat major.
3. Considering every melody tone as the seventh factor of a seventh chord, proper resolution of the seventh factor (in the soprano voice) could occur only when the seventh chords occur at (a) notes 5 and 6 only; (b) notes 1, 2, and 3; (c) notes 4, 5, and 6; (d) notes 6 and 7 only; (e) notes 2 and 3 only.
4. If a Cm7 chord (iv^7 in G minor) were placed at note 6, it would have (a) a type 1 treatment, (b) to be followed by a supertonic triad, (c) a type 3 treatment, (d) to be in root position, (e) a type 2 treatment.
5. The diatonic vii°^{7} (in G minor) would fit well at two places in this composition. These are at: (a) notes 3 and 4, (b) notes 2 and 5, (c) notes 2 and 4, (d) notes 5 and 7, (e) notes 3 and 5.

Here is one possible selection. It leans heavily toward the tonic and dominant and includes one nondominant seventh chord.

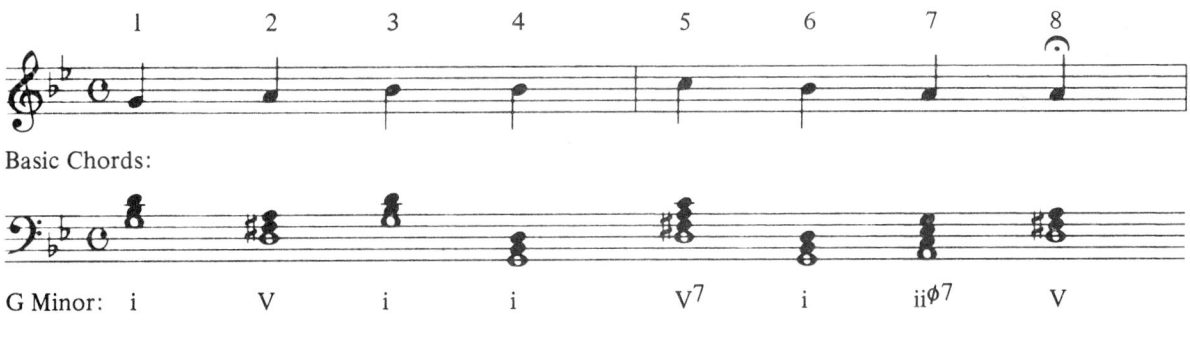

A bass line created only through the use of chord roots is too angular, lacks direction, and does not allow for the full potential of musical shaping. Thus, the bass line in the following excerpts, reduces the angularity to one leap and permits a directional line (stepwise) from the fourth note through the eighth.

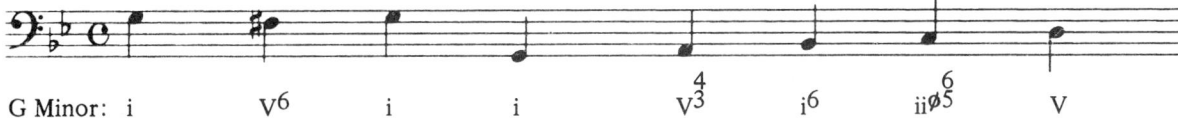

The alto and tenor are added to complete the harmonization:

To illustrate a later type of writing that would permit nonresolution of seventh chords and a greater saturation of such chords, the same chorale melody is harmonized with a majority of seventh chords:

ASSIGNMENT 6

Chart the possible harmonizations (according to the procedures already described) of the following chorale melody. Then answer the questions.

Herzlich lieb hab ich dich, O Herr   Chorale
(Lord, All My Heart Is Fixed on Thee)

Questions:

1. The cadence tones (the final two tones A and G) will support an authentic cadence in how many keys?
2. Is a plagal cadence possible? A half cadence? A deceptive cadence?
3. Could the entire phrase be harmonized in G major?
4. Could the melody be harmonized entirely with descending P5 progressions?
5. How many of the melody tones could be harmonized as the seventh factor of a seventh chord and also effect either normal or alternate resolution?

ASSIGNMENT 7

Harmonize each of the following chorale melodies.

1. Use the procedure described earlier.
2. Limit each phrase to one nondominant seventh chord.
3. Use a harmonic rhythm of one chord per quarter note.
4. Use prescribed four-part writing procedures outlined earlier in this chapter.

ASSIGNMENT 7 (continued)

5. Make a complete analysis of each chord selected.
6. Divide the class into four sections (soprano, alto, tenor, and bass) and sing one harmonization written by each student.
7. Add nonharmonic tones to the harmonization, and arrange it for four instruments.

1.
Wir Christenleut Chorale
(We Christians May Rejoice Today)

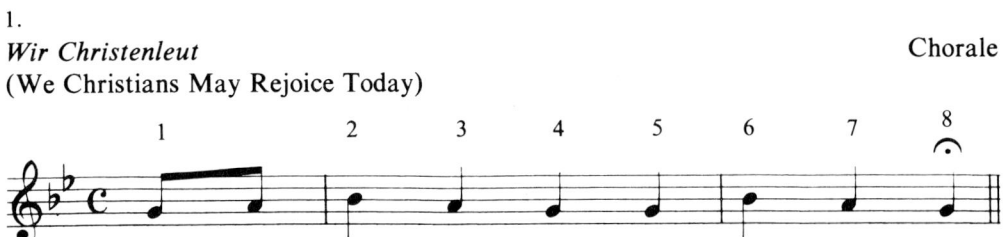

2.
Wie schön leuchtet der Morgenstern Chorale
(How Brightly Shines the Morning Star)

ASSIGNMENT 8

1. Compose a short composition in the following form:

MEASURES	KEY	PHRASE RELATIONSHIP	CADENCE
1-4	A MAJOR	A	HALF IN A MAJOR
5-8	MODULATE TO E MAJOR	AP	AUTHENTIC IN E MAJOR
9-12	MODULATE TO A MAJOR	B	HALF IN A MAJOR
13-16	A MAJOR	A	AUTHENTIC IN A MAJOR

2. Employ a homophonic style (one melody with accompaniment).
3. Use a number of nondominant seventh chords.
4. Write for any instrument (or voice) or combinations that interest you.
5. Perform the compositions in class.

15 Secondary Dominant Chords

V/ V⁷/ vii°/ vii°⁷/
vii⌀⁷/
Characteristics
Tonicized Chord Inversions

Secondary Dominant Types
History
Treatment of Secondary Dominants

Part-writing
Selecting Secondary Dominants in Chord Progressions

SECONDARY DOMINANT CHORDS

Any major or minor diatonic triad may be preceded by a chord that is in effect its dominant. Analysis using *secondary dominant chords* is simply another way of implying very short modulations (in reality a modulation of two chords only).

Characteristics

Secondary dominant chords may be regarded as very short modulations, but since they consist of two chords only, they are not effective in establishing a new key.

The following illustration shows how the same passage may be analyzed first as a modulation and then as a secondary dominant:

Tonicized Chord

A *tonicized chord* temporarily functions as a tonic having been preceded by a secondary (temporary) dominant.

1. The root of the tonicized chord lies a P5 below the root of the V/ or V⁷/ chords.
2. The root of the tonicized chord lies a half step above the root of the vii°/, the vii°⁷/, and the vii⌀⁷/ chords.

243

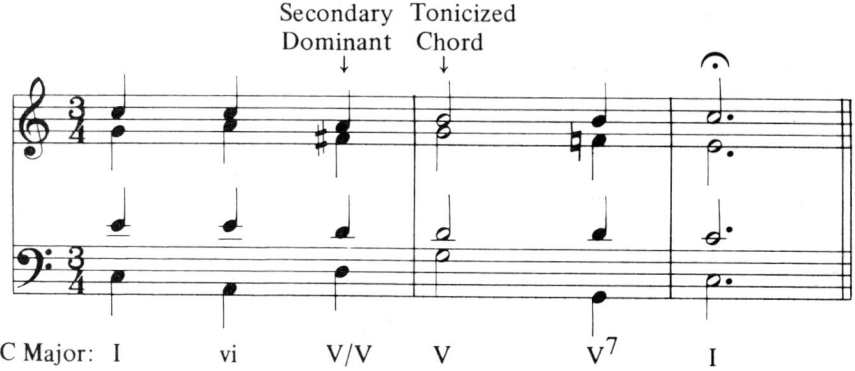

The secondary dominant is used immediately before its tonicized chord so that it will function as a dominant. In order to function as a dominant, the secondary dominant must have the same sound as a dominant or a leading tone chord (i.e., major, diminished, major-minor, etc.). The simplest secondary dominant is a major triad.

The following illustrates a series of chord progressions. In each pair the first chord is diatonic; then it is changed to major in the second progression to form a secondary dominant.

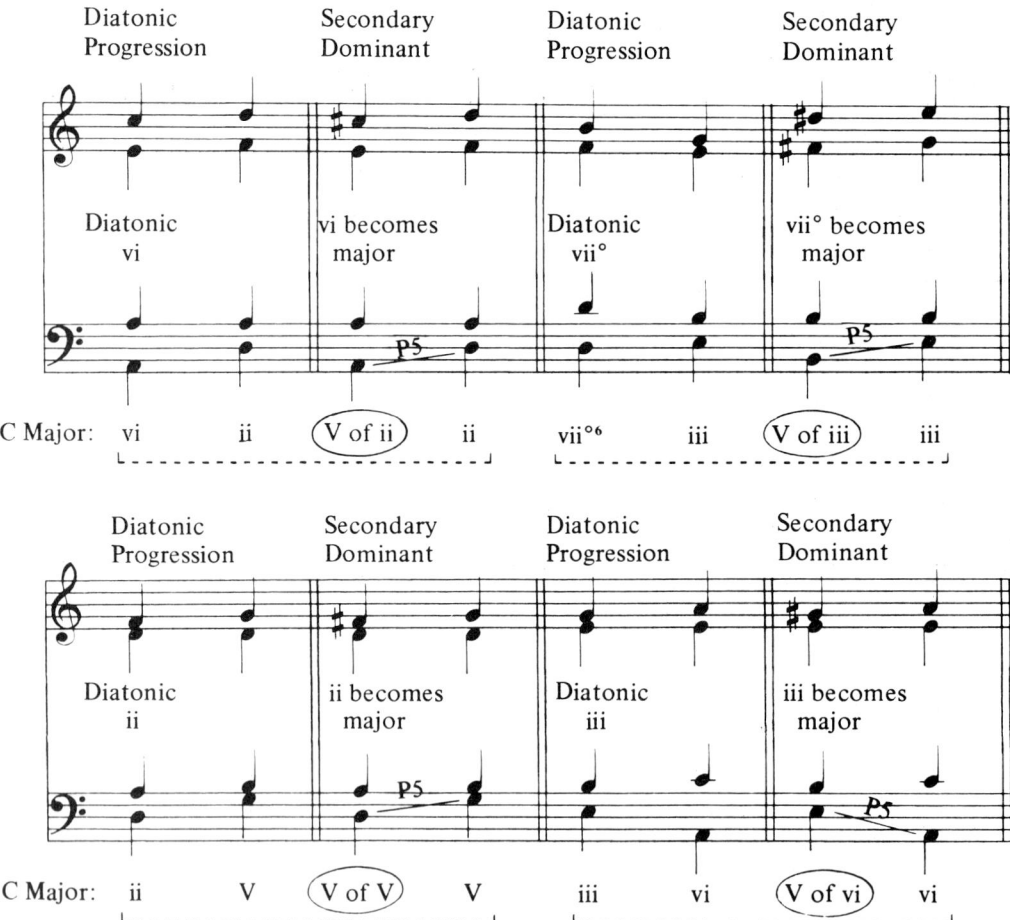

244   Secondary Dominant Chords

Secondary Dominant Types

Secondary dominants are of five types. Any major or minor triad may be tonicized, but for purposes of illustration the dominant V will be used here:

1. V of V (expressed as V/V) is a major triad whose root lies a P5 above the root of the tonicized chord.
2. V⁷ of V (expressed as V⁷/V) is a major-minor seventh chord whose root lies a P5 above the root of the tonicized chord.
3. vii° of V (expressed as vii°/V) is a diminished triad whose root lies a half step below the root of the tonicized chord.
4. vii⌀⁷ of V (expressed as vii⌀⁷/V) is a diminished-minor seventh chord whose root lies a half step below the root of the tonicized chord.
5. vii°⁷ of V (expressed as vii°⁷/V) is a diminished-diminished seventh chord whose root lies a half step below the root of the tonicized chord.

If all five types were combined, they would form a single dominant ninth chord whose root lies a P5 above that of the tonicized chord. Such a chord might assist as an expedient reminder of the five various forms of the secondary dominants.

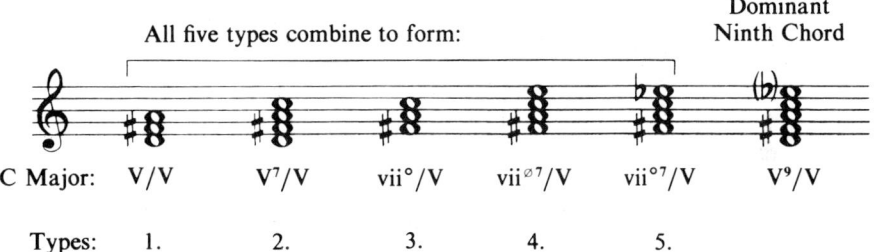

Here are illustrations showing each of the five types of secondary dominants used in context. Each illustration contains the same chords except for the secondary dominants:

Chords reduced to simple position:

Secondary Dominant Chords 245

Chords reduced to simple position:

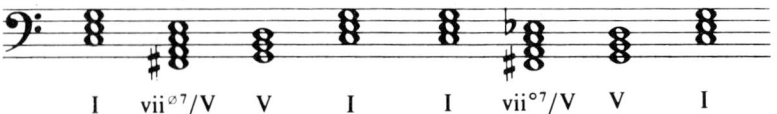

I   vii^{ø7}/V   V   I   I   vii^{o7}/V   V   I

Inversions   Secondary dominants are subject to inversion just as are their diatonic counterparts.

Secondary dominant in inversion:

Chords reduced to simple position:

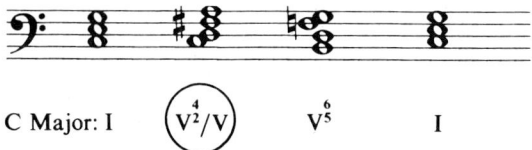

C Major: I   (V$^4_2$/V)   V$^6_5$ I

ASSIGNMENT 1   At the end of each staff, a tonicized chord is given. For instance, the first tonicized chord is V in the key of F major, and measures 1 through 5 are secondary dominants related to it.

Write each requested secondary dominant chord in simple position. Numbers 1 and 10 are written for you.

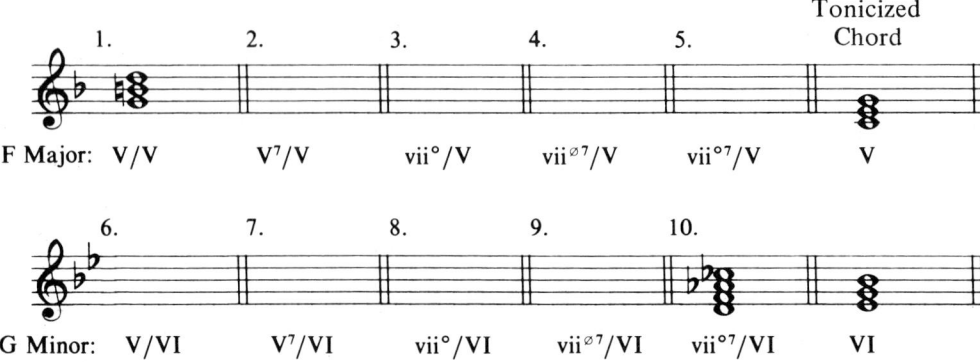

246   Secondary Dominant Chords

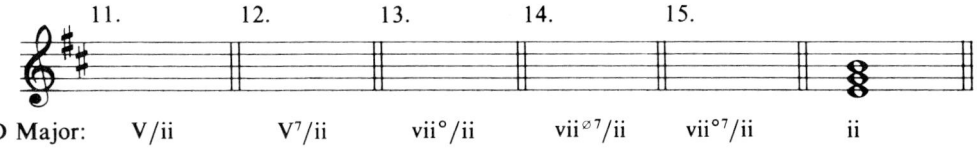

D Major: V/ii   V⁷/ii   vii°/ii   viiø⁷/ii   vii°⁷/ii   ii

ASSIGNMENT 2   Each exercise contains (1) a potential secondary dominant followed by (2) a tonicized chord.

1. Write the analysis of each chord as it appears without accidentals.
2. Then, change the first chord in each exercise to a secondary dominant by adding one or more accidentals as necessary to give it the proper sound.
3. Do not change the letter name of any pitch.
4. Write the analysis of both chords after the accidental or accidentals have been added to the first. (The analysis of the second chord will remain the same in both analyses.)

EXAMPLE   Exercise as printed: Same exercise as completed:

A Major   A Major

Without alteration: vi   ii
With alteration: __   __   V/ii   ii

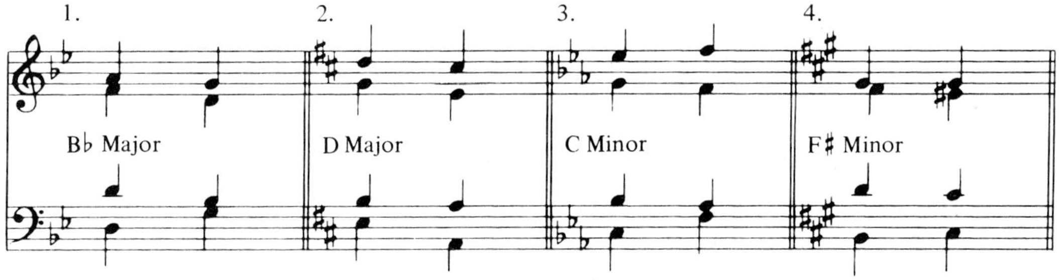

1. B♭ Major
2. D Major
3. C Minor
4. F♯ Minor

Without alteration: __ __ __ __ __ __ __ __
With alteration: __ __ __ __ __ __ __ __

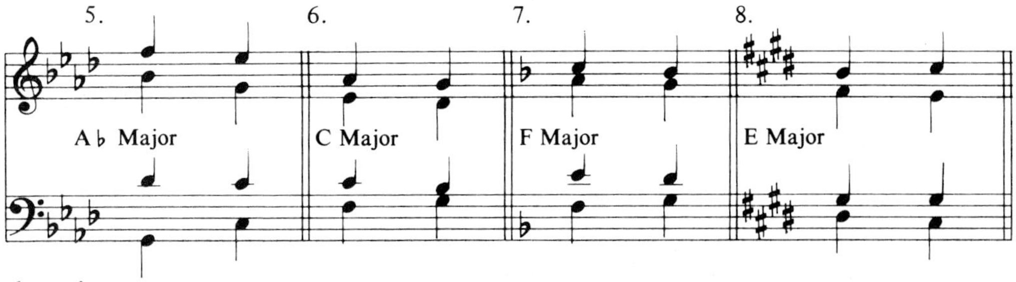

5. A♭ Major
6. C Major
7. F Major
8. E Major

Without alteration: __ __ __ __ __ __ __ __
With alteration: __ __ __ __ __ __ __ __

Secondary Dominant Chords

HISTORY The historical use of secondary dominant chords varied in the style periods:

Baroque Period (1600–1750) Secondary dominants developed during the Baroque period and occurred in moderate frequency.

Frequently found:	V of	V⁷ of	vii°⁶ of
Less frequently found:	vii⌀⁷ of	vii°⁷ of	

Conservative part-writing, resolution of seventh factors of seventh chords, and avoidance of parallel P5s and P8s marked the style of Baroque usage. Chord progression from the secondary dominants was most often to the tonicized chord.

Here are some illustrations from the Baroque period:

Bach: *Wahrlich, ich sage euch*   Cantata
(Truly I Say Unto You)

E Major: I   V   IV⁶   I   V   V⁶/V   V   I

Purcell: *Suite 8 in F Major*

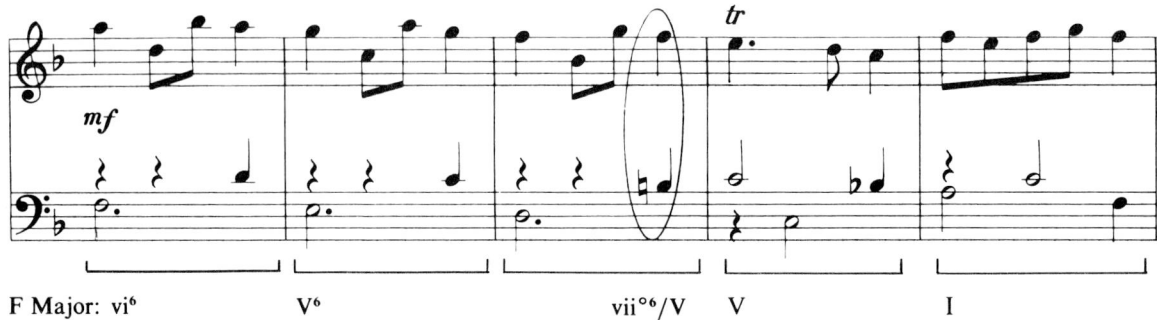

F Major: vi⁶   V⁶   vii°⁶/V   V   I

Classical Period (1750–1825) In the Classical period, as a natural development of the Baroque period, the secondary dominants occurred somewhat more frequently, and the usage was less conservative. The order of frequency changed from the earlier period since seventh chords were also gaining in popularity and secondary dominants followed this trend.

Became more frequent:	V⁷ of	vii°⁷ of	vii⌀⁷* of
Became less frequent:	vii°⁶ of	V of	

Conservative part-writing, resolutions of the seventh factors of seventh chords, and avoidance of parallel P5s and P8s still prevailed but with slightly less intensity. Chord progressions from the secondary dominant followed for the most part the patterns of Baroque practice. Type 3 resolutions (although by no means common) did, however, begin to appear.

*This chord has in all style periods received less use than other secondary dominants.

Here are two representative examples of secondary dominant use in the Classical period:

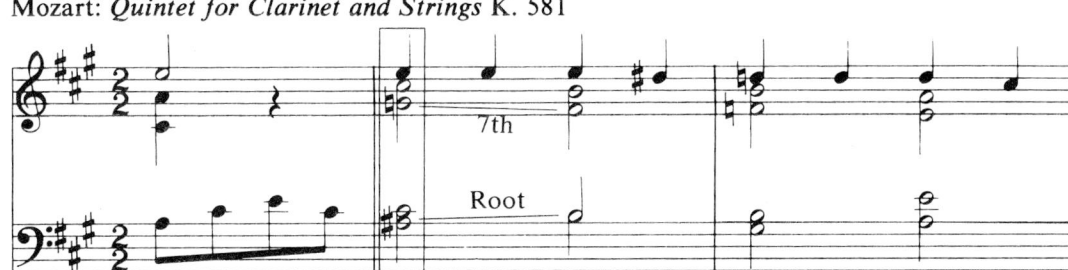

Mozart: *Quintet for Clarinet and Strings* K. 581

Mozart: *Sonatina in C Major*

The following illustration shows both typical and atypical use of secondary dominants in the Classical period. At no. 1 and no. 2, the chords are resolved in the usual fashion. But, at no. 3, the secondary dominant is followed by another diminished seventh, leaving the first (at no. 3) without a resolution:

Mozart: *String Quartet* K. 458

Romantic Period (1825–1900)

In the Romantic period, the use of secondary dominants increased still more in frequency from the Classical period, and preference for those that are seventh chords continued to be more popular.

Secondary Dominant Chords 249

Part-writing became more daring (wider leaps, occasional augmented intervals in the melodic line), sevenths were sometimes not resolved, but in general parallel P5s and P8s were still avoided.

As the Romantic period progressed, the style became more and more chromatic and less adherent to diatonic key systems. Thus, the secondary dominants, altered chords as they are, became more prominent, and the use of them became freer and less restrictive.

Here is a typical example from Romantic literature showing three successive secondary dominants:

Chopin: *Polonaise* op. 26 no. 1

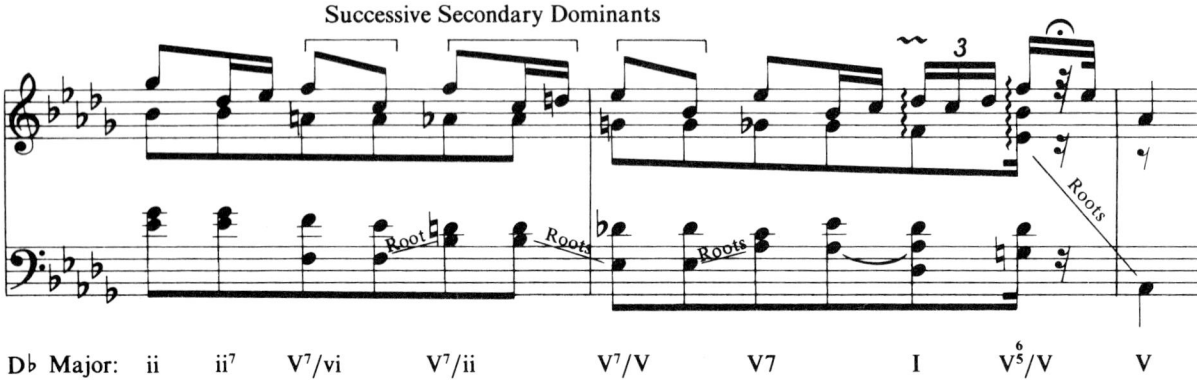

Here is another illustration showing a secondary dominant that takes a type 3 resolution. Quite often the chord that appears to be a vii°7/iii progresses to a I6 triad, thus effecting a nonresolution of the seventh:

Chopin: *Polonaise* op. 53

Here are two other examples of secondary dominants from Romantic literature. Both have somewhat conventional resolutions.

Brahms: *Intermezzo in C* op. 119 no. 3

Schumann: *Happy Farmer* op. 68

Post-Romantic and Impressionistic Period (1875–1920)

Since the strong dominant-tonic relationship began to wane during this period, the secondary dominant function became less and less common. Other devices, such as parallel chords, found favor among composers, and the more traditional practices, including secondary dominants, failed to meet the stylistic and expressive requirements of the Post-Romantic and Impressionistic period.

Here is an illustration of the use of a secondary dominant, but in a manner quite different from that found in more traditional Romantic literature. The fleeting suggestion of a foreign key (F-sharp major) is brought about by a secondary dominant modifying the leading tone triad that is in itself altered (the leading-tone chord traditionally diminished has been made major).

Debussy: *Minstrels*

Copyright 1910, Durand et Cie. Used by permission of the publisher. Elkan-Vogel, Inc., sole representative, United States.

TREATMENT

The treatment of the secondary dominant is as follows:

As V of (V/)

This secondary dominant (V) generally progresses to its tonicized chord. Infrequently, the chord progresses to another whose root is a step above that of the secondary dominant. The effect is similar to that of a deceptive cadence where the true dominant ignores its natural progression to the tonic and chooses the vi chord instead. It is found in either root position or in first inversion.

In four-part writing, it is handled in much the same way as its unaltered counterpart except that the third of the chord has the function of a leading tone and should not be doubled. All other conventional part-writing practices apply.

Secondary Dominant Chords 251

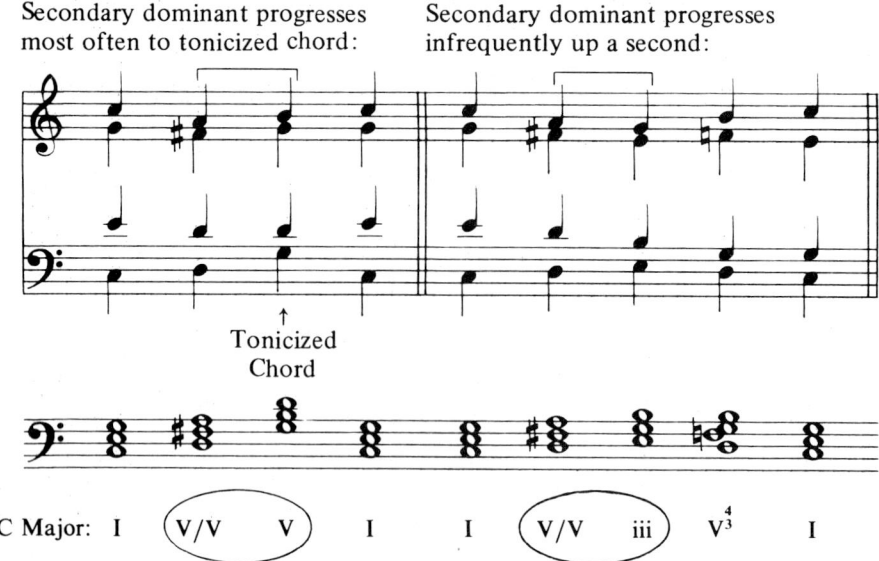

As V⁷ of (V⁷/)

Type 1: This major-minor seventh chord (V⁷) regularly progresses to its tonicized chord (roots down a P5). This is by far the most common progression from a secondary dominant seventh chord.

Type 2: Infrequently, the chord progresses to another that allows the seventh of the chord to resolve properly down one step, but does not lie in fifth relationship with the root of its tonicized chord. Most often an alternate resolution is to a chord whose root is one step above that of a secondary dominant seventh chord.

Type 3: Rarely, the chord progresses to another that provides no resolution for the seventh factor of the seventh chord.

It is found in root position or in any of its inversions.

In four-part writing, it is handled in much the same way as its unaltered counterpart. Be sure to resolve the seventh of the chord down one step except when a nonresolution is intended. All other conventional part-writing practices apply.

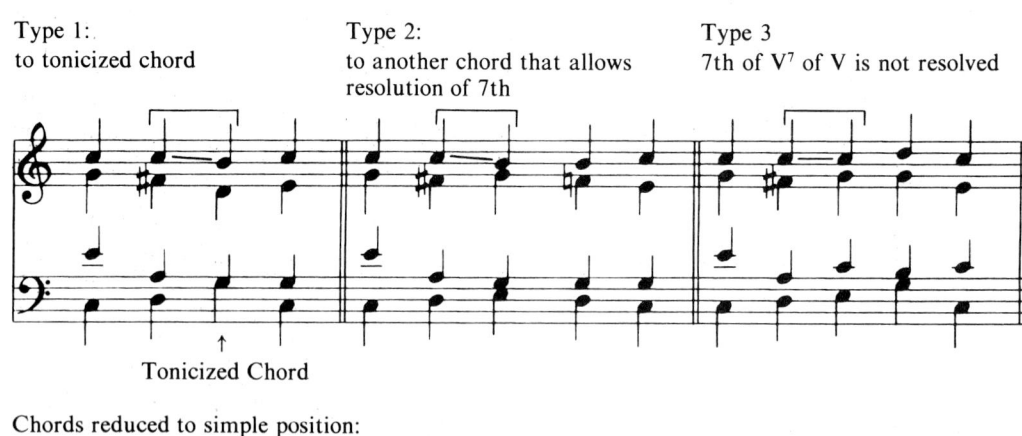

Chords reduced to simple position:

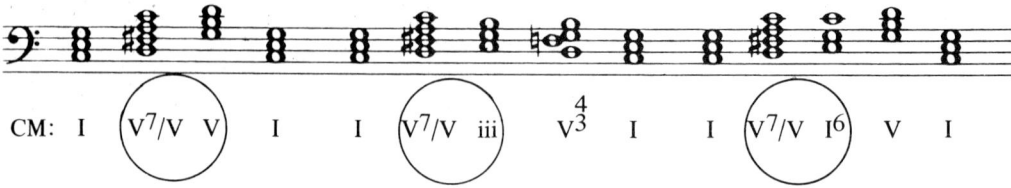

252 Secondary Dominant Chords

As vii°⁶ of (vii°⁶/) The secondary vii°⁶ progresses to its tonicized chord. It is found most frequently in first inversion.

In four-part writing, it is handled in the same manner as a diatonic vii°⁶. The root of the chord is not doubled. It is, so to speak, a secondary leading tone. All other conventional part-writing practices apply.

This chord was found mostly in the Baroque period, and its use fell off sharply thereafter.

Secondary vii°⁶ progresses to its tonicized chord:

Chords reduced to simple position:

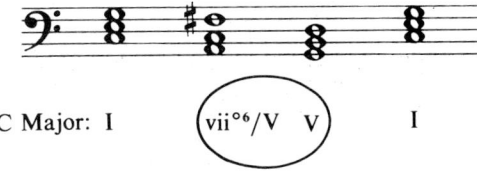

C Major: I   (vii°⁶/V V)   I

As vii⌀⁷ of (vii⌀⁷/) This secondary dominant chord appears much less frequently in literature than the vii⌀⁷ does. When it does appear, it is used when the tonicized chord is major since it is diatonic only in the major key.

Type 1: The resolution (root movement to the next chord is down a P5) that is afforded most other seventh chords *is not used,* since this secondary dominant has a leading tone chord function.

Type 2: This is the usual resolution pattern for the secondary dominant with a leading tone chord function. The root of the chord moves by half step up to the root of the tonicized chord. Thus, the seventh of the secondary dominant is resolved and so is the tritone (root to fifth factor).

Type 3: Rarely does the chord progress to another that provides no resolution for the seventh factor of the seventh chord.

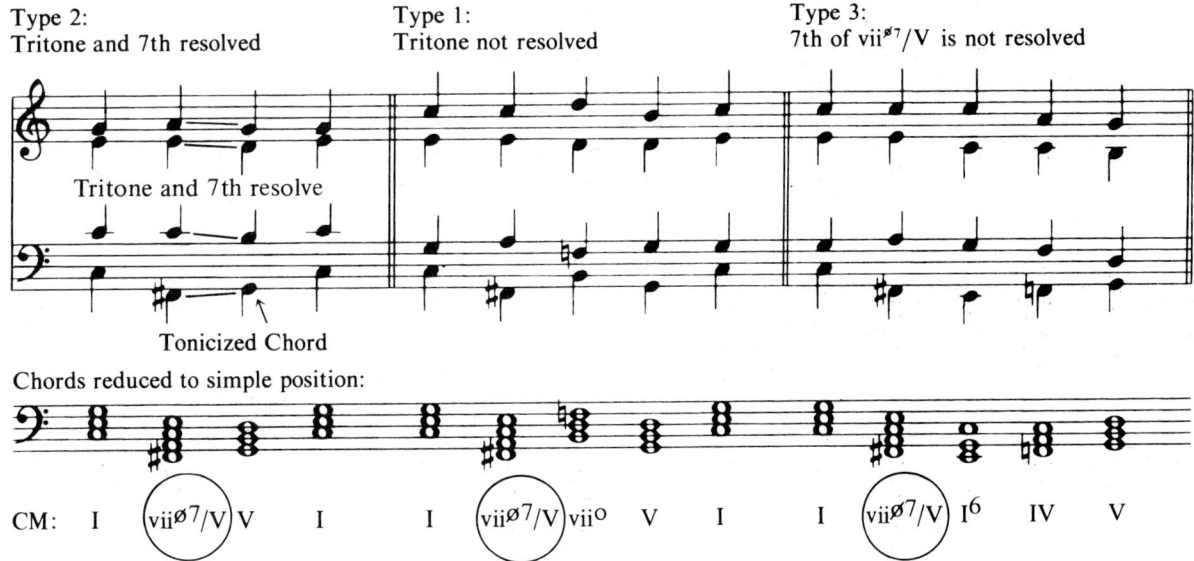

Secondary Dominant Chords   253

It is found in root position or in any of its inversions.

In four-part writing, the ideal solution is to resolve the tritone inward in the same two voices as a d5 and outward in the same two voices as an A4. Unfortunately, this cannot always be accomplished because P5s sometimes intervene. The seventh factor of the chord should resolve down a half step.

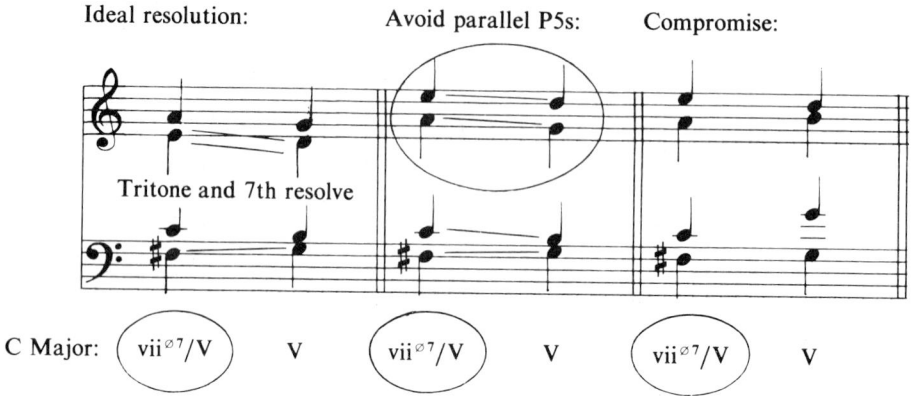

As vii°⁷ of (vii°⁷/)

Developed in the Baroque period, this secondary dominant (vii°⁷) became increasingly popular during the Classical and Romantic periods and reached a peak in the late Romantic. It appears in both major and minor tonalities.

Type 1: The resolution (root movement to the next chord is down a P5) that is afforded most other seventh chords is seldom used, since this secondary dominant has a leading-tone chord function.

Type 2: This is the usual resolution pattern for the secondary dominant with a leading-tone chord function. The root of the chord moves by half step up to the root of the tonicized chord. Thus, the seventh factor of the secondary dominant is resolved and so too is the tritone (root to fifth factor).

Type 3: Rarely does the chord progress to another that provides no resolution for the seventh factor of the seventh chord. Sometimes this chord occurs in a succession of seventh chords.

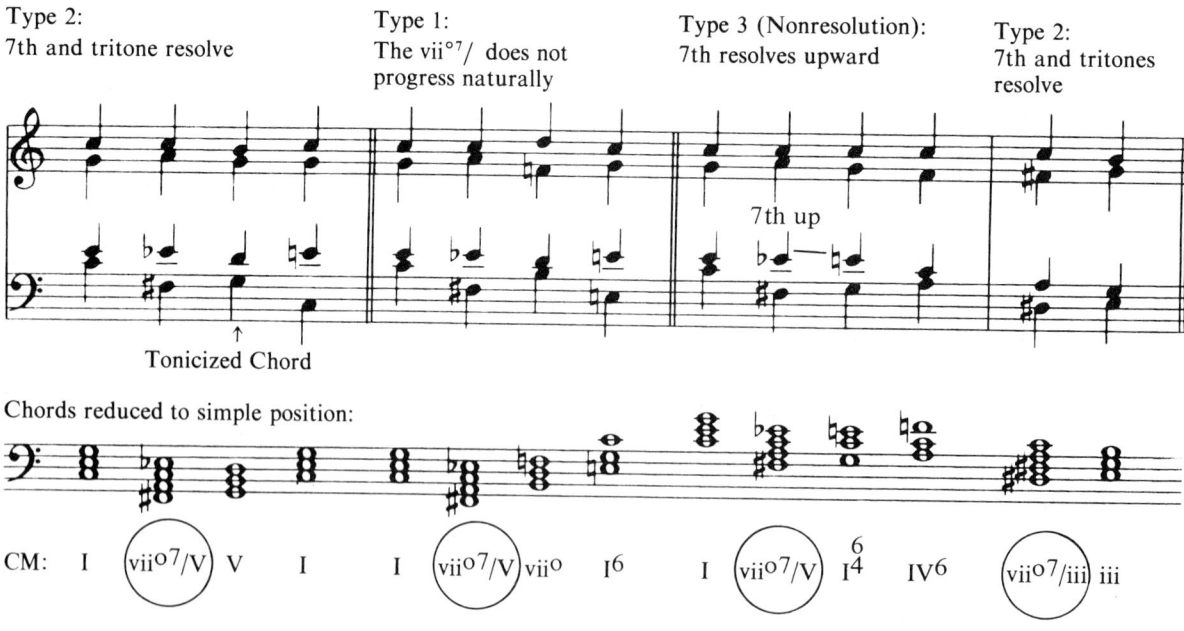

254 Secondary Dominant Chords

It is found in root position or in any of its inversions.

In four-part writing, the vii°7/ chord is handled in the same manner as the diminished-minor seventh except that part-writing is somewhat easier because of the two tritones that exist in this chord.

All of the following are excellent examples of type 2 resolution of the vii°7/V. The roots are not a P5 apart, but the seventh resolves properly.

7th factor and lower tritone of each resolves:

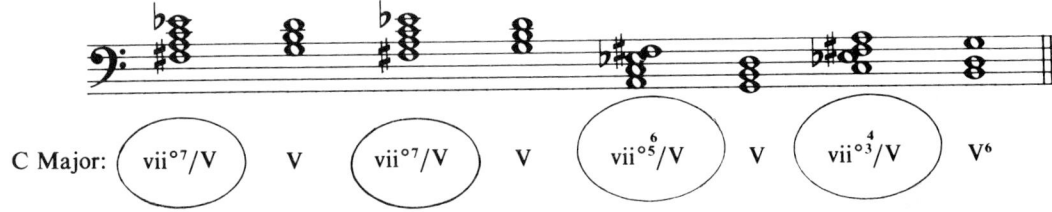

Here is an example of the most common type of resolution:

Bach: *Prelude no. 1 in C Major* from *The Well-Tempered Clavier*, Book 1

Secondary Dominant Chords 255

This is an example of the vii°⁷/V by Beethoven. It is distinctive in that (1) two vii°⁷ chords are used successively, and (2) the resolution of the secondary dominant is delayed by a $^6_4$ chord.

Beethoven: *Piano Sonata* op. 10 no. 1 (second movement)

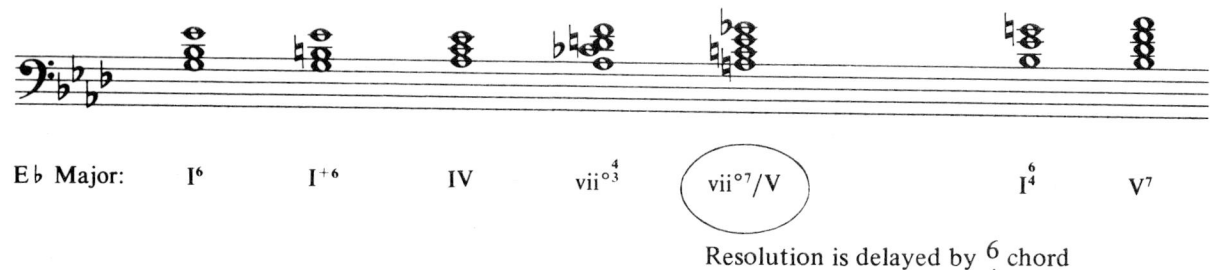

E♭ Major: I⁶   I⁺⁶   IV   vii°$^4_3$ (vii°⁷/V)   I$^6_4$ V⁷

Resolution is delayed by $^6_4$ chord

SUMMARY   A summary of the secondary dominant chords:

SECONDARY DOMINANT CHORD	MOST COMMON PROGRESSION OF ROOTS FROM SECONDARY DOMINANT	THE SUCCEEDING CHORD
V/?	DOWN A P5	The tonicized chord (Example: V/ii proceeds to ii)
V⁷/?	DOWN A P5	The tonicized chord (Example: V⁷/vi proceeds to vi)
vii°⁶/?	UP A HALF STEP	The tonicized chord (Example: vii°⁶/V proceeds to V)
vii⌀⁷/?	UP A HALF STEP	The tonicized chord (Example: vii⌀⁷/IV proceeds to IV)
vii°⁷/?	UP A HALF STEP	The tonicized chord (Example: vii°⁷/iii proceeds to iii)

Part-writing Procedures   This is a continuation of the list that begins on page 135. All part-writing procedures are summarized in Appendix 2.

26. *Part-writing procedures for secondary dominants are the same as for primary dominant types (V, V⁷, vii°⁶, vii⌀⁷, vii°⁷).*
27. *When the secondary dominant V⁷/ occurs consecutively,*
    a. *Some of the chords are frequently incomplete:*

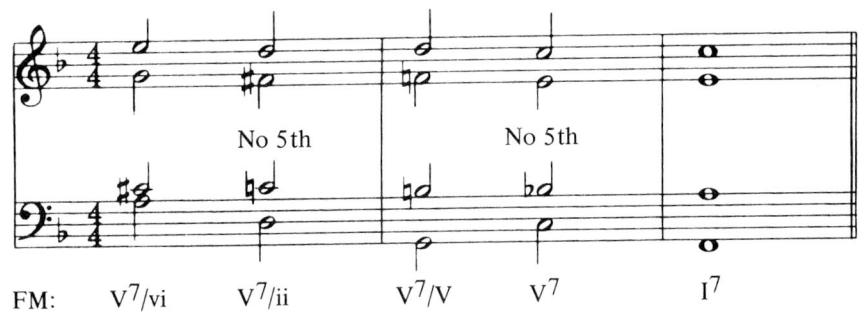

FM: V⁷/vi   V⁷/ii   V⁷/V   V⁷   I⁷

b. *The sevenths of some chords ascend rather than resolving downward conventionally (see page 234).*

Review the part-writing procedures for:

Triads V/ and vii°⁶/   (on pages 251 and 256)
The V⁷/ chord   (on page 252)
The vii⌀⁷/ and vii°⁷/   (on pages 253–54)

ASSIGNMENT 3   The following are chorale phrases used by Bach and many of his contemporaries.

1. Add the alto and the tenor according to the figured bass symbols. Remember that figured bass numbers represent intervals above the bass notes.
2. Provide a complete harmonic analysis of each chorale phrase.
3. In class, put several harmonizations on the blackboard and have class members sing them.
4. From the German titles, look up some of the chorale harmonizations by Bach and sing them in class also. Any good edition of the 371 chorale harmonizations of J. S. Bach will provide these.

In no. 1 double the soprano in the diminished triad.

1.
Wie bist du, Seele
(Why Art Thou, Soul, So Troubled Within Me)

2.
Wir Christenleute
(We Christian Folk)

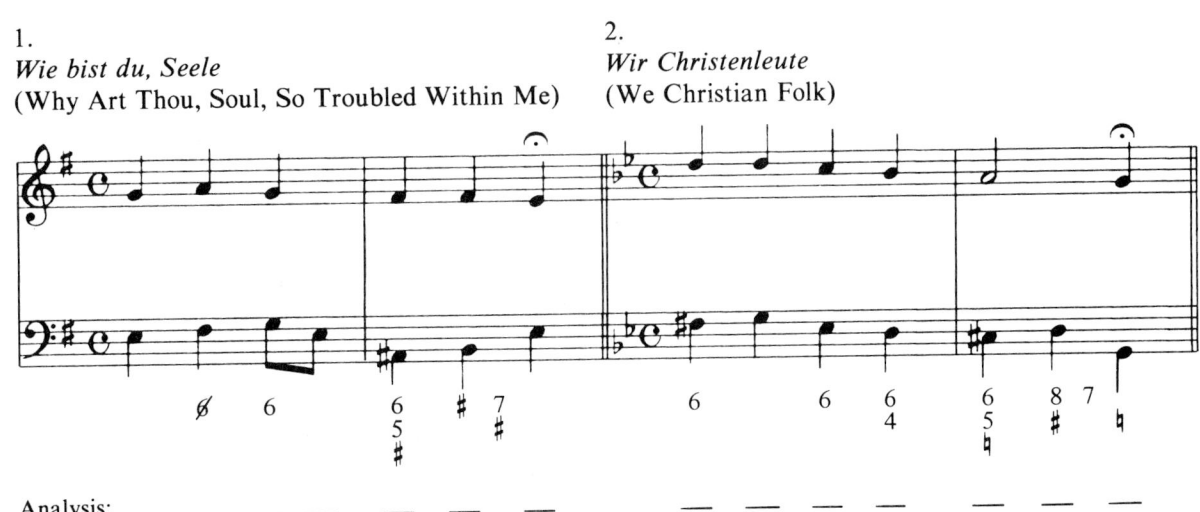

Analysis: __ __ __ __ __ __ __ __ __ __ __ __ __

Secondary Dominant Chords   257

ASSIGNMENT 3 (continued)

3.
Was betrübst du dich
(What Makes You Grieve, My Heart)

Analysis: __ __ __ __ __ __

In the final measure of no. 4, overlapping cannot be avoided.

4.
Meinen Jesum lass' ich nicht
(I Will Not Leave My Jesus)

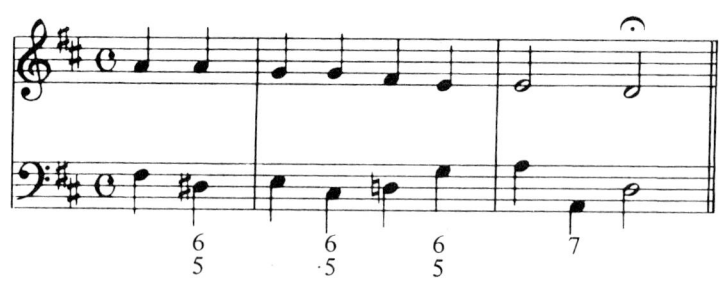

Analysis: __ __ __ __ __

5.
Wenn ich in Angst und Not
(When I in Anxiety and Need)

Analysis: __ __ __ __ __ __

ASSIGNMENT 3 (continued)

Put the first two chords of no. 6 in one key and the remainder in another. Other analyses are possible also.

6.
Herr Christ, der ein'ge Gott's sohn
(Lord Christ, the Only Son of God)

Analysis: __ __ __ __ __ __ __

ASSIGNMENT 4

After completing the six figured-bass chorales in assignment 3, decorate each with nonharmonic tones.

Passing tones, neighboring tones, and suspensions should be the most frequently used nonharmonic tones, but others such as anticipations, changing tones, escape tones, and appoggiaturas can also be effectively applied.

Try to add one nonharmonic tone per beat although sometimes it is not possible. Do not put all the nonharmonic tones in one voice.

As an illustration, phrase no. 3 in assignment 3 (page 258) is shown below with nonharmonic decorations by Bach.

Bach: *Was betrübst du dich*
(What Makes You Grieve, My Heart)

ASSIGNMENT 5

A *chorale prelude* is a type of composition based on the chorale itself. In the seventeenth century, it was customary for the organist to introduce the chorale in the Protestant church by playing the tune with accompaniment before it was to be sung by the congregation. This served to refresh the memories of the members in case they had forgotten the tune. At the same

ASSIGNMENT 5 (continued)

time, it offered the organist an opportunity to elaborate on the melody and/or harmony. As time progressed, organists developed very sophisticated contrapuntal compositions using chorale melodies, and these came to be called chorale preludes.

1. Write a very short chorale prelude.
2. Use both the harmony and melody of one of the four-part exercises in assignment 3.
3. Compose a very short melodic or rhythmic figure that can be used to decorate each note of the soprano voice.
4. Apply this figure successively to each tone of the melody and keep at least part of the harmony tones beneath it.
5. Two possible beginnings of phrase 6 in assignment 3 are shown here as illustrations. In both, the melody appears in the soprano voice and is simply an arpeggiation of the original harmony. Each chord of the four-part phrase is given an entire measure in this illustration.

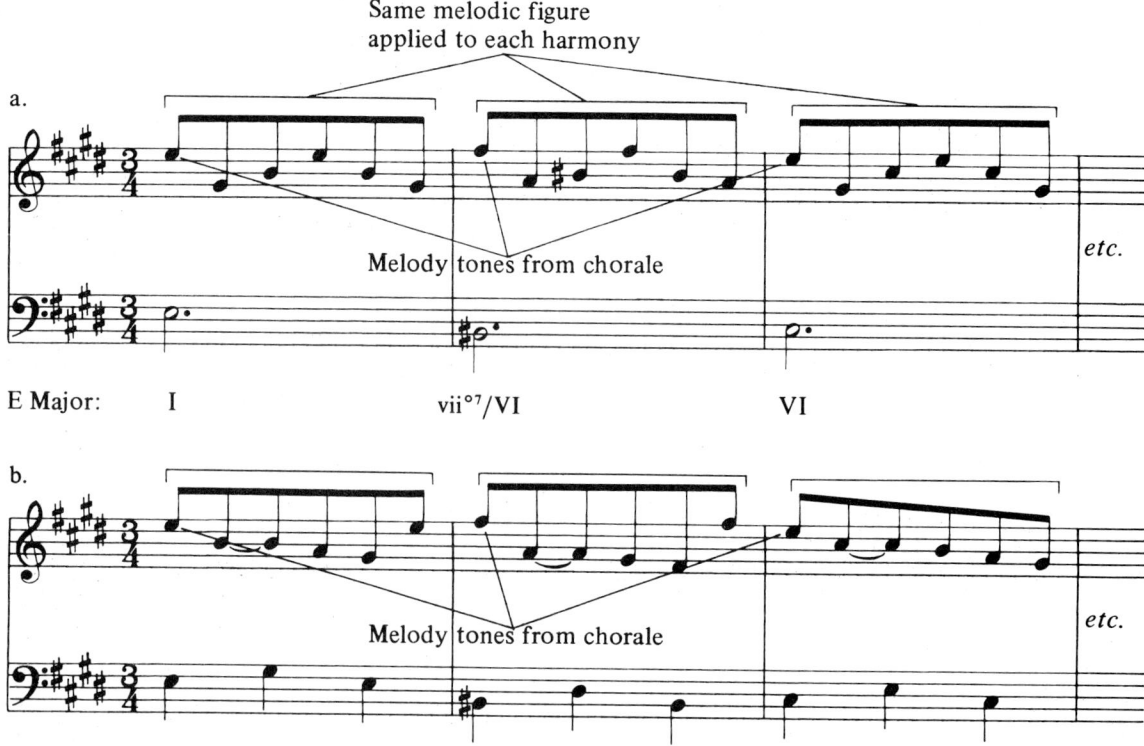

6. The figure you select should be different from either of the above. With each different melody tone it may be necessary to deviate slightly from the figure as you first present it. Thus, if your figure is designed for a triad in root position, it will probably have to be altered to fit a first inversion triad or a seventh chord.
7. Complete your chorale prelude here:

ASSIGNMENT 5 (continued)

SELECTING FOR CHORD PROGRESSIONS

The task of identifying and analyzing secondary dominants is far simpler than selecting and incorporating such chords in harmonic progressions. Until familiarity with these altered chords is developed, the following step-by-step illustration will be of assistance.

The melody to be harmonized is:

Wach' auf mein Herz Chorale
(Awake, My Heart)

Since this is a chorale melody, the harmonic rhythm will be that of one chord per beat although on occasion a chord may be repeated from one beat to the next.

The possible diatonic triads that can be used with each melody tone are:

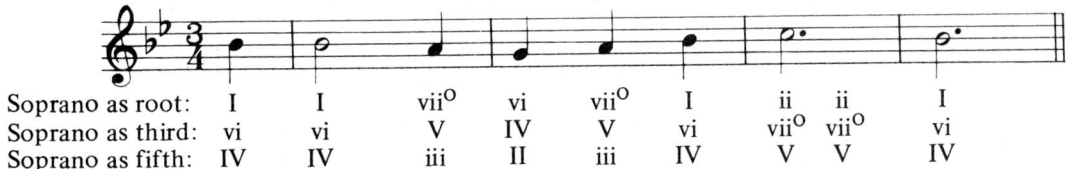

Soprano as root:	I	I	vii°	vi	vii°	I	ii	ii	I
Soprano as third:	vi	vi	V	IV	V	vi	vii°	vii°	vi
Soprano as fifth:	IV	IV	iii	II	iii	IV	V	V	IV

To obtain a sufficient number of strong progressions (descending P5s) and an appropriate balance of primary triads (I, IV, and V), both are marked—the strong progressions with a line from one chord to the next, the primary triads with circles.

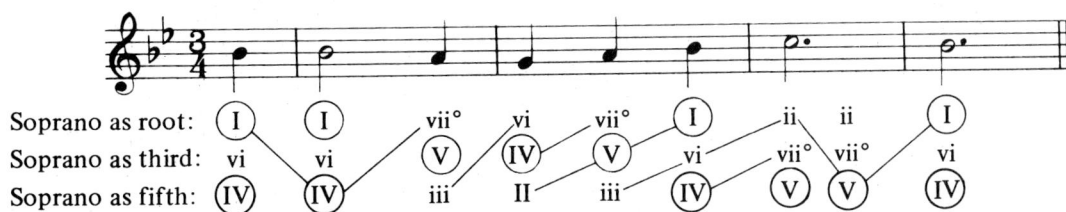

Soprano as root:	(I)	I	vii°	vi	vii°	(I)	ii	ii	(I)
Soprano as third:	vi	vi	(V)	(IV)	(V)	vi	vii°	vii°	vi
Soprano as fifth:	(IV)	(IV)	iii	II	iii	(IV)	(V)	(V)	(IV)

In selecting from among all possible harmonizations, it is important to keep in mind the following:

1. By far the largest number of V/ and V^7/chords are found in the type 1 descending P5 progression since the root of the tonicized chord lies a P5 below the root of the secondary dominant.

Secondary Dominant Chords

2. The vii°/, vii⌀7/, and vii°7/ chords take type 2 resolution (root ascends a half step up to the root of the tonicized chord). Thus, the more descending P5 and ascending stepwise progressions selected, the more opportunities there are for including such chords in the harmonizations.
3. The following choice is made because it contains a number of both descending P5 and ascending 2nd progressions.

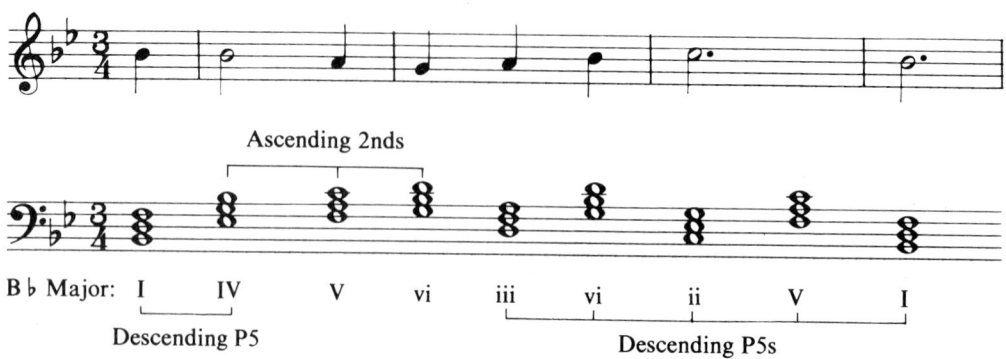

At this point, it is necessary to investigate the number of possible secondary dominants in the series.

1. The first of two chords in any descending P5 progression is a potential V/ or V⁷/ chord.
2. The first of two chords in an ascending 2nd progression is a potential vii°/, vii⌀7/, or vii°7/ chord.

Whether these potential secondary dominants will provide unity and balance to the phrase is as yet undetermined, but for the moment it is imperative that the various possibilities be examined.

The necessary accidentals, along with seventh factors (optional), will be added to the diatonic triads to form suitable secondary dominants.

Thus, the phrase harmonized with possible secondary dominants is:

Line A—The melody
Line B—Possible secondary dominants substituted for diatonic triads.
Line C—Other forms of secondary dominants that could be substituted for those included in line B.

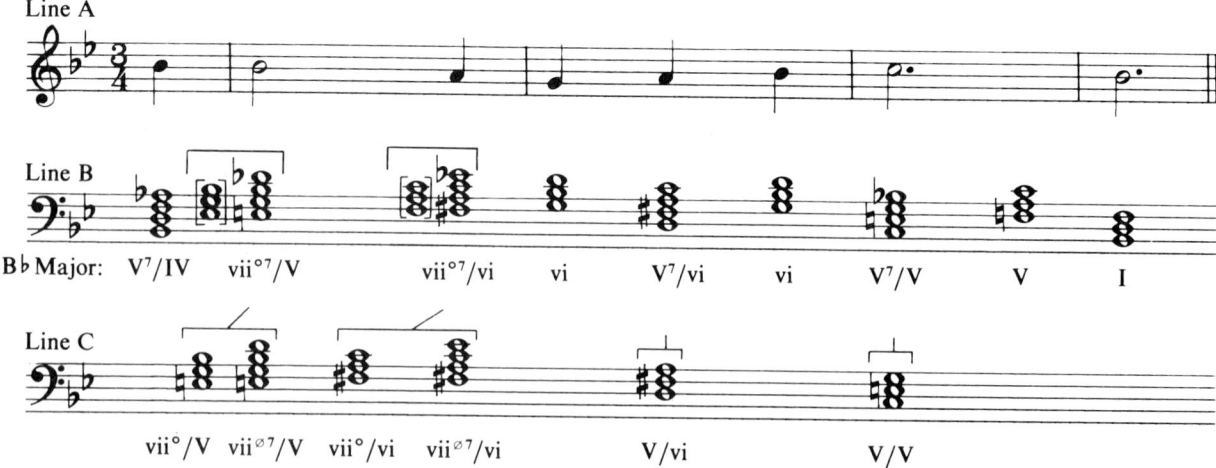

262   Secondary Dominant Chords

From the preceding illustration showing possible secondary dominant harmonizations, it can be seen that to use all such chords would introduce more chromaticism than is desirable and would create a tonal unrest that might be detrimental to the smoothness desired. Consequently, the following harmonization that comprises a balance of diatonic and altered (secondary dominant) chords is submitted as a final choice:

From this basic harmonization, the following bass line is fashioned to provide (1) contrary motion to the melody, and (2) an interesting and directional line or lines in its own right.

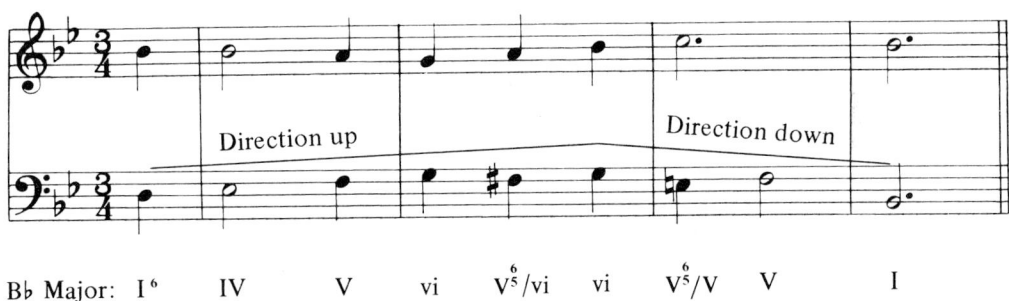

The inner voices are then added:

Nonharmonic tones are included, and the harmonization is complete:

ASSIGNMENT 6 Using the same procedures described in the step-by-step illustration, harmonize the two chorales that follow. Each contains two phrases. Try to use at least one secondary dominant in each phrase.

Werde Munter, mein Gemute
(Be Glad, My Soul)   Chorale

Jesu Leiden, Pein und Tod
(Jesus Suffering Pain and Death)   Chorale

264   Secondary Dominant Chords

ASSIGNMENT 7 The following excerpt is a folk song with chord symbols for an accompaniment.

1. Sing the melody over several times.
2. Add the Roman numeral analysis symbols above the requested chords.
3. Play the block chords on the piano as you sing.
4. Add at least one secondary dominant to the existing chord symbols. (Measure 6 is one possibility.)
5. Compose an appropriate accompaniment pattern from the chord symbols and any additions that you make.
6. Arrange the complete song (with accompaniment) for piano or a group of two or three instruments played by class members.
7. In class, sing your version of the song with your own accompaniment.
8. Ask class members to criticize your performance.

Billy the Kid Folk Song

ASSIGNMENT 8 Look over the music carefully, then answer the five questions.

Bach: *O Welt, sieh hier dein Leben*
(O World, Behold Thy Life)

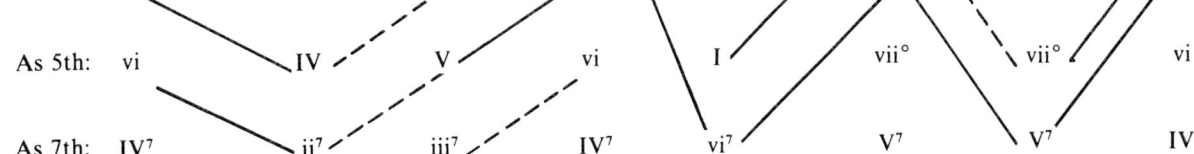

_____ Indicates descending P5th progressions
- - - - - - Indicates descending 5th progressions that are not perfect or that produce progressions where the 7th of a 7th chord cannot resolve.

Secondary Dominant Chords 265

ASSIGNMENT 8 (continued)

Questions:

1. Secondary dominant major triads (V/) could occur at which numbers?
   a. 1, 4, and 6 only
   b. 2, 3, 4, and 6
   c. 1, 2, 3, 4, and 6
   d. 4, 5, and 6
   e. 1, 3, and 4 only

   Hint: Look for minor or diminished triads that can be altered to become major and have the possibility of a descending P5 progression to the next chord.

2. Considering every melody note as the seventh factor of a seventh chord, at which number or numbers could a secondary dominant seventh chord (V^7/) be placed and allow the seventh of the chord to resolve down one step in the next chord?
   a. 2 and 5 only
   b. 1 and 3 only
   c. 5 only
   d. 2, 4, and 6
   e. 2, 3, and 5

   Hint: Look on the fourth line (as 7th:) for seventh chords that form usable descending P5 progressions with the next chord. Remember that every melody note is the seventh factor of a seventh chord.

3. Considering every melody note as the seventh of a seventh chord, at which number could a secondary dominant diminished seventh chord (vii°^{7}/) be placed and allow the seventh of the chord to resolve down a half step?
   a. 4
   b. 1
   c. 6
   d. 7
   e. 5

   Hint: Look for a melody note that descends a half step to the next note and a seventh chord that has the possibility of descending a half step to the next chord.

4. Considering triads only, numbers 7 and 8 (cadence) could be harmonized with both a half and a plagal cadence in which key?
   a. F#m
   b. Bm
   c. EM
   d. Am
   e. AM

5. Beginning at 4 (C#), it is possible to continue to the end of the phrase in descending P5 progressions if one begins with
   a. I
   b. vi
   c. iii
   d. IV^7
   e. ii

266 Secondary Dominant Chords

ASSIGNMENT 9   Underline the correct answers to the questions regarding the following excerpt from *Sonata in D Major* by Mozart.

1. Possible pivot chords between G major and D major at numbers 3 through 9 are:
   a. 4 only
   b. 4, 6, and 8
   c. 5 only
   d. 3, 5, and 7
   e. 7 and 9 only
2. The chord at no. 14 is
   a. V^6_5/iii
   b. V^6_5/vi
   c. $\text{vii}^{\varnothing 7}/\text{vi}$
   d. V^4_3
   e. $\text{vii}^{\circ 7}/\text{IV}$
3. The chord at no. 21 is
   a. V^6
   b. V^6/ii
   c. V^6/V
   d. $\text{vii}^{\circ 6}/\text{ii}$
   e. $\text{vii}^{\circ 6}/V$
4. A chord that is tonicized is
   a. 5
   b. 4
   c. 2
   d. 24
   e. 13
5. The chord at no. 8 is
   a. V^6_5/vi
   b. $\text{vii}^{\circ 6}/\text{IV}$
   c. V^6/V
   d. $\text{vii}^{\circ 6}$
   e. $\text{vii}^{\circ 6}/V$
6. Two dominant seventh chords, one of which is secondary, occur successively at
   a. 18 and 19
   b. 17 and 18
   c. 25 and 26
   d. 32 and 33
   e. 16 and 17
7. Of the secondary dominants at 4, 8, 21, and 32 the only type that is not represented is:
   a. V of
   b. V^7 of
   c. vii° of
   d. $\text{vii}^{\varnothing 7}$ of
   e. vii° of

Secondary Dominant Chords

ASSIGNMENT 9 (continued)

8. A series of chords whose roots lie in descending P5 relationship (from one chord to the next) appears in three places. Name the location of all 3:

   a. at 8 9 10 11,
       at 12 13 14 15 16,
       and at 19 20 21

   b. at 2 3 4,
       at 8 9 10 11,
       and at 17 18 19 20 21

   c. at 0 1 2 3,
       at 4 5 6 7 8,
       and at 12 13 14

   d. at 2 3 4,
       at 12 13 14 15,
       and at 17 18 19 20 21

   e. at 0 1 2 3,
       at 4 5 6 7 8,
       and at 17 18 19

9. Of the three series above in no. 8,
   a. only the chords of the first (in order of appearance) are diatonic
   b. only the chords of the second are diatonic
   c. only the chords of the third are diatonic
   d. the chords of all three series are diatonic
   e. only the chords of the second and third series are diatonic

Mozart: *Sonata in D Major* K. 311 (second movement)

Andante con espressione

G Major: I   V⁶   I   V⁶₅   I   IV⁶ I⁶₄ IV   I⁶ vii°   I   V

etc.   (GM:)   I

ASSIGNMENT 9 (continued)

Secondary Dominant Chords

ASSIGNMENT 9 (continued)

ASSIGNMENT 10

Following is a recitative and aria from the cantata *Ein feste Burg* by J. S. Bach.

The figured bass was intended to be realized (played at sight) by an organist. Since the art of reading figured bass requires considerable practice and skill, it would be too difficult at the moment to play at sight. Nevertheless, much can be learned about the art through preparing the figured bass in manuscript:

1. Write the requested chords above the figured bass symbols in block style (on scratch paper).
2. Then, arrange the chords in a keyboard idiom for organ, piano, or harpsichord. Add nonharmonic tones to make interesting lines but avoid unnecessary distractions from the vocal soloist.
3. Analyze each chord. Different analyses are possible, as with most music, but the recitative and aria can be analyzed entirely in the key of F♯ minor if desired.
4. When the figured bass has been interpreted and placed on the staff in a keyboard idiom, perform the composition in class. A bass vocalist sings the voice line, an organist, a harpsichordist, or a pianist plays the figured bass realization, and a cellist, a bassoonist, or another instrumentalist in the range plays the printed notes of the continuo line.

Figured bass realizations in recitatives are characteristically simple and often consist of no more than block chords. Arias are rendered quite simply too, but decorations of the basic harmony are not uncommon.

Slight differences exist in figured bass terminology. This particular type varies somewhat from that previously described:

$7^\flat$ —Means to lower the seventh above the bass tone a half step but does not necessarily mean that a flat will be written.

4^+ —Means to raise the fourth above the bass tone a half step, ($4\sharp$), but does not necessarily mean that a sharp will be written.

The accidentals are placed to the right of the numbers in this particular figured bass example.

270   Secondary Dominant Chords

ASSIGNMENT 10 (continued)

Bach: *Ein feste Burg*
(A Mighty Fortress Is Our God)

Cantata

Secondary Dominant Chords

ASSIGNMENT 10 (continued)

272 Secondary Dominant Chords

ASSIGNMENT 10 (continued)

ASSIGNMENT 10 (continued)

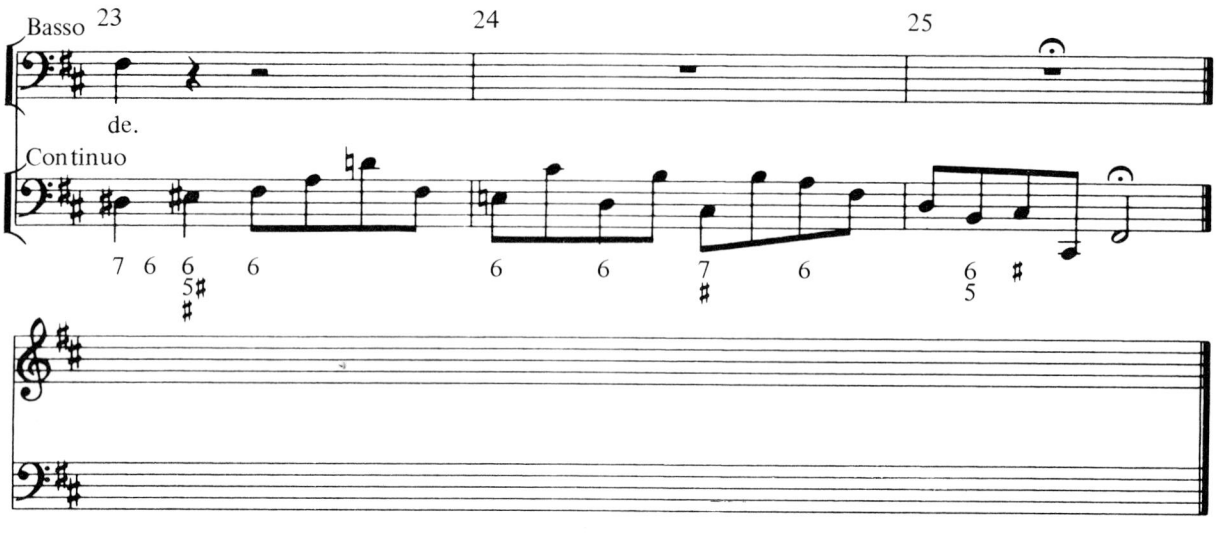

274 Secondary Dominant Chords

16 Two-Part (Binary) Form

Two-Part Form
Binary Form
Suite
Rounded Binary Form

Minnesingers
Meistersingers
Bar Form
Stollen

Abgesang
Canzo
German Part Song
German Lied

TWO-PART FORM Also called *binary,* the *two-part form* consists of two main sections. It may occur at the period, double period, or song form level. Some authorities reserve the term *song form* for three-part form only.

In its simplest configuration, the first part may consist of a period only, while in a more expanded construction a double period or larger section could comprise part A. The second part (part A′ or part B, as will be seen later) may also be composed in the same manner, but on frequent occasions the second part is longer than the first. Both parts may share the same key or a related key. In any case, the second part ends with an authentic cadence in the original key. Within this concept, three possibilities exist.

Similar Material The binary form may consist of two sections of essentially the same material, the second section being shaped to balance the first.

Illustrated below are two phrases containing the same melodic material. Each phrase is designed to complement the other. Two phrases would seldom be contemplated in terms of a complete form, yet embodied in this small musical period is a microcosm of two-part form. For analysis purposes, the first section is designated A and the second section A′ although at the period level AP is perhaps more apt.

Similar material in both parts:

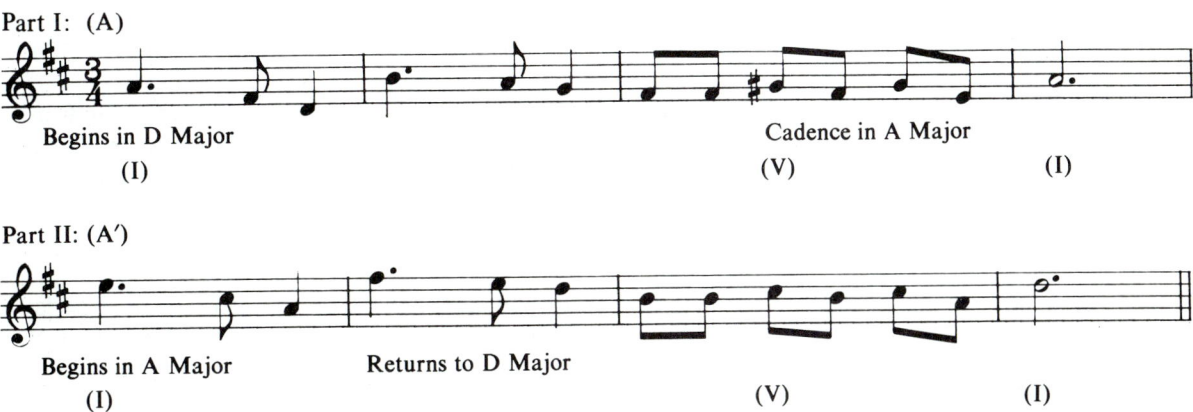

Part I: (A)
Begins in D Major (I)   Cadence in A Major (V)   (I)

Part II: (A′)
Begins in A Major (I)   Returns to D Major   (V)   (I)

275

Different Material

The two sections of the binary form may be related successfully to each other through means other than simply a similarity of thematic material. The mere shaping of melodic material, the balancing of key relationships, or the molding of complementary harmonic patterns are other techniques available to the composer.

The four phrases of *Londonderry Air* demonstrate the way in which different material may be used in the two parts:

Londonderry Air — Old Irish Air

ANALYSIS OF COMPOSITION

MEASURES	KEY	TYPE OF CADENCE	PHRASE RELATIONSHIPS	TWO-PART FORM
1–4	E-FLAT MAJOR	HALF	a	A
5–8	E-FLAT MAJOR	PERFECT AUTHENTIC	a′	A
9–12	E-FLAT MAJOR	HALF	b	A′
13–16	E-FLAT MAJOR	PERFECT AUTHENTIC	b′	A′

One important element that unifies the four phrases and welds them firmly into the two-part, or binary, form is that each section (A and A′) ends on a perfect authentic cadence with a half cadence dividing the two periods. Notice also the similarity in rhythmic structure between the two parts—except for the last three measures of each.

Both Similar and Different Material

A type of two-part form very popular in the Baroque and Classical periods (especially in the Baroque) consisted of motivic material common to both the A and the B sections. The excerpt below by Haydn typifies this treatment in the Classical period. It is essentially *homophonic* (a single line of melody with supporting harmony).

Haydn: *Sonata no. 8 in A Major* Hob. 16/5 (second movement)

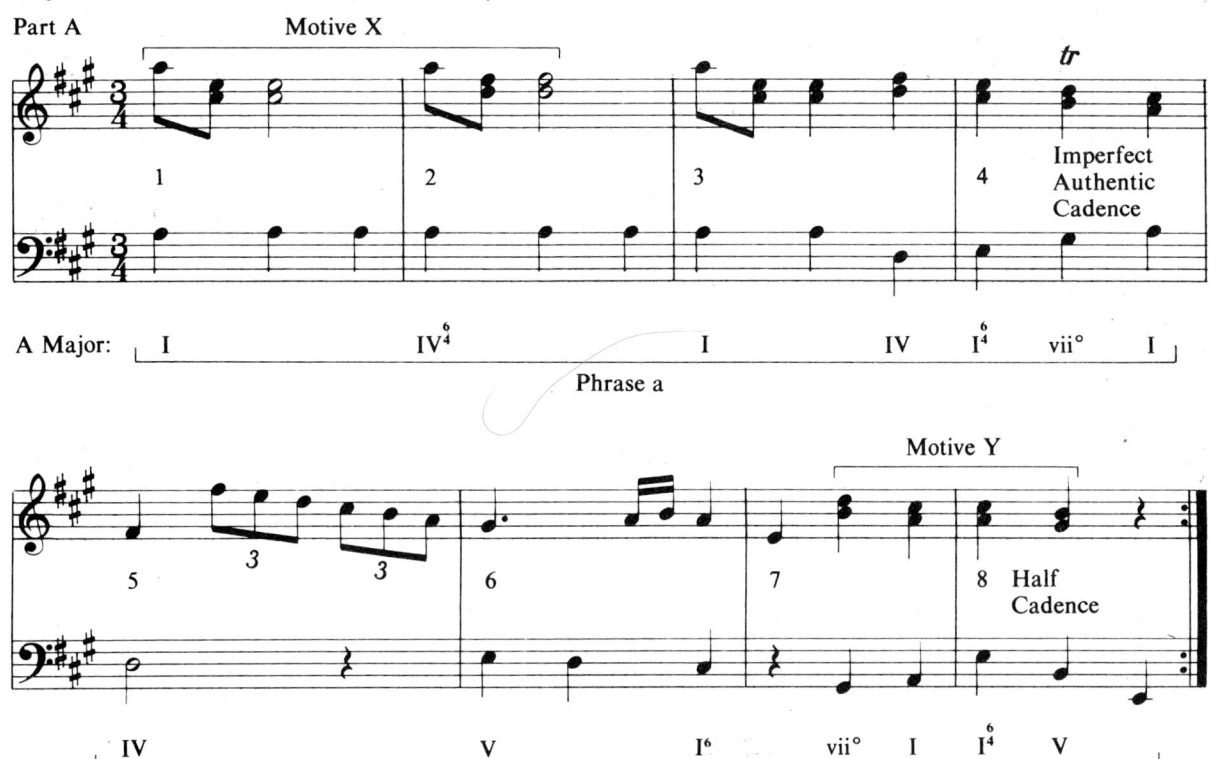

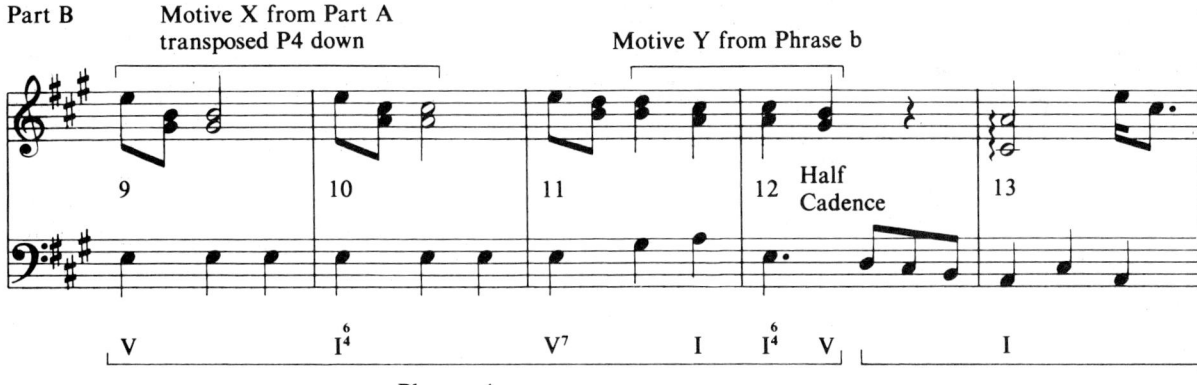

Two-Part (Binary) Form 277

ANALYSIS OF COMPOSITION

MEASURES	KEY	TYPE OF CADENCE	PHRASE RELATIONSHIPS	TWO-PART FORM
1–4	A MAJOR	IMPERFECT AUTHENTIC	a ⎤	
5–8	A MAJOR	HALF	b ⎦ A
9–12	A MAJOR	HALF	a′ ⎤	
13–18	A MAJOR	PERFECT AUTHENTIC	c ⎦ B

Note—

1. that phrase a′ is related to a in that it contains the same motive transposed.
2. that the only perfect authentic cadence occurs at the end of the composition.
3. that there is an absence of sequences.

The following illustration is an additional example of the two-part or binary, form where both parts (A and B) utilize similar (but not exactly the same) material. This work by Bach is taken from one of the *English Suites* written for keyboard. Each suite is composed of a number of dances, all of which are in the same key. Most often a prelude introduces the dances. The dance types employed in the Baroque period include the *allemande, courante, sarabande, gigue* (jig), *gavotte, bourrée, minuet,* and others. These had begun as popular dances, but by the time of the Late Baroque, they had gradually entered into the domain of art music. Such dances of peasant origin injected an earthy flavor into the formal surroundings of the period.

This particular composition is an excellent example of suite movements written in the Baroque period where a majority are in binary form and embrace the kind of motivic or thematic unity so characteristic of the genre.

Bach: *Gavotte* from *English Suite no. 3 in G Minor* BWV 808

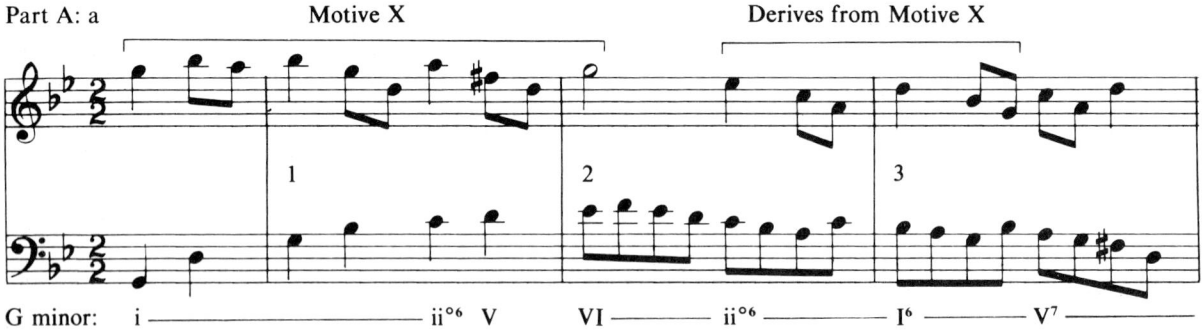

278 Two-Part (Binary) Form

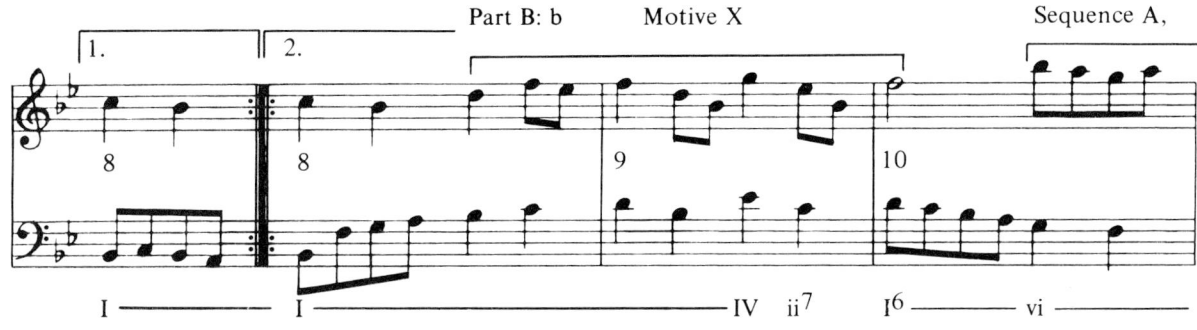
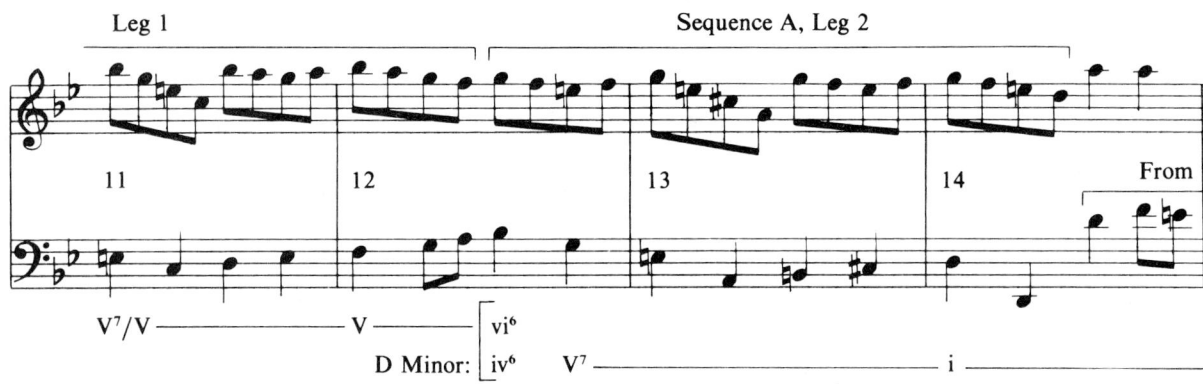
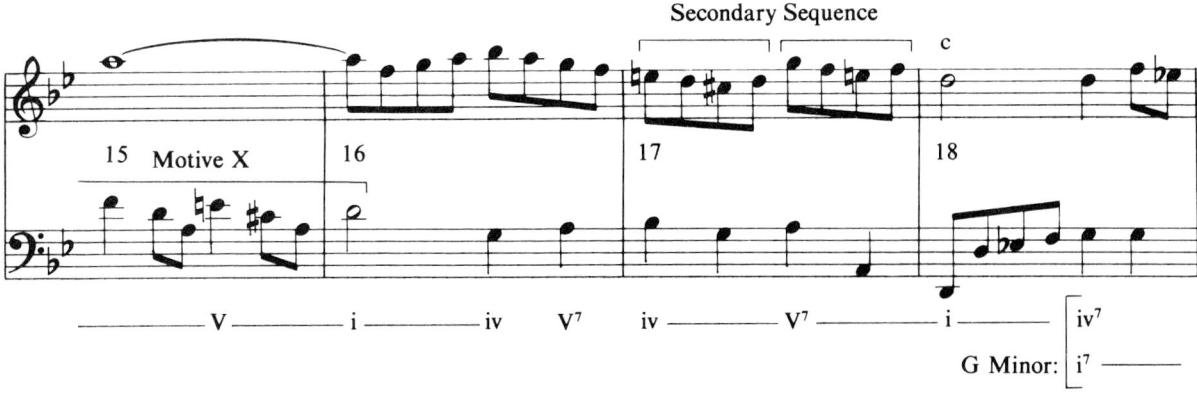

*This will be discussed in volume 2.

Two-Part (Binary) Form 279

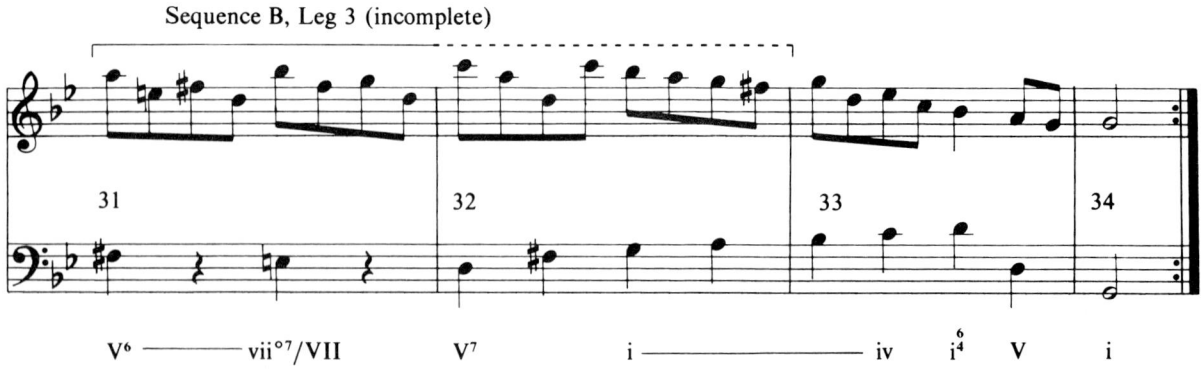

*$vii°^7/iv$ over a G (i) pedal tone

280   Two-Part (Binary) Form

ANALYSIS OF COMPOSITION

MEASURES	KEY	TYPE OF CADENCE	PHRASE RELATIONSHIPS	TWO-PART FORM
1–4	G MINOR	IMPERFECT AUTHENTIC	a ⎤	⎫
4–8	G MINOR TO B-FLAT MAJOR	PERFECT AUTHENTIC	a′ ⎦	⎬ A
8–18	B-FLAT MAJOR TO D MINOR	PERFECT AUTHENTIC	b ⎤	⎫
18–26	D MINOR TO G MINOR	HALF	c	⎬ B
26–34	G MINOR	PERFECT AUTHENTIC	d ⎦	⎭

The Bach *Gavotte* is an excellent example of the style of tonal counterpoint (as opposed to modal counterpoint of the sixteenth century) found in the Baroque period. Here the counterpoint is governed by the functional harmony it implies. Although the composition lacks the organic intensity of a fugue or canon, it is essentially a polyphonic rather than homophonic work. The basic binary form is reinforced by the key relationships:

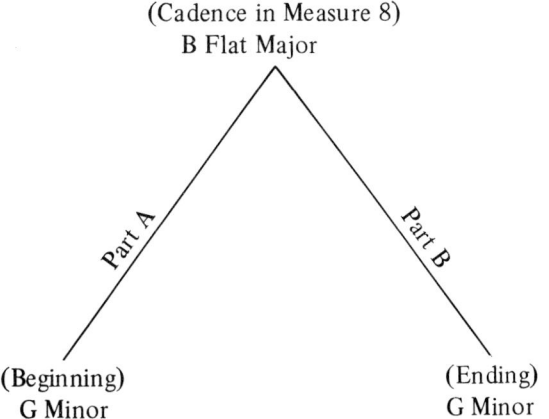

Either motive X itself or derivatives of it appear frequently (six times) in part A or in part B. This is a compelling force for unification of the two parts and insures organization in the composition. Motivic material appears only once in the lower voice (in measures 14–16). The lower voice for the most part simply provides supporting counterpoint for the upper voice, which contributes most of the elements of interest.

Two important sequences occur—one in measures 10–14 (sequence A) and the other in measures 27–33 (sequence B). Secondary sequences (sequences of less structural significance) are also found in measures 17 and 25.

The cadences in measures 4 and 26 are considered weak since the melodic line allows only a brief pause at those moments and immediately picks up the next phrase. Thus, the force of the cadence is reduced.

ROUNDED BINARY FORM

The rounded binary form differs from true two-part or binary form in that the first section (A) is repeated (sometimes in part) at the end of the second section.

The difference between the rounded binary form and the three-part form will be discussed in the next chapter, "Three-Part (Ternary) Form."

Four-Phrase Level   Rounded binary form at the four-phrase level is common. Most often the phrases combine to form a double period. The A section consists of two phrases (a period). The B section has one phrase only, and the return of the first section has also one phrase. The return of A is frequently not exact, and is thus analyzed as A′. The following excerpt is an example of a four-phrase, rounded binary form.

Mozart: *Sonata in D Major* K. 284 (third movement)

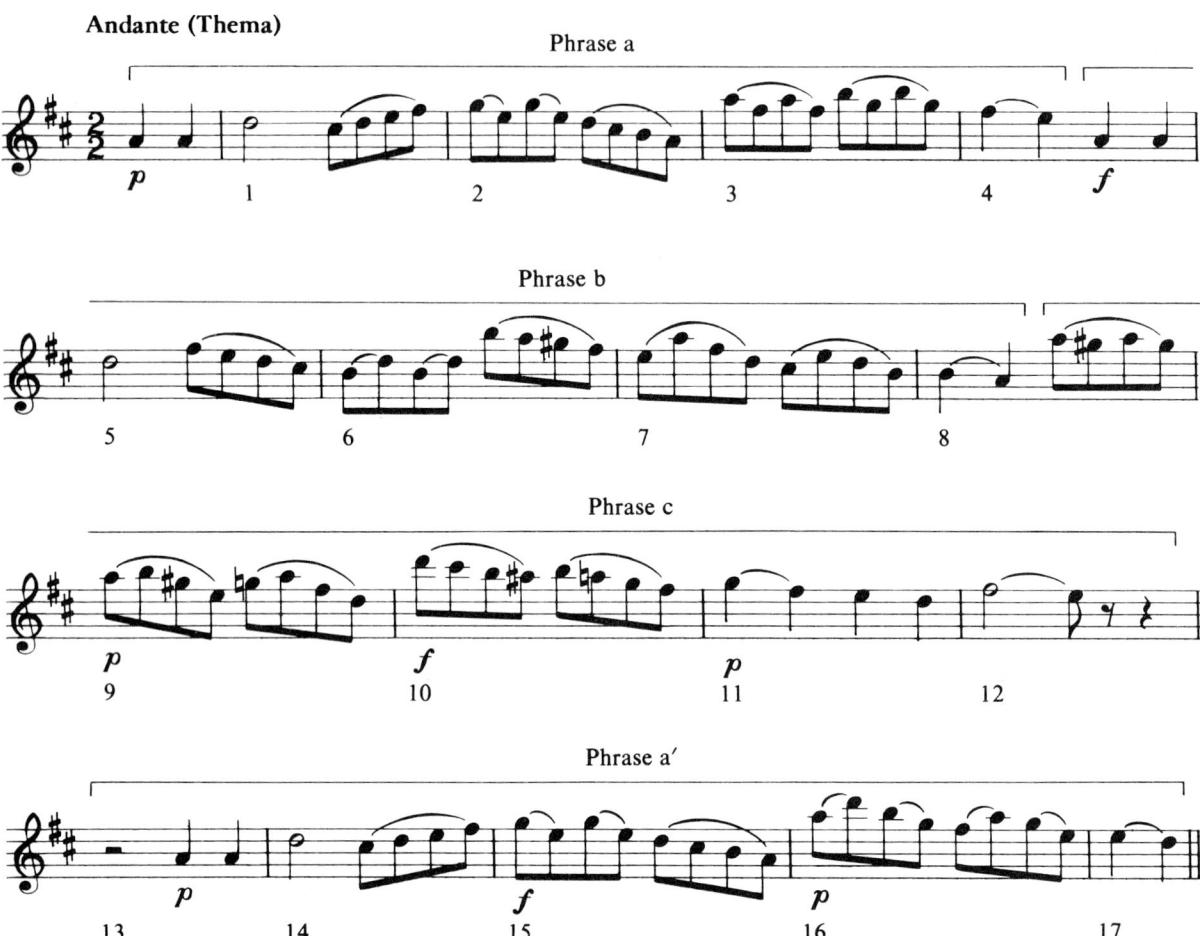

ANALYSIS OF COMPOSITION

MEASURES	PHRASE RELATIONSHIP	ROUNDED BINARY FORM	PERIOD
1–4	a ⎤		
5–8	b ⎦	A	1ST
9–13	c ⎤		
14–17	a ⎦	BA	2ND

Five-Phrase Level   Also a rounded binary form, the five-phrase level is common. The phrases generally result in a period (A), followed by a single phrase (B), and ending with another period (A or A′). The following is a typical example:

Mozart: *Sonata in E-flat Major* K. 282 (second movement)

Two-Part (Binary) Form 283

ANALYSIS OF COMPOSITION

MEASURES	KEY	TYPE OF CADENCE	PHRASE RELATIONSHIP	PERIOD	ROUNDED BINARY FORM
1–4	B♭ MAJOR	IMPERFECT AUTHENTIC	a ⎫	A	A
5–12	B♭ MAJOR TO F MAJOR	PERFECT AUTHENTIC	b ⎭		
13–18	F MAJOR TO B♭ MAJOR	HALF	c	B	
19–22	B♭ MAJOR	IMPERFECT AUTHENTIC	a′ ⎫	A′	BA
23–32	B♭ MAJOR	PERFECT AUTHENTIC	b′ ⎭		

HISTORY

Middle Ages (500–1450)

The forerunner of binary two-part form was the *Bar form*. This is a name given to a song form used by the *Minnesingers* (aristocratic poet-musicians from the twelfth to fourteenth centuries) and *Meistersingers* (middle-class, poet-musicians from the fourteenth to sixteenth centuries).

Bar form consists simply of an A part (called *Stollen*) that is repeated and a B part (*Abgesang*) that is not repeated. As Bar form developed, the B part began to contain either a section or all of the A part.

The following illustration is an example of the *canzo*, which resembles the Bar form. The form has a *rounded-binary* aspect in that part of the A section is repeated in B. The canzo is a form associated with the troubadours, twelfth- and thirteenth-century poet musicians of southern France. The composition shown below was written toward the end of the twelfth century and may have been performed as an unaccompanied solo song.

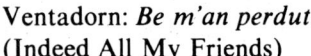

Ventadorn: *Be m'an perdut* (Indeed All My Friends)

Canzo

Be m'an per-dut lay en-ves Ven-ta dorn Tuih mei a-mic pos ma do-na no m'a ma
Non ay ra-zon que ieu ia mays lai torn Tant es mi bra-va e nos re- cla-ma

284 Two-Part (Binary) Form

This is a repetition of the last section of Part A

Renaissance (1450–1600)

The Bar form continued into the Renaissance although its use was not extensive. The two-part concept found its way into a variety of compositions of this period, among them the *German Part Song* and the *German Lied*.

Baroque (1600–1750)

It was during the Baroque period that the use of two-part form became most extensive. Suite movements of extended length (allemande, courante, sarabande, gigue, minuet, bourrée, gavotte, etc.) were written using this construction, and only the basic elements of the older Bar form remained.

Seventeenth-Century Binary Forms

Many two-part compositions of the seventeenth century have the following characteristics (examples of such writing may be found in the *Fitzwilliam Virginal Book,* a collection of English seventeenth-century instrumental music):

1. No modulations.
2. First section ends with an authentic or a half cadence in the original key.
3. Second section ends with an authentic cadence in the original key.
4. Second section may or may not contain material similar to that of the first.

Eighteenth-Century Binary Forms

Refinements and expansion of the binary form in the late seventeenth and early eighteenth century led to the following type of construction (typical examples are the dance movements from the *English Suites* for keyboard by Bach):

1. The first section modulates to a closely related key, usually the dominant or relative major.
2. The second section starts out in a new key but modulates back to the original key.
3. The first section ends with an authentic cadence in a new key.
4. The second section ends with an authentic cadence in the original key.
5. The second section often begins with the theme of the first section in the new key and contains material derived from the first section.

Classical Period (1750–1825)

The Classical period, especially the early part, saw considerable use of the two-part form. From the concise shape of the Baroque suite movements, the Classical composers began to evolve embryonic development sections at the beginning of the second section, the theme (or themes) from the first section were repeated at the end of the second section in the original key, and the result was the *sonata allegro* form.

Following is a movement from a sonata by Haydn showing a step in the transition from the binary to the sonata allegro form. This movement satisfies the qualifications for the rounded binary form (also known as *incipient three-part form*) and at the same time contains in miniature many of the principles of the sonata allegro form:

Haydn: *Sonata no. 3 for Piano* Hob. XVI/9 (first movement)

286 Two-Part (Binary) Form

First Theme in Recapitulation (F Major)

Transition (F Major)

Second Theme in Recapitulation (F Major)

Romantic Period (1825–1900)

The use of the binary form continued through the Romantic period although its application was greatly diminished in numbers and much greater freedom was taken in adapting the construction to nineteenth-century musical thought.

Examples of binary form may be found in the works of Schubert, Berlioz, Mendelssohn, Bizet, and Schumann.

Post-Romantic and Impressionistic Period (1875–1920)

Although examples can be found during this period, the binary form was not an essential element in this era.

Contemporary Period (1920–Present) Works by Bartók, Villa-Lobos, and Britten, as well as those of many other composers, employ two-part form, but this type of construction is not a common practice of contemporary composers.

ASSIGNMENT 1 Following are three compositions for analysis. The first is a movement from *Suite no. 7 in B-flat Major for Harpsichord* by Handel. Somewhat less complex contrapuntally than most works of Bach, this composition is ideal for analysis at this point.

The second composition, a product of the Romantic period, is a bit more venturesome harmonically.

The third work by Mozart is in a form discussed in this chapter. See if you can recognize the form as described.

1. Become familiar with each of these compositions by playing them on the piano or listening to recordings. If possible, get a class member who is an accomplished pianist to discuss the interpretation of each work.
2. Make a complete analysis of each composition using the guidelines stated in chapter 10, "Approach to Style Analysis."
3. Place special emphasis in your analysis on the following:
   a. Phrase relationships
   b. Analysis of form
   c. Key schemes and modulations
   d. Compositional devices such as imitation, sequence, phrase extension, harmonic elaboration, etc.
   e. Harmonic vocabulary
   f. Cadence types

1.
Handel: *Gigue* from *Suite no. 7 for Harpsichord*

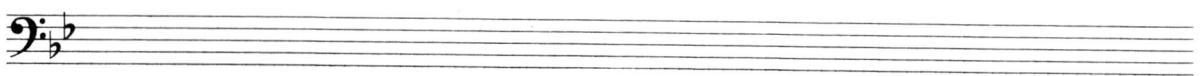

288   Two-Part (Binary) Form

ASSIGNMENT 1 (continued)

Two-Part (Binary) Form

ASSIGNMENT 1 (continued)

2.
Schumann: *Davidsbündlertänze* op. 6 no. 8

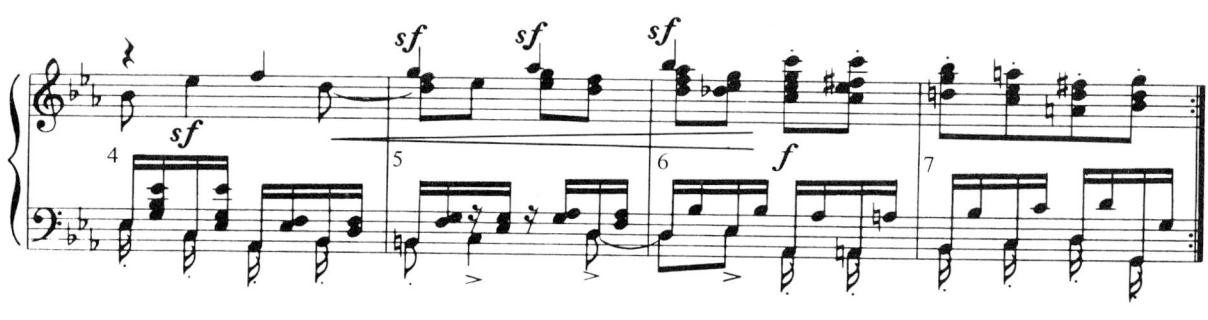

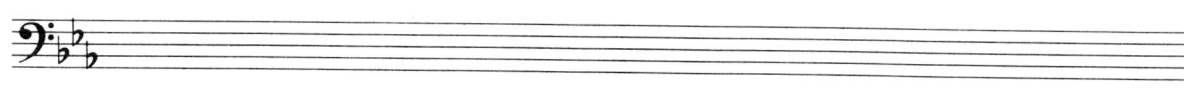

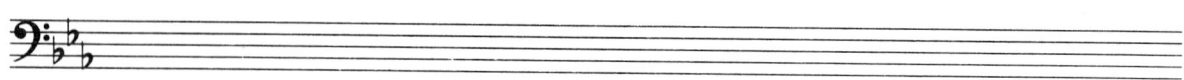

ASSIGNMENT 1 (continued)

A number of chords in this composition lack at least one factor. In writing the chords on the blank staves, fill in the factors you think are implied (but not stated).

3.
Mozart: *Piano Sonata* K. 282 (second movement)

Two-Part (Binary) Form 291

ASSIGNMENT 1 (continued)

292   Two-Part (Binary) Form

ASSIGNMENT 2   Below is the first section (A) of a two-part Baroque suite movement.

1. Compose the second section (B).
2. Analyze carefully the first section.
3. Begin the B section in the same key as the final cadence of the A section.
4. Adapt some material from A for use in B.
5. B may be somewhat longer than A.
6. End B in the same key as the first phrase of A.
7. When the composition is completed, arrange it as an oboe solo with accompaniment. If the class has no student of oboe, arrange the solo for another appropriate instrument.
8. Have each student play his or her completed composition while the others provide an oral analysis.

ASSIGNMENT 3   Write a composition in two-part (binary) form.

1. Begin in E-flat major.
2. Make the A section about eight to sixteen measures long.
3. Let the A section modulate to B-flat major.
4. Start the B section in B-flat major and return to E-flat major.
5. The B section should be somewhat longer than the A section.
6. Have each student play his or her composition in class while the others provide an oral analysis.

ASSIGNMENT 4 Additional examples of the binary, or two-part, form are listed here. Selections from the list should be played by students or listened to in recordings for oral analysis.

Bach:	*Goldberg Variations* (the theme or any variation)
	English Suite no. IV (*Sarabande*)
	English Suite no. VI (*Courante*)
	English Suite no. III (*Courante*)
	(Nearly all of the dance movements from the *English Suites* are in two-part form. The particular movements listed above are somewhat shorter and require less advanced piano technique than others in the collection.)
Handel:	*Suite no. 4 for Klavier* (*Sarabande*)
	Suite no. 7 for Klavier (*Andante*)
Scarlatti:	*Sonata in E Major* K. 380 Longo 23
Chopin:	*Prelude* op. 28 no. 20
	Prelude op. 28 no. 10

17 Three-Part (Ternary) Form

Three-Part Form
Three-Part Song Form
Expanded Three-Part Form
Song-Form with Trio

THREE-PART FORM A *three-part*, or *ternary*, form is a sectional form consisting of three principal parts following the scheme A B A in which each of the letters refers to one of the distinctive parts.

Part I	Part II	Part III
A	B	A
Statement	Contrast	Restatement

The *three-part form* may exist at any dimension of musical relationship from small to large. In order of increasing length, the three-part forms may be listed as follows:

1. Three-phrase level
2. Three-part song form
3. Expanded three-part song form
4. Song form with trio

In volume 2 of the text, you will discover that some rondo forms and the sonata allegro form include aspects of ternary design with the sonata allegro representing the highest level of this three-part pattern.

Three-Phrase An independent, or complete, three-part form at the very lowest level (*three-phrase*) is somewhat rare. The following is an example of this construction:

Schumann: *Kinder Sonata no. 1*

295

Phrase a

Song Form

The *three-part song form* is one of the most prevalent small homophonic forms in music. In this pattern, both As are at least a period in length. The B as well is usually at least a period in length, although it may be only a single phrase. The following is a typical example:

Chopin: *Mazurka no. 24* op. 33 no. 3

296   Three-Part (Ternary) Form

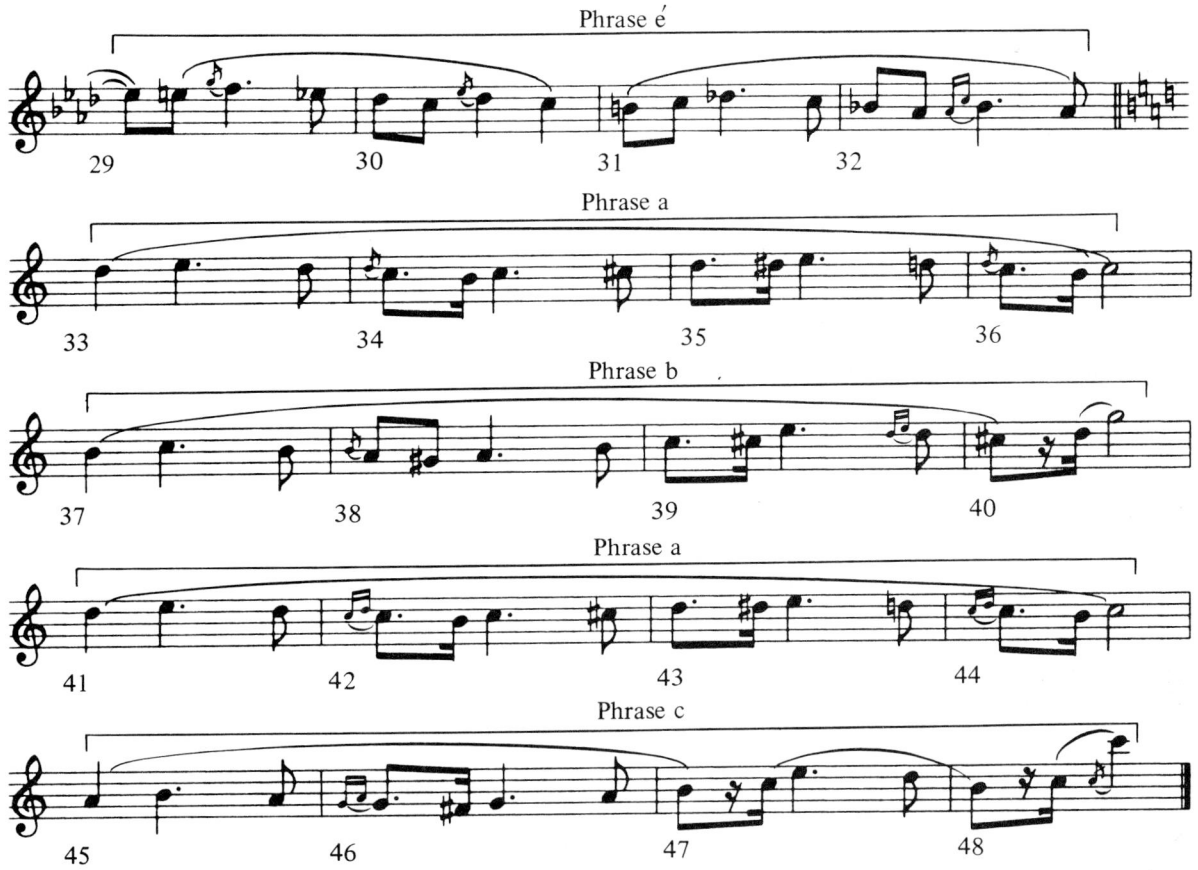

ANALYSIS OF COMPOSITION

MEASURES	PHRASE RELATIONSHIP	PART	ORGANIZATION
1–4	a ⎤		
5–8	b ⎥	A	DOUBLE PERIOD
9–12	a ⎥		
13–16	c ⎦		
17–20	d ⎤		
21–24	e ⎥	B	PERIOD REPEATED
25–28	d' ⎥		
29–32	e' ⎦		
33–36	a ⎤		
37–40	b ⎥	A	DOUBLE PERIOD
41–44	a ⎥		
45–48	c ⎦		

This example clearly illustrates the function of the B part in this form: to provide contrast with the A part and to create a need to return to the A part to complete the pattern. The degree of contrast between the A and B parts varies considerably from composition to composition. In some examples, the thematic material of B may be derived from that of A resulting in a slight degree of contrast. In other examples, such as the Chopin, the B may provide a sharp contrast with A.

Song Form Expanded

Repetition

The song form may be expanded by the use of repetitions, which are found in a standard pattern:

$$A//B//A//$$

Any combination of these repeats may be used. The repeats may be made with double-bars and repeat signs, or any repeat may be written out so that the composer may provide a different setting of the music when it is repeated. The first A is always repeated alone. The B and the final A section are always repeated together. When repetitions are made, the form is described as an *expanded three-part song form.*

Auxiliary Members

The three-part song form may be expanded by the use of *auxiliary members* such as an *introduction* to precede the first A, a *transition* between the sections, or a *coda* after the final A part that serves to bring the composition to a close. (If this closing material is brief, it is called a *codetta.*) In more extensive three-part song forms, a codetta may be found at the end of any section. Suggested examples of the expanded three-part form:

Chopin:	*Mazurka in A minor* op. 17 no. 4
Chopin:	*Waltz in D-flat Major* op. 64 no. 1 *Minuet*
Prokofiev:	*Classical Symphony in D Major* op. 25 *Gavotte* (third movement)
Mendelssohn:	*Songs Without Words* op. 19 no. 3, op. 30 no. 2, op. 30 no. 4, op. 38 no. 4, op. 53 no. 1, op. 53 no. 3, op. 53 no. 5.

Song Form with Trio

In the *song form with trio,* the most complex of the small homophonic forms, each of the three sections (A B A) is a song form in itself. The A sections are usually in ternary design while the B section may be either binary or ternary. This is the standard form of the dance-related movements (usually the third in a four-movement sequence of symphonies, sonatas, chamber works, etc., composed in the last half of the eighteenth and early nineteenth centuries. The dance style employed most frequently was that of the minuet. Beethoven eventually replaced the minuet with the faster *scherzo* (literally "joke"), which in his earlier works essentially maintains the structural design (if not the style) of the minuet.

The song form with trio is outlined as follows:

MINUET	TRIO	MINUET
A	B	A
(Song Form I)	(Song Form II)	(Song Form I)

The minuet-trio-minuet in the following illustration is the second movement of one of Haydn's early sonatas for piano. The sonata as a whole is not representative of his later and more mature works in this form. The minuet-trio-minuet, however, is typical of the period and provides a worthy specimen for analysis. (Incidentally, "Hob." refers to the chronology of Haydn sonatas established by Anthony van Hoboken in his *Haydn Catalog* published in Mainz, Germany, in 1957.)

Haydn: *Piano Sonata in C Major* Hob. XVI/10 *Minuet* (second movement)

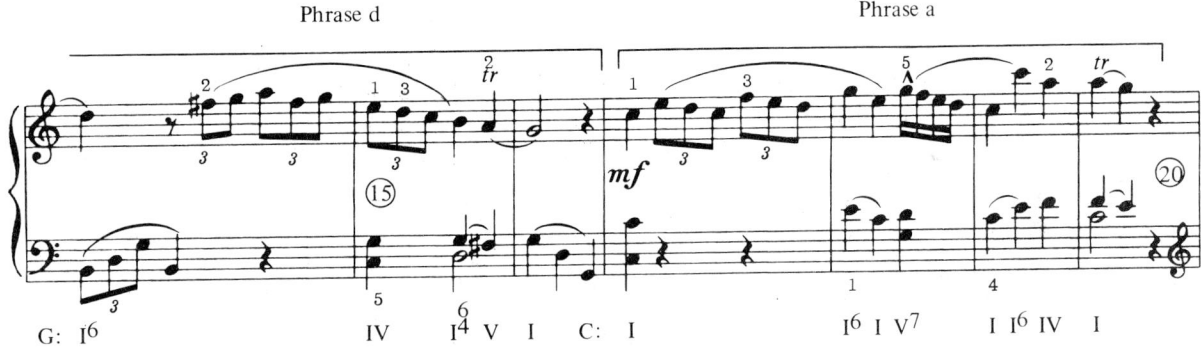
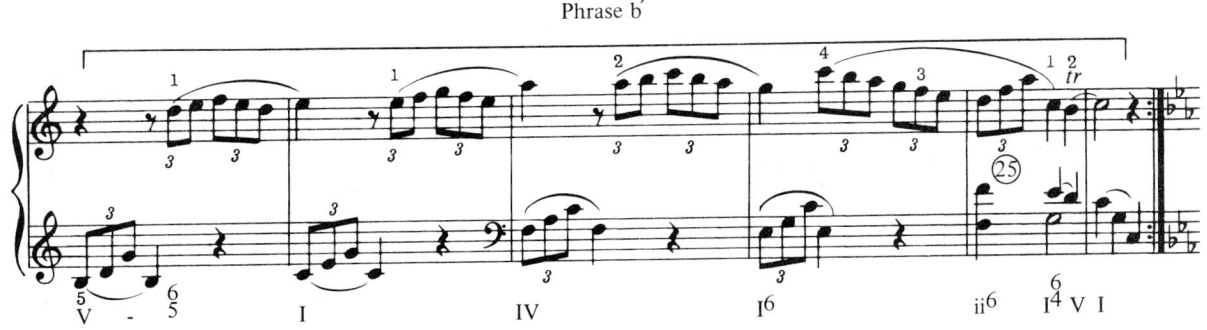

Three-Part (Ternary) Form

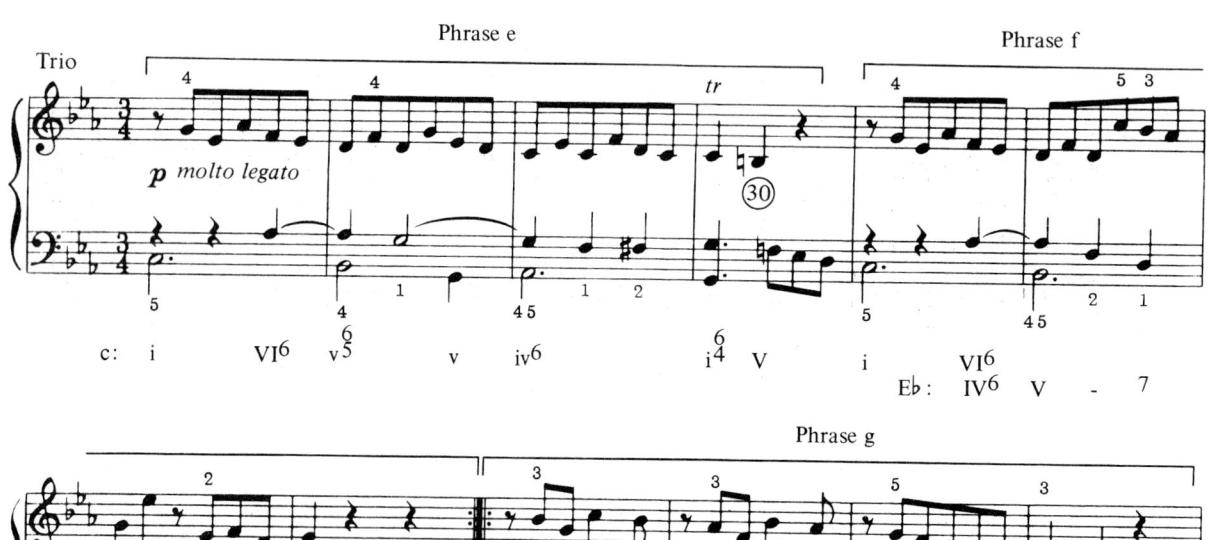

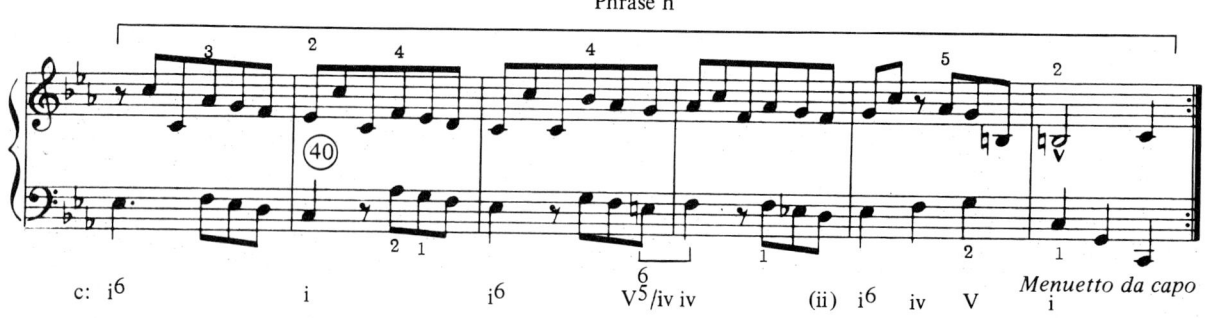

300　Three-Part (Ternary) Form

ANALYSIS OF COMPOSITION

MEASURES	KEY	TYPE OF CADENCE	PHRASE RELATION-SHIP		FORM OF ENTIRE COMPOSITION

FORM OF MINUET

MEASURES	KEY	TYPE OF CADENCE	PHRASE		
1–4	C MAJOR	IMPERFECT AUTHENTIC	a ⌉	A	
5–8	C MAJOR	PERFECT AUTHENTIC	b ⌋		
9–12	G MAJOR	IMPERFECT AUTHENTIC	c ⌉	B	A
13–16	G MAJOR	PERFECT AUTHENTIC	d ⌋		*TERNARY
17–20	C MAJOR	IMPERFECT AUTHENTIC	a ⌉	A′	
21–26	C MAJOR	PERFECT AUTHENTIC	b′ ⌋		

FORM OF TRIO

27–30	C MINOR	HALF	e ⌉	A	
31–34	E♭ MAJOR	PERFECT AUTHENTIC	f ⌋		B
					BINARY
35–38	C MINOR	HALF	g ⌉	B	
39–44	C MINOR	PERFECT AUTHENTIC	h ⌋		

(*MINUET DA CAPO*)

FORM OF MINUET

1–4	C MAJOR	IMPERFECT AUTHENTIC	a ⌉	A	
5–8	C MAJOR	PERFECT AUTHENTIC	b ⌋		
9–12	G MAJOR	IMPERFECT AUTHENTIC	c ⌉	B	A
13–16	G MAJOR	PERFECT AUTHENTIC	d ⌋		TERNARY
17–20	C MAJOR	IMPERFECT AUTHENTIC	a ⌉	A′	
21–26	C MAJOR	PERFECT AUTHENTIC	b′ ⌋		

*The location of the repeat signs in the *Minuet* suggests the possibility of a rounded binary form. However, the use of period forms, complete with perfect authentic cadences for each (m. 8, 16, 26), suggests the sectional ternary design. In effect, the *Minuet* includes aspects of both.

HISTORY	The history of ternary design in Western music can be traced back to the liturgical chants of the early Christian church. The principle is present in chant settings of the *Kyrie eleison (Lord Have Mercy)* and the *Agnus Dei (Lamb of God)*. It also appears in the structure of medieval secular song.
Medieval and Middle Ages (500–1450)	

Mass V: *Kyrie eleison* (Mode 8: Hypomixolydian)*

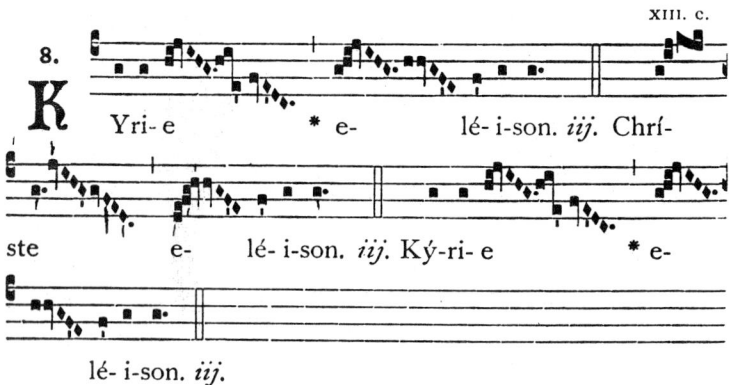

Kyrie eleison (in modern notation)

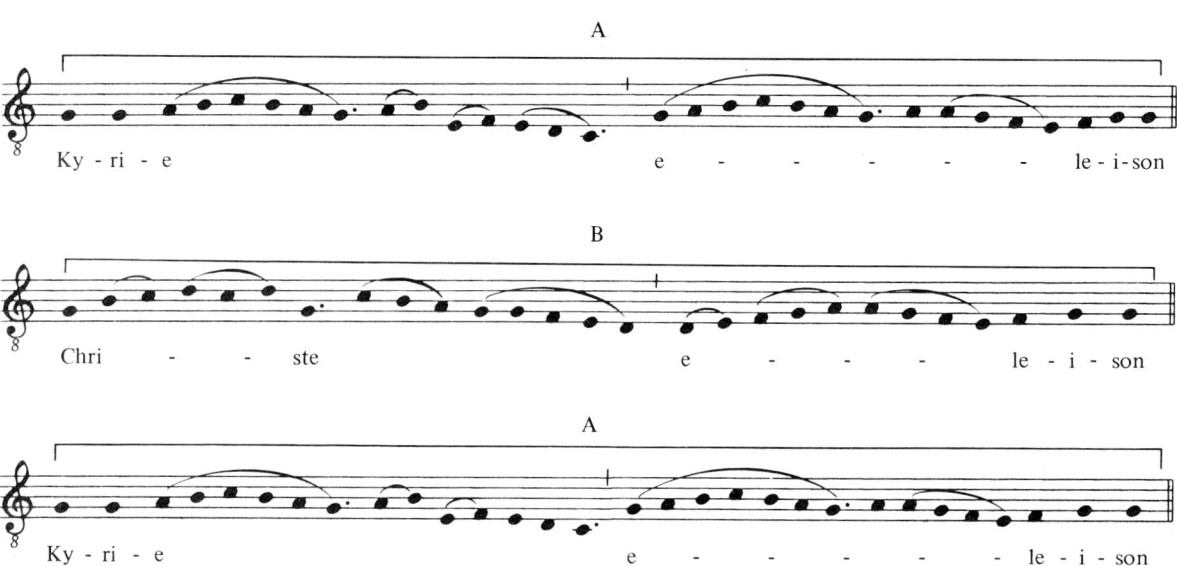

Renaissance (1450–1600) and Baroque (1600–1750)	Josquin des Prés (1440?–1521) in *Faulte d'argent (Lack of Money)* observes the principle of ternary design as do many composers of the sixteenth-century *chansons* (songs). The arias found in seventeenth-century and early eighteenth-century operas, oratorios, and chamber cantatas utilize the principle in the form of the *da capo* (A B A) aria. In the Baroque *suite,* the ternary design is achieved by alternating two dances, repeating the first after the second, e.g., Bourrée I, II or Minuet I, II resulting in an A B A sequence.
Classical Period (1750–1825)	A more significant aspect of ternary design occurs when it is combined with a binary scheme as found in the song form with trio. This form appears in the dance-related movements (usually the third movement in a four-movement sequence) of the late eighteenth- and early nineteenth-century symphonies, sonatas, chamber works, etc. The ternary (A B A) aspect of the song-form section is organized in such a way as to isolate the first A, usually with a perfect

Liber usualis, p. 28.

authentic cadence and repeat signs, while B A (or B A′) are combined into a single structural unit also set off with repeat signs. Thus the song-form section of the song form with trio includes aspects of binary and ternary design (‖: A :‖: B A :‖). The same design may also appear in the trio. The sequence of song form-trio-song form, however, constitutes unequivocally a sectional ternary design in much the same manner as the alternating dances cited above.

Romantic Period to present (1825–   )

The basic ternary design persisted through the nineteenth century in the character pieces of Schubert, Schumann, Mendelssohn, Chopin, and Brahms, to name only a few, and made its way into the twentieth century, notably in the shorter works of Debussy and Bartók.

The ternary principle was extended by means of repetitions of trio sections found in dance-related movements. Beethoven repeated these trio sections in the dance-related movements of his *Fourth, Sixth, Seventh,* and *Ninth* symphonies. The once ternary form took on a broadened, five-part scheme (not unlike that of the *rondo form* to be discussed in volume 2 of the text):

```
    A      //  B    //    A      //  B    //    A
Song Form  —  Trio  —  Song Form  —  Trio  —  Song Form
```

ASSIGNMENT 1

Following is the third movement of the *Eine kleine Nachtmusik* (literally, A Little Night Music) by Mozart. This four-movement work for strings (violin 1, violin 2, viola, and cello) was written in 1787.

1. Become familiar with this work by listening to a recording of it several times. If possible, listen to two different recordings and compare the interpretations.
2. Make a complete analysis using the guidelines stated in chapter 10, "Approach to Style Analysis."
3. Place special emphasis on the following:
   a. Phrase relationships
   b. Analysis of the form
   c. Key schemes and modulations
   d. Compositional devices such as imitation, sequence, phrase extension, harmonic elaboration, etc.
   e. Harmonic vocabulary
   f. Cadence types
4. Compare the style of this orchestral (string) work with that of the *Minuet* by Haydn analyzed in this chapter. Consider the topics listed in no. 2 above.

ASSIGNMENT 1 (continued)

Mozart: *Eine kleine Nachtmusik* (A Little Night Music) K. 525 (third movement)

Menuetto

304 Three-Part (Ternary) Form

ASSIGNMENT 1 (continued)

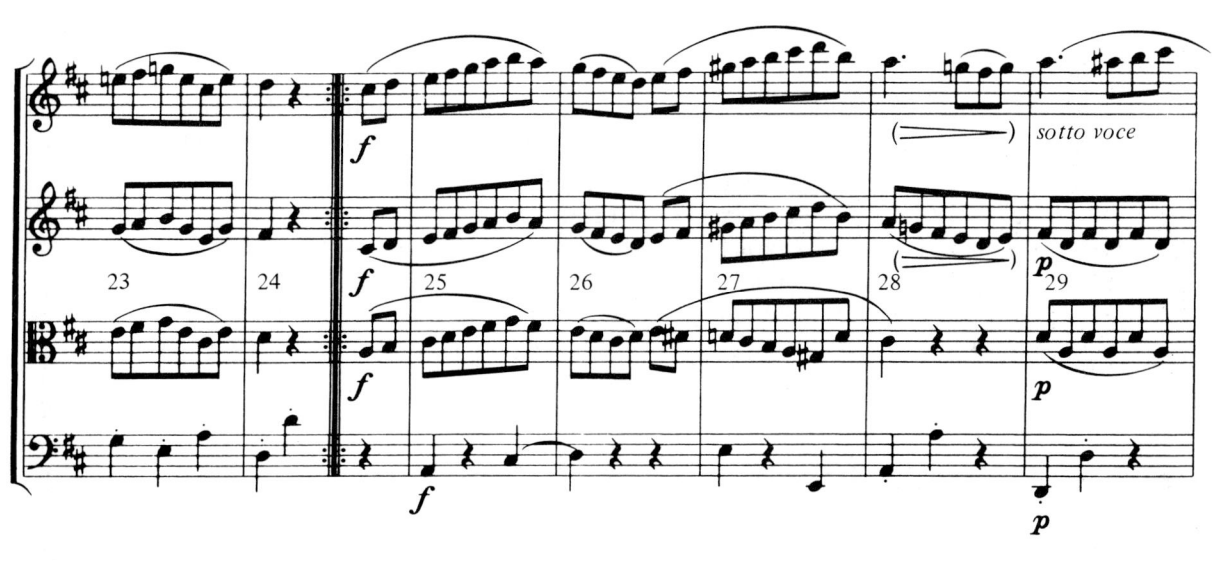

ASSIGNMENT 1 (continued)

Menuetto da capo

ASSIGNMENT 2   Additional examples of three-part form are listed. Selections from this list should be played in class by students or in recordings for oral analysis.

Smaller Ternary Forms:
- Brahms: *Four Piano Pieces* op. 119 nos. 1, 2, 3
- Chopin: *Prelude in F-sharp Major* op. 28 no. 13
- Chopin: *Mazurka no. 16 in A-flat Major* op. 24 no. 3
- Chopin: *Etude in C Minor* op. 10 no. 12 *(Revolutionary)*
- Schumann: *Album for the Young* op. 68 no. 3 *Trällerliedchen* (Humming Bird)
- Schumann: *Scenes from Childhood* op. 15 no. 6 *(An Important Event)*
- Schumann: *Papillons* op. 2 nos. 4, 5

Larger Ternary Forms:
- Beethoven: *Piano Sonata* op. 2 no. 1 (third movement)
- Beethoven: *Piano Sonata* op. 2 no. 2 (third movement)
- Beethoven: *Piano Sonata* op. 2 no. 3 (third movement)
- Beethoven: *Piano Sonata* op. 27 no. 2 *(Moonlight)* (second movement)
- Beethoven: *Symphony no. 1* (third movement)
- Beethoven: *Symphony no. 2* (third movement)
- Haydn: *String Quartet in D Minor* Hob. III/76
- Mozart: *Piano Sonata in A Major* K. 331 (second movement)
- Mozart: *Symphony no. 40 in G Minor* K. 550 (third movement)

ASSIGNMENT 3 Write a composition using the following guidelines:

1. Key of A major
2. 6/8 meter
3. Form: three-part according to the following analysis:

MEASURES	KEY	CADENCE	OVERALL FORM
1-4	A MAJOR	HALF	A
5-8	A MAJOR	AUTHENTIC	
9-12	E MAJOR	HALF	B
13-16	E MAJOR	AUTHENTIC	
17-20	A MAJOR	HALF	A
21-24	A MAJOR	AUTHENTIC	

4. Incorporate at least two secondary dominants in the composition.
5. Write for whatever instrument or instruments you wish.
6. Write in a homophonic style (single melody with accompaniment).

18 American Popular Song

Popular Music Symbols	Melody	dm^7 to Mm^7 Chords	Diatonic Stepwise
Triad Types	Harmony	Augmented Triad	Progressions
Seventh, Ninth, Eleventh,	Circle of P5s	Diminished Seventh	Four-Chord Formulas
and Thirteenth Chords	mm^7 to Mm^7 to Triad	Chromatic Descending	Four-Chord Formulas in
Forms	Secondary Dominants in	Chord Progressions	Succession
Key	Succession	Substitute Mm^7 Chords	Ostinato Bass
Rhythm and Meter	Successions of mm^7		Turnarounds (Turnbacks)
	Chords		

Popular song as now found in the United States evolved near the beginning of the twentieth century. Some notable composers of the music are George Gershwin, Cole Porter, Richard Rodgers, Irving Berlin, Vernon Duke, and Burt Bacharach.

In this country, popular songs by composers like those just mentioned were the dominant music with mass appeal until rock 'n' roll became firmly entrenched in the 1960s. Today, popular songs in the earlier sense still exist as a separate and developing style, but they have also been assimilated into rock and vice versa. Note too that popular songs are often a vehicle for jazz improvisation.

POPULAR MUSIC SYMBOLS

Figured bass was to the eighteenth century what *popular music symbols* are to the twentieth century—a shorthand system of notating chords involving a modicum of improvisation.

Instead of writing out the exact chords on score paper, popular music composers and arrangers indicate the chord symbols they wish used for accompaniment above the melody line of the composition. Such a score, with the melody and the popular music symbols, is called a *lead sheet* or *fake sheet*.

Chorus

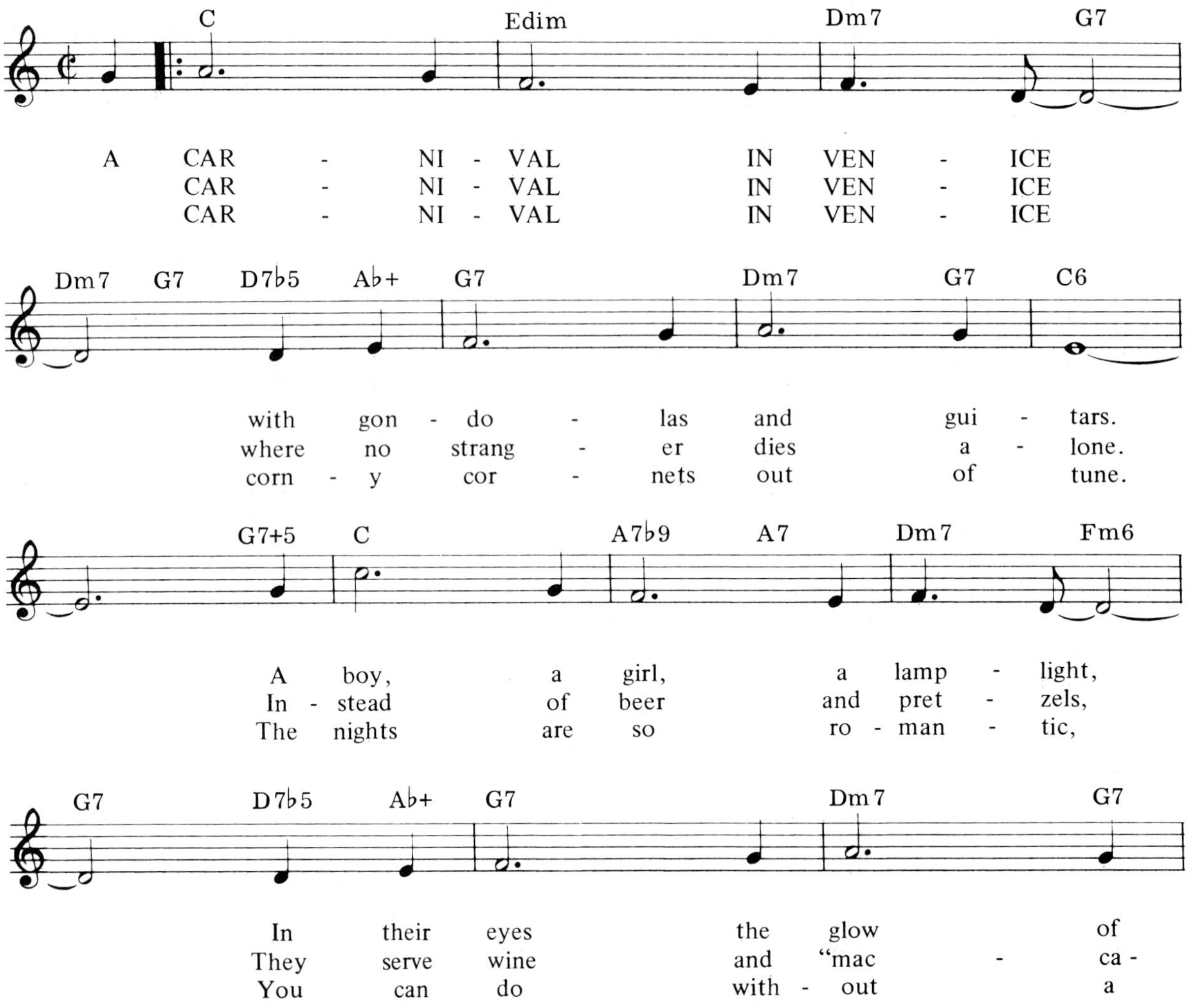

| C | Edim | Dm7 | G7 |

A CAR - NI - VAL IN VEN - ICE
  CAR - NI - VAL IN VEN - ICE
  CAR - NI - VAL IN VEN - ICE

| Dm7 G7 D7♭5 A♭+ G7 | Dm7 G7 | C6 |

with gon - do - las and gui - tars.
where no strang - er dies a - lone.
corn - y cor - nets out of tune.

| G7+5 C | A7♭9 A7 | Dm7 | Fm6 |

A boy, a girl, a lamp - light,
In - stead of beer and pret - zels,
The nights are so ro - man - tic,

| G7 D7♭5 A♭+ G7 | Dm7 | G7 |

In their eyes the glow of
They serve wine and "mac - ca -
You can do with - out a

The chord indications are quite simple to master and generally refer to *root* position. They may be read and interpreted by guitar players, and keyboard players alike. The addition of rhythmic patterns and arrangements of the chord factors is left entirely to the performer, and most of these musicians are well trained in the art of improvisation. Although chord indications are given in root position, most performers will *voice* the chords, that is, arrange them for the best voice leading, which may mean placing them in inversion.

The following examples illustrate popular music chord symbols.

Major Triad   A major triad is shown by a capital letter designating the root.

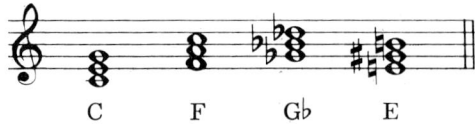

C   F   G♭   E

Minor Triad — A minor triad is shown by a capital letter with a lowercase m added (Dm). Sometimes the minor triad is indicated simply by a lower case letter (d).

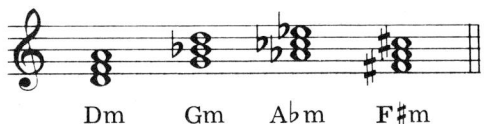

Dm   Gm   A♭m   F♯m

Diminished Triad — A diminished triad is shown by a capital letter with "dim" added (Bdim), or by a lowercase letter with ° added (b°).

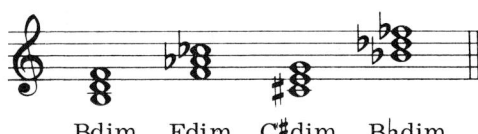

Bdim   Fdim   C♯dim   B♭dim

Augmented Triad — An augmented triad is shown by a capital letter with either "aug" (Caug) or + added (C+).

C+   F+   B♭+   A♭+

Added Sixth Chord — A triad with an added tone a major sixth above the triad root is indicated by adding 6 after the letter designating the triad (C6).

C6   Fm6   A6   E♭6

Major-Minor Seventh Chord — A four-tone chord based on a major triad with the interval of a minor seventh added (from root to seventh) is indicated by adding 7 after the letter designation of the triad (C7). The major-minor seventh chord is known also as a dominant seventh-type chord.

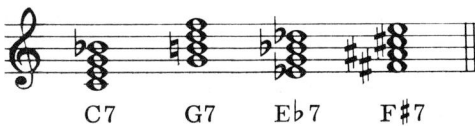

C7   G7   E♭7   F♯7

Minor-Minor Seventh Chord — A four-tone chord based on a minor triad with the interval of a minor seventh (from root to seventh) added is indicated by adding m7 to the letter designating the triad (Dm7).

Dm7   Fm7   E♭m7   G♯m7

Major-Major
Seventh Chord

A four-tone chord based on the major triad with the interval of a major seventh (from root to seventh) added is indicated by adding maj7 after the letter designating the triad (Cmaj7).

Cmaj7   Dmaj7   A♭maj7   F♯maj7

Major-Minor-Major
Ninth Chord

A five-tone chord based on the major-minor seventh chord with a major ninth (from root to ninth) added. A ninth is an octave and a second. The chord is indicated by adding 9 to the letter designating the triad (A9).

A9   F9   A♭9   C♯9

Other Chords

Many other chords can be indicated by this shorthand system. The following are but a few:

B♭m7 (♭5) = B♭m7 with fifth factor lowered a half step.
F7 (♭9)   = F7 with minor ninth.
C7 + 5 (♭9) = C7 with augmented fifth and minor ninth.
A13   = To the triad add the seventh, ninth, eleventh, and thirteenth factors. Usually two or three factors are left out of this chord in practical use.

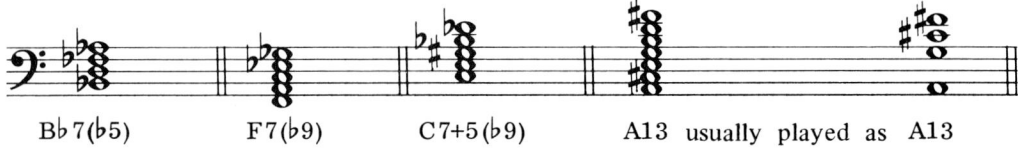

B♭7(♭5)   F7(♭9)   C7+5(♭9)   A13 usually played as A13

The following illustration is a popular melody with chord symbols as they would appear in music notation. Of course, the guitar player, the pianist, or other performers who play from these chord symbols may change the distribution of the chord tones (as shown) and will probably add an interesting rhythm.

The Tailgate Ramble

Mercer and Malone: © 1944 Michael H. Goldsen, Inc. © 1972 renewed Michael H. Goldsen, Inc.

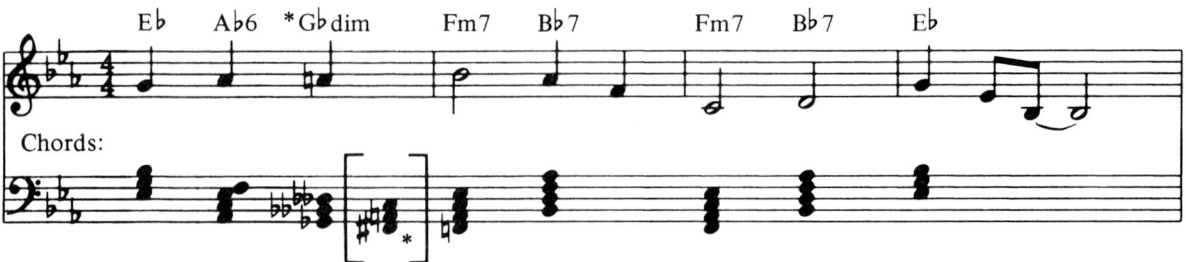

* Same as G♭dim and easier to read.

312   American Popular Song

Appendix I, in the back of this volume, contains a complete list of popular chord symbols for those who wish further information.

The following chords are among the most common found in popular song accompaniments:

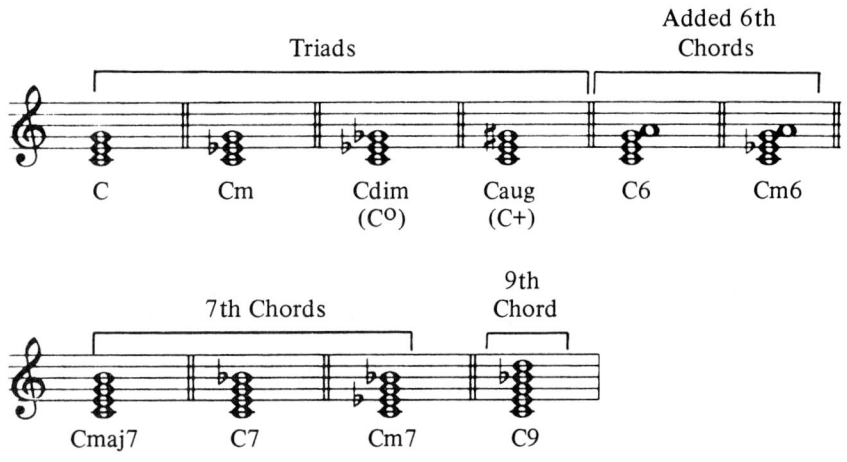

ASSIGNMENT 1   Below are twenty chord types found frequently in popular music. Write the popular music symbol for each in the blank provided. Examples 1 and 2 illustrate the correct procedure.

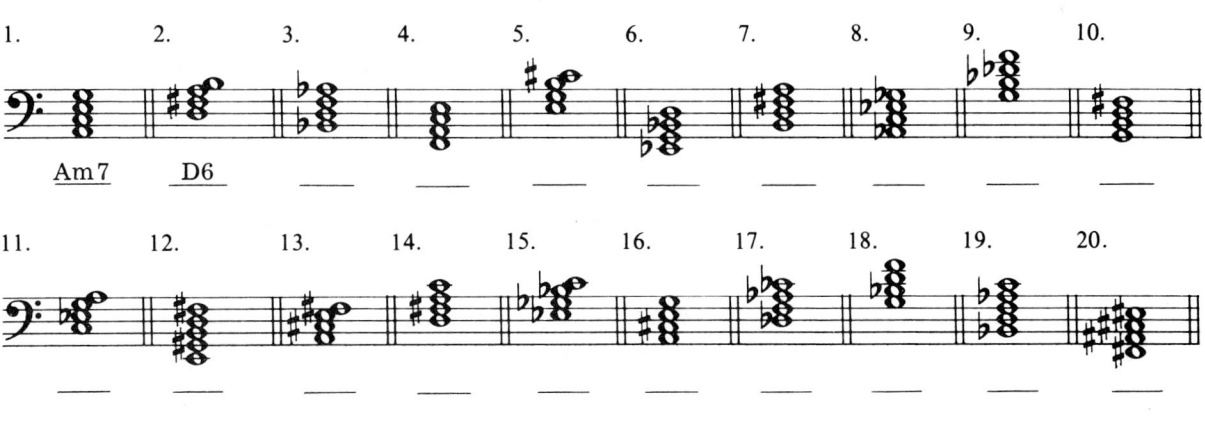

American Popular Song   313

FORM The popular song is constructed of a verse and a chorus (refrain), although many songs consist only of a chorus. The chorus is usually of the most musical interest. Typically, it is thirty-two measures long divided into four eight-measure periods. In the following illustrations, each capital letter indicates an eight-measure period:

COMMON POPULAR CHORUS FORMS

A A B A   A A′ B A   A A B A′   A A′ B A″

On the other hand, the chorus may be of any reasonable length and may be constructed in a great many other ways:

OTHER POPULAR CHORUS FORMS ALSO FOUND

A B C A   A B A B′   A B A C D   A B C A D E   (ETC.)

The example that follows is a thirty-two bar popular song with the form: A A B A′.

Schmidt: *Try to Remember*

Copyright © 1960 by Tom Jones and Harvey Schmidt. Chappell & Co., Inc., owner of publication and allied rights. All rights reserved. Used by permission.

ANALYSIS OF COMPOSITION

PHRASE MEASURES	RELATIONSHIP	CADENCE	KEY	CHORDS AND ROOT MOVEMENT
1–8	A	HALF	G MAJOR	G |AM D7 G| |AM D7| (DESCENDING P5S DESCENDING P5S)
9–16	A	HALF	G MAJOR	|G| |AM D7 G| |AM D7| (DESCENDING P5S DESCENDING P5S)
17–24	B	HALF	G MAJOR	|BM7 EM7 AM7 D7 GMAJ7 CMAJ7 F| |D7| (DESCENDING P5S)
25–32	A′	AUTH	G MAJOR	|G| |AM D7 G CMAJ7| G (DESCENDING P5S)

KEY

Until the 1960s, the great majority of popular songs were written in major keys. This is still true of the period after 1960, but songs in minor keys have become somewhat more common.

Many songs do not modulate but do often contain a number of secondary dominant seventh chords, which are sometimes in succession. An example of four secondary dominants, two of these in chains of chords whose roots descend in P5s, is found in *Georgia On My Mind:*

Carmichael and Gorrell: *Georgia On My Mind*

GEORGIA ON MY MIND by Hoagy Carmichael and Stuart Gorell. Copyright 1930 by Peer International Corporation. Copyright renewed. Used by permission. All rights reserved.

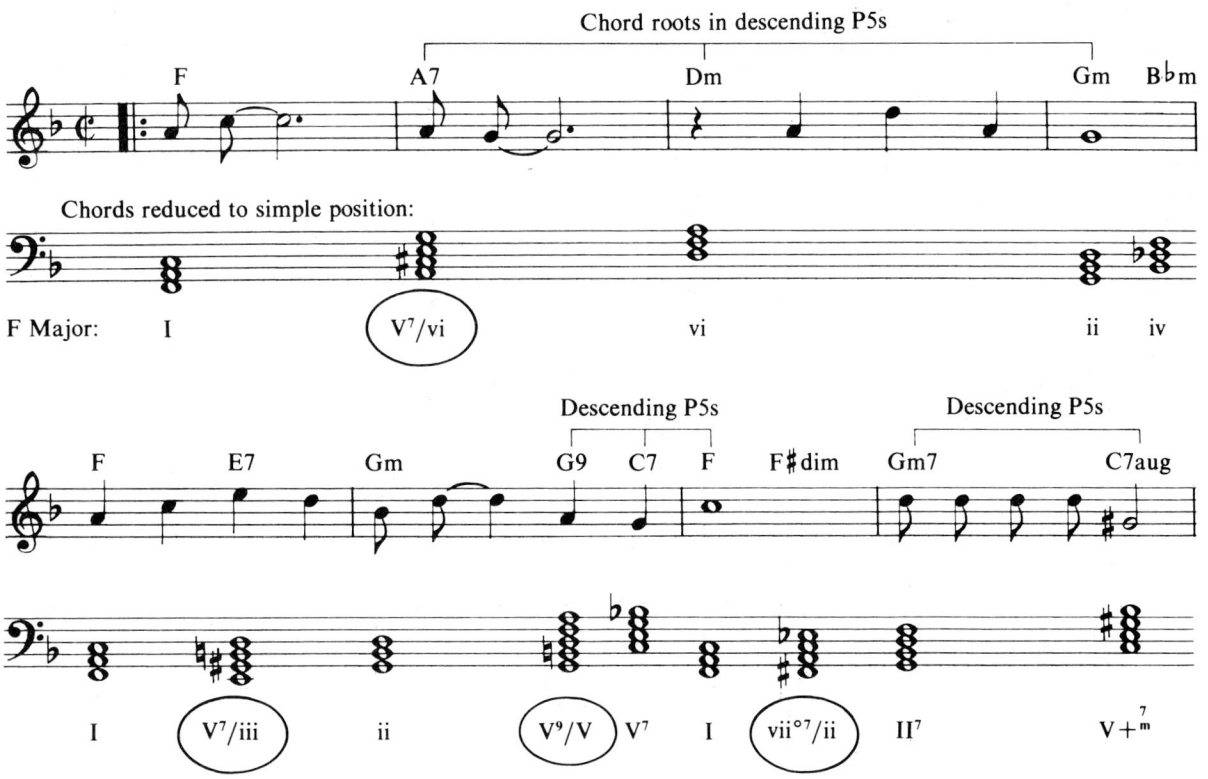

American Popular Song   315

In a song that does modulate, a progression of chords in the new key will usually contain a major seventh chord whose root is other than the first or fourth degree of the previous scale.

This popular song, which modulates from G major to B-flat major, illustrates the major seventh chord (B-flat) preceded by Cm7 to F7 that can be interpreted in B-flat major as ii⁷ to V⁷.

Raye, DePaul, and Johnston: *I'll Remember April*

Words and Music by DON RAYE, GENE DE PAUL, and PAT JOHNSTON.
© Copyright 1941, 1942 by MCA Music, A Division of MCA Inc., New York, N.Y.
Copyright renewed. USED BY PERMISSION. ALL RIGHTS RESERVED.

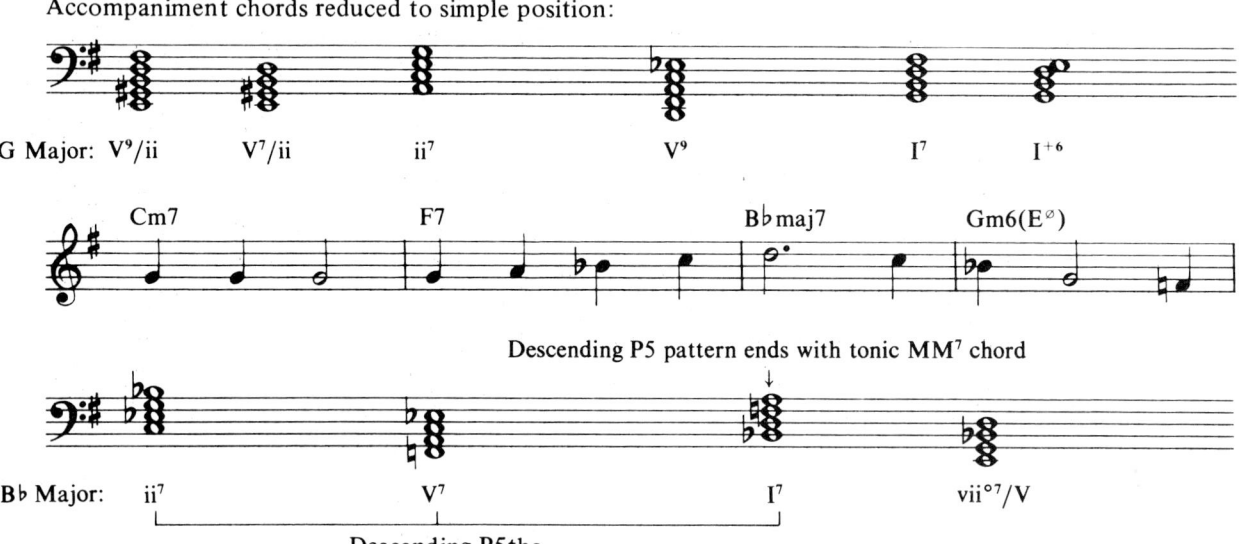

RHYTHM AND METER

Most popular songs are in 4/4 meter, although 2/4 and 3/4 are not uncommon. In general, melodies are rhythmically simple and are composed of whole notes, half notes, quarter notes, eighth notes, and occasionally sixteenth notes.

MELODY

In popular song melody, stepwise motion predominates. Leaps of a third or a fourth are common. Leaps of a fifth, a sixth, a seventh, or of an octave occur less frequently, and leaps of more than an octave are unusual.

A majority of melodies are largely diatonic. As with many other styles, melody tones are frequently factors of the accompanying harmony.

Most popular songs are easy to sing, direct in appeal, and simple in design.

HARMONY

Elements of harmony in popular music have their origin in the Baroque, Classical, and Romantic period styles. The following is an excerpt from a well-known Chopin prelude that utilizes four basic harmonic progressions or devices evident in much of popular music:

1. A series of chords whose roots lie in a pattern of descending P5s.
2. A series of chords whose roots move chromatically downward.

3. A series of diatonic chords whose roots move by step.
4. The frequent use of four-chord cadential formulae that serve to structure a phrase.

Chopin: *Prelude* op. 28 no. 20

*A *French augmented sixth chord* (Augmented sixth between $A^\flat$ and $F^\sharp$) to be explained next semester.

American Popular Song

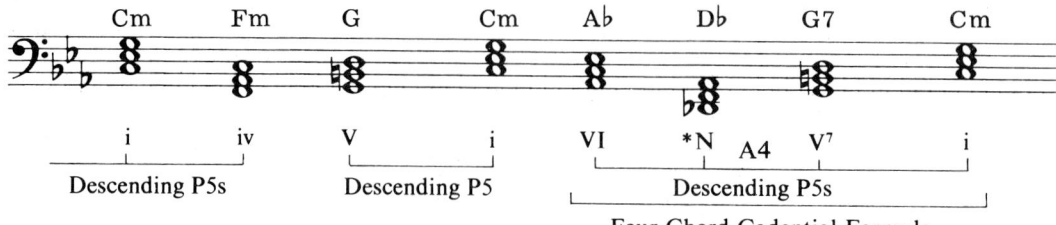

In measure 6 of the Chopin prelude, the popular music symbols and the traditional analysis do not correspond exactly. This is intentional and serves to illustrate the different manner in which a person familiar with popular music and a person conversant with the historical periods hear chord patterns. The chromatic progression $A^{\emptyset}$ to $A\flat 9 \sharp 11$ to G may also be thought of as $A^{\emptyset}$ to $D7\flat 5$ (Fr6) to G in which case the root movement is descending P5s.

Note further the use of the four-chord cadential formulas such as i iv V i in the second to last measure and VI N* V^7 i in the last measure. The frequent occurrence of patterns such as these connotes a harmonic style common to much popular music.

Harmonic Progressions

The harmonic progressions and devices used in popular music are now to be explored in greater depth:

Circle of P5s

First mentioned on page 143 in chapter 8, this progression type becomes even more important in the study of the American popular song. The following figure illustrates the pattern of root movement in the circle of P5 progressions.

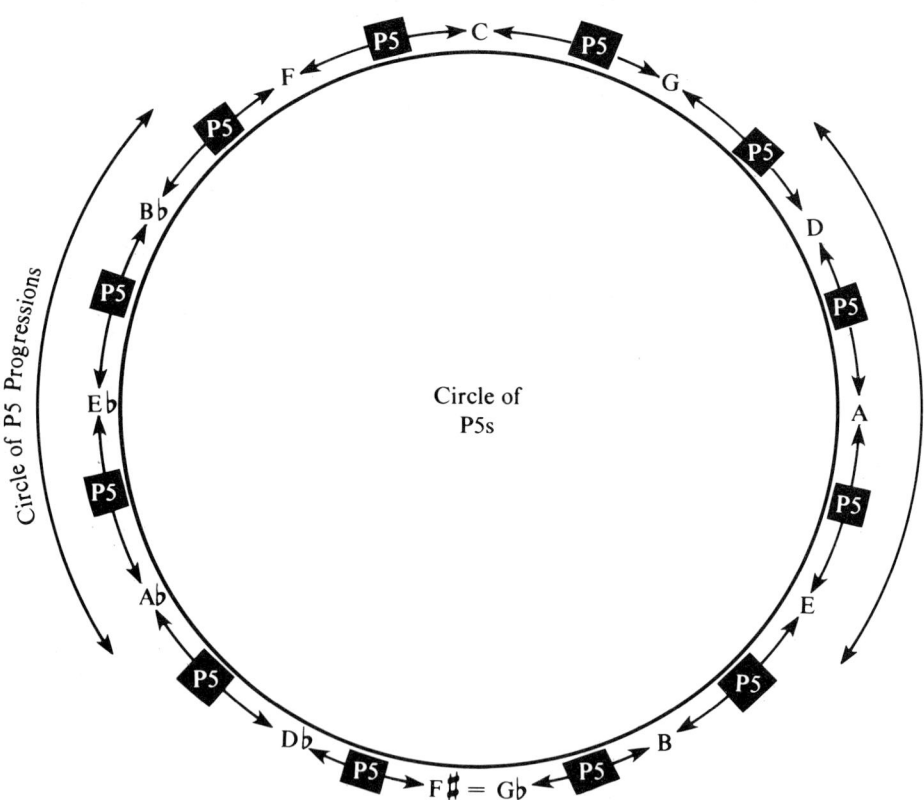

Neapolitan chord (major triad on lowered second degree of scale) to be explained next semester.

Thus, in the circle progression:

ANALYSIS		ANALYSIS	POPULAR MUSIC SYMBOLS	(C MAJOR)		POPULAR MUSIC SYMBOL (C MAJOR)
vii⁰⁷	PROCEEDS TO	iii⁷	=	B⌀	PROCEEDS TO	Em7
iii⁷	PROCEEDS TO	vi⁷	=	Em7	PROCEEDS TO	Am7
vi⁷	PROCEEDS TO	ii⁷	=	Am7	PROCEEDS TO	Dm7
ii⁷	PROCEEDS TO	v⁷	=	Dm7	PROCEEDS TO	G7
v⁷	PROCEEDS TO	I⁷	=	G7	PROCEEDS TO	Cmaj⁷ or C6 or C

Progressions of chords based on the circle-of-P5s movement occur repeatedly in most popular songs as shown in the previous musical examples and in this phrase from *Misty:*

Garner: *Misty*

MISTY by: Erroll Garner. © 1954 and 1955 by Vernon Music Corporation (by arrangement with Octave Music Publishing Corporation). All rights reserved. Used by permission.

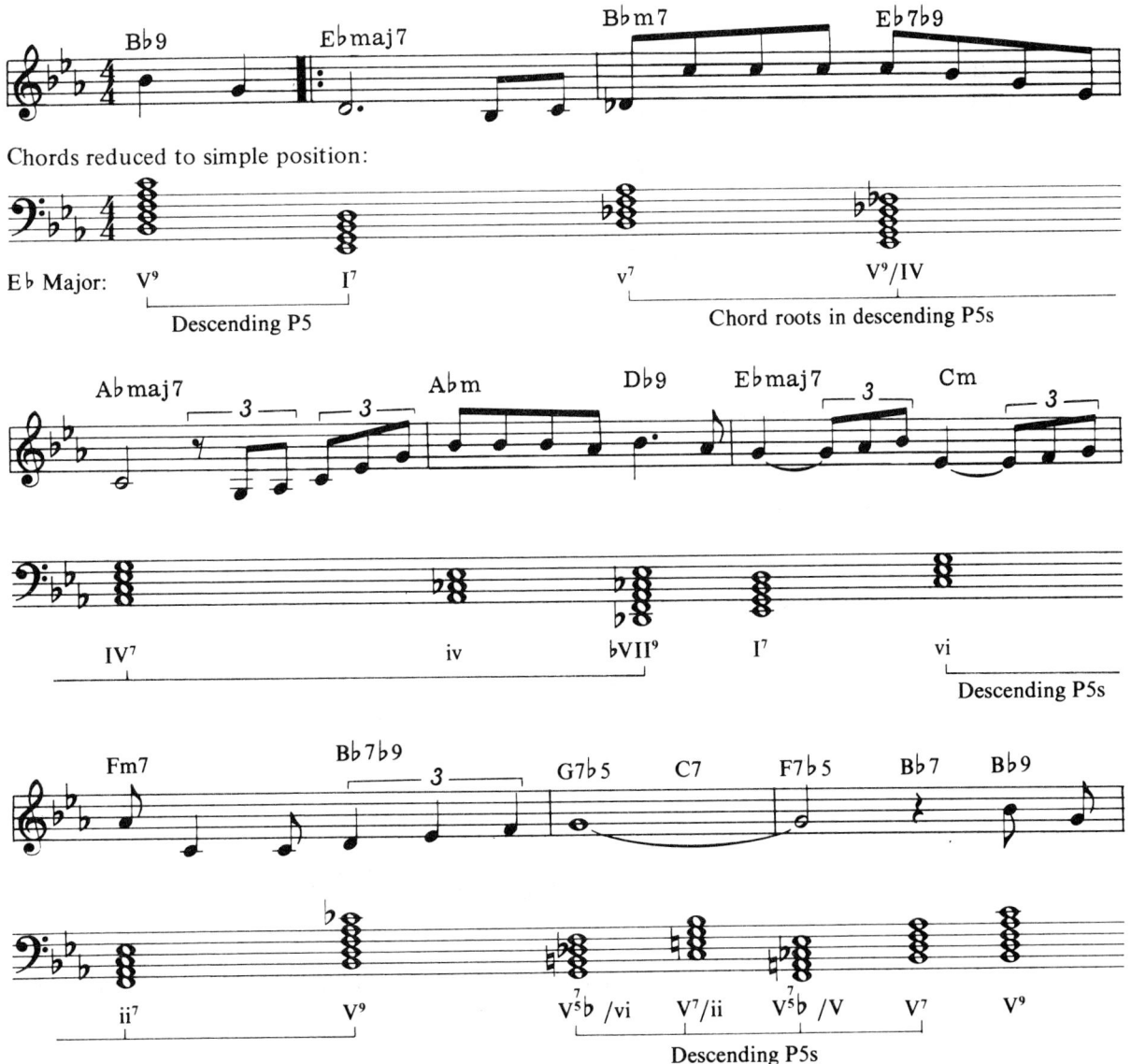

American Popular Song 319

Typical Circle of 5ths Chord Patterns

mm7 to Mm7 to Triad — Minor seventh chord (mm7) to dominant seventh chord (Mm7) to triad (triad alone, with added sixth, or with M7) is perhaps the most common chord pattern in all of popular music, and is frequently referred to as a II V I progression.

CONVENTIONAL CHORD PROGRESSION

POPULAR MUSIC SYMBOLS	C MAJOR:	Dm7	G7	C (OR C6 OR Cmaj7)
TRADITIONAL ANALYSIS SYMBOLS	C MAJOR	ii^7	V^7	I (OR I^{+6} OR I^7)

Here is an example:

My Way

Words by Paul Anka. Original French Lyric by Gilles Thibault. Music by J. Revaux and C. Francois. © Copyright 1967 by Societe des Nouvelles editions Eddie Barclay, Paris, France. © Copyright 1969 for U.S. and Canada by Spanka Music Corporation, 445 Park Avenue, New York, N.Y. 10022. Used by permission. All rights reserved.

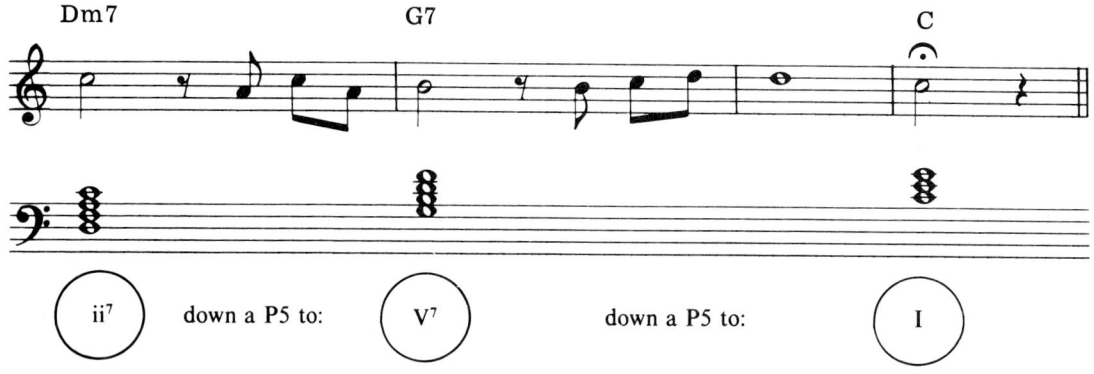

ii^7 down a P5 to: V^7 down a P5 to: I

Successions of Mm7 — This pattern of dominant seventh chords creates a series of altered chords (except for the final dominant seventh in the key) that are secondary dominants:

Thomas: *Spinning Wheel*

By David Clayton Thomas. © 1968 Blackwood Music, Inc., and Bay Music Ltd. Administered by Blackwood Music, Inc., 1350 Avenue of the Americas, New York, New York 10019. International copyright secured. All rights reserved. Used by permission.

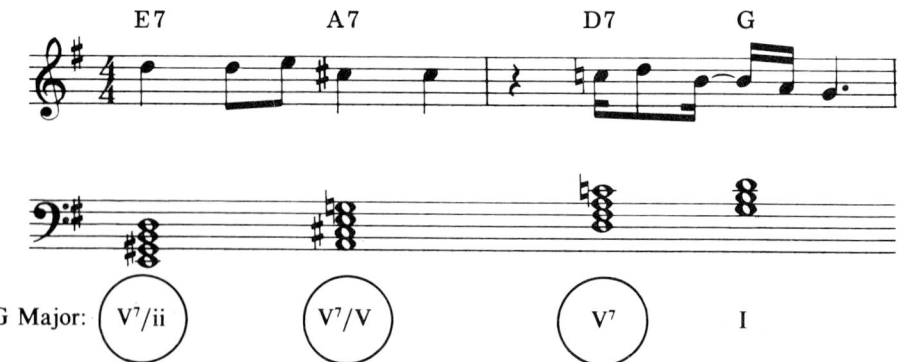

G Major: V^7/ii   V^7/V   V^7 I

Successions of mm7 — In this series of minor sevenths, chord tones are often unaltered notes of the scale (diatonic):

320 American Popular Song

Schmidt: *Try to Remember*

Copyright © 1960 by Tom Jones and Harvey Schmidt. Chappell & Co., Inc., owner of publication and allied rights. All rights reserved. Used by permission.

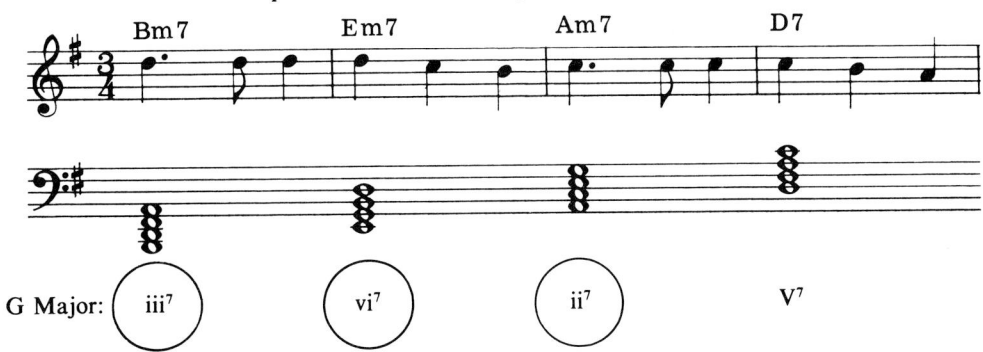

| Mixtures of mm7 and Mm7 | Frequently this mixture of minor and dominant seventh chords is an alternation between mm7 and Mm7. The Mm7 chords often act as secondary dominants: |

Bacharach: *Raindrops Keep Fallin' On My Head*

By Burt Bacharach and Hal David. Copyrighted in 1969 by Blue Seas Music, Inc., New York, N.Y. 10022. Reprinted by permission of the publishers.

Chords reduced to simple position:

| dm7 to Mm7 | This progression of half-diminished seventh chord (dm7) to dominant seventh chord (Mm7) functions in much the same way as the progression from a mm7 chord to a Mm7 chord. Indeed, the half-diminished is most properly thought of as a mm7 chord with a flatted fifth. The half-diminished chord sometimes provides more harmonic interest than the mm7 chord.

Use of the half-diminished chord also frequently makes the transition from chord to chord smoother:

| Popular Music Symbols: | B-flat Major: | Em7–5 | A7 |
| Analysis Symbols: | B-flat Major: | vii^{ø7}/V | V^7/iii |

Gershwin: *Bess, You Is My Woman Now*

Copyright © 1935 by Gershwin Publishing Corp. Copyright renewed. All rights reserved. Used by permission of Chappell & Co., Inc.

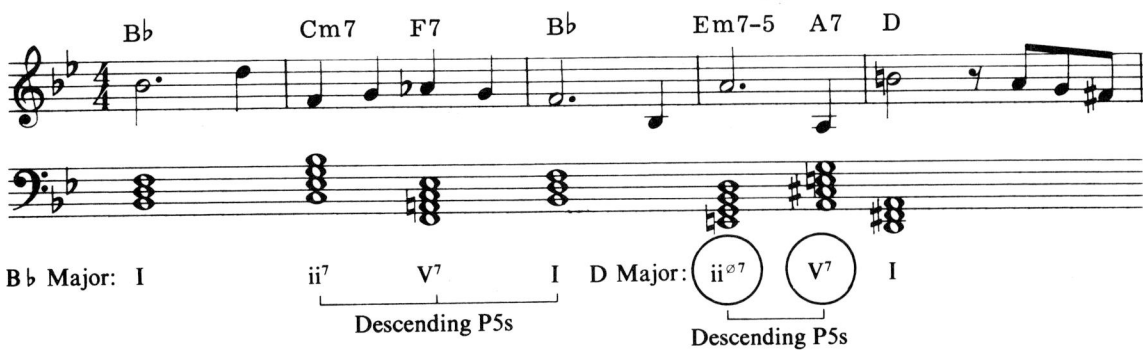

American Popular Song 321

Augmented Chords *Augmented chords* are an augmented triad or seventh chord followed by a triad or seventh chord in the circle-of-P5s pattern. The augmented chord may be considered an inversion, if necessary, to treat it as part of a circle-of-P5s progression. The same-sounding augmented triad (enharmonically spelled) may progress in any of three circle-of-P5s patterns:

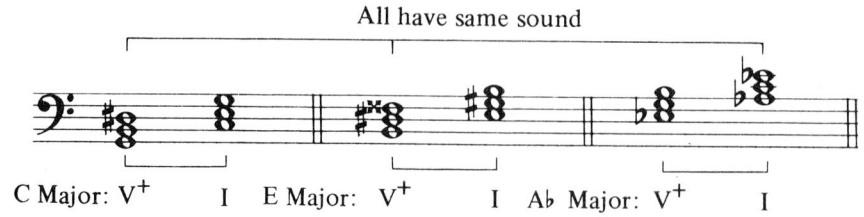

An augmented triad in context:

Haggart: *What's New?*

© 1939 M. Witmark & Sons. Copyright renewed. All rights reserved. Used by permission of Warner Bros. Music.

Diminished Seventh A diminished seventh chord resolves conventionally to a chord whose root is a half step above one of its component notes: diminished seventh Chord (dd7) to any major (MM7), minor (mm7) or dominant (Mm7) seventh chord. Such chords are often spelled for convenience of reading rather than for accuracy of function. Diminished seventh chords frequently progress to chords that are not in a circle-of-P5s pattern:

Gershwin: *Embraceable You*

By George Gershwin. © 1930 New World Music Corporation. Copyright renewed. All rights reserved. Used by permission of Warner Bros. Music.

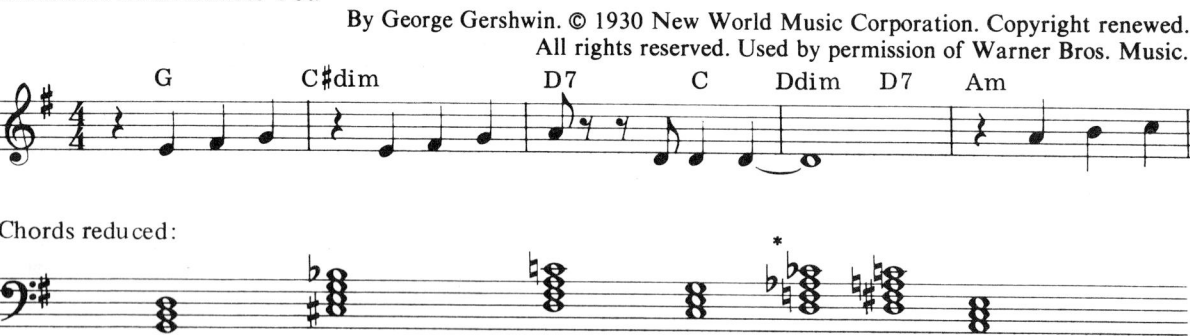

*Type 2 resolution would be to ♭VI♭, but the chord acts simply as a decoration (somewhat like an appoggiatura) to the V^7 following it.

322 American Popular Song

As the illustration shows, the strong sense of movement imparted by the circle-of-descending-P5s type of pattern is due to the descending P5 interval from root to root. The ear experiences the strong root movement toward the tonic, a phenomenon found in all tonal music. The types of chords (Mm, dm, or dd) built from these roots are of less importance than the actual root relationships themselves.

SUMMARY

A summary of circle-of-P5 patterns:

PROGRESSION	**WHERE FOUND (ILLUSTRATIONS ARE IN C)**
DOMINANT 7TH TO MAJOR 7TH	Usually occurs at cadence points or in other parts of a song where the V^7 to I^7 is used.
DOMINANT 7TH TO DOMINANT 7TH	Occurs as one of a series of secondary dominants: V^7/II to V^7/V to V^7 to I A^7 to D^7 to G^7 C
MINOR 7TH TO MINOR 7TH	When the circle-of-P5s pattern begins at either the iii^7 or vi^7 chord and continues to the V^7 diatonically the result is a succession of minor 7th chords. iii^7 to vi^7 to ii^7 to V^7 to I Em^7 to Am^7 to Dm^7 to G^7 to C
MINOR 7TH TO DOMINANT 7TH	Probably the most common chord movement in popular music. ii^7 to V^7 to I Dm^7 to G^7 to C
HALF-DIMINISHED 7TH TO DOMINANT 7TH	Often found in lieu of minor 7th to dominant 7th. $ii^{ø7}$ to V^7 to I Dm7-5 to G^7 to C
AUGMENTED CHORD	An augmented triad or seventh chord followed by a triad or seventh chord in the circle-of-descending P5s pattern. V^+ to I $V7^+$ to I G^+ to C $G7^+$ to C
DIMINISHED 7TH CHORD	To any major (MM), minor (mm), or dominant (Mm) seventh chord—especially one whose root is a half step above that of the diminished seventh chord. vii^{o7}/V to V F♯ dim to G

Chromatic Descending Chord Progression

In the chromatic descending chord progression, the root of each succeeding chord is a half step below that of the previous chord:

The chromatic descending pattern is followed in Hoagy Carmichael's "Lazy River":

Carmichael and Arodin: *Lazy River*

LAZY RIVER by Hoagy Carmichael and Sidney Arodin. Copyright 1931 by Peer International Corporation. Copyright renewed. Used by permission. All rights reserved.

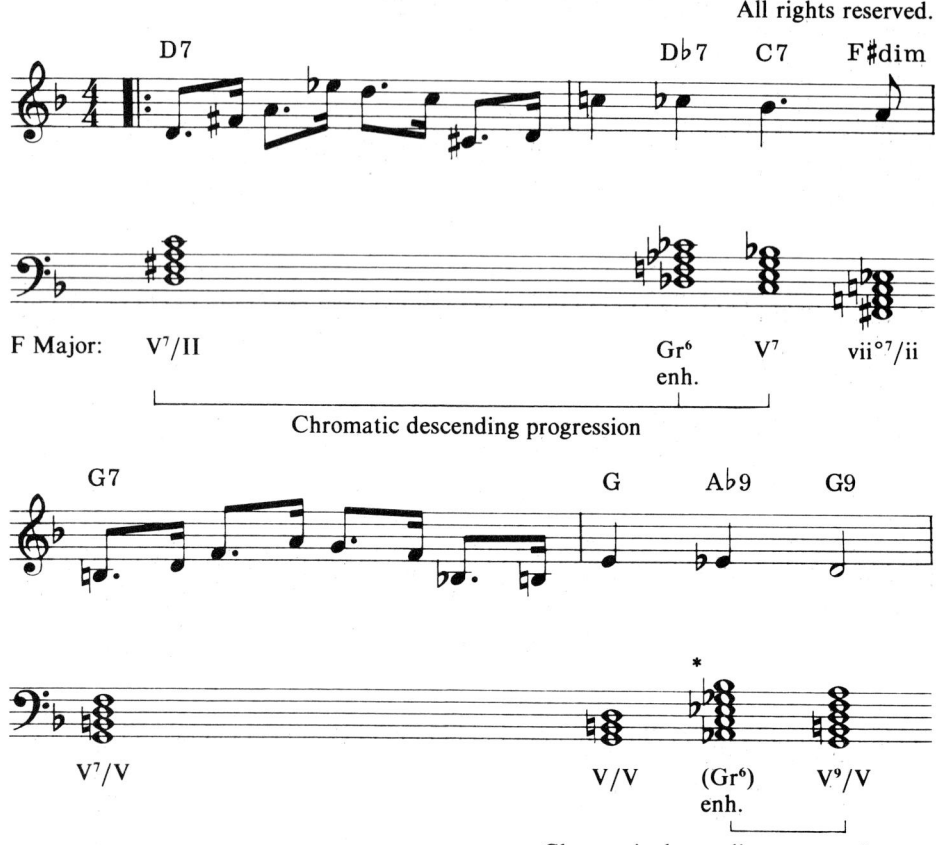

The chromatic descending pattern is closely related to the circle-of-P5s progression. The illustration below shows how the root of every other chord coincides—regardless of type so long as the progression is consistently maintained—in both the chromatic and in the circle-of-P5s chord progression.

ROOT MOVEMENT

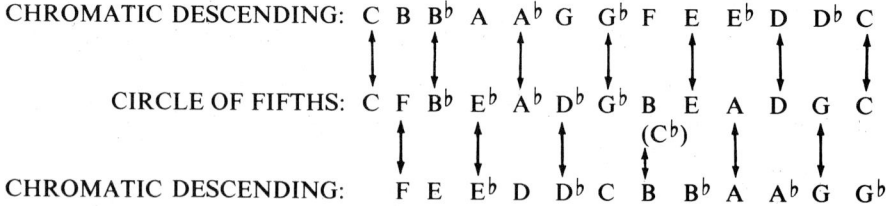

*The sound of this chord coincides with that of the augmented sixth chord in European traditional music. An augmented sixth chord is so named because of its characteristic A6 interval. This chord will be discussed in detail in volume 2 of the text.

324   American Popular Song

The coincidence of roots of Mm7 chords in circle-of-P5s and chromatic descending progressions:

Circle of descending P5s

Chromatic descending progressions:

Substitute Mm7 Chords

The similarity of the chromatic descending progression and the circle-of-P5s progression may be used to practical advantage in providing smoother chord resolution or diversion from stereotyped or monotonous chord movement.

A Mm7 chord in a circle-of-P5s chord progression may often be replaced by the Mm7 chord whose root is an augmented fourth above or below. This turns a circle-of-P5s progression into a chromatic descending progression.

A harmonic accompaniment using circle-of-P5s pattern exclusively:

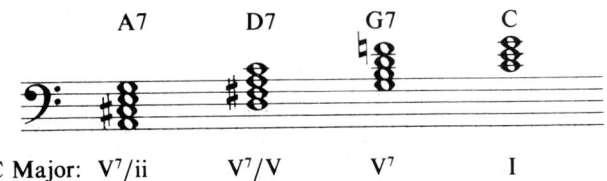

C Major: V^7/ii V^7/V V^7 I

The same accompaniment pattern except for the substitute chord whose root lies a tritone above or below:

C Major: V^7/ii V^7/V Sub.   I

The following two illustrations demonstrate harmonic substitutions that transform a circle-of-P5s progression into a chromatic descending progression:

Gershwin: *Nice Work If You Can Get It*

Copyright © 1937 by Gershwin Publishing Corp. Copyright renewed. All rights reserved. Used by permission of Chappell & Co., Inc.

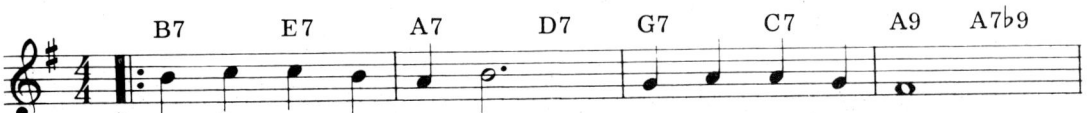

Chords reduced to simple position:

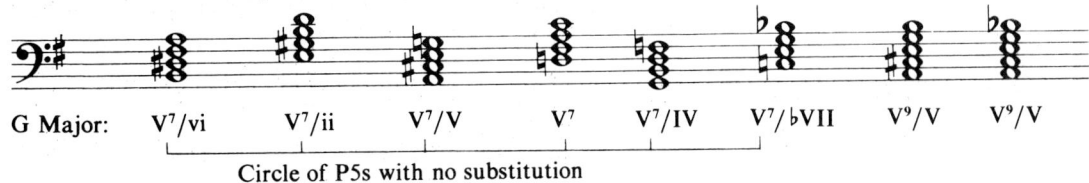

G Major: V^7/vi V^7/ii V^7/V V^7 V^7/IV $V^7/\flat VII$ V^9/V V^9/V

Circle of P5s with no substitution

American Popular Song

The same composition with substitutions:

A Mm7 chord in a chromatic descending progression may often be replaced by the Mm7 chord whose root is an augmented fourth above or below. This turns a chromatic descending progression into a circle-of-P5s progression.

The following harmonic accompaniment uses chromatic progression exclusively:

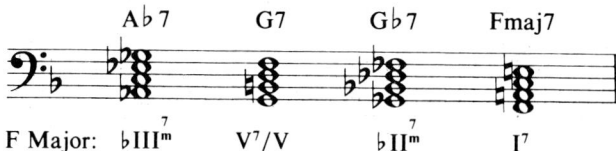

Here is the same accompaniment with an augmented-fourth substitute:

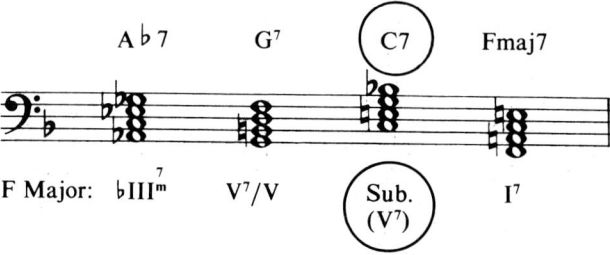

An illustration of how a harmonic substitute transforms a chromatic descending progression into a circle-of-P5s progression:

Brodszky and Kahn: *I'll Never Stop Loving You*

Copyright © 1954, 1955 Metro-Goldwyn-Mayer, Inc. Rights throughout the world controlled by Leo Feist, Inc.

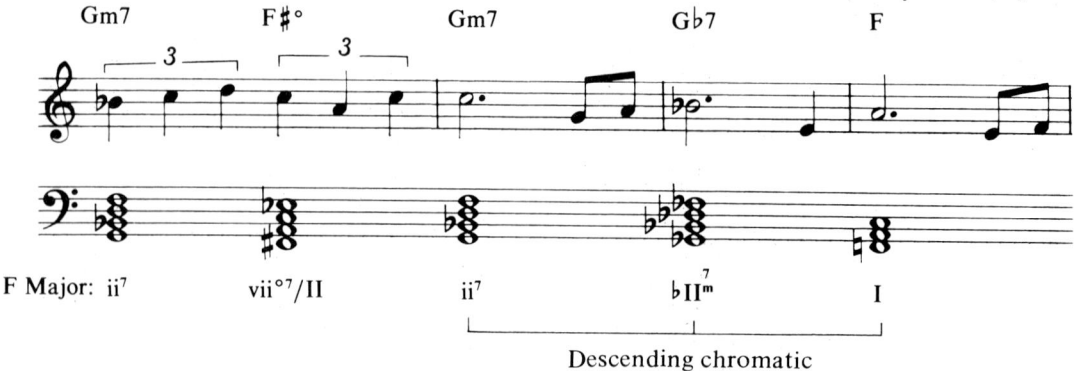

The same composition with substitution for G♭7:

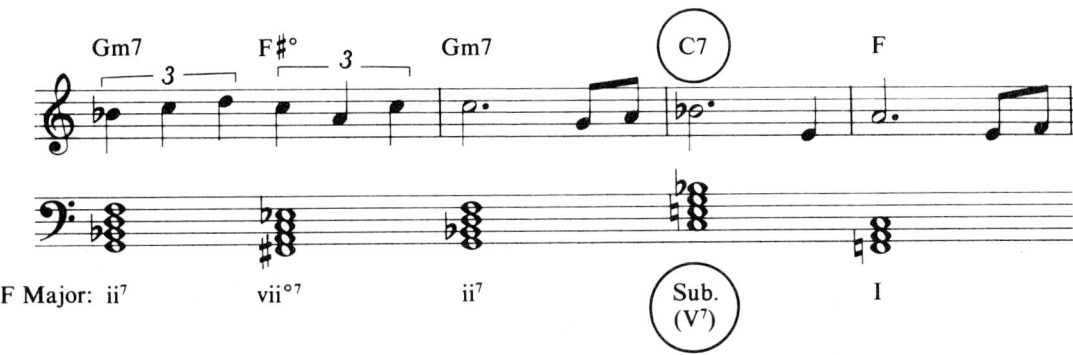

Part of the musical logic permitting the substitution of chromatic progressions for the circle-of-P5s pattern and vice versa is that each matched pair of Mm7 chords contains the same tritone.

In the following examples, the tritone in each coinciding pair of chords has the same pitch.

Circle-of-P5s pattern:

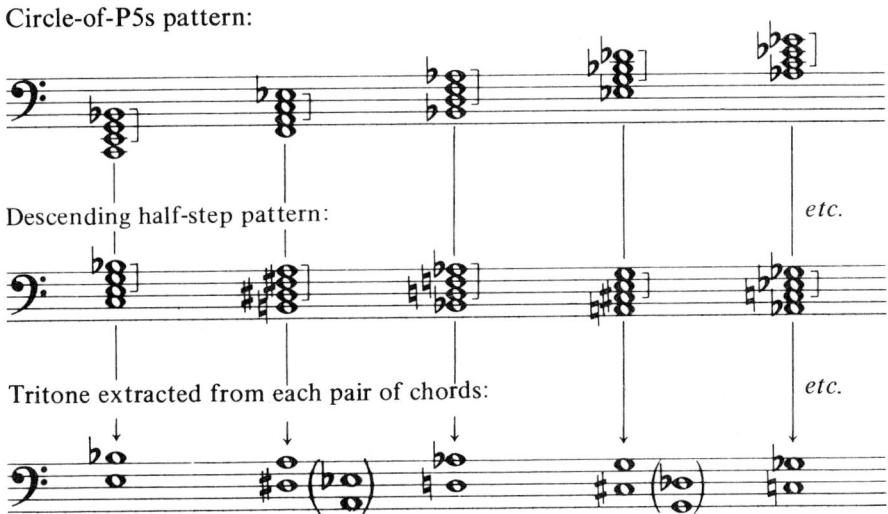

Descending half-step pattern:

Tritone extracted from each pair of chords:

The following chart indicates how each Mm7 chord in a circle-of-P5s pattern can be replaced with a chord from the corresponding chromatic descending progression.

THE CHORDS IN THE BOXES MAY BE SUBSTITUTED ONE FOR ANOTHER:

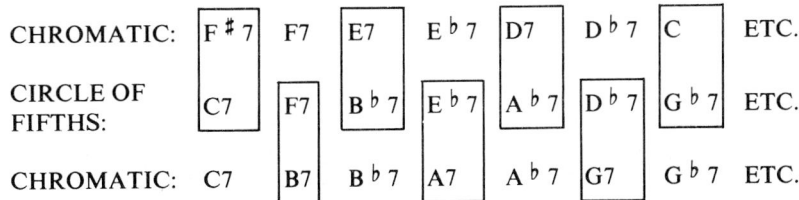

The usefulness of substitute Mm7 chords in converting a circle-of-P5s pattern into a chromatic descending pattern is greater than in converting a chromatic descending pattern into a circle of P5s. The reason is that circle-of-P5s patterns are prominent in a great many more popular songs than chromatic descending movements.

American Popular Song

Diatonic Stepwise Chord Patterns

In these patterns, the root of each successive chord moves diatonically stepwise up or down. The factors of each chord are diatonic also.

Common patterns are:

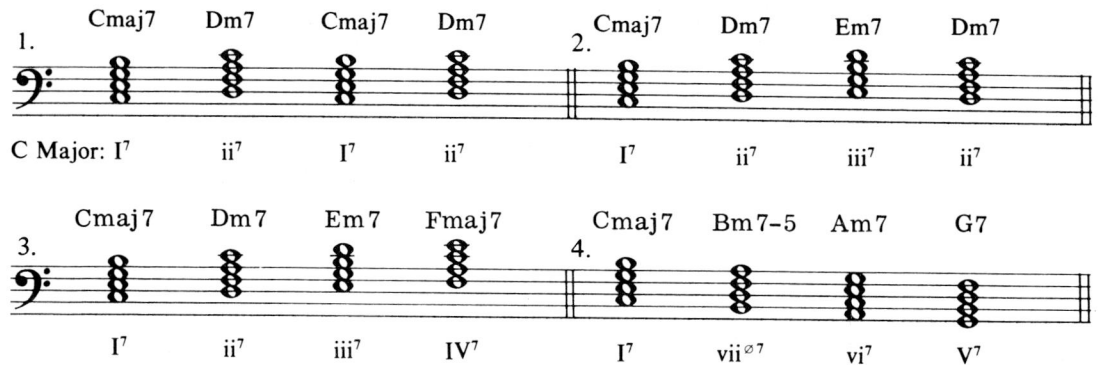

Diatonic stepwise movement provides the basic harmonic structure for the first four measures of the following song:

Wilder: *I'll Be Around*

Words and music by Alec Wilder. TRO © Copyright 1942 and renewed 1970 Ludlow Music, Inc., New York, N.Y. Used by permission.

Occasionally, it is appropriate to reharmonize a portion of a popular tune to provide more interesting harmonic movement. Substituting a diatonic step progression for a particular sequence of chords is one of the ways this can be accomplished. Substitutions of this sort must be made with care and musical intelligence.

The following excerpt, reharmonized in a diatonic-stepwise chord pattern, provides a refreshing contrast to the original tonic-dominant harmonization.

The first phrase as originally published:

Brandt and Haymes: *That's All*

Copyright © 1952 Travis Music Company. Copyright © 1952 Unart Music Corporation. Used by permission.

The same phrase reharmonized using diatonic stepwise progression:

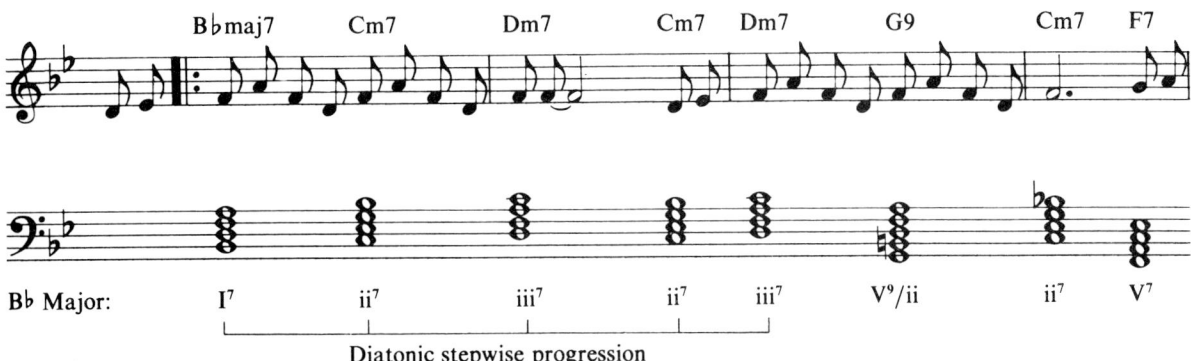

Four-Chord Formulas Certain four-chord formulas are contained in a great many popular songs. These four-chord progressions usually begin with I, V^7/IV, I^7, or iii^7, and end with V^7 or its augmented-fourth substitute $\flat$II$_m^7$. In a popular song in $^4_4$ meter, the four-chord formula is generally two measures long, each chord receiving two beats. Such a series is sometimes found, however, in a single measure or spread across three or four.

An illustration of one of the most conventional varieties appears in this excerpt from a Richard Rodgers song:

R. Rodgers: *Mountain Greenery*

Copyrighted in 1926 by Harms, Inc. Copyrighted, renewed by Warner Bros. Music.

The conventional four-chord sequence is characteristic of harmony found in popular music since it is largely based on the circle of descending P5s or chromatic chord movement.

The following chart outlines typical four-chord formulas:

TYPICAL CHORD FORMULAS

ANALYSIS SYMBOLS					POPULAR MUSIC SYMBOLS IN KEY OF C			
I^7	vi^7	ii^7	V^7	=	Cmaj7	Am7	Dm7	G7
V^7/IV	V^7/ii	V^7/V	V^7	=	C7	A7	D7	G7
I^7	$\flat$iii^7	ii^7	$\flat$II$_m^7$	=	Cmaj7	E$\flat$m7	Dm7	D$\flat$7
I	vii^{o7}/ii	ii^7	V^7	=	C	C$\sharp$°	Dm7	G7
iii^7	vi^7	ii^7	V^7	=	Em7	Am7	Dm7	G7
iii^7	$\flat$iii^7	ii^7	$\flat$ii$_m^7$	=	Em7	E$\flat$m7	Dm7	D$\flat$7
V^7/IV	$\flat$VII$_m^7$	$\flat$VI^7	V^7	=	C7	B$\flat$7	A$\flat$7	G7
V^7/IV	$\flat$III$_m^7$	$\flat$VI^7	V^7	=	C7	E$\flat$7	A$\flat$7	G7

American Popular Song

These formulas may also be constructed, in part, of simple triads by omitting the sevenths except where diminished chords occur.

In Succession Often the harmonic structure of a phrase consists of a succession of four-chord formulas. When used in this manner, the patterns impart a distinct orderliness and logic to the music that is immediately perceived by the listener.

The student composition that follows is an eight-measure phrase made up entirely of four-chord formulas. It exemplifies the use of various four-chord formulas:

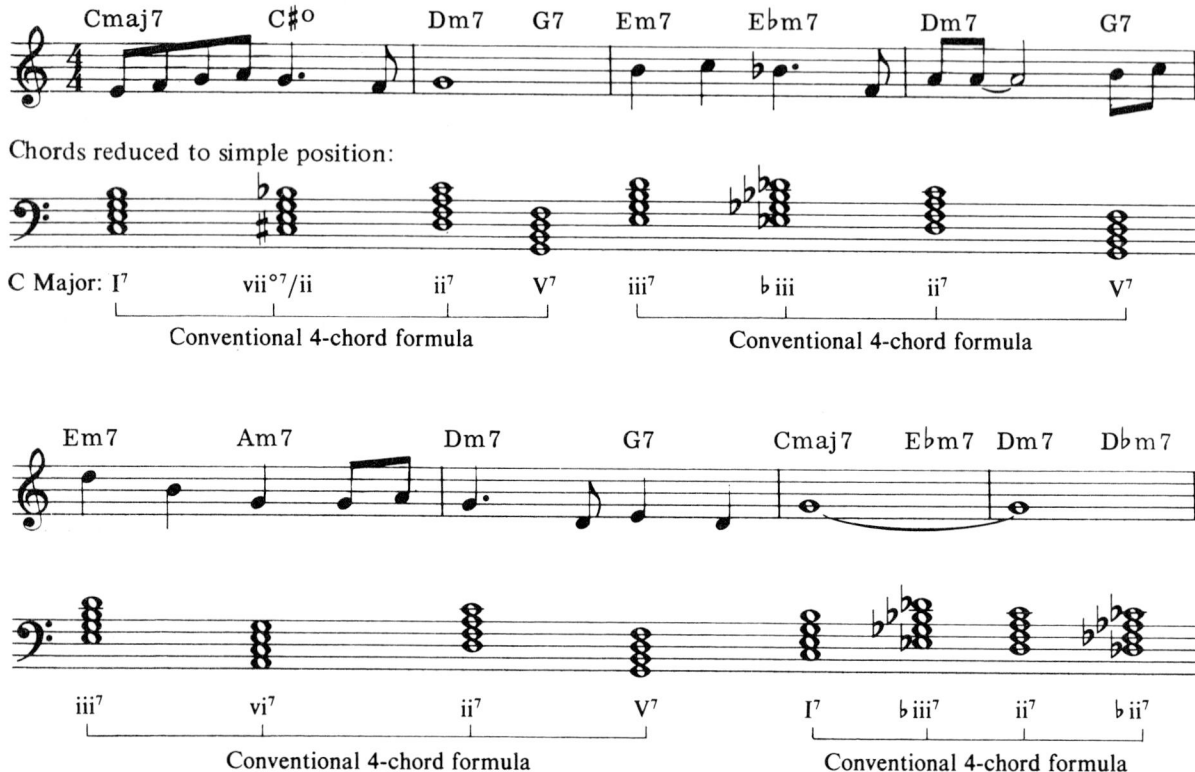

Ostinato Bass In popular songs, it is not uncommon for a single four-chord formula to be repeated once or even several times. This repetition of the same progression is called *ostinato bass* (repeated bass line). The most frequently used four-chord formula in ostinato bass is: I vi ii V
(C Am Dm G)

Strachey, Link, and Marvell: *These Foolish Things*

THESE FOOLISH THINGS music by Jack Strachey and Harry Link, words by Holt Marvell. Copyright © 1935 by Boosey & Co. Ltd., London, England. Copyright renewed. All rights for United States, Canada, and Newfoundland assigned to BOURNE CO. N.Y., N.Y. All rights reserved. Used by permission.

330 American Popular Song

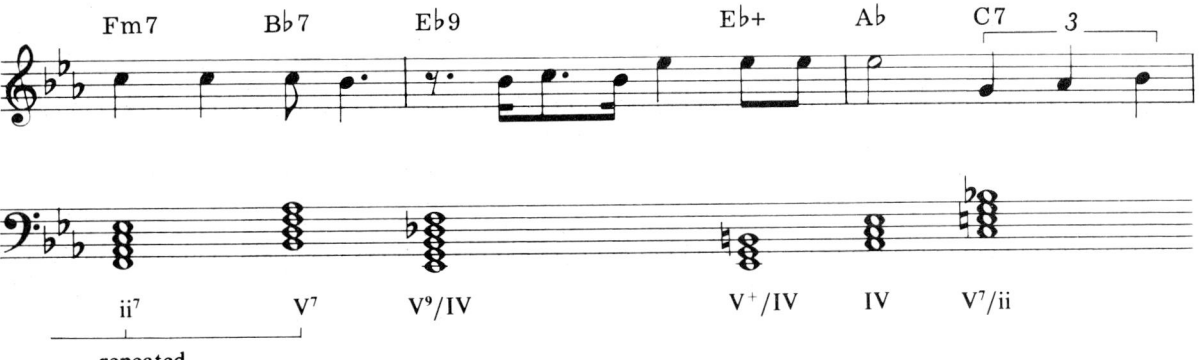

Turnarounds *Turnarounds* (or *turnbacks*) are terms used in popular music (and especially in jazz) to denote four-chord formulas that signal the repetition of a period or return to a previous period. A schematic outline is useful for showing the position of turnarounds in a thirty-two measure popular song of the form A A B A′:

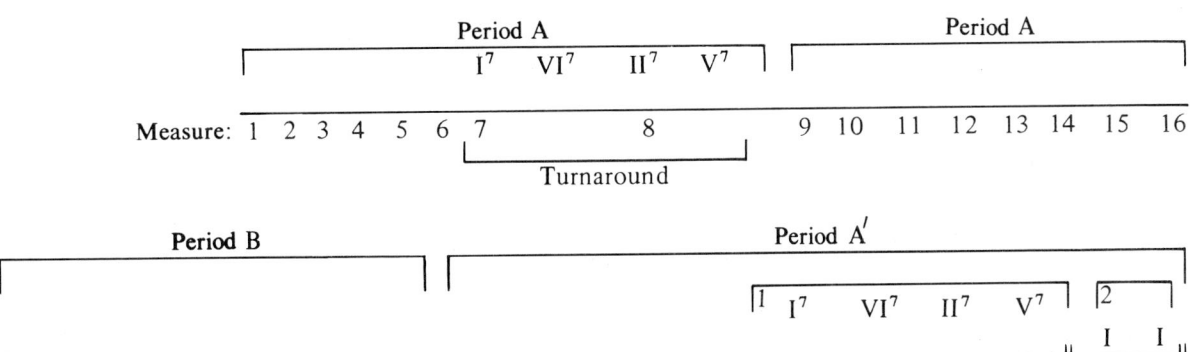

The turnaround in *Days of Wine and Roses* is typical of the device employed in many popular songs:

Mancini and Mercer: *Days of Wine and Roses*

© 1962 Warner Bros. Inc. All rights reserved. Used by permission.

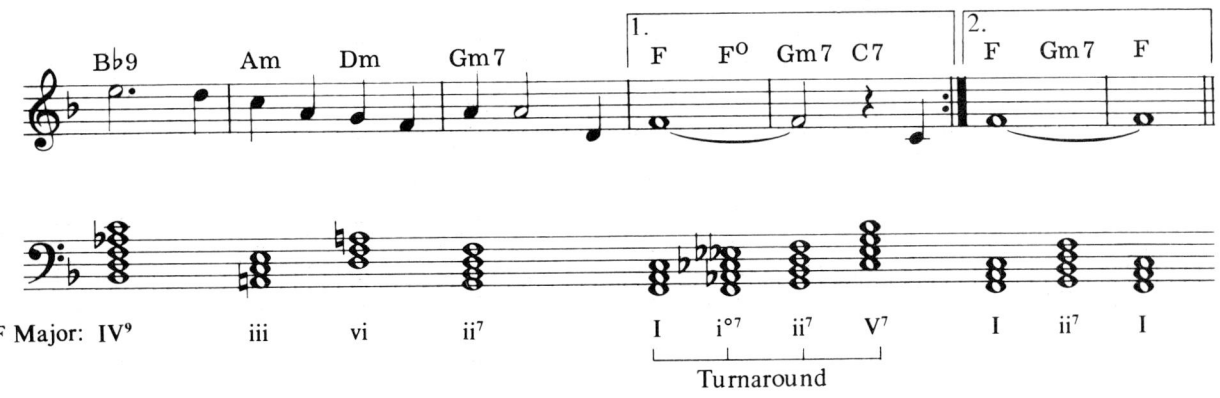

American Popular Song   331

ASSIGNMENT 2 On a separate sheet of score paper, analyze the melody, *Try to Remember* (page 314) identifying structural, secondary, embellishing tones, melodic step progressions, themes, motifs, the breadth of leaps from tone to tone, altered tones, the duration of the melody tones, and any possible modulations.

ASSIGNMENT 3 Harmonize the following three melody fragments with II–V–I progressions. Determine the harmonic rhythm first. Use block chords.

ASSIGNMENT 4 Harmonize the following excerpt with Mm7 (dominant seventh) chords in a circle-of-P5s pattern. Determine the harmonic rhythm first. Block chords will suffice for the moment. A few of the chords are indicated for you.

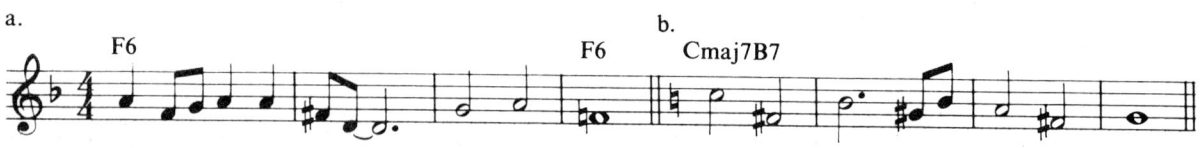

ASSIGNMENT 5 Complete the harmony with a circle-of-P5s progression that employs only diatonic chords.

ASSIGNMENT 6 Form a circle-of-P5s progression that alternates between dominant and minor seventh chords. Then reharmonize the melody fragment with a circle-of-P5s progression that alternates between dominant seventh and half-diminished chords.

ASSIGNMENT 7 Provide the missing chords furnishing the melody with a chromatic descending progression of Mm7 (dominant seventh) chords.

ASSIGNMENT 8 Reharmonize the following melody fragments using substitute Mm7 chords.

a.

b.

c.
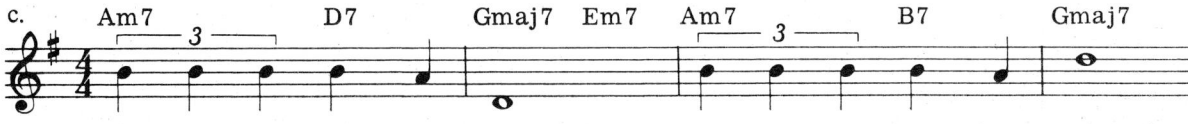

ASSIGNMENT 9 Harmonize the following melody fragment using diatonic stepwise chord progressions.

ASSIGNMENT 10 Reharmonize the following melody fragment using a diatonic chord progression.

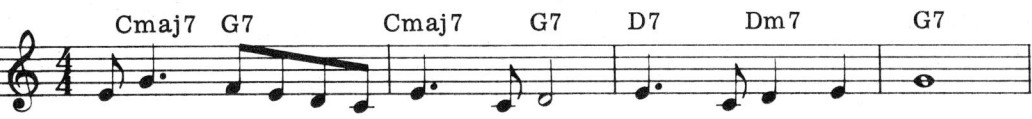

ASSIGNMENT 11   Compose a melody (only) for a thirty-two measure popular song of the form A A B A′.

ASSIGNMENT 12   Compose a melody (only) for a thirty-two measure popular song of the form A B C A.

ASSIGNMENT 13   Compose an eight-measure period with underlying harmony consisting entirely of conventional four-chord formulas.

ASSIGNMENT 14   Compose an eight-measure period with an underlying harmony that is largely an ostinato bass.

ASSIGNMENT 15   Compose the first two eight-measure periods of a thirty-two measure popular song having the form A A B A′. Use a turnaround to signal the repetition. Sketch in the block chords first, then, arrange the chords in a typical piano idiom. Try to voice the chords (use inversions) to obtain maximum smoothness.

ASSIGNMENT 16   Compose a thirty-two measure popular song (both melody and harmony) that repeats itself in the form A A′ B A″.

19 Blues, Boogie, and Jazz

Blues
Standard Twelve-Bar
 Blues
Twelve-Bar Jazz Blues
Modified Twelve-Bar
 Jazz Blues
Melody
Blue ("Worried") Notes
Blues Scales
Chords Underlying the
 Blues Scale

Melodies Based on Mm7
 Chords
Riff
Tetrachords
Blues Scale and Added
 Notes
Boogie-Woogie
Rhythm: Boogie-Woogie
 Bass
Thick-Textured Boogie-
 Woogie

Thin-Textured Boogie-
 Woogie
Jazz
Jazz Rhythm
Syncopation
Rhythmic Modulation
Odd-Length Motives
Polyrhythm
Polymeter

Harmonic Syncopation
Rhythmic
 Superimposition
Swing
Jazz Harmony and
 Altered Chords
Bebop
Improvisation

Black American music is among the most notable expressions of religious, folk, and art music in the United States. The various styles have numerous elements indigenous to African music and thus are largely distinct from the European classical tradition.

BLUES

The *blues* refers to a black American song of sorrow supported by I, IV, and V harmony. It extends usually to twelve measures, although blues of eight, sixteen, twenty-four, and thirty-two bars are not uncommon. The blues arose from the black country and gospel music of the Deep South, where these roots contributed a vital and penetrating melodic quality. The blues has not only been perpetuated as a unique style but has infused and inspired nearly all types of Afro-American music, some twentieth-century classical music, and popular songs. The blues also provided the underpinnings of much rock 'n' roll.

Harmony

Most early blues structures are extremely simple, generally containing only I, IV, and V chords either in the form of triads or dominant sevenths. Later blues are more complex. Most early blues begin on the I chord and maintain this chord until it gives way to the IV chord in the fifth measure. The progression ends on either a I or a V chord and is repeated as many times as necessary to accommodate the vocal or instrumental choruses.

Standard
Twelve-Bar Blues

The following are typical *standard twelve-bar blues* that consist entirely of major-minor seventh chords. A minor blues may also be formed by treating each chord as a minor-minor seventh instead. In this chapter, a seventh chord will be assumed to be a major-minor seventh chord unless stated otherwise.

**STANDARD TWELVE-
BAR BLUES** (4/4 Meter)

		1	2	3	4	5	6	7	8	9	10	11	12
Progression	A:	I^7	I^7	I^7	I^7	IV^7	IV^7	I^7	I^7	V^7	IV^7	I^7	V^7
Progression	B:	I^7	I^7	I^7	I^7	IV^7	IV^7	I^7	I^7	V^7	IV^7	I^7	I^7
Progression	C:	I^7	I^7	I^7	I^7	IV^7	IV^7	I^7	I^7	IV^7	V^7	I^7	V^7
Progression	D:	I^7	IV^7	I^7	I^7	IV^7	IV^7	I^7	I^7	V^7	IV^7	I^7	V^7
Progression	E:	I^7	I^7	I^7	I^7	IV^7	IV^7	I^7	I^7	V^7	V^7	I^7	I^7

Progression A is perhaps the most common of the twelve-bar blues. Several widely used variants of the standard twelve-bar blues are also shown in B, C, D, E. *Sweet Home Chicago*, recorded by Robert Johnson in 1936, is a blues sung over the first chord progression (A):

Johnson: *Sweet Home Chicago*

Robert Johnson, composer. Special permission from Horoscope Music Co.

| Twelve-Bar Jazz Blues | A *twelve-bar jazz blues* is characterized by the chord movement from II^7 to V^7 in the ninth and tenth bars. An often-used pattern is: |

**TWELVE-BAR
JAZZ BLUES**

1	2	3	4	5	6	7	8	9	10	11	12
I^7	IV^7	I^7	I^7	IV^7	IV^7	I^7	I^7	ii^7	V^7	I^7	V^7

| Modified Twelve-Bar Jazz Blues | A *modified twelve-bar jazz blues* is one of the countless progressions that incorporate chord patterns found in popular music. Often there are two or more chords per measure (all chords are Mm7s unless otherwise marked): |

$\frac{4}{4}$ Meter:

	1	2	3	4	5	6	7	8	9	10	11	12
1	I^7	IV^7	I^7	I^7	IV^7	IV^7	I^7 VII^7	$\flat VII^7$ VI^7	ii^7	V^7	I^7	V_7
2	I^7	ii^7 V^7	I^7	I^7	IV^7	iv^7	iii^7	VI^7	ii^7	V^7	I_7 $\flat iii^7$	ii^7 $\flat II^7_m$
3	I^7	IV^7	I^7	I^7	IV^7	IV^7	I^7 ii^7	iii^7 $\flat iii^7$	ii^7	V^7	I^7 $\sharp i^{\circ 7}$	ii^7 V^7

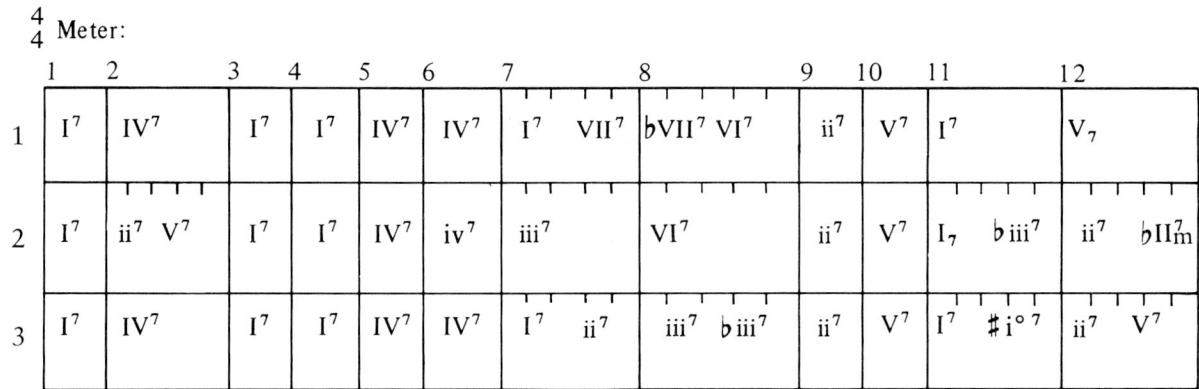

Another modified twelve-bar jazz-blues progression underlies this theme:

Parker: *Au Privave*

By Charlie Parker. © 1956. Atlantic Music Corp.

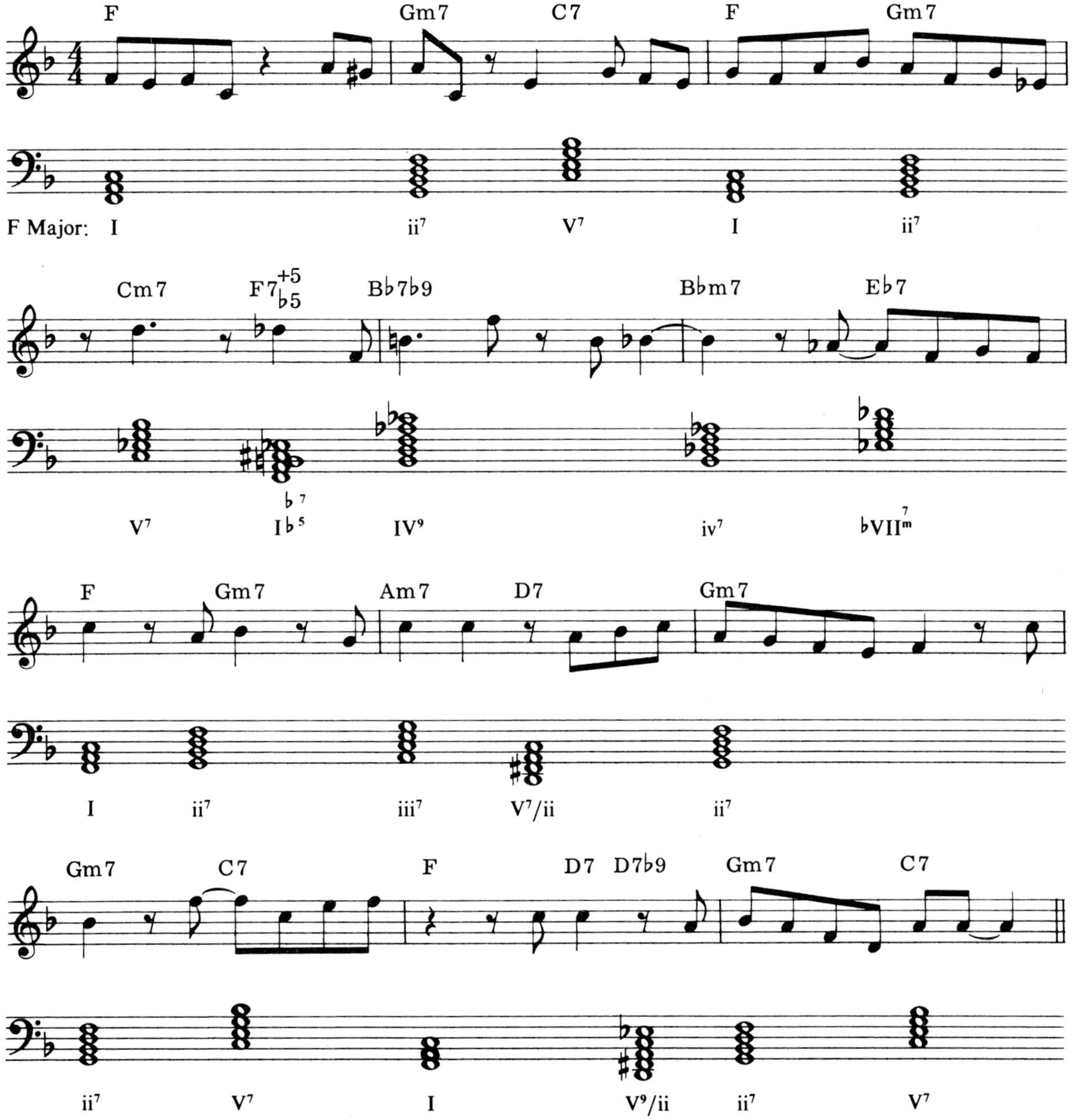

Melody Blues melody is not easily notated since vocalists and instrumentalists tend to bend and stretch certain notes, sometimes flatting or sharping the pitch by a semitone or more. The "worrying" of so-called *blue notes* gives the blues its distinct emotional impact and is not fully appreciated until heard.

Blues Scales A *blues scale* has a flat third and flat seventh. The notes most often given the blues intonation are the flat third and the flat seventh of the major scale. In the blues scale in the key of C that follows, the blues notes are placed in parentheses to show variable pitch:

Blues scale in key of C

Major-Minor Chords of the Blues Scales Blues scales consist only of notes that are factors of the I^7, IV^7, and V^7 chords. In the key of C, these chords are C^7, F^7, and G^7. In the following illustration, the three chords used in a standard twelve-bar blues contain all the notes of the blues scale:

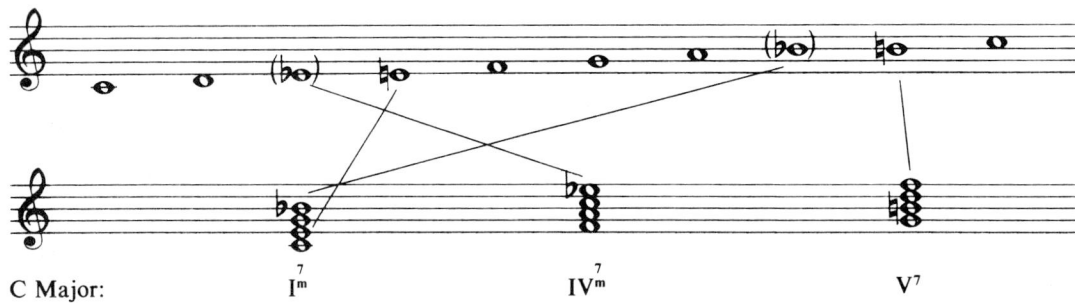

C Major: I^7_m IV^7_m V^7

Melodies Based on Mm7s A common melodic technique is to build melodies on the factors of the I^7, IV^7, and V^7 chords underlying the blues scale. Blues melodies often arpeggiate the chords that accompany them.

I^7_m IV^7_m I^7_m I^7_m

Repeated Melodic Figures Short melodic figures known as *riffs* are often repeated and superimposed over successive chords of the blues progression:

Garland: *Soul Junction*

By Red Garland. Copyright 1964. Prestige Music, 10th and Parker Sts., Berkeley, Ca. Used by permission. All rights reserved.

Riff

338 Blues, Boogie, and Jazz

| Division into Two Tetrachords | The blues scale may also be regarded as a combination of two tetrachords, as in the following scale in C Major: |

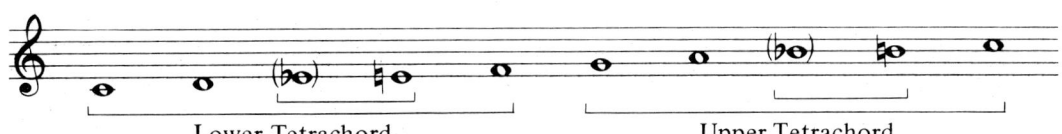

Melody, especially in early blues, tends to focus on the tonic and dominant of the scale (the beginning tones of the tetrachords). Typical movement of melody notes is indicated by the arrows:

Often the tonic and the dominant are approached from a minor third below or from a major second or minor third above.

| Scale with ♭3, ♭7, ♭5, ♭9 | Many musicians and composers employ a blues scale that adds a flatted fifth to the above scale, and, one might argue, a flatted ninth blue note as well: |

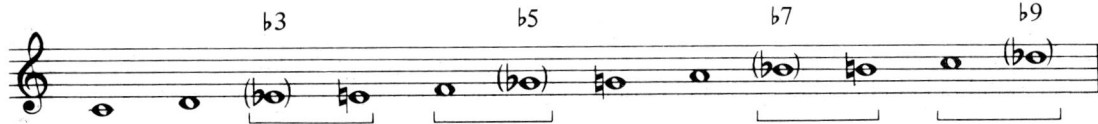

| +11 Chords | This scale may be generated by the notes of three augmented eleventh (+11) chords that, in the key of C major, are:

♯11   ♯11   ♯11
C7(9), F7(9), and G7(9).

In any key, this blues scale is derived tonally from the factors of a +11 chord built on the tonic, subdominant, and dominant degrees of the major scale.

Here is a blues scale (with ♭3, ♭5, ♭7, ♭9) derived from altered Mm7 (+9 +♯11): |

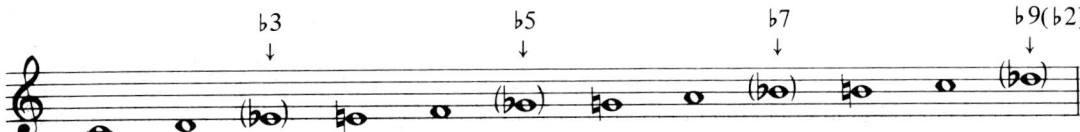

Blues, Boogie, and Jazz 339

The scale on the preceding page is derived from these chords:

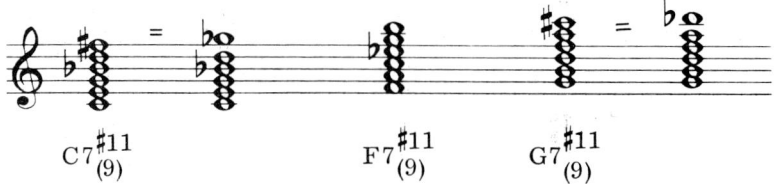

Division into Tetrachords

The blues scale with a ♭5 and ♭9 may also be regarded as two tetrachords combined:

C Major:

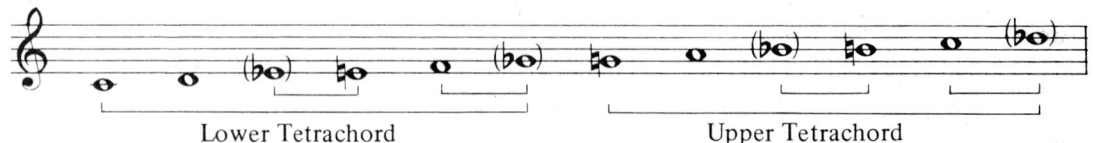

Lower Tetrachord   Upper Tetrachord

This blues scale is partly distinguished from the scale with only ♭3 and ♭7 by a melodic focus on the subdominant that is in addition to the focus on the tonic and dominant of the scale:

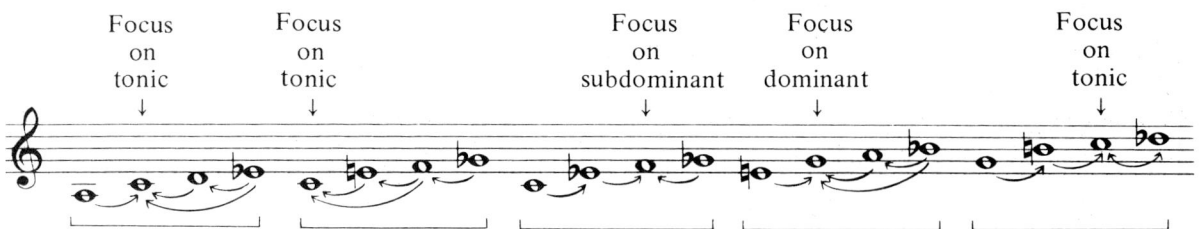

In earlier blues, musicians generally gave preference to the ♭3 and ♭7 blue notes. This blues, recorded by Gertrude "Ma" Rainey in 1924, makes use of only the ♭3 blue note.

Suddath: *Booze and Blues*

By J. Guy Suddath. © Copyright 1924, renewed 1952 by Northern Music Company. Used by permission. All rights reserved.

Went to bed last night, of course I was in my feet e-e-e I went to bed last night, and I was in my feet woke up this mornin: the po-lice was takin' me.

340 Blues, Boogie, and Jazz

More modern blues players and composers occasionally add the ♭5 and ♭9 in an effort to create greater tension in their music. The following is a typical blues figure with a ♭5 and a ♭9:

Indeed, the tension inherent in the blues is partly due to the conflict between the blue notes and the factors of the underlying chords. Blues artists who wish to minimize the tension, play the ♭3 blue note against the IV^7 chord, and the ♭7 blue note against the I^7 which creates a consonance between the blue notes and the chord factors. Greater tension is achieved by playing the ♭3 blue note against the I^7 or the ♭7 against the IV^7 or V^7 chord. Tension is maximized when, for example, the ♭5 or ♭9 is played over the I^7 chord:

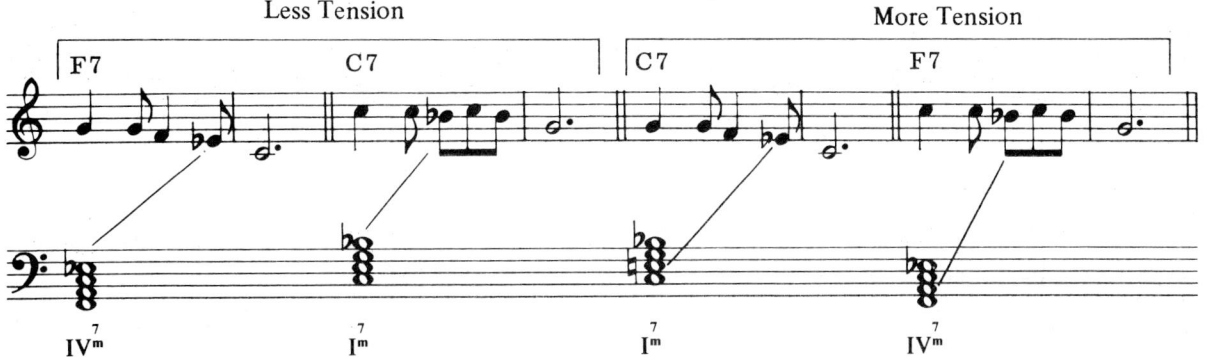

BOOGIE-WOOGIE

Boogie-woogie is a modern blues style originally created by black pianists who performed in local dives and at rent parties in the 1920s. To be heard over the noisy crowds and to compensate for the partly broken-down and out-of-tune pianos, the pianists developed such idiomatic tendencies as playing highly repetitive and rhythmic figures in both the left and right hands. The bass lines that characterize boogie-woogie have been adapted to other instruments besides the piano and are the stock in trade of nearly all blues and most rock 'n' roll artists.

Harmony

Boogie-woogie generally employs a standard twelve-bar blues although sometimes an eight-bar blues is used.

Melody

A blues scale is used in boogie-woogie.

With the piano, it is not possible to bend blue notes as vocalists and most instrumentalists do. To obtain a blues intonation, the pianist crushes (*acciaccatura*) and slurs notes or plays repetitive figures through the blue notes:

Crushes and slurs

Repetitive figures

Rhythm   The rhythmic thrust of boogie-woogie comes from the bass pattern that consists of a single- or double-note bass line repeated over and over. The rhythmic pattern typically consists of dotted eighth and sixteenth notes or simply eighth notes.

Base lines in key of C:

Texture   Boogie-woogie may have a texture that varies from thick to thin.

Thick Texture   Thick-textured boogie-woogie occurs when melodies embedded in chords or chord fragments are set against a double-note bass line:

Thick-textured Boogie-woogie:

342   Blues, Boogie, and Jazz

Thin Texture

Thin-textured boogie-woogie occurs when single-note figures are played against a single-note bass line, as in the following piano solo from *East Saint Louis Blues*:

Yancey: *East Saint Louis Blues*

By Jimmy Yancey. © Copyright 1940, renewed 1967 by MCA Music, a division of MCA, Inc. Used by permission. All rights reserved.

JAZZ

The blues influence in jazz is less noticeable than in boogie-woogie because jazz has drawn so heavily on the popular music tradition. Also, since the early 1940s, jazz has developed a highly sophisticated improvised melodic line that sometimes appears convoluted and anarchic to the uninitiated ear. Nevertheless, blues figures are evident in many jazz themes and in much improvisation.

In a typical jazz performance, first the theme is stated, supported by a sequence of chords. Then, the theme is abandoned while the chords are retained, and the musicians take turns improvising a new melody often based on the original theme. The performance concludes with a restatement of the initial melody.

Jazz Rhythm

The great majority of jazz compositions are written in $\frac{4}{4}$ meter. Jazz in waltz meter ($\frac{3}{4}$) is now common, but other meter signatures are employed less often. What distinguishes jazz rhythmically from other musical styles is its ability to "swing." There are several ingredients that contribute to this phenomenon.

Melodic Syncopation — *Syncopation* puts melodic stress on beats not normally accented. Syncopation creates rhythmic interest by injecting melodic highlights that anticipate or follow the underlying pulse, thus disturbing the metric regularity—

1. by introducing a note of different duration from the rhythmic pulse and by using tied notes and rests (simple syncopation).

Simple syncopation: Use of tied notes
Rhythmic Pattern: Musical Illustration:

Simple syncopation achieved with rests
Rhythmic Pattern: Musical Illustration:

2. by shifting the metric accent from the normally strong beats to weaker beats (syncopation through accent):

Parker: *Au Privave*

By Charlie Parker. © 1956. Atlantic Music Corp.

Rhythmic Modulation — *Rhythmic modulation* provides alternations of beat or beat-subdivision groupings involving duplets, triplets, and quadruplets. Rhythmic modulation most often contributes to the unique jazz idiom when melody tones that are an even division or multiple of the underlying meter shift from or to a series that is an uneven division or multiple of the metric pulse. Quarter notes followed by half-note triplets, quarter-note triplets followed by several eighth notes, and half-note triplets followed by quarter-note triplets are instances of rhythmic modulation. The following rhythmic modulation from *West End Blues* performed by Louis Armstrong is an example:

Williams: *West End Blues*

By Joe Oliver-Clarence Williams. © Copyright 1928, renewed 1955 by MCA Music, a division of MCA, Inc. Used by permission. All rights reserved.

344 Blues, Boogie, and Jazz

Odd-Length Motives in Succession

An *odd-length motive* is a melodic figure of such odd length that its entrance and exit do not coincide with the accents of the metric pulse. Here the notes of the melody coincide with the underlying pulse but are arranged as motives or figures of rhythmic length different from that of the prevailing meter. This device is referred to by some as *polyrhythm* and by others as *polymeter*. One common example sets a motive of three eighth notes against the 4/4 meter found in most jazz:

3 note melodic figure in sequence

Here is an example of five-beat figure in 4/4 meter:

Harmonic Syncopation

In *harmonic syncopation,* the chords supporting the theme are placed on weak beats or subdivisions of beats:

Rhythmic Superimposition

Frequently in jazz, at least three rhythms of different basic duration are played simultaneously. One rhythm occurs on the melodic level, the second at the harmonic, and the third at the purely rhythmic level. The melody's basic duration is the eighth or sixteenth note; harmony, usually provided by piano and guitar, is presented in chords of half note duration; and, the purely rhythmic, furnished by stringed bass and drums, is basically a quarter note beat (metric).

RHYTHMIC SUPERIMPOSITION

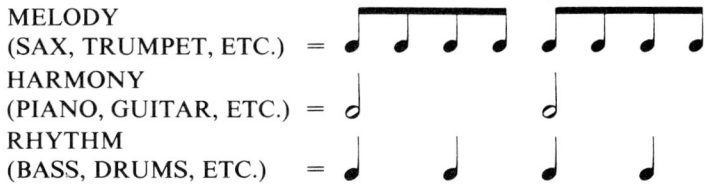

MELODY
(SAX, TRUMPET, ETC.) =

HARMONY
(PIANO, GUITAR, ETC.) =

RHYTHM
(BASS, DRUMS, ETC.) =

All of the elements in rhythmic superimposition are found in other types of music, but when combined by skilled musicians with the phrasing and attack peculiar to jazz, the result is music that does indeed swing.

Swing

Much controversy rages among jazz musicians themselves about the true meaning of *swing*, but regardless of the various definitions the effect of this free rhythmic interpretation is that of an easy undulation, relaxed and tranquil in slower tempi, and compelling and persistent at the faster pace. In essence, swing is a feeling and not an objective entity. Seldom does a listener have difficulty identifying swing in music, but performers must be quite experienced before the natural effect comes to full bloom.

Perhaps the most common of all jazz rhythms is the eighth note pattern:

Although the written music would seem to intend notes of equal value, the jazz artist will interpret such rhythm as:

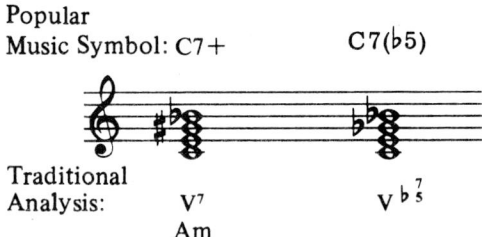

Jazz Harmony and Altered Chords

The harmonic vocabulary of jazz consists frequently of blues progressions and progressions from popular music. Jazz also makes extensive use of altered chords that are not found as often in popular music. Most altered chords (chords with nondiatonic tones) in jazz can be classified as one of the following:

Secondary dominants
Augmented triad + m7
Mm7 chord with lowered fifth

In traditional terms, the latter two chords—C7+ and C7 ♭ 5—are known as *altered dominants* or *whole-tone dominants* (each factor of the chord is a note in a whole-tone scale).

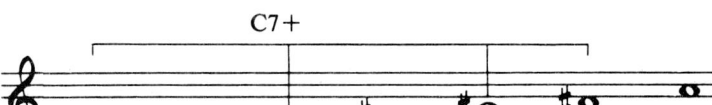

Actually both are whole-tone chords:

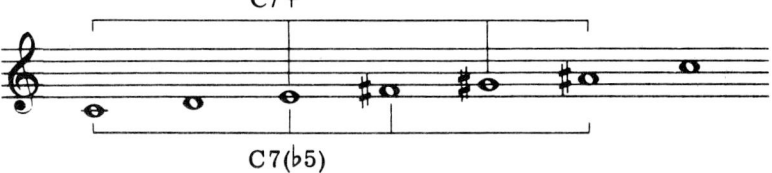

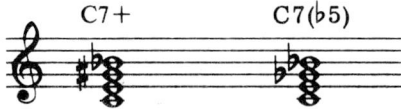

Also, in traditional music as well as in jazz, the chords have both dominant and secondary-dominant functions.

The use of an augmented seventh chord and a whole-tone dominant seventh chord is especially prominent in the jazz style known as *bebop*, which was created by such musicians as Charlie Parker, Dizzy Gillespie, and Thelonius Monk.

The following example illustrates the use of augmented seventh and whole-tone dominant seventh chords in bebop:

Monk: *52nd Street Theme*

By Thelonius Monk. Copyright Music Sales Corporation, New York, 1948, renewed 1975. All rights reserved. Used by permission.

Diminished Seventh Chords	Jazz uses *diminished sevenths,* altered chords built on degrees of the scale other than the leading tone in the harmonic minor scale.
Altered Factors above the Seventh	Altered chords are also formed by adding raised or lowered ninths, elevenths, and thirteenths to the seventh chords. Extensions of seventh chords add considerable harmonic interest and tension and sometimes cause extreme dissonance. Generally, the ear must be relied on to determine the appropriateness of a given sound.

Additional factors above the seventh:

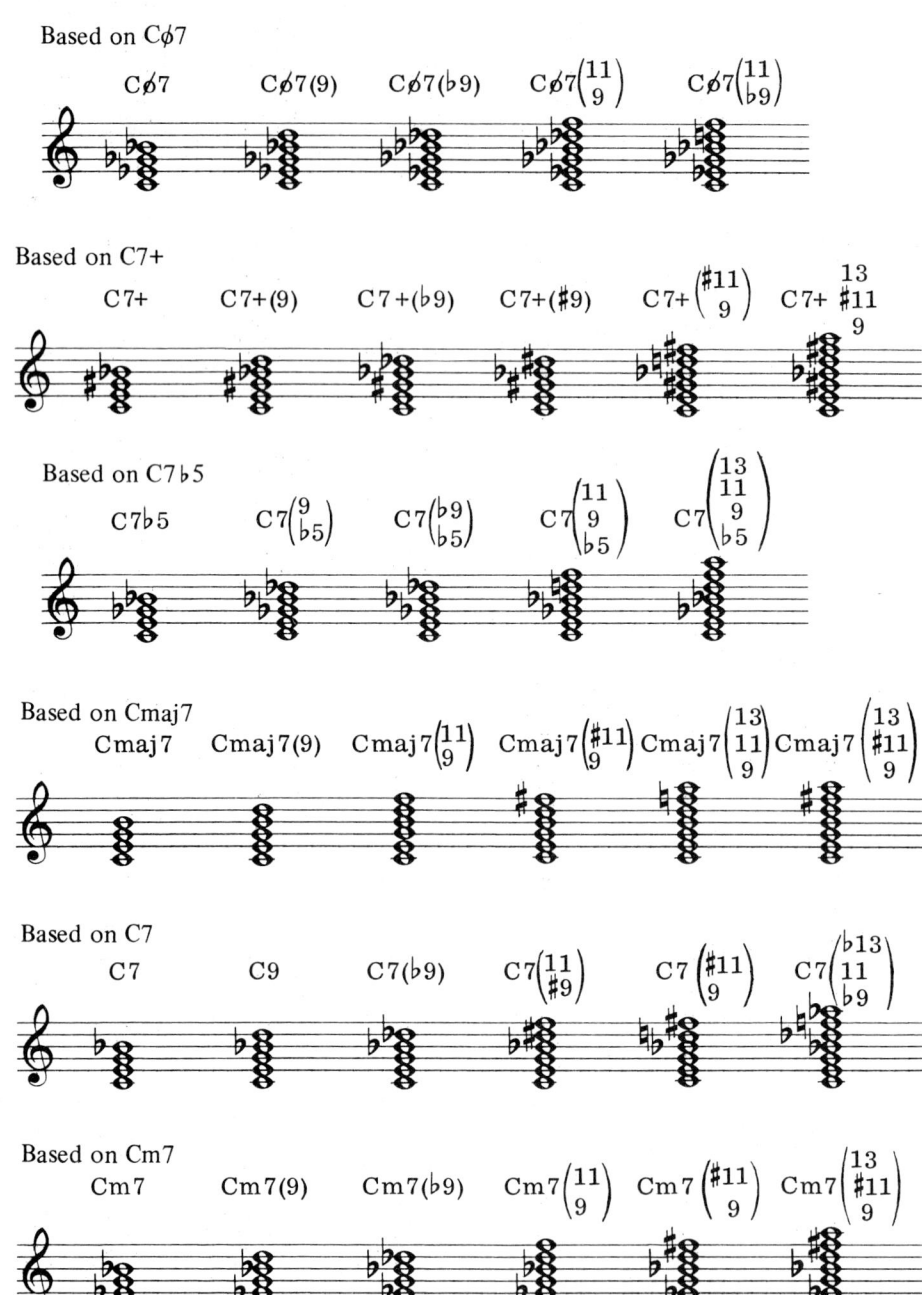

The following solo piano passage, transcribed from a Bill Evans recording, employs numerous extended seventh chords.

348 Blues, Boogie, and Jazz

Evans: *Only Child*

ONLY CHILD by Bill Evans, TRO © Copyright 1966 and 1969 LUDLOW MUSIC, INC., New York, N.Y. Used by permission.

Atonality

In modern jazz, to add interest, musicians often strive to negate tonality through free use of all pitches. Thus, improvisation on a tonal melody often gives way to atonal excursions accompanied by tonal chord progressions. As a result, the improvisation contains many altered (nondiatonic) notes. In jazz that is purely atonal both melodically and harmonically, such terms as "altered tones" have no meaning since atonal music by definition seeks a balance among all twelve tones of the chromatic scale.

Jazz Melody and Improvisation

The melodic material of jazz themes comes from a variety of sources but primarily blues, popular songs, and compositions written expressly for jazz performance. While a jazz theme is usually well established in advance of performance, jazz improvisation is partly spontaneous and often very original. Ideas for jazz improvisation come from:

1. Recordings.
2. Transcriptions of recordings.
3. Practice exercises and "woodshedding changes" (practicing improvisation over a set of chord changes).
4. Experience in playing with other musicians.
5. The prompting of an inventive and fertile mind.

The more skilled and the more creative musicians are, the less they will rely on previous performance and the more they are likely to produce music that is entirely new.

In order to learn to improvise well, listen to as much jazz as possible. The more involved and critical in listening, the sooner and better the listener will learn to improvise. Singing or playing along with recorded jazz themes and improvisations and making transcriptions of them are helpful aids in learning to improvise. Also, careful analysis of the harmonic implications of melody is required. In addition, many jazz musicians increase their facility by creating melodic patterns or other exercises based on scales suitable to a given chord or sequence of chords. Finally, since jazz is generally collective improvisation, play with other musicians as much as possible.

One way to organize material for jazz improvisation is to distinguish between a vertical and a horizontal approach for accommodating the improvised melody to chords.

Horizontal Approach (Diatonic)

To the extent possible, the improvised line lies within the diatonic scale and thus is strongly oriented to the tonic and the key. For example, the improviser playing a melody over a diatonic seventh chord in the key of C might play only tones that are found in the C major scale. Further, she or he might continue to play diatonic tones even over chords that contain altered tones.

The following illustration shows the horizontal accommodation of improvised melody to chords:

Vertical Approach (Chromatic)

With this approach, the improvised line is dictated by the structure of each underlying chord. The arrival of each new chord brings about a change in scalar or modal structure of the improvised line. As a result, the vertical approach leads to the use of many altered tones that tend to weaken the relationship between the improvised line and the key.

One example of the vertical approach is the accommodation of a mixolydian mode to a Mm7 chord:

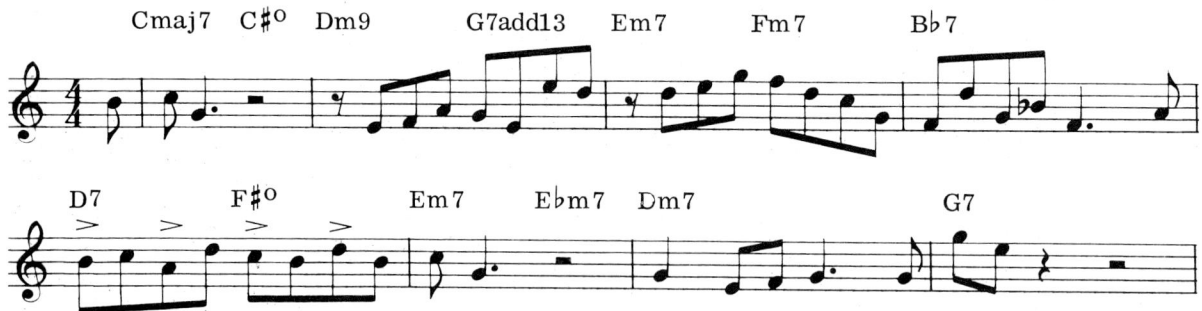

CHORD	FUNCTION IN KEY OF C	ACCOMMODATION OF MIXOLYDIAN MODE
C7	V^7/IV	Mixolydian Mode on C
D7	V^7/V	Mixolydian Mode on D
E7	V^7/vi	Mixolydian Mode on E

Mixolydian Mode on F

F7 V^7/VII =

Mixolydian Mode on G

G7 V^7 =

Mixolydian Mode on D♭

D♭7 $V^7/{}^\flat V$ =

Mixolydian Mode on E♭

E♭7 $V^7/{}^\flat VI$ =

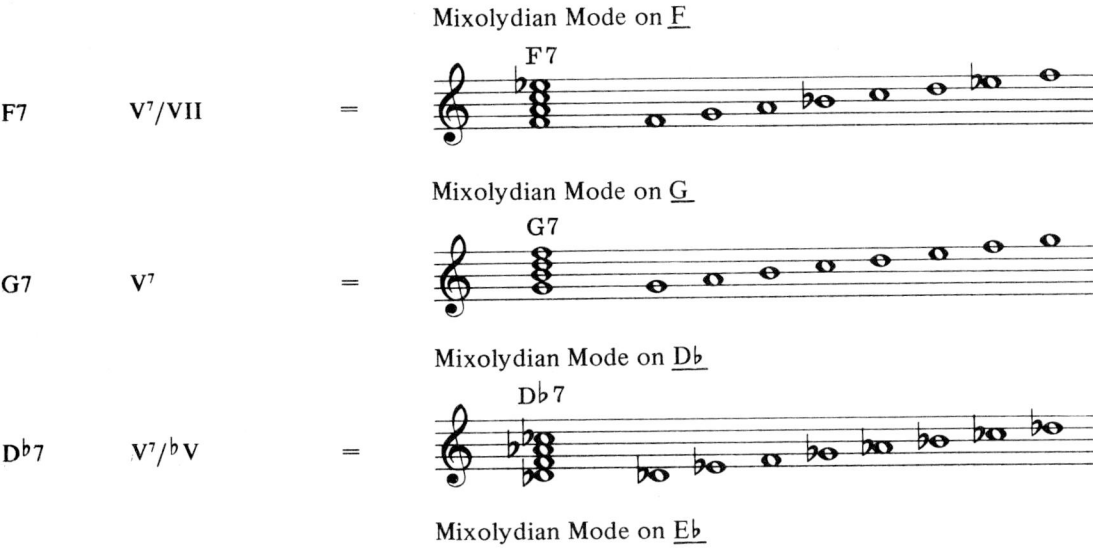

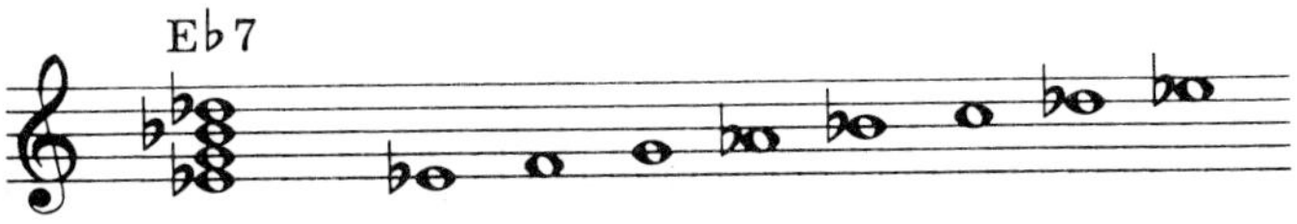

In the example below, the improvised line consists of notes of the mixolydian mode compatible with each Mm7 chord. The resultant line is an example of the vertical approach to improvisation:

Vertical accommodation of improvised melody to chords

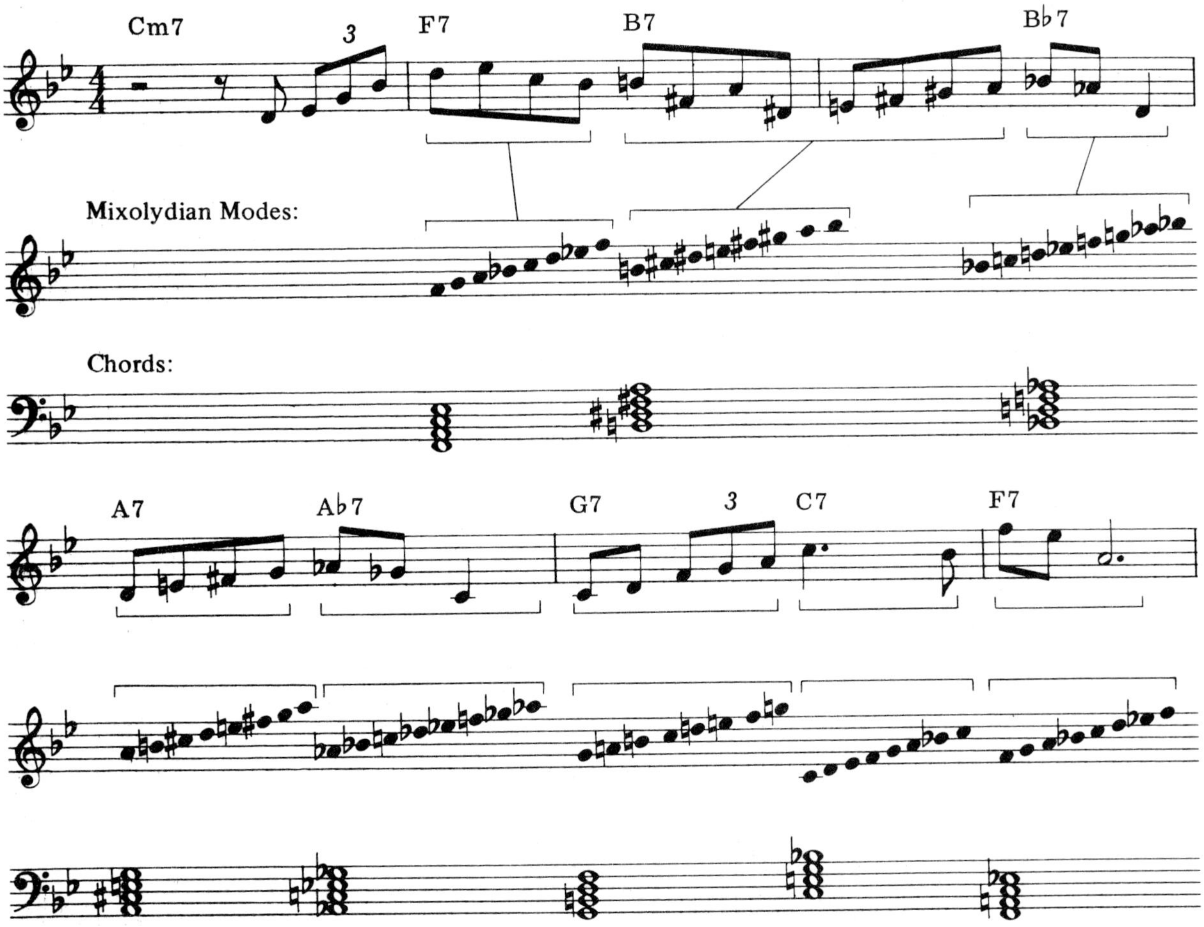

Other examples of the vertical approach are the accommodations of:
1. A Lydian or Ionian mode (major scale) to the MM7 chord.
2. A Phrygian, Aeolian, or Dorian mode to the mm7 chord.
3. A Locrian mode to the dd7 chord.
4. A whole-tone scale to the whole-tone dominant seventh chord.

CHORD **FUNCTION** **MODE**

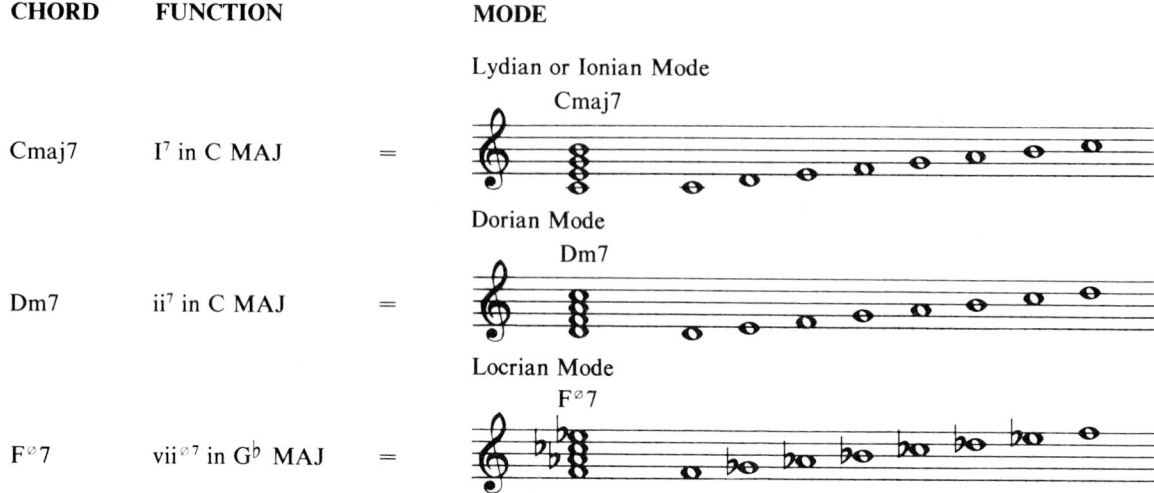

Unless the improviser wishes to play atonal jazz, he or she must choose between the horizontal or vertical approach or select some combination in between. Complete adherence to the horizontal approach generally results in uninteresting jazz that is too diatonic. On the other hand, an excessively vertical approach may leave the listener disoriented. Jazz is not easily codified. To improvise well requires the same good taste, creativity, and technical mastery that is necessary to compose traditional music or improvise in any other style.

ASSIGNMENT 1   Analyze the following musical passages. Identify:

1. Blues progressions.
2. Blues scales.
3. Blue notes and the manner in which they are approached.
4. Repeated figures or motifs.
5. Figures based on chords underlying the blues scale.
6. Rhythmic elements idiomatic to jazz.

1.
Davis: *Bag's Groove*   (take no. 1) trumpet solo transcription

Bag's Groove by Miles Davis. Copyright by WEMAR MUSIC CORP. All rights reserved. Used by permission of Wemar Music Corp. 6515 Sunset Blvd., Hollywood, Calif. 90028.

352   Blues, Boogie, and Jazz

ASSIGNMENT 1 (continued)

2.
Matthews: *Pastime Rag, A Slow Drag, no. 3*

By Artie Matthews. Carol Hyolt—Rights and Permissions. Published by Dover Publications, Inc. (1973), New York, N.Y.

3.
Smith: *Backwater Blues*

BACKWATER BLUES by Bessie Smith. © 1927, 1974 FRANK MUSIC CORP. © Renewed 1955 FRANK MUSIC CORP. International copyright secured. All rights reserved. Used by permission.

ASSIGNMENT 1 (continued)

4.
Rollins: *Tenor Madness*

By Sonny Rollins. Copyright 1957 Prestige Music, 10th and Parker Sts., Berkeley, Ca. Used by permission. All rights reserved.

ASSIGNMENT 2

Compose a boogie-woogie based on a standard twelve-bar blues. Use the following bass line:

ASSIGNMENT 3

Compose a boogie-woogie based on a standard eight-bar blues of the form:

Measures:	1	2	3	4	5	6	7	8
Chords:	I^7	I^7	IV^7	IV^7	I^7	V^7	I^7	I^7

Use this bass line:

| ASSIGNMENT 4 | Enrich the harmony of a popular song of your choosing by extending the seventh chords. |

| ASSIGNMENT 5 | Compose a blues over the chord changes underlying *Au Privave*, illustrated in this chapter on page 337. |

| ASSIGNMENT 6 | Compose a variation of Thelonius Monk's *52nd Street Theme*, page 347. |

| ASSIGNMENT 7 | On your instrument, improvise a solo over the chord progression underlying the popular song *Try to Remember* on page 314 of chapter 18, "The American Popular Song." Does the sequence of chords lend itself to a horizontal or vertical approach to improvisation? Write out a melody that might serve as an improvised chorus. |

| ASSIGNMENT 8 | What modes or scales may be superimposed on these chords without creating dissonance?

Cm7 F♯7 B♭° D♭° Amaj7 E7+ G♯7$^{(♭5)}$ B7 Bm7
B° B° Bmaj7 B7+ B7$^{(♭5)}$

Play the modes and scales consistent with these chords on your instrument. |

| ASSIGNMENT 9 | Determine the modes and scales consistent with each chord in the twelve-bar jazz blues progressions on page 336 in the keys of C major, F major, B-flat major, D major, A major, and E-flat Major. Play the progression on your instrument as follows:

1. Play the scale or mode consistent with each chord (in eighth notes).
2. Arpeggiate each chord in eighth notes.
3. Improvise a chorus over the blues progression. |

| ASSIGNMENT 10 | Apply the procedure described in no. 1 of assignment 9 to no. 3 of the modified twelve-bar jazz blues progressions on page 337. |

| ASSIGNMENT 11 | Transcribe a vocal blues from a recording by one of the following artists: |

Ma Rainey	Charlie Patton	Muddy Waters
Bessie Smith	Roosevelt Sykes	B. B. King
Robert Johnson	Champion Jack Dupree	James Cotton
Lightnin' Hopkins		

Singing along with the recording until the melody is memorized makes transcribing considerably easier. After the transcription is completed, play the blues composition on your instrument after which a variation of the same blues melody should be improvised.

| ASSIGNMENT 12 |

1. Transcribe a jazz theme and at least one improvised chorus from a recording. Before attempting the transcription, learn to sing the theme and the improvised chorus if you can. If the tempo is too fast, play the recording at half speed on your record player or tape recorder, and you will hear the details more clearly.
2. Take your transcription from one of the following:
   a. Any Miles Davis recording. Recordings made after 1965 are not particularly suitable for this purpose, although they are of considerable musical interest.
   b. Any Charlie Parker recording.
   c. Any Louis Armstrong recording.
   d. Any other recording that seems noteworthy and suitable for this purpose.
3. In addition to transcribing the melodic line:
   a. Determine the harmony.
   b. Then, on your instrument, play the theme and improvised chorus either by ear or from the transcription.
   c. Finally, improvise several choruses of your own.

REFERENCES

Books

Baker, David. *Jazz Improvisation.* Chicago: Maher, 1969.

Mehegan, John. *Jazz Improvisation.* Volumes 1–4. New York: Watson-Guptil, 1962.

Russell, George. *Lydian Chromatic Concept of Tonal Organization.* New York: Concept Publishing, 1959.

Sargeant, Winthrop. *Jazz, Hot and Hybrid.* 3rd ed. New York: Da Capo Press, 1975.

Schuller, Gunther. *Early Jazz, Its Roots and Musical Development.* New York: Oxford University Press, 1968.

Recordings

1. *The Story of the Blues.* Columbia G30008
2. *Bessie Smith, Any Woman's Blues.* Columbia G30126 (part of a five volume set of double albums)
3. *The Louis Armstrong Story.* Vols. 1–4, Columbia Cl 851–854

4. *Charlie Parker Memorial.* Vol. 1, Savoy MG–12000
5. *Miles Davis, Workin' and Steamin'.* Prestige P–24034
6. *Song for My Father, Horace Silver Quintet.* Blue Note 84185
7. *Bill Evans, Village Vanguard Sessions.* Milestone 47002
8. *Sonny Rollins, Saxophone Colossus.* Prestige 7326
9. *Herbie Hancock, Maiden Voyage.* Blue Note 84195
10. *Coltrane.* Prestige 24003
11. *Night Train: The Oscar Peterson Trio.* Verve V6–8538
12. *Ballads, John Coltrane Quartet.* Impulse A–32
13. *Cannonball Adderley, Cannonball and Eight Giants.* Milestone 47001
14. *Collaboration: Modern Jazz Quartet with Laurindo Almeida.* Atlantic 1429
15. *Kansas City Boogie, Anthology #10.* Folkways Records FJ 2810
16. *Barrelhouse, Blues, and Boogie.* Vol. 2, Storyville (Danish Import) 183
17. *Freddie Hubbard, Red Clay.* CTI 6001
18. *Chick Corea, Return to Forever.* ECM 1022 ST
19. *Thelonius Monk's Greatest Hits.* Columbia CS 9775

Appendix 1

Comprehensive List of Chords Found in Popular Music

Following is a comprehensive list of chords found in popular song accompaniments. All are based on C but may be transposed to any other tone:

C   Cm   Cdim (C°)   Caug (C+)   C6   Cm6   C(♭5)   C7

Cm7   Cdim7   Cmaj7   C7♯5   C7♭5   C7sus   Cmaj7♯5   Cm7♭5

Cm(maj7)   C9   C9♯5   C7♭9   C9♭5   C7♯9   Cm9   Cmaj7add9

C11   C13   C13(♭9)   Caug11   C6/9   Cm6/9   C7♯5♭9   C7♯5♯9

Cm9(♭5)   C13(♯11)

Appendix 2

Summary of Part-Writing Procedures Based on Practices Followed by Eighteenth-Century Composers of Chorale Harmonizations

There are no exceptions to these practices:

1. Avoid parallel perfect eighths (P8s), perfect fifths (P5s), and perfect unisons. When such successive intervals remain on the same pitch, they are not considered parallel. (p. 135)
2. Never double the leading tone of the scale. (p. 135)
3. Keep all voices within their ranges. (p. 135)
4. Avoid augmented seconds (A2s) and augmented fourths (A4s) in the melodic line of any of the four voices. (p. 135)

These practices should be carefully observed unless a particular situation permits no other alternative:

5. First choice: Double the root in root position major and minor triads. (p. 136)
   Second choice: Double the first, fourth, or fifth degree of the scale. (p. 136)
6. First choice: Double the soprano note in first-inversion major and minor triads. (p. 136)
   Second choice: Double the bass note. In a series of first inversions, double the soprano and bass alternately. (p. 136)
7. In second inversion, the triads double the bass note (fifth factor). (p. 136)
8. First choice: Double the third (bass note) in first-inversion diminished triads. The root position of the diminished triad is seldom used. (p. 136)
   Second choice: Double the fifth factor (fourth degree of the scale). For the ii°⁶ in minor, double the root or the third. (p. 136)
9. All factors of triads should be present except for the final chord of a phrase or section. This chord may contain a tripled root and a single third. (p. 136)
10. Avoid large melodic leaps of a sixth or more. The exceptions are octave leaps in the bass voice. (p. 136)

11. Do not overlap voices from one chord to the next. Overlapping occurs between adjacent chords when one voice leaps above (or below) the pitch of an adjacent voice. This is best explained through the following illustration: (p. 136)

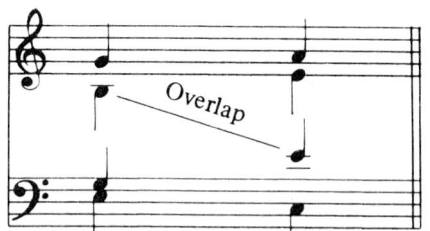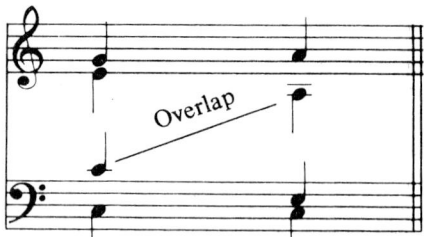

Tenor G leaps up to E, which is higher than the alto B in the previous chord.

Alto E leaps down to A, which is lower than the previous tenor note C.

Half-step overlap used on occasion

Bass D leaps to G which is above the previous tenor F-sharp

12. In the outer voices, do not leap in the same direction to perfect intervals (P8s, P5s, or P1s). (p. 136)

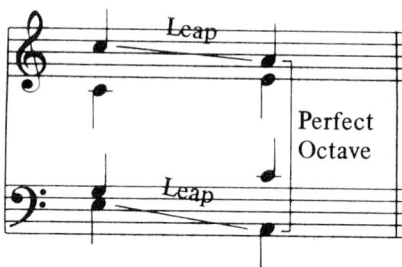

13. Maintain the regular order of voices. Bass is lowest, then tenor, then alto, and the highest is soprano. (p. 137)
14. Maintain an octave or less (harmonic interval) between the soprano and alto and between the alto and tenor voices. Intervals of more than an octave frequently occur between the tenor and bass voices. (p. 137)
15. Although augmented seconds and fourths are always to be avoided, leaps downward of a diminished fifth (d5) or a diminished fourth (d4) occur occasionally. (p. 137)

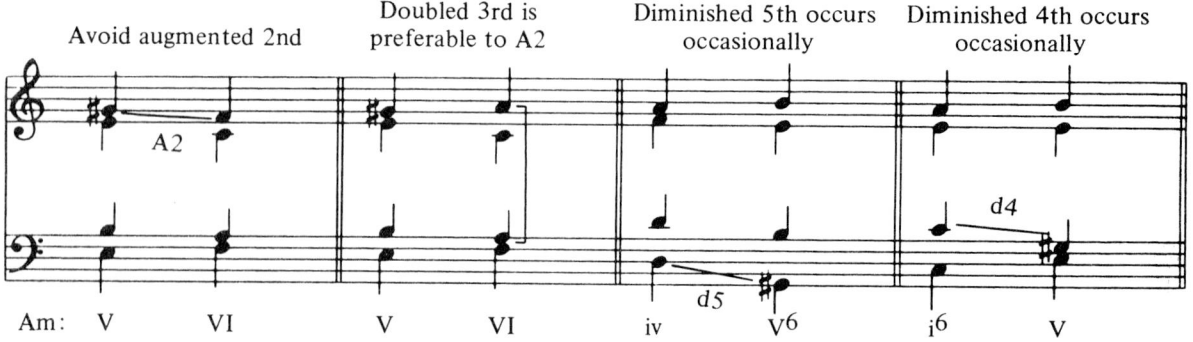

16. Resolve the seventh of the V⁷ chord in the same voice except when the resolution tone (one scale step down from the seventh factor) is not present in the following chord. (p. 185)
17. The V⁷ usually contains all four factors, but on occasion, for smoothness in part-writing, the root is doubled and the fifth omitted. (p. 185)
18. Omit the fifth (by tripling the root) that occasionally follows the V⁷ to avoid parallel fifths. (p. 185)
19. Resolve the seventh of the vii^{ø7} in the ensuing chord (tonic). (p. 194)
20. Resolution of the tritone (inward if a d5 and outward if an A4) in the same two voices is desirable but not always possible. (p. 194)
21. Resolve the seventh of the vii°⁷ in the ensuing chord (tonic). (p. 195)
22. Resolve at least the lower tritone (root to fifth) whenever possible. Music literature reveals a variety of part-writing procedures in the progression vii°⁷ to i. Parallel uneven fifths (d5 to P5) are observed in literature but are comparatively rare. (p. 195)
23. Resolve the seventh factor of a nondominant seventh chord whenever possible. (p. 233)
24. Make sure all factors are present in nondominant seventh chords. (p. 233)
25. Exceptions to rule 24 when seventh chords occur consecutively: (p. 234)
    a. Frequently, some of the chords are incomplete.
    b. The sevenths of some chords ascend rather than resolving downward in the conventional manner.
26. Part-writing procedures for secondary dominants are the same as for primary dominant types (V, V⁷, vii°⁶, vii^{ø7}, and vii°⁷). (p. 256)
27. When the secondary dominant V⁷/ occurs consecutively: (p. 256)
    a. Some of the chords are frequently incomplete.
    b. The sevenths of some chords ascend rather than resolving downward.

Appendix 3

Expression Marks Expression marks represent a composer's attempt to convey aspects of interpretation to a prospective performer. The most frequently used expression marks include *tempo* marks and *dynamics* symbols. Tempo symbols are concerned with setting the pace of a given work, while dynamics symbols focus on relative degrees of intensity.

Representative Tempo Marks

	presto	very fast (with a sense of haste)
	allegro	fast (with a sense of cheerfulness)
	allegretto	moderately fast (literally, a "little" or small *allegro*)
	moderato	moderate (neither fast nor slow)
	andante	an easy walking pace
	lento	slow (with a sense of laziness)
	adagio	quite slow (in a quiet, easy manner)
	largo	very slow (with a sense of breadth and expansiveness)
	grave	very slow (with a sense of solemnity, sternness, and seriousness)

Representative Dynamic Marks

	pp	*pianissimo*	very soft
	p	*piano*	soft
	mp	*mezzo piano*	moderately soft (literally, "half" soft)
	mf	*mezzo forte*	moderately loud
	f	*forte*	loud (literally, "strong")
	ff	*fortissimo*	very loud
	sfz	*sforzato*	with a forced accent (literally, "excessive" or "coerced")
	sf	*sforzando*	synonymous with *sforzato* for musical purposes

A third category of expression marks consists of terms and phrases (usually in Italian) intended to suggest the character and/or mood of a given work or smaller sections within a larger work. For example:

accelerando	becoming faster (literally, "accelerating")
animato	animated
con brio	with energy, spirited
calando	becoming softer (with a sense of waning or sinking)
cantabile	in a singing style (literally, "singable")
crescendo	increasing in intensity (literally, "growing")
diminuendo	becoming softer (with a gradual sense of lessening or reducing)
giocoso	in a playful or joking manner
legato	to be performed smoothly (literally, "bound" or "linked" together)
marcato	marked or stressed (emphasizing each note)
morendo	fading, becoming softer (literally, "dying")
rallentando	gradually slowing down (literally, to "relax" or "slacken")
ritardando	gradually slowing down (literally, to "delay" or "defer")
scherzando	joking, whimsical
smorzando	dying away (literally, "becoming extinguished")
sperdendosi	fading away (literally, "disappearing" or "becoming dispersed")
staccato	detached (literally, "separated")
vivace	lively (literally, "full of life, flourishing")

While some of these musical terms seem to be synonymous, the serious composer is sensitive to subtle shades of meaning and will often prefer one over another. The equally serious and responsible performer must also be sensitive to the composer's choices.

Glossary

Accidental A symbol used to indicate the momentary raising or lowering of a pitch—as opposed to a pitch raised in the key signature. Accidental symbols include: ♯ ♭ ♮ 𝄪 ♭♭

Blues Although earlier examples exist, blues as a type of popular music developed in the United States about 1909. In general, blues music embodies the following characteristics:

1. Each section or "strain" of blues consisted of twelve bars (measures).
2. Blues works feature the blues scale (a major scale with alternate use of flatted thirds and sevenths).
3. Blues music is characterized by blue ("worried") notes—tones between the diatonic and flatted thirds and sevenths.
4. The melody is in the style of spirituals and work songs.
5. Blues began as vocal music.

Blues scale A major scale with a flat third and seventh. It must be remembered that the flat third and seventh were sometimes "worried" notes; thus, their pitches did not always correspond to equal-tempered tuning.

Blues scale with added flat fifth A classic blues scale (flat third and seventh) but with an additional flat fifth. This scale is a somewhat later development in blues. Flat ninths are also included on occasion.

Boogie-woogie A modern blues style created for instrumental application. Boogie-woogie is characterized by an adaptation of the ground bass principle—a repetitious bass figure that suggests the blues chord progression.

Cadence—authentic A cadence consisting of the dominant to tonic harmonic progression.

Cadence—deceptive A cadence made up of a harmonic progression from the dominant to a chord other than the tonic. V to VI is the one most often found.

Cadence—half A cadence consisting of a harmonic progression ending on the dominant. Most half cadences conform with one of the following: IV to V, I to V, or II to V.

Cadence—harmonic A formula consisting of two chords that brings a phrase, section, or composition to a conclusion.

Cadence—plagal	A cadence made up of a harmonic progression from subdominant to tonic. The Amen cadence (IV to I) is a typical example.
Chorale	Lutheran melodies that are the counterparts of English hymn tunes. These melodies were adapted from (1) well-known popular songs of the period, (2) Catholic hymn tunes, and (3) German hymn melodies predating the Reformation. A few chorale melodies were original. Most were established before the seventeenth century but were modified for use in the eighteenth century.
Chord-progression types	The progression of chords by: (1) descending fifths or ascending fourths, (2) descending fourths or ascending fifths, (3) ascending seconds or descending sevenths, (4) descending thirds or ascending sixths, (5) ascending thirds or descending sixths, (6) descending seconds or ascending sevenths.
Clef—alto	A C clef or "movable" clef. The indentation in the signature signifies that middle C is on the middle line of the staff.

Clef—bass	Called the F clef because dots are placed on the *fourth line* of the staff to indicate the F below middle C.

Clef—soprano	A C clef or movable clef. The indentation signifies that middle C is on the bottom line of the staff.

Clef—tenor	A C or movable clef. The indentation in the sign signifies that middle C is on the fourth line of the staff.

Clef—treble	Called the G clef because the curved line of the signature terminates on the second line of the staff to establish G above middle C.

Closely related keys	In the major key: (1) the dominant major, (2) the subdominant major, (3) the relative minor, (4) the relative minor of the dominant, and (5) the relative minor of the subdominant.
	    In the minor key: (1) the dominant minor, (2) the subdominant minor, (3) the relative major, (4) the relative major of the dominant, and (5) the relative major of the subdominant.
	    Stated in another way, two keys may be regarded as closely related if their key signatures do not differ by more than one sharp or flat.

Common chord	In a modulation a common chord is one that is diatonic to both keys (the original and the new).

Consonance	A relative term denoting a combination of sounds producing a feeling of repose or relaxation, or sounds that create little tension (desire for resolution). Consonances during the so-called common practice period are: perfect unisons, P5s, P8s, and major and minor sixths and thirds.
Conventional four-chord formula	In popular music, a harmonic progression pattern containing four chords. Most four-chord patterns occupy two measures. Example: I vi ii^7 V^7. Such formulas occur so often in popular songs as to be critical components of style.
Cross relation	A conflict, produced by a tone in one voice followed in another voice by the same tone (same letter name) altered a half step. Example: D-sharp in one voice followed immediately by D-natural in another voice.
Diatonic	A seven-note scale consisting of whole steps and half steps. The eighth note or step of the scale is regarded as a repetition of the first. A major scale places half steps between scale steps 3 and 4 and steps 7 and 8. All three forms of the minor scale place a half step between scale steps 2 and 3. The placement of other half steps depends on the specific form of the minor scale: natural, harmonic, or melodic.
Dissonance	A relative term denoting a combination of sounds producing harsh or discordant results, or sounds that heighten the tension (increase the desire for resolution). Dissonances during the so-called common practice period are: M and m seconds, M and m sevenths, and all augmented and diminished intervals.
Double period	A succession of four phrases in which each of the first three is punctuated by a half cadence and the fourth is terminated by an authentic cadence.
Embellishing tone	Melodic decorations and ornaments to structural and secondary tones.
Enharmonic	Two tones having the same pitch but different spelling. Example: F-sharp and G-flat are enharmonic.
Figured bass	A bass melody with numbers and musical symbols beneath it to indicate the chords to be played. Known also as *basso continuo* and *thorough bass*. A device of the seventeenth to mid-eighteenth centuries.
Harmonic progression	Movement from one chord to the next; a succession of chords or a chord progression.
Harmonic rhythm	The frequency of harmonic changes in a composition; the rate of chord change.
Harmony	The study of simultaneously sounding tones or concern with the chordal structure of a musical composition.
Homophonic (texture)	A single, clearly defined melody with chordal accompaniment. Examples: a popular song, a Mozart minuet, a Johann Strauss waltz, and nearly all music of the nineteenth century.
Imitation	The repetition of a melody or melodic group in close succession but in a different voice; the repetition of a melody at a different pitch level in a polyphonic texture.
Imitation—real	An imitation with no modifications except for the usual diatonic adjustment of half and whole steps. The exact transposition of a melody at different pitch levels.

Improvise	To extemporize; to play on the spur of the moment. To perform without a prepared text or composed material.
Incipient three-part form	*See* Three-part form—incipient.
Interval	The difference in pitch between two tones.
Interval—compound	Any interval greater than an octave. Usually compound intervals are expressed as simple equivalents (the octave is subtracted). Example: A major tenth interval—a compound major third.
Inversion (of a melody)	A procedure for deriving another form of a given melody. An ascending interval in a melody becomes a descending interval (and vice versa) of the same size in the inversion of the melody.
Inversion (of intervals)	Occurs when the lower tone forming the interval becomes the upper tone (or vice versa). Example: major third becomes a minor sixth when inverted at the octave.
Jazz	A nearly indefinable term. Jazz was influenced by several other types of music, among them blues and the popular song. It is characterized by a highly sophisticated improvised melodic line; chord progressions that utilize seventh, ninth, eleventh, and thirteenth chords; and syncopated rhythms.
Melody	An organized succession of pitches.
Meter	The system of regularly recurring pulses most often grouped by periodic accents. Example: 3/4 meter indicates that the beats are grouped by three's with the quarter note representing one beat or pulse.
Meter—asymmetrical	Those meters in which the pulse cannot be divided into equal groupings of two, three, or four in the measure. Examples: 7/4, 5/4, 11/8, and so on.
Meter—compound	Meter in which the basic pulse may be subdivided into groups of three. Examples: 6/8, 9/8, 12/8, and so on.
Meter—simple	Meter signatures whose upper numbers are 1, 2, 3, or 4. The basic subdivision of the pulse is in duplets.
Mode—Aeolian	A system of seven tones with the same arrangement as the natural minor key (A to A on the white keys of the piano). Not one of the original church modes; developed with the advent of polyphony.
Mode—Dorian	A system of seven tones with the same arrangement as from D to D on the white keys of the piano.
Mode—Ionian	A system of seven tones with the same arrangement as our major key scale (C to C on the white keys of the piano). Not one of the original church modes; developed with the advent of polyphony.
Mode—Locrian	A system of seven tones with the same arrangement as from B to B on the white keys of the piano. Seldom found in music literature because of tritone relationships.

Mode—Lydian	A system of seven tones with the same arrangement as from F to F on the white keys of the piano.
Mode—Mixolydian	A system of seven tones with the same arrangement as from G to G on the white keys of the piano.
Mode—Phrygian	A system of seven tones with the same arrangement as from E to E on the white keys of the piano.
Modes—authentic	Associated with Gregorian chants. The octave ranges of the Dorian, Phrygian, Lydian, and Mixolydian modes coincide with each modal scale, each with the *final* as first note.
Modes—church (or medieval or ecclesiastical)	Classified at the time of Pope Gregory I (about 600 A.D.). The church modes consist of a system of eight scales derived from the codification of liturgical chants. These scales served as the basis for musical composition until the sixteenth century, when the system was expanded to twelve modes with modes nine to ten and eleven to twelve emerging as the natural minor and major scales respectively.
Modes—Plagal	Associated with Gregorian chants. The octave ranges of Hypodorian, Hypophrygian, Hypolydian, and Hypomixolydian modes begin a P4th below and extend to the P5th above the *final*.
Modified twelve-bar jazz blues	Variants of the standard twelve-bar blues and twelve-bar jazz blues progressions. Most variants incorporated progressions found in the popular songs of the period. In some variants the harmonic rhythm was increased to more than one chord per measure. Although blues provided the ingredients for jazz in the beginning, later blues music was influenced by some of the newer jazz idioms.
Modulation	Change of key; a shift of tonal center. Generally refers to diatonic (key-centered) music, but may also be applied to free tonality and modality in certain instances.
Modulation—chromatic	A modulation that takes place at the point of a chromatic progression (a progression that involves the chromatic inflection of one of the chord tones). At such a point no common chord exists.
Modulation—common chord	A modulation that is effected through a chord that is diatonic in both keys (the original and the new). Example: In a modulation to G major from C major, the C major triad is a *common chord:* I in C and IV in G.
Modulation—enharmonic	A modulation that involves the enharmonic spelling of a chord. Example: F-sharp, A-sharp, C-sharp = I in F-sharp major and G-flat, B-flat, D-flat = IV in D-flat major. The two chords have the same sound but are spelled differently.
Modulation—static	A modulation that takes place between phrases, sections, or other musical portions of a composition. A modulation that occurs at a static point in the music, sometimes referred to as a tonal shift.
Motive	The smallest meaningful and self-contained fragment of musical thought. May consist of as few as two tones.

Neume	A symbol used in the early notation of music (circa 650 A.D. to 1350 A.D.)
Nondominant seventh chord	A diatonic seventh chord that does not have dominant function. Since the dominant and leading tone seventh chords (V^7 and VII^7) are the only ones that do have dominant function, all others I^7, II^7, III^7, IV^7, and VI^7) are nondominant.
Nonharmonic tone	A tone that is not a part of the chord sounding at the particular moment.
Nonharmonic tone—anticipation	A chord tone that becomes a nonharmonic tone by moving stepwise *before* the next chord is actually sounded to become a tone in that next chord.
Nonharmonic tone—appoggiatura	A nonharmonic tone preceded by a leap and resolved by step.
Nonharmonic tone—changing tone	Two successive nonharmonic tones. Leads from a chord tone by step, leaps to another nonharmonic tone, then leads to a chord tone by step.
Nonharmonic tone—escape tone	A nonharmonic tone that leads from a chord tone by step, then leaps to another of different pitch. In the so-called common practice period, this meant a step up and a leap of a third down.
Nonharmonic tone—neighboring tone	A nonharmonic tone that leads from one chord tone by step to another of the same pitch.
Nonharmonic tone—passing tone	A nonharmonic tone leading from one chord tone by step to another of different pitch.
Nonharmonic tone—pedal tone (pedal point)	A held or repeated note, usually in the lowest-sounding voice, that alternates between consonant and dissonant relationships with the chord structures above it.
Nonharmonic tone—retardation	A nonharmonic tone that is similar to a suspension except that the resolution is upward instead of downward.
Nonharmonic tone—suspension	Leads by repetition from a chord tone, then by step downward to another chord tone. Suspensions are most frequently found on stressed beats. The three phases of suspension are preparation, suspension, and resolution.
Nontransposing instruments	Instruments in which the produced pitch is the same as the written pitch.
Notation—mensural	Measured notation. First drawn up by Franco of Cologne in the thirteenth century. Bar lines did not appear until the seventeenth century.
Notation—tablature	Notation using letters, numbers or a diagram. In the case of the vihuela, lute, and guitar, the diagrams frequently represented the strings of the instruments.
Parallels (major and minor)	Major and minor scales that have the same tonic.
Period	A combination of two (less frequently three) phrases that are in some way related so that a new and larger complete musical unit is formed.
Period—three part	Three phrases that form a period, the first two ending with a half cadence and the last with a full or authentic cadence.

Phrase	A complete musical thought that usually ends with a half cadence. Phrases are typically four measures in length, but occasionally appear as three- or five-measure units.
Phrase member	A portion of a phrase clearly divided from the remainder of the phrase. This term is usually used to describe contrasting elements of a phrase.
Phrases—contrasting	Two phrases, the second of which (although a complement of the first) has had different contour and makeup.
Phrases—parallel	A period in which the first portion of both phrases is essentially the same, but each ends in a different manner.
Phrases—repeated	Two phrases that occupy the duration of a period; the second is a repetition or a modified repetition of the first.
Picardy third	A major triad used to end a composition or section in the minor key. Substitution of the tonic major triad for the tonic minor triad; a borrowed chord.
Pitch inventory	A list of all the tones in a composition or excerpt.
Polyphonic (texture)	A musical style or texture that includes at least two (and more often three or four) levels of melody, each maintaining some degree of individuality without comprising compatibility with the other parts.
Popular music symbols	A shorthand system of indicating the chords to be played with the melody in popular songs. The symbols are usually printed above the melody. Examples: An F major triad = F, a minor-minor seventh chord whose root is D = Dm7, an A minor triad with an added 6th = Am6, and so on.
Popular song, American	A form and style indigenous to the United States that evolved near the beginning of the twentieth century. Characterized by (1) a chorus of about thirty-two measures (recent songs tend toward varying lengths), (2) a verse of about eight measures (though some recent songs have no verse), (3) eight-measure phrase combinations in A A B A form (although songs of the last ten years vary widely in form), (4) texts dealing with love, and (5) simple harmony (that does, however, show much jazz influence).
Relatives (major and minor)	Major and minor scales that have the same key signature, but whose tonics are a minor third apart.
Rest	A silence. Indicated in notation by symbols that are equal in value to pitch duration symbols. Examples: 𝄽 = quarter rest; 𝄾 = eighth rest.
Rhythmic modulation	Alternations of beat or beat subdivision groups involving duplets, triplets, and quadruplets. A gradual shift from one meter to another and then quickly back to the original (without meter change).
Rhythmic superimposition (or superposition)	The simultaneous sounding of more than one rhythm. In jazz, a rhythm made up essentially of eighth or sixteenth notes played by one group of instruments, another rhythm made up of quarter notes played by the drums, and still another rhythm with slower note values played by the harmonic instruments such as the guitar and piano come together to produce a typical rhythmic superimposition. Frequently the periodicity (time span) of each is different, creating an even more intricate web of sound.

Root (of a chord)	The root of the lowest, most stable interval in the chord.
Root (of an interval)	The tone (of the two forming the interval) that is supported or strengthened most by the resultant combination of tones.
Rounded binary form	*See* Three-part form—incipient.
Scale—chromatic	A scale consisting entirely of half-step intervals.
Scale—harmonic minor	A seven-tone scale in which half steps occur between the second and third, fifth and sixth, and seventh and eighth (first) degrees.
Scale—major	A seven-tone scale in which half steps occur between the third and fourth degrees and the seventh and eighth (first) degrees.
Scale—melodic minor	A seven-tone scale in which half steps occur between the second and third degrees and the seventh and eighth (first) degrees in the ascending form. (The scale follows the natural minor scale when descending.)
Scale—natural minor	A seven-tone scale in which half steps occur between the second and third degrees and the fifth and sixth degrees.
Scale—pentatonic	A five-tone scale. One example: C D E G A.
Scale—synthetic	A scale *synthesized* or invented by a composer for a particular composition.
Scale—whole-tone	A six-tone scale made up entirely of whole-step intervals.
Scale degrees—names	First degree = tonic Fifth degree = dominant Second degree = supertonic Sixth degree = submediant Third degree = mediant Seventh degree = leading tone Fourth degree = subdominant Seventh degree = subtonic (in natural minor)
Secondary dominant chord	A diatonic triad or chord that is temporarily given dominant status by two conditions: (1) it is given the sound quality of a dominant chord (example: ii [minor triad] is changed to II [major triad]), and (2) it is followed by a diatonic chord (either major or minor) whose root lies in descending P5th (ascending P4th) relationship. In analysis a slash symbol (/) is used to designate secondary dominant chords. Since the leading-tone chords also have dominant function, diatonic chords may be temporarily changed to leading-tone chords to make secondary dominant chords.
Secondary tones	The elaboration of a structural tone by leap (usually arpeggiating a chord).
Sequence	The immediate restating of a melodic figure at a higher or lower pitch, so that the structure of the figure is maintained. Each unit of restatement is called a *leg*.
Sequence—diatonic	Each leg of a diatonic sequence accommodates the diatonic scale so that occasionally a half step is sequenced as a whole step and vice versa.
Sequence—exact	Each successive leg of an exact sequence maintains exactly the same intervallic distance as the previous leg.

Sequence—false	Partly sequence and partly repetition. A portion of a melodic figure is repeated while the remainder is sequenced.
Sequence—modified	A sequenced melodic group that has been elaborated or embellished in a way that does not destroy its original character.
Sequence—modulating	A sequence that leads from one tonal center to the next. In some sequences of this type, each leg is technically in a different key.
Seventh chord	A triad with an added factor a third above the fifth (seventh above the root).
Seventh chord—Type 1 resolution	1. The root of the seventh chord descends a P5th to the root of the following chord. 2. The seventh of the seventh chord resolves down one step to a factor of the following chord. Generally this takes place in the same voice, but in instrumental music the resolution is sometimes in another voice (implied).
Seventh chord—Type 2 resolution	1. The root of the seventh chord proceeds to the root of another that is *not* a P5th below (P4th above). 2. The chord following must contain the resolution tone for the seventh of the seventh chord. The most frequent example of a type 2 resolution is that of a seventh chord that progresses to a triad whose root is a step above that of the seventh chord.
Seventh chord—Type 3 resolution	1. The root of the seventh chord does *not* progress down a P5th (up a P4th). 2. The chord following does *not* contain the resolution tone for the seventh of the seventh chord. Example: D♯ F♯ A C progressing to EG C (C major triad in first inversion).
Solfeggio	Melodic lines sung to the syllables *do re mi fa sol la ti*. In the movable *do* system *do* is always the tonic of the major scale. In the fixed *do* system *do* is always C.
Song form	The combination of two or three periods or double periods to form a larger, yet concise musical unit. The minuet movement of the typical classical sonata or symphony is an example.
Spacing	The interval distance between voices or factors of a chord.
Standard twelve-bar blues	Twelve-bar units repeated as many times as lyrics dictate. Accompanying each twelve-bar unit is a routine harmonic progression (with several variants): I, IV, I, V, IV, I, V. Although the best-known blues melodies were published (St. Louis Blues, Memphis Blues, and so on) a large number were improvised on the spot above the blues harmony. Even those blues melodies that were "written down" often underwent considerable interpretation by the singers themselves, who assumed wide latitude for individual expression.
Step progression	Selected tones from a melody that give it direction. Certain tones (usually not adjacent) proceed by stepwise motion either up or down to provide direction to the melody. Tones forming a step progression may occur in the space of a measure or two or may extend to an entire phrase of a melody.
Structural tone	A melody tone of the highest importance to the existence of the melody; a tone that is the focal point of a melody or portion thereof.

Temperament—equal	A system of tuning in which an octave is divided in twelve equal half steps. This leaves no pure intervals except the octave, but makes possible the use of all twelve keys.
Temperament—just	A system of tuning in which both the fifths and thirds are pure (according to the natural overtone series).
Temperament—mean-tone	A system of tuning in which the pure fifths are compromised in favor of pure thirds.
Temperament—Pythagorean	A system of tuning in which the tones of the scale are arrived at by selecting a series of twelve pure fifths. This, of course, does not provide 2 : 1 octaves.
Ternary form	*See* Three-part form.
Tessitura	The average range of a particular voice or instrument in a composition. If a tessitura is "high" the notes tend to be in the higher extreme of the total range of that voice or instrument.
Theme	A melodic figure or phrase that is the basis for a composition or section of a composition.
Three-part form	A form most often found in homophonic music but existing as well in three-part polyphony, the first and third parts of which are either the same or nearly so. Usually designated by the letters A B A, three-part form is also known as *ternary* form.
Three-part form—incipient	Related both to two- and three-part form. Consists of three sections with the first and third similar, but with a middle section that is often shorter than the other two and that is frequently repeated along with the third section. The fine line of difference between incipient and full three-part form lies in the strength of the middle section. Incipient three-part form is also known as *rounded binary* form.
Tonality	A system of tones (example: the tones of a major scale) used in such a way that one tone becomes central and the remaining tones assume a hierarchy based on their intervallic relationship to the central tone or tonal center.
Tonicized chord	A chord that functions temporarily as a tonic (having been preceded by a secondary dominant).
Transposing instruments	Instruments that produce a pitch other than that written.
Triad	Strictly speaking, a triad is any three-tone chord. In tertian harmony, a triad is a chord built in superposed thirds. The four types of triads are major, minor, diminished, and augmented.
Triad—augmented	A triad consisting of a major third and an augmented fifth above the root.
Triad—diminished	A triad consisting of a minor third and a diminished fifth above the root.
Triad—first inversion	The position of a chord in which the third factor is the lowest-sounding tone.

Triad—major	A triad consisting of a major third and a perfect fifth above the root.
Triad—minor	A triad consisting of a minor third and a perfect fifth above the root.
Triad—root position	The position of a chord in which the root is the lowest-sounding tone.
Triad—second inversion	The position of a chord in which the fifth factor is the lowest-sounding tone.
Turnaround (Turnback)	A term used in popular song to denote four-chord formulas that signal the repetition of a period or return to a previous period. Typical turnabout: I to vii°^{7} to ii^7 to V^7 (in popular music symbols: C major: C to C$^\sharp$ dim to Dm7 to G7).
Twelve-bar jazz blues	A variant of the twelve-bar blues harmony characterized by ii^7 to V^7 progression in the ninth and tenth bars.
Twelve-bar jazz blues—modified	*See* Modified twelve-bar jazz blues.
Twelve-bar blues—standard	*See* Standard twelve-bar blues.
Two-part (binary) form	A form, often found in homophonic as well as polyphonic compositions, consisting of two organically related parts. Frequently the two parts are bound together by the same thematic material, but this is not always the case. Two-part and three-part form differ considerably in their respective makeups and are, obviously, not consanguineous.

Index

Abgesang, 284
A cappella, 166
Accidentals, 15
Acoustics, 4
Added sixth chord, 311
American popular song, 309–34
   form, 314–15
   harmonic progressions, 318–19
   harmony, 316–23
   key, 315–16
   melody, 316
   meter, 316
   rhythm, 316
Amplitude, 4. *See also* Intensity
Analysis, 171
Analytical procedure, 171
Anticipation, 79
Appoggiatura, 77
Asymmetrical divisions (of meter), 19
Augmented intervals, 49–50
Augmented triad, 58
   symbol in popular music, 311
Authentic cadence, 72–73
   imperfect, 73
   perfect, 72

Bar form, 284–85
   as forerunner of binary form, 284–85
   rounded binary aspect, 284

Baroque period, 166
   secondary dominants in, 248
   three-part form in, 302
   two-part form in, 276–81, 285
   vii$°^7$ chord in, 198
Bass clef, 12
Binary form, 275–94
Black American music, 335
Black notation, 9
Blues, 335–41
   harmony of, 335–37
   melody of, 338–41
Blues scale, 338
   major-minor chords of, 338
Boogie-woogie, 341–43
   harmony, 341
   melody, 341
   rhythm, 342
   texture, 342
      thick, 342
      thin, 343

Cadence, 72–74
   authentic, 72
   deceptive, 74
   half, 73
   imperfect authentic, 73
   perfect authentic, 72
   plagal, 73
Canon, 53
Canzo, 284
C clef, 13
   alto, 13
   baritone, 13
   mezzo soprano, 13
   soprano, 13
   tenor, 13

Changing tone, 80
Chorale, 127–31
   analysis of, 129–31
Chorale harmonizations
   fixed practices in, 135
   preferred practices, 136–37
Chord, 57–60
   patterns, 142–51
   progressions, 142–51
   selecting for, 261–63
   relationship, 141–42
   roots, 59
Chromatic descending chord progression, 323–24
Chromatic scale, 42
Church modes, 44–47
   Aeolian, 45–46
   Dorian, 45–46
   Ionian, 45–46
   Lydian, 45–46
   Mixolydian, 45–46
   Phrygian, 45–46
Circle of P5s, 318–19
   typical chord patterns in, 320–23
Circle progression, 179–81
Classical period, 166–67
   secondary dominants in, 248–49
   seventh chord in, 199–200
   three-part form in, 302
   two-part form in, 276–78, 285–87

Clef, 12
   alto, 13
   baritone, 13
   bass, 12
   C, 13
   mezzo soprano, 13
   soprano, 13
   tenor, 13
   treble, 12
Composer, 3
Composition, 3
Compression, 3
Contemporary period, 168
   three-part form in, 303
   two-part form in, 288
Continuo, 66
Counterpoint, 57

Deceptive cadence, 74
Decibels, 4
Descant, in mensural notation, 8
Diatonic scales, 28–41
   tonic in, 28
Diatonic sequence, 112–13
Diatonic stepwise chord patterns, 328–29
Diminished intervals, 49–50
Diminished triad, 58
   symbol in popular music, 311
Dot, 16
Double flat, 15
Double period, 109
Double sharp, 15
Doubling, 134
Duration, 3, 4
   notation of, 16–19
   patterns of, 4

Dynamic marks, 20
  in instrumental music, 23
  in piano music, 23
  in vocal music, 23

Embellishing tone, 98. See also Nonharmonic tone
Enharmonic
  equivalents, 15, 31
  intervals, 50
  tones, 50
Equal temperament system (of tuning), 34
Equal temperament tuning, 35–37
Escape tone, 76
Exact sequence, 112
Expanded three-part song form, 298

False sequence, 113
Fermata, 130
Figured bass, 66
  symbols, 67–72
Final, 44. See also Tonic
Five-line staff, 10
Flat, 15
  above the bass note, 68
  number in major key signatures, 30
  number in major-relative minor relationships, 38
Form
  bar, 284–85
  song, 110
  song, with trio, 298–301
  three-part (ternary), 295–307
  two-part (binary), 275–94
Four-chord formulas, 329–30
  in succession, 330
Four-line staff, 8
  in Gregorian chant, 8
Frequency, 4

G clef, 12. See also Treble clef
German lied, 285
German part song, 285
G major scale, 29
Grand staff, 12
Greek modes, 44

Half cadence, 73
Harmonic progression, 141–64
  ascending perfect fifth, 144–45
  ascending second (M2 or m2), 145–48
  ascending third, 150–51
  chord selection in, 153–60
  circle progression, 143–44
  deceptive cadence, 146
  descending second (M2 or m2), 151–52
  descending third (M3 or m3), 148–50
Harmonic rhythm, 83–88
Harmonics, 5. See also Partials
Harmonic series, 5–6
Harmonic syncopation, 345
Harmonization
  of melodies that modulate, 218–22
  nondominant seventh chords, 238–41
  procedure, 153–60
Harmony, 57–92
  in four-part chorale writing, 130–31
Hexachord, 11
Homophonic music, 276

Impressionism, 167
Innovations in twentieth-century music, 19
Instrumental ranges, 119–22
Instruments (and voices), 119–26
Intensity, 3, 4
Interval, 14, 48–54
  augmented, 49–50
  diminished, 49–50
  enharmonic, 50
  inversion of, 51–52

Jazz, 343–52
  altered chords, 346–49
  harmony, 346–49
  improvisation, 349–52
  melody, 349–52
  rhythm, 343–46

Key, 54
Key signature, 29
  and key notes in major-relative minor relationships, 38
  and tonic note in major key signatures, 30

Lead sheet, 309
Ledger lines, 12
Letter names, 10

Major-major seventh chord, 312
Major-minor dominant seventh chord, 175–92
  symbol in popular music, 311
Major-minor-major ninth chord, 312
Major scale, 28–31
Major triad, 58
  chord symbol in popular music, 310
Manuscript notation, 20–26
Mean-tone tuning, 35
Meistersingers, 284
Melodic components, hierarchy of, 94
Melodic minor scale, 33–34
Melodic organization, 103–18
Melody, 93–102
Mensural notation, 8–9
Meter, 4, 17
  asymmetrical, 19
  compound, 18
  duple, 4–5
  signatures, 17
  simple, 17
  triple, 4–5
Middle ages
  bar form in, 284–85
  three-part form in, 302

Middle C, 12
Minnesingers, 284
Minor triad, 58
  chord symbol in popular music, 311
Modes, 44
  Aeolian, 45–46
  Dorian, 45–46
  Greek, 44
  Ionian, 45–46
  Lydian, 45–46
  Mixolydian, 45–46
  Phrygian, 45–46
Modified sequence, 113
Modified twelve-bar jazz blues, 336–37
Modulating sequence, 113
Modulation, 135, 203–24
  chromatic, 207–8
  common chord, 203–6, 207
  enharmonic, 208–9
  related keys, 203–5
  static, 206
Motive, 103
Musical grammar, 6
Musical tone, 5–6

Natural, 15
  above the bass note, 68
  sign, 15
Natural minor scale, 31–32
Neighboring tone, 76
Neumatic notation, 7–8
Neumes, 7–8
  early types of, 7–8
Noncircle progression, with resolution, 182–83
Nondiatonic scales, 42–44
  chromatic, 42
  whole-tone, 43–44
Nondominant seventh chords, 225–42
  analysis symbols for, 226–27
  harmonizing, 238–41
  part-writing of, 233–38
  resolutions of, 227–32
Nonharmonic tones, 74
  in pairs, 80
  types, 76–80

Nonresolution, 183–84
Nontransposing instruments, 119
Notation, 7–26
 black, 9
 history of, 7–10
 neumatic, 7–8
 tablature, 9

Octave identification, 14
Odd-length motives, 345
 in succession, 345
Open position, 134
Organum, 57
Ostinato bass, 330
 in popular music, 330–31

Parallel relationship, 39–40
Partials, 5–6
 fundamental, 5–6
Parts, in mensural notation, 8
Part-writing procedures, 135–37, 185, 194–95, 233–34, 256–60
Passing tone, 76
Pedal tone, 80
Pentatonic scale, 41
Perfect fifth, 29
Performer, 3
Period, 104
 double, 109
 three-part, 107
Phrase, 104
 contrasting, 107
 extension of, 110–11
  cadential, 111
  internal, 111
  near the beginning, 111
 member, 104
 modifications of, 110–11
 mutation, 111
 parallel, 105–6
 repeated, 104
 modified, 105
Pitch, 3, 4
 notation of, 10–13
Pitch inventory, 54
Plagal cadence, 73
Polymeter, 345
Polyrhythm, 345
Popular music symbols, 309

Post-Romantic and Impressionistic period, 167
 secondary dominants in, 251
 seventh chord in, 201–2
 two-part form in, 287
Present notation, 10
Pure fifth, 34–35
Pure third, 35
Pythagorean tuning, 34–35

Rarefaction, 3
Relative major, 37
Relative minor, 37
Relative relationships (of scales), 37–39
Renaissance period, 166
 three-part form in, 302
Repetition, 112
Resolution (of seventh chords), 179–92
 general types, 179–92
Retardation, 80
Rhythm, 4, 5
 in four-part chorale writing, 131
 harmonic, 83–88
Rhythmic modulation, 344
Rhythmic superimposition, 345
Riffs, 338
Romantic period, 167
 secondary dominants in, 249–51
 three-part form in, 303
 two-part form in, 287
Root relationships, 141–42
Roots, 59
 of augmented triads, 59
 of diminished triads, 59
 of minor triads, 59
Rounded binary form, 281–84
 five-phase level, 282–83
 four-phase level, 282

Scale(s), 27–44
 chromatic, 42
 diatonic, 28–41
 G major, 29
 harmonic minor, 32–33
 major, 28–31, 38
 melodic minor, 33–34
 natural minor, 31–32
 nondiatonic, 42–44
 pentatonic, 41
 relative minor, 37–39
 whole-tone, 43
Scale degree names, 60–64
Scale relationships, 37–40
 parallel, 39–40
 relative, 37–39
Scale tuning, 34–37
Secondary dominant chords, 243–74
 characteristics of, 243
 inversions, 246
 part-writing procedures for, 256–60
 treatment of, 251–56
 types, 245
Secondary tone, 97–98
Second dot, 16
Sequence, 112–13
 characteristics of, 112
 diatonic, 112–13
 exact, 112
 false, 113
 modified, 113
 modulating, 113
Seventh chord, 175–78
 analysis symbols for, 176–78
 history of, 175–76
 inversion of, 178–79
 resolution of, 179–92
Sharp, 15
 above the bass note, 68
 number in major key signatures, 30
 number in major–relative minor relationships, 38
$^6_4$ chords, 152–53
 uses for, 152
Solfeggio syllables, 11
Sonata allegro form, 285–87

Song form, 110
 with trio, 298–301
Sound, 3
 properties of, 3–6. See also Pitch, Intensity, Duration, and Timbre
Sound wave, 3. See also Vibration
Spacing, 134–35
Staff, 10
 grand, 12
Standard twelve-bar blues, 335–36
Step progression, 93–94
 conditions for formation of, 93–94
Stollen, 284
Structural tone, 94
 elements to produce, 94
 relationship to step progressions, 95
Style, 171
 factors that produce, 171–73
Style analysis, 171–73
Style periods, 165–69
 approximate dates of, 165
Substitute Mm^7 chords, 325–27
Suspension, 77–79
Swing, 345–46
Syncopation, 344
Synthesis, 171

Tablature notation, 9
 pitch in, 9
Ternary form, 295–307
Tessitura, 123
Three-part form, 295–307. See also Ternary form
 history of, 302–3
Three-part period, 107
Three-part song form, 296–98
 expansion of, 298
Three-phrase construction, 295
Tie, 16
Timbre, 3, 5
Tonal center, 54
Tonality, 54–55
Tone, 4

Tonic, 28
    in church modes, 44
    in diatonic scales, 28
    in major key
        signatures, 30
Tonicized chord,
    243–44
Transposing
    instruments, 119
Transposition, 29
Treble clef, 12
Triad analysis symbols,
    65
Triad inversion, 64
Triad position, 64
    first inversion, 64
    root position, 64
    second position, 64
Triads, 57–60
    augmented, 58
    diminished, 58
    major, 58
    minor, 58
    roots, 58–59
    on scale tones, 61
    types in diatonic
        scales, 62
Triad stability, 64
Turnarounds, 331
Turnbacks, 331
Twelve-bar jazz blues,
    336
Two-part form,
    275–94. *See also*
    Binary form
    history of, 284–88

Vibration, 3
vii$^{\phi 7}$ and vii^{o7} chords,
    193–202
    dominant tendencies
        of, 193
    historical use,
        198–202
    part-writing, 194–98
    resolution of, 194–95
Voice leading, in four-
    part choral writing,
    127–40
Voice ranges, 119

White notation, 9
Whole-tone scale, 43